TOUCHED WITH FIRE

THE FREE PRESS
New York   London   Toronto   Sydney   Tokyo   Singapore

TOUCHED WITH FIRE

Manic-Depressive Illness
and the Artistic Temperament

Kay Redfield Jamison

Copyright © 1993 by Kay Redfield Jamison

All rights reserved. No part of this book may be reproduced
or transmitted in any form or by any means, electronic or
mechanical, including photocopying, recording, or by any
information storage and retrieval system, without permission
in writing from the Publisher.

The Free Press
A Division of Simon & Schuster Inc.
1230 Avenue of the Americas
New York, N.Y. 10020

First Free Press Paperback Edition 1994

Printed in the United States of America

printing number

5 6 7 8 9 10

Designed by REM Studio, Inc.

Library of Congress Cataloging-in-Publication Data

Jamison, Kay R.
    Touched with fire : manic-depressive illness and the artistic
temperament / Kay Redfield Jamison.
        p.   cm.
    ISBN 0–02–916003–0
    1. Manic-depressive psychoses.   2. Artists—Mental health.
3. Authors—Mental health.   4. Creative ability.   I. Title.
RC516.J36   1993
616.89'5'00887—dc20   92-18327
                                                        CIP

Grateful acknowledgment is given to the publishers for permission to reprint excerpts from the following works:

"I Think Continually of Those Who Were Truly Great," from *Collected Poems 1928–1953* by Stephen Spender. Copyright 1934 and renewed 1952 by Stephen Spender. Reprinted by permission of Random House, Inc. Reprinted by permission of Faber and Faber Ltd.

Excerpt from "Elegy," from *Field Work* by Seamus Heaney. Copyright © 1976, 1979 by Seamus Heaney. Reprinted by permission of Farrar, Straus & Giroux, Inc. Reprinted by permission of Faber and Faber Ltd.

Excerpts from "Visitors" and "Suicide" from *Day by Day* by Robert Lowell. Copyright © 1975, 1976, 1977 by Robert Lowell. Reprinted by permission of Farrar, Straus & Giroux, Inc. Reprinted by permission of Faber and Faber Ltd.

Excerpt from "Elegy," copyright © 1955 by New Republic, Inc., from *The Collected Poems of Theodore Roethke* by Theodore Roethke. Used by permission of Doubleday, a division of Bantam Doubleday Dell Publishing Group, Inc. Reprinted by permission of Faber and Faber Ltd.

Excerpt from "May's Truth and May's Falsehood," in Delmore Schwartz: *Selected Poems: Summer Knowledge*. Reprinted by permission of New Directions Publishing Corporation. Reprinted by permission of Laurence Pollinger Limited.

Excerpt from "It's After One" by Vladimir Mayakovsky, in Edward J. Brown, *Mayakovsky: A Poet in Revolution*. Copyright © 1973 by Princeton University Press. Reprinted by permission of Princeton University Press.

Excerpt from "The First Day's Night Had Come" (poem 410): Reprinted by permission of the publishers and the Trustees of Amherst College from *The Poems of Emily Dickinson*, Thomas H. Johnson, ed., Cambridge, Mass.: The Belknap Press of Harvard University Press, Copyright © 1951, 1955, 1979, 1983 by the President and Fellows of Harvard College.

Excerpt from "In a Dark Time," copyright © 1960 by Beatrice Roethke, Administratrix of the Estate of Theodore Roethke, from *The Collected Poems of Theodore Roethke* by Theodore Roethke. Used by permission of Doubleday, a division of Bantam Doubleday Dell Publishing Group, Inc. Reprinted by permission of Faber and Faber Ltd.

Excerpt from "90 North" from *The Complete Poems* by Randall Jarrell. Copyright © by Mrs. Randall Jarrell. Renewal copyright © 1968 by Mrs. Randall Jarrell. Reprinted by permission of Farrar, Straus & Giroux, Inc. Reprinted by permission of Faber and Faber Ltd.

Excerpt from "The Deceptive Present, The Phoenix Year" in: Delmore Schwartz: *Selected Poems: Summer Knowledge*. Copyright © 1959 by Delmore Schwartz. Reprinted by permission of New Directions Publishing Corporation. Reprinted by permission of Laurence Pollinger Limited.

Excerpt from "Little Gidding" in *Four Quartets*, copyright 1943 by T. S. Eliot and renewed 1971 by Esme Valerie Eliot, reprinted by permission of Harcourt Brace Jovanovich, Inc. Reprinted by permission of Faber and Faber Limited.

For
Richard Jed Wyatt, M.D.

To those who, by the dint of glass and vapour,
Discover stars, and sail in the wind's eye—

—BYRON

I think continually of those who were truly great.
Who, from the womb, remembered the soul's history
Through corridors of light, where the hours are suns,
Endless and singing. Whose lovely ambition
Was that their lips, still touched with fire,
Should tell of the Spirit, clothed from head to foot in song.
And who hoarded from the Spring branches
The desires falling across their bodies like blossoms.

What is precious, is never to forget
The essential delight of the blood drawn from ageless springs
Breaking through rocks in worlds before our earth.
Never to deny its pleasure in the morning simple light
Nor its grave evening demand for love.
Never to allow gradually the traffic to smother
With noise and fog, the flowering of the spirit.

Near the snow, near the sun, in the highest fields,
See how these names are fêted by the waving grass
And by the streamers of white cloud
And whispers of wind in the listening sky.
The names of those who in their lives fought for life,
Who wore at their hearts the fire's centre.
Born of the sun, they travelled a short while toward the sun
And left the vivid air signed with their honour.

—STEPHEN SPENDER

CONTENTS

1.
THAT
FINE MADNESS

Introduction

. . . his raptures were,
All air, and fire, which made his verses clear,
For that fine madness still he did retain,
Which rightly should possess a poet's brain.

—MICHAEL DRAYTON[1]

An Angel Descending: *Dante's Divine Comedy*. William Blake, c. 1826
(The Pierpont Morgan Library, New York)

"We of the craft are all crazy," remarked Lord Byron about himself
and his fellow poets. "Some are affected by gaiety, others by melancholy, but all are more or less touched."[2] This book is about
being "more or less touched"; specifically, it is about manic-
depressive illness—a disease of perturbed gaieties, melancholy,
and tumultuous temperaments—and its relationship to the artistic
temperament and imagination. It is also a book about artists and
their voyages, moods as their ships of passage, and the ancient,
persistent belief that there exists such a thing as a "fine madness."

The fiery aspects of thought and feeling that initially compel
the artistic voyage—fierce energy, high mood, and quick intelligence; a sense of the visionary and the grand; a restless and feverish temperament—commonly carry with them the capacity for
vastly darker moods, grimmer energies, and, occasionally, bouts of
"madness." These opposite moods and energies, often interlaced,
can appear to the world as mercurial, intemperate, volatile, brooding, troubled, or stormy. In short, they form the common view of
the artistic temperament, and, as we shall see, they also form the
basis of the manic-depressive temperament. Poetic or artistic ge-

nius, when infused with these fitful and inconstant moods, can become a powerful crucible for imagination and experience.

That impassioned moods, shattered reason, and the artistic temperament can be welded into a "fine madness" remains a fiercely controversial belief. Most people find the thought that a destructive, often psychotic, and frequently lethal disease such as manic-depressive illness might convey certain advantages (such as heightened imaginative powers, intensified emotional responses, and increased energy) counterintuitive. For others it is a troubling or unlikely association that conjures up simplistic notions of the "mad genius," bringing with it images of mindless and unaesthetic reductionism as well as concerns about making into disease something that subsumes vital human differences in style, perception, and temperament. Indeed, labeling as manic-depressive anyone who is unusually creative, accomplished, energetic, intense, moody, or eccentric both diminishes the notion of individuality within the arts and trivializes a very serious, often deadly illness. There are other reasons for such concerns. Excesses of psychoanalytic speculation, along with other abuses of psychobiography, have invited well-deserved ridicule. Due to the extraordinary advances in genetics, neuroscience, and psychopharmacology, much of modern psychiatric thought and clinical practice has moved away from the earlier influences of psychoanalysis and toward a more biological perspective. Some fear that the marked swing from psychoanalysis to psychopharmacology is too much, too soon, and that there exists the risk of a similar entrenchment of ideas and perspectives. The erosion of romantic and expressive language into the standardization of words and phrases necessary for a scientific psychiatry has tempted many to dismiss out of hand much of modern biological psychiatry. Almost by definition, the idea of using formal psychiatric diagnostic criteria in the arts has been anathema, and, in any event, biological psychiatrists have displayed relatively little interest in studying mood disorders in artists, writers, or musicians. Certainly those in the arts have been less than enthusiastic about being seen through a biological or diagnostic grid. Those in the best position to link the two worlds—scholars of creativity—only recently have begun to address the problem. Having previously focused on the relationship between creativity and "schizophrenia" (often misdiagnosed manic-depressive illness) or diffuse notions of psychopathology, these researchers have left largely unexamined the specific role of mood disorders in creative work.

Complicating matters further, certain life-styles provide cover for deviant and bizarre behavior. The arts have long given latitude to extremes in behavior and mood; indeed, George Becker has observed that the Romantic artists used the notion of mad genius to "provide recognition of special status and the freedom from conventional restraints that attended it."[3]:

> The aura of "mania" endowed the genius with a mystical and inexplicable quality that served to differentiate him from the typical man, the bourgeois, the philistine, and, quite importantly, the "mere" man of talent; it established him as the modern heir of the ancient Greek poet and seer and, like his classical counterpart, enabled him to claim some of the powers and privileges granted to the "divinely possessed" and "inspired."[4]

Robert Burton wrote in the seventeenth century that "all poets are mad," a view shared by many since. Such a view—however appealing to some, and whatever its accuracy—tends to equate psychopathology with artistic expression. A common assumption, for example, is that within artistic circles madness is somehow normal. This is well illustrated by an episode described by Ian Hamilton in his biography of the poet Robert Lowell; it illustrates the reactions of Lowell's colleagues to one of his many escalations into mania:

> Lowell had announced to all his Cincinnati acquaintances that he was determined to remarry, and had persuaded them to stand with him on the side of passion. Some members of the faculty found him excitable and talkative during this period, but since the talk was always brilliant and very often flattering to them, they could see no reason to think of Lowell as "ill," indeed, he was behaving just as some of them hoped a famous poet would behave. They undertook to protect this unique flame against any dampening intrusions from New York. Thus, when Hardwick [Lowell's wife] became convinced that Lowell was indeed sick—over a period of two weeks his telephone calls to New York became more and more confused, lengthy and abusive—she ran up against a wall of kindly meant hostility from

Lowell's campus allies. Her version of Lowell was not theirs, even when they were discussing the same symptoms; what to her was "mad" was to them another mark of Lowell's genius.[5]

The main purpose of this book is to make a literary, biographical, and scientific argument for a compelling association, not to say actual overlap, between two temperaments—the artistic and the manic-depressive—and their relationship to the rhythms and cycles, or temperament, of the natural world. The emphasis will be on understanding the relationship between moods and imagination, the nature of moods—their variety, their contrary and oppositional qualities, their flux, their extremes (causing, in some individuals, occasional episodes of "madness")—and the importance of moods in igniting thought, changing perceptions, creating chaos, forcing order upon that chaos, and enabling transformation.

The book begins with a general overview of manic-depressive illness: what it is, whom it affects, and how it shows itself. Mania, depression, mixed manic and depressive states, and suicide are described both from a clinical perspective and through the words and experiences of artists, musicians, and writers who have suffered from severe mood disorders. The biographical and scientific evidence for a relationship between manic-depressive illness and artistic creativity is given in chapter 3. Recent research strongly suggests that, compared with the general population, writers and artists show a vastly disproportionate rate of manic-depressive or depressive illness; clearly, however, not all (not even most) writers and artists suffer from major mood disorders. There remains skepticism and resistance to the idea of *any* such association, however—some of it stemming understandably from the excesses of psychobiography alluded to earlier (especially those of a highly speculative and interpretive nature), but much of it arising from a lack of understanding of the nature of manic-depressive illness itself. Many are unaware of the milder, temperamental expressions of the disease or do not know that most people who have manic-depressive illness are, in fact, without symptoms (that is, they are psychologically normal) most of the time. When many individuals—even those who are generally well versed in psychology and medicine—think of manic-depressive illness, they tend to imagine the back wards of insane asylums and unremitting mental illness or madness, and rightly conclude that no meaningful or sustained creative work can occur under such circumstances. Madness, or psychosis, represents only one end of the manic-depressive continuum, however; most people who have the illness, in fact, never become insane. Likewise, work that may be inspired by, or partially executed in, a mild or even psychotically manic state may be significantly shaped or partially edited while its creator is depressed and put into final order when he or she is normal. It is the interaction, tension, and transition between changing mood states, as well as the sustenance and discipline drawn from periods of health, that is critically important; and it is these same tensions and transitions that ultimately give such power to the art that is born in this way.

The psychological and biological arguments for a relationship between "madness" and artistic creativity are presented in chapter 4; the overlapping natures of the artistic and manic-depressive temperaments, as well as similarities in patterns of thought and behavior, are also explored. The importance to the creative process of certain types of experiences whose existence is due to extreme emotional states is discussed in some detail; however, the need for discipline, control, and highly reasoned thought is also stressed. The creative significance of the tension and reconciliation of naturally occurring, opposite emotional and cognitive states in artists with manic-depressive illness or cyclothymia (its milder temperamental variant), and the use of art by artists to heal themselves, are examined as well. The rhythms and cycles of manic-depressive illness, a singularly cyclic disease, are strikingly similar to those of the natural world, as well as to the death-and-regeneration and dark-and-light cycles so often captured in poetry, music, and painting. Seasonal cycles are particularly important, and these are discussed in the context of the scientific evidence for seasonal patterns in moods and psychosis, as well as illustrated by the seasonal patterns of artistic productivity evident in the lives of Robert Schumann, Vincent van Gogh, and others.

Any discussion of temperament and art is best served by examining one life in some depth, and none better illustrates the

complexity of overlap between heredity, individual will, circum-
stance, and poetic temperament than that of George Gordon, Lord
Byron. Heir to madness, virulently melancholic, and in lifelong
fear of going insane, Byron represents the fine edge of the fine
madness—the often imperceptible line between poetic temperament and psychiatric illness. His terrible struggles with melancholy and his "savage moods,"[6] yet his work's indebtedness to
them, bring up many of the medical, social, and ethical issues that
are discussed in the final chapters. Manic-depressive illness is a
genetic disease, and that fact is fundamental not only to understanding its origins but also to the many medical and ethical issues
raised later in the book. The scientific arguments for the genetic
basis of manic-depressive illness are presented in chapter 6, put
into the context of the family psychiatric histories, or pedigrees, of
several major literary and artistic families (including those of Byron, Tennyson, Melville, William and Henry James, Schumann,
Coleridge, van Gogh, Hemingway, and Woolf).

Clearly, a close association between the artistic temperament
and manic-depressive illness has many implications—for artists,
medicine, and society. Modern psychopharmacology and genetic
research raise almost endless possibilities, both liberating and disturbing, but the ethical waters remain disconcertingly uncharted.
No psychiatric illness has been more profoundly affected by the
advances in clinical and basic neuroscience research than manic-
depressive illness. The efficacy of a wide range of medications has
given clinicians unprecedented options and patients lifesaving
choices. The fact that lithium, antidepressants, and anticonvulsants
are now the standard of care for manic-depressive illness (and
psychotherapy or psychoanalysis *alone*, without medication, is usually considered to be malpractice) raises particularly interesting
questions about the treatment of writers and artists. Some artists
resist entirely the idea of taking medication to control their mood
swings and behaviors; interestingly, however, there is some evidence that, as a group, artists and writers disproportionately seek
out psychiatric care; certainly many—including Byron, Schumann,
Tennyson, van Gogh, Fitzgerald, and Lowell—repeatedly sought
help from their physicians. Other writers and artists stop taking
their medications because they miss the highs or the emotional
intensity associated with their illness, or because they feel that

drug side effects interfere with the clarity and rapidity of their thought or diminish their levels of enthusiasm, emotion, and energy.

Although manic-depressive illness has long been assumed to be genetic in origin, and its strong tendency to run in some families but not in others has been observed for well over a thousand years, only the recent radical advances in molecular biology have provided the techniques to enable highly sophisticated searches for the genes involved. Similarly, an almost unbelievable increase in the rate of study of brain structure and function has resulted in a level of biological knowledge about manic-depressive illness—this most humanly expressed, psychologically complicated, and moody of all diseases—that is without parallel in psychiatry. The ethical issues arising from such knowledge, and from the possibility that such a devastating illness can confer individual and societal advantage, are staggering: Would one want to get rid of this illness if one could? Sterilization of patients with hereditary psychoses, most directly applicable to those with manic-depressive illness, was once practiced in parts of the United States, and large numbers of individuals with manic-depressive illness were systematically killed in German concentration camps. Even today many provinces in China enforce mandatory sterilization and abortion policies for those with hereditary mental illness. What will be the roles of amniocentesis, other types of prenatal diagnosis, and abortion once the manic-depressive genes are found? What are the implications for society of future gene therapies and the possible early prevention of manic-depressive illness? Does psychiatric treatment have to result in happier but blander and less imaginative artists? What does it mean for biographers and critics that manic-depressive illness and its temperaments are relatively common in the writers and artists they study? These and other issues are discussed in the final chapter.

Ultimately this book is about the temperaments and moods of voyagers: It is about the thin line that exists between the fate of Icarus, who—burned by rather than touched with fire—"felt the hot wax run, / Unfeathering him,"[7] and the fates of those artists who survive the flight, "without self-loss through realms of chaos and 'old night.' "[8] It is about the "Night Ferry," as Seamus Heaney described poet Robert Lowell; it is about the conjurer and setter of moods, the guide through the "ungovernable and dangerous." It is about voyages:

> You were our night ferry
> thudding in a big sea,
>
> the whole craft ringing
> with an armourer's music
> the course set wilfully across
> the ungovernable and dangerous.[9]

2.
ENDLESS NIGHT, FIERCE FIRES AND SHRAMMING COLD

Manic-Depressive Illness

I come to ferry you hence across the tide
To endless night, fierce fires and shramming cold.

—DANTE[1]

"Come on, sir." "Easy, sir."
"Dr. Brown will be here in ten minutes, sir."
Instead, a metal chair unfolds into a stretcher.
I lied secured there, but for my skipping mind.
They keep bustling.
"Where you are going, Professor,
you won't need your Dante."

—ROBERT LOWELL[2]

Dante's Inferno. Gustave Doré, c. 1860

"I feel the jagged gash with which my contemporaries died,"[3] wrote Robert Lowell about his generation of feverishly brilliant, bruised, and wrathful poets. There was, he felt,

> personal anguish everywhere. We can't dodge it, and shouldn't worry that we are uniquely marked and fretted and must somehow keep even-tempered, amused, and in control. John B[erryman] in his mad way keeps talking about something evil stalking us poets. That's a bad way to talk, but there's some truth in it.[4]

Robert Lowell and John Berryman, along with their contemporaries Theodore Roethke, Delmore Schwartz, Randall Jarrell, and Anne Sexton, were—among other things—"stalked" by their manic-depressive illness. Mercurial by temperament, they were subject to disastrous extremes of mood and reason. All were repeatedly hospitalized for their attacks of mania and depression; Berryman, Jarrell, and Sexton eventually committed suicide.

What is the nature of this disease of mood and reason that so often kills and yet so often is associated with the imaginative arts?

What kind of illness takes those who have it on journeys where they, like Robert Lowell, both do and do not need their Dantes?

Manic-depressive, or bipolar, illness encompasses a wide range of mood disorders and temperaments. These vary in severity from cyclothymia—characterized by pronounced but not totally debilitating changes in mood, behavior, thinking, sleep, and energy levels—to extremely severe, life-threatening, and psychotic forms of the disease. Manic-depressive illness is closely related to major depressive, or unipolar, illness; in fact, the same criteria (described in detail in Appendix A) are used for the diagnosis of major depression as for the depressive phase of manic-depressive illness. These depressive symptoms include apathy, lethargy, hopelessness, sleep disturbance (sleeping far too much or too little), slowed physical movement, slowed thinking, impaired memory and concentration, and a loss of pleasure in normally pleasurable events. Additional diagnostic criteria include suicidal thinking, self-blame, inappropriate guilt, recurrent thoughts of death, a minimum duration of the depressive symptoms (two to four weeks), and significant interference with the normal functioning of life. Unlike individuals with unipolar depression, those suffering from manic-depressive illness also experience episodes of mania or hypomania (mild mania). These episodes are characterized by symptoms that are, in many ways, the opposite of those seen in depression. Thus, during hypomania and mania, mood is generally elevated and expansive (or, not infrequently, paranoid and irritable); activity and energy levels are greatly increased; the need for sleep is decreased; speech is often rapid, excitable, and intrusive; and thinking is fast, moving quickly from topic to topic. Hypomanic or manic individuals usually have an inflated self-esteem, as well as a certainty of conviction about the correctness and importance of their ideas. This grandiosity can contribute to poor judgment, which, in turn, often results in chaotic patterns of personal and professional relationships. Other common features of hypomania and mania include spending excessive amounts of money, impulsive involvements in questionable endeavors, reckless driving, extreme impatience, intense and impulsive romantic or sexual liaisons, and volatility. In its extreme forms mania is characterized by violent agitation, bizarre behavior, delusional thinking, and visual and auditory hallucinations. In its milder variants the increased energy, expansiveness, risk taking, and fluency of thought associated with hypomania can result in highly productive periods. The range in severity of symptoms is reflected in the current psychiatric diagnostic system. Bipolar I disorder, what one thinks of as "classic" manic-depressive illness, refers to the most severe form of affective illness; individuals diagnosed as bipolar I must meet the full diagnostic criteria for both mania and major depressive illness. (The standard diagnostic criteria for mania, hypomania, major depression, and cyclothymia, as well as more clinically descriptive criteria for cyclothymia, are given in Appendix A.) Bipolar II disorder, on the other hand, is defined as the presence or history of at least one major depressive episode, as well as the existence or history of less severe manic episodes (that is, hypomanias, which do not cause pronounced impairment in personal or professional functioning, are not psychotic in nature, and do not require hospitalization).

Cyclothymia and related manic-depressive temperaments are also an integral and important part of the manic-depressive spectrum, and the relationship of predisposing personalities and cyclothymia to the subsequent development of manic-depressive psychosis is fundamental. Cyclothymic temperament can be manifested in several ways—as predominantly depressive, manic, hypomanic, irritable, or cyclothymic. German psychiatrist Ernst Kretschmer described the fluidity inherent to these manic-depressive temperaments:

> Men of this kind have a soft temperament which can swing to great extremes. The path over which it swings is a wide one, namely between cheerfulness and unhappiness. . . . Not only is the hypomanic disposition well known to be a peculiarly labile one, which also has leanings in the depressive direction, but many of these cheerful natures have, when we get to know them better, a permanent melancholic element somewhere in the background of their being. . . . The hypomanic and melancholic halves of the cycloid temperament relieve one another, they form layers or patterns in individual cases, arranged in the most varied combinations.[5]

Clearly not all individuals who have cyclothymia go on to develop the full manic-depressive syndrome. But many do, and the temperamental similarities between those who meet all the diagnostic criteria for mania or major depression (that is, are "syndromal") and those who meet them only partially (that is, are "subsyndromal," or cyclothymic) are compelling. British psychiatrists Dr. Eliot Slater and Sir Martin Roth have given a general description of the "constitutional cyclothymic," emphasizing the natural remissions, vague medical complaints, and seasonal patterns often intrinsic to the temperament. The alternating mood states—each lasting for days, weeks, or months at a time—are continuous in some individuals but subside, leaving periods of normality, in others. Slater and Roth also discuss the occurrence of the cyclothymic constitution in artists and writers:

> Its existence in artists and writers has attracted some attention, especially as novelists like Bjørnson and H. Hesse have given characteristic descriptions of the condition. Besides those whose swings of mood never intermit, there are others with more or less prolonged *intervals of normality*. In the hypomanic state the patient feels well, but the existence of such states accentuates his feeling of insufficiency and even illness in the depressive phases. At such times he will often seek the advice of his practitioner, complaining of such vague symptoms as headache, insomnia, lassitude, and indigestion. . . . In typical cases such alternative cycles will last a lifetime. In cyclothymic artists, musicians, and other creative workers the rhythm of the cycles can be read from the dates of the beginning and cessation of productive work.
>
> Some cyclothymics have a *seasonal rhythm* and have learned to adapt their lives and occupations so well to it that they do not need medical attention.[6]

The distinction between full-blown manic-depressive illness and cyclothymic temperament is often an arbitrary one; indeed, almost all medical and scientific evidence argues for including cyclothymia as an integral part of the spectrum of manic-depressive illness. Such milder mood and energy swings often precede overt clinical illness by years (about one-third of patients with definite manic-depressive illness, for example, report bipolar mood swings or hypomania predating the actual onset of their illness). These typically begin in adolescence or early adulthood and occur most often in the spring or autumn, on an annual or biennial basis. The symptoms, whose onset is usually unrelated to events in the individual's life, generally persist for three to ten weeks and are often characterized by changes in energy level as well as mental discomfort.[7] These subsyndromal mood swings, frequently debilitating, are as responsive to lithium treatment as full-blown manic-depressive illness is.[8] In addition to the overlapping nature of symptoms in cyclothymia and manic-depressive illness, and the fact that cyclothymia responds to treatment with lithium, two further pieces of evidence support the relationship between the temperament and the illness. First, approximately one out of three patients with cyclothymia eventually develops full syndromal depression, hypomania, or mania; this is in marked contrast to a rate of less than one in twenty in control populations.[9] Additionally, patients who have been diagnosed as cyclothymic have many more bipolar manic-depressive individuals in their family histories than would be expected by chance.[10] Particularly convincing are the data from studies of monozygotic (identical) twin pairs, which show that when one twin is diagnosed as manic-depressive, the other, if not actually manic-depressive, very frequently is cyclothymic.[11] Manic-depressive illness is indisputably genetic; the fundamental importance of heritability in the etiology and understanding of this disease is elaborated upon in chapter 6 (within the context of literary and artistic families characterized by generations of individuals who suffered from depressive or manic-depressive illness). While the specific genes responsible for manic-depressive illness have not yet been identified, promising regions on the chromosomes have been located. It is probable that at least one of the genes will be isolated within the next few years.

Manic-depressive illness, often seasonal, is recurrent by nature; left untreated, individuals with this disease can expect to experience many, and generally worsening, episodes of depression and mania. It is important to note, however, that most individuals who have manic-depressive illness are normal most of the time; that is, they maintain their reason and their ability to function personally and professionally. Prior to the availability and widespread use of lithium, at least one person in five with manic-depressive illness committed suicide. The overwhelming majority of all adolescents and adults who commit suicide have been determined, through postmortem investigations, to have suffered from either bipolar manic-depressive or unipolar depressive illness.

Manic-depressive illness is relatively common; approximately one person in a hundred will suffer from the more severe form and at least that many again will experience milder variants, such as cyclothymia. One person in twenty, or 5 percent, will experience a major depressive illness. Men and women are equally likely to have manic-depressive illness, in contrast to major depressive illness, which is more than twice as likely to affect women. The average age of onset of manic-depressive illness (18 years) is considerably earlier than that of unipolar depression (27 years).

Highly effective treatments exist for both manic-depressive and major depressive illness. Lithium has radically altered the course and consequences of manic-depressive illness, allowing most patients to live reasonably normal lives. In recent years anticonvulsant medications such as carbamazepine and valproate have provided important alternative treatments for patients unable to take, or unresponsive to, lithium. A wide variety of antidepressants has proven exceptionally powerful in the treatment of major depression. Psychotherapy, in conjunction with medication, is often essential to healing as well as to the prevention of possible recurrences. Drug therapy, which is primary, frees most patients from the severe disruptions of manic and depressive episodes. Psychotherapy can help individuals come to terms with the repercussions of past episodes, take the medications that are necessary to prevent recurrence, and better understand and deal with the often devastating psychological implications and consequences of having manic-depressive illness.

Although we will be emphasizing the bipolar form of manic-depressive illness in our discussion of writers and artists, manic-depressive illness, in its European and historical sense, encompasses the severe, recurrent melancholias as well. The clinical, genetic, and biological overlaps between recurrent depressive and manic-depressive illness are stronger than existing differences.[12] Although the melancholic side of an imaginative individual may be more striking, the subtler manic states are often also there in a fluctuating pattern. We turn next to descriptions of these mood disorders, given by those who have experienced them.

—I am groaning under the miseries of a diseased nervous System; a System of all others the most essential to our happiness—or the most productive of our Misery. . . . Lord, what is Man! Today, in the luxurance of health, exulting in the enjoyment of existence; In a few days, perhaps in a few hours, loaded with conscious painful being, counting the tardy pace of the lingering moments, by the repercussions of anguish, & refusing or denied a Comforter.—Day follows night, and night comes after day, only to curse him with life which gives him no pleasure.

—ROBERT BURNS[13]

The depressive, or melancholic, states are characterized by a morbidity and flatness of mood along with a slowing down of virtually all aspects of human thought, feeling, and behavior that are most personally meaningful. Occasionally these changes reflect only a transient shift in mood or a recognizable and limited reaction to a life situation. When energy is profoundly dissipated, the ability to think is clearly eroded, and the capacity to actively engage in the efforts and pleasures of life is fundamentally altered, then depression becomes an illness rather than a temporary or existential state. As with most kinds of illness, symptoms of depression can range widely in their severity. Thinking, for example, may be only mildly slowed or it can be stuporous; mood may be only slightly downcast or it can be unrelentingly bleak and suicidal; the mind may retain its reason or it can be floridly delusional. In depression (as with the manic states) the degree, type, number, and duration of symptoms largely determine whether or not they meet diagnostic criteria for a mood, or affective, disorder.

Mood, in the more serious depressive states, is usually bleak, pessimistic, and despairing. A deep sense of futility is frequently accompanied, if not preceded, by the belief that the ability to experience pleasure is permanently gone. The physical and psychological worlds are experienced as shades of grays and blacks, as having lost their color and vibrancy. Irritability, quick anger, suspiciousness, and emotional turbulence are frequent correlates of depressed mood; morbid and suicidal thinking are common. The mood of misery and suffering that usually accompanies depression was expressed by Edgar Allan Poe in a letter written when he was in his mid-twenties:

My feelings at this moment are pitiable indeed. I am suffering under a depression of spirits such as I have never felt before. I have struggled in vain against the influence of this melancholy—*You will be-lieve me* when I say that I am still miserable in spite of the great improvement in my circumstances. I say you will believe me, and for this simple reason, that a man who is writing for *effect* does not write *thus*. My heart is open before you—if it be worth reading, read it. I am wretched, and know not why. Console me—for you can. But let it be quickly—or it will be too late. Write me immediately. Convince me that it is worth one's while—that it is at all necessary to live, and you will prove yourself indeed my friend. Persuade me to do what is right. I do not mean this—I do not mean that you should consider what I now write you a jest—oh pity me! for I feel that my words are incoherent—but I will recover myself. You will not fail to see that I am suffering under a depression of spirits which will [not fail to] ruin me should it be long continued.[14]

In his *Memoirs* French composer Hector Berlioz also wrote of the agonies attendant upon his frequent spells of depression, this most "terrible of all the evils of existence":

> It is difficult to put into words what I suffered—the longing that seemed to be tearing my heart out by the roots, the dreadful sense of being alone in an empty universe, the agonies that thrilled through me as if the blood were running ice-cold in my veins, the disgust with living, the impossibility of dying. Shakespeare himself never de-scribed this torture; but he counts it, in *Hamlet*, among the terrible of all the evils of existence.
>
> I had stopped composing; my mind seemed to become feebler as my feelings grew more intense. I did nothing. One power was left me—to suffer.[15]

Berlioz suffered throughout his life from these black depressions. He described in detail the two types of melancholia, or "spleen," he had experienced: an active, painful, and tumultuous one (almost certainly a mixed state, in which manic and depressive symptoms exist together), and another type, characterized by ennui, isolation, lethargy, and a dearth of feeling. "I again became prey to that frightful affliction—psychological, nervous, imaginary, what you will," he wrote, and then went on to describe one of his attacks in some detail:

> The fit fell upon me with appalling force. I suffered agonies and lay groaning on the ground, stretching out abandoned arms, convul-

sively tearing up handfuls of grass and wide-eyed innocent daisies, struggling against the crushing sense of *absence*, against a mortal isolation.

Yet such an attack is not to be compared with the tortures that I have known since then in ever-increasing measure.

What can I say that will give some idea of the action of this abominable disease? . . .

There are . . . two kinds of spleen; one mocking, active, passionate, malignant; the other morose and wholly passive, when one's only wish is for silence and solitude and the oblivion of sleep. For anyone possessed by this latter kind, nothing has meaning, the destruction of a world would hardly move him. At such times I could wish the earth were a shell filled with gunpowder, which I would put a match to for my diversion.[16]

The active and malignant spleen was described by Scottish poet Robert Burns as well: "Here I sit, altogether Novemberish, a damn'd mélange of Fretfulness & melancholy; not enough of the one to rouse me to passion; nor of the other to repose me in torpor; my soul flouncing & fluttering round her tenement, like a wild Finch caught amid the horrors of winter newly thrust into a cage."[17] And Shakespeare, in his portrayal of the weary and melancholic Hamlet, describes the bleeding out of hope, color, beauty, and belief:

I have of late—but wherefore I know not—lost all my mirth, forgone all custom of exercises. And indeed it goes so heavily with my disposition that this goodly frame the earth seems to me a sterile promontory. This most excellent canopy, the air, look you, this brave o'erhanging firmament, this majestical roof fretted with golden fire— why, it appeareth nothing to me but a foul and pestilent congregation of vapours.[18]

Eighteenth-century poet William Cowper, who was confined to an asylum for his manic-depressive illness, spoke of the terrors of being hunted "by spiritual hounds in the night season" as well as of the deadening side to his melancholy:

The weather is an exact emblem of my mind in its present state. A thick fog invelops every thing, and at the same time it freezes intensely. You will tell me that this cold gloom will be succeeded by a cheerful spring, and endeavor to encourage me to hope for a spiritual change resembling it. But it will be lost labour: Nature revives again, but a soul once slain, lives no more. The hedge that has been apparently dead, is not so, it will burst into leaf and blossom at the appointed time; but no such time is appointed for the stake that stands in it. It is as dead as it seems, and will prove itself no dissembler.[19]

Austrian composer Hugo Wolf, who died from tertiary syphilis but whose volatility and extremes in mood predated the symptoms of his paresis, focused on the painful contrast between the subjective experience of an arid, sterile reality and a sense of the external world as an unobtainable, visible, but not for him habitable place of light, warmth, and creation:

What I suffer from this continuous idleness I am quite unable to describe. I would like most to hang myself on the nearest branch of the cherry trees standing now in full bloom. This wonderful spring with its secret life and movement troubles me unspeakably. These eternal blue skies, lasting for weeks, this continuous sprouting and budding in nature, these coaxing breezes impregnated with spring sunlight and fragrance of flowers . . . make me frantic. Everywhere this bewildering urge for life, fruitfulness, creation—and only I, although like the humblest grass of the fields one of God's creatures, may not take part in this festival of resurrection, at any rate not except as a spectator with grief and envy.[20]

He also described the gap that frequently exists between public appearance and private despair: "I appear at times merry and in good heart, talk, too, before others quite reasonably, and it looks as if I felt, too, God knows how well within my skin; yet the soul maintains its deathly sleep and the heart bleeds from a thousand wounds."[21]

Depression affects not only mood but the nature and content of thought as well. Thinking processes almost always slow down, and decisiveness is replaced by indecision and rumination. The ability to concentrate is usually greatly impaired and willful action and thought become difficult if not impossible. English poet Edward Thomas spoke of a "dulness and thickness of brain"[22] and

Cowper wrote with bitter irony about the existence of only enough
sense and intellect to allow him awareness of his damaged mind:

> Oh wretch! to whom life and death are alike impossible! Most mis-
> erable at present in this, that being thus miserable I have my senses
> continued to me only that I may look forward to the worst. It is
> certain at least, that I have them for no other purpose, and but very
> imperfectly even for this. My thoughts are like loose dry sand, which
> the closer it is grasped slips the sooner away. Mr. Johnson reads to
> me, but I lose every other sentence through the inevitable wander-
> ings of my mind, and experience, as I have these two years, the same
> shattered mode of thinking on every subject and on all occasions. If
> I seem to write with more connextion, it is only because the gaps do
> not appear.[23]

Irrational fears, feelings of panic (including actual panic attacks), obsessions, and delusions are also present in many types of
severe depression. Robert Schumann described his panic and terrors during one of his many bouts of melancholy.

> I was little more than a statue, neither cold nor warm; by dint of
> forced work life returned gradually. But I am still so timid and fearful
> that I cannot sleep alone. . . . Do you believe that I have not the
> courage to travel alone . . . for fear something might befall me?
> Violent rushes of blood, unspeakable fear, breathlessness, momen-
> tary unconsciousness, alternate quickly.[24]

Excessive preoccupation with sin and religion are not uncommon in depression; likewise, thoughts of suicide often accompany
feelings of despair and apathy. David Cecil, in *The Stricken Deer*,
wrote about one of Cowper's anguished periods of melancholic
insanity, which was followed, in turn, by the resumption of a relatively normal existence:

> A mood of lassitude and dejection took possession of his spirits. He
> lost all pleasure in society, would sit for hours at his table, unable to
> bring himself to work at anything.
>   So passed December; and now January, fatal January, was here.
> Sure enough, the old symptoms began to reappear. His sleep was
> troubled by dreams, his waking hours by accusing voices. . . . His

shaken nerves could muster up no power of resistance. Every day he grew rapidly worse. Melancholy swelled to obsession, obsession to delusion. . . . For the third time in his life Cowper was a raving maniac. . . .

The disease followed its old course. Once again he tried to kill himself. Once again he shrank from all other friends . . . this time it lasted much less long than before. There was no period of gradual recovery. One day in July he returned to his right mind; and by September he was working and writing letters and dining out, to outward appearance just the same as he had been before the attack.[25]

Like thought and verbal expression, activity and behavior are almost always slowed in the depressed phase of manic-depressive illness. Fatigue, lassitude, and a marked inability to exercise will are part and parcel of depression as well. In his 1936 autobiographical essay *The Crack-Up*, F. Scott Fitzgerald traced the ebbings and flowings of several of his breakdowns, describing in the process the backing off from friends and social ties of all sorts, endless and fearful sleeping, obsessive list making, the great effort required for even the slightest of everyday transactions, and the frenetic pace that led up to the "cracking":

I found I was good-and-tired. I could lie around and was glad to, sleeping or dozing sometimes twenty hours a day and in the intervals trying resolutely not to think—instead I made lists . . . hundreds of lists. . . .

I realized . . . that every act of life from the morning toothbrush to the friend at dinner had become an effort . . . hating the night when I couldn't sleep and hating the day because it went toward night. I slept on the heart side now because I knew that the sooner I could tire that out, even a little, the sooner would come that blessed hour of nightmare which, like a catharsis, would enable me to better meet the new day. . . .

All rather inhuman and undernourished, isn't it? Well, that, children, is the true sign of cracking up.[26]

Bleak weariness with life, very much a hallmark of his recurrent melancholy, was also described by poet Edward Thomas:

There will never be any summer any more, and I am weary of everything. I stay because I am too weak to go. I crawl on because it

is easier than to stop. I put my face to the window. There is nothing
out there but the blackness and the sound of rain. Neither when I
shut my eyes can I see anything. I am alone. . . . There is nothing
else in my world but my dead heart and brain within me and the rain
without.[27]

Irish poet James Clarence Mangan described not only the
absolute psychic and physical exhaustion of depression but also the
psychosis that, in his case, had preceded it:

> My nervous and hypochondriacal [melancholic] feelings almost
> verged upon insanity. I seemed to myself to be shut up in a cavern
> with serpents and scorpions and all hideous and monstrous things,
> which writhed and hissed around me, and discharged their slime and
> venom over my person. . . .[28]
>
> A settled melancholy took possession of my being. A sort of
> torpor and weariness of life succeeded to my former over-excited
> sensibilities. Books no longer interested me as before; and my own
> unshared thoughts were a burden and torment to me.[29]

"It was," he said, "woe on woe, and 'within the lowest deep a lower
deep.' "[30] It is not surprising that despair should find its way into
so many of his poems:

> Tell thou the world, when my bones lie whitening
>   Amid the last homes of youth and eld,
> That there was once one whose veins ran lightning
>   No eye beheld.
>
> .   .   .   .
>
> And tell how trampled, derided, hated,
>   And worn by weakness, disease, and wrong,
> He fled for shelter to God, who mated
>   His soul with song—
>
> .   .   .   .
>
> Tell how this Nameless, condemned for years long
>   To herd with demons from hell beneath,
> Saw things that made him, with groans and tears, long
>   For even death.[31]

Gerard Manley Hopkins, English poet and Jesuit, died of a fever in Dublin in 1889. At the time he was relatively young, morbidly depressed, and in fear of going mad. The depressions from which he suffered were clearly becoming more chronic. In 1885 he wrote that "The melancholy I have all my life been subject to has become of late years not indeed more intense in its fits but rather more distributed, constant, and crippling . . . my state is much like madness."[32] Later in the year he wrote, "soon I am afraid I shall be ground down to a state like this last spring's and summer's, when my spirits were so crushed that madness seemed to be making approaches."[33] In January of the year he died he stated, "All my undertakings miscarry: I am like a straining eunuch. I wish then for death."[34] "The body cannot rest when it is in pain," said Hopkins, "nor the mind be at peace as long as something bitter distills in it and it aches."[35] Hopkins's poetry, like his prose, is palpable with his anguish. His "Dark Sonnets," among the great poems of despair, were, he said, "written in blood."[36] This takes no convincing to believe:

> No worst, there is none. Pitched past pitch of grief,
> More pangs will, schooled at forepangs, wilder wring.
> Comforter, where, where is your comforting?
> Mary, mother of us, where is your relief?
> My cries heave, herds-long; huddle in a main, a chief-
> Woe, world-sorrow; on an age-old anvil wince and sing—
> Then lull, then leave off. Fury had shrieked 'No ling-
> Ering! Let me be fell: force I must be brief'.
> O the mind, mind has mountains; cliffs of fall
> Frightful, sheer, no-man-fathomed. Hold them cheap
> May who ne'er hung there. Nor does long our small
> Durance deal with that steep or deep. Here! creep,
> Wretch, under a comfort serves in a whirlwind: all
> Life death does end and each day dies with sleep.[37]

Moods are by nature compelling, contagious, and profoundly interpersonal, and disorders of mood alter the perceptions and behaviors not only of those who have them but also of those who are related or closely associated. Manic-depressive illness—marked as it is by extraordinary and confusing fluctuations in mood, personality, thinking, and behavior—inevitably has powerful and often painful effects on relationships. The anger, withdrawal, and blackness of melancholic moods are captured graphically in this passage from *Cloud Howe*, by Scottish novelist Lewis Grassic Gibbon:

> Sometimes a black, queer mood came on Robert, he would lock himself up long hours in his room, hate God and Chris and himself and all men, know his Faith a fantastic dream; and see the fleshless grin of the skull and the eyeless sockets at the back of life. He would pass by Chris on the stairs if they met, with remote, cold eyes and a twisted face, or ask in a voice that cut like a knife, *Can't you leave me alone, must you always follow?*
>
> The first time it happened her heart had near stopped, she went on with her work in a daze of amaze. But Robert came back from his mood and came seeking her, sorry and sad for the queer, black beast that rode his mind in those haunted hours.[38]

Disrupted and fitful sleep, or sleeping far too much or far too little, are among the most pervasive and consistent symptoms of depression. Quentin Bell, in his biography of his aunt, Virginia Woolf, described her sleepness nights and their aftermath: "After such nights the days brought headaches, drilling the occiput as though it were a rotten tooth; and then came worse nights; nights made terrible by the increasing weight of anxiety and depression."[39] Bell continued on with Woolf's own description of such nights from her novel *The Voyage Out*, drawn in part from her own experience with manic-depressive illness: "those interminable nights which do not end at twelve, but go on into the double figures—thirteen, fourteen, and so on until they reach the twenties, and then the thirties, and then the forties . . . there is nothing to prevent nights from doing this if they choose."[40] Sylvia Plath, who was hospitalized for severe depression and ultimately committed suicide, described her awful and sleepless nights in the autobiographical novel *The Bell Jar*:

> I hadn't washed my hair for three weeks. . . .
> I hadn't slept for seven nights.
> My mother told me I must have slept, it was impossible not to sleep in all that time, but if I slept, it was with my eyes wide open, for I had followed the green, luminous course of the second hand and

the minute hand and the hour hand of the bedside clock through their circles and semicircles, every night for seven nights, without missing a second, or a minute, or an hour.

The reason I hadn't washed my clothes or my hair was because it seemed so silly.

I saw the days of the year stretching ahead like a series of bright, white boxes, and separating one box from another was sleep, like a black shade. Only for me, the long perspective of shades that set off one box from the next had suddenly snapped up, and I could see day after day glaring ahead of me like a white, broad, infinitely desolate avenue.

It seemed silly to wash one day when I would only have to wash again the next.

It made me tired just to think of it.

I wanted to do everything once and for all and be through with it.[41]

And finally, Theodore Roethke, who, like so many of his fellow poets suffered from manic-depressive illness, described an almost unbearable pain:

> I have myself an inner weight of woe
> That God himself can scarcely bear.
>
> .   .   .   .
>
> What you survived I shall believe: the Heat,
> Scars, Tempests, Floods, the Motion of Man's Fate;
> I have myself, and bear its weight of woe
> That God that God leans down His heart to hear.[42]

In striking contrast to the melancholic states are the manic ones, in which, wrote Hugo Wolf, the "blood becomes changed into streams of fire."[43] Mania is characterized by an exalted or irritable mood, more and faster speech, rapid thought, brisker physical and mental activity levels, quickened and more finely tuned senses, suspiciousness, a marked tendency to seek out other people, and impulsiveness. In hypomania, the less severe form of mania, these changes tend to be moderate and may or may not result in serious difficulties for the individual experiencing them. As the hypomania intensifies, however, it profoundly disrupts the lives of those who are manic, their families and acquaintances, and the society in which they live. The range of symptoms in the manic states, from those found in the mild hypomanias to florid psychosis in acute mania, is as wide as that found in the depressive states.

Mood in hypomania is usually ebullient, self-confident, and often transcendent, but it almost always exists with an irritable underpinning. Hypomanic mood, although elevated, is generally both fluctuating and volatile. Manic mood, frequently character-ized as elated and grandiose, is often as not riddled by depression, panic, and extreme irritability. The perceptual and physical changes that almost always accompany hypomania and mania gen-erally reflect the close and subtle links that exist between elevated mood, a sense of well-being, expansive and grandiose thought, and intensified perceptual awareness.

Examples of manic grandiosity, visionary expansiveness, and unbridled euphoria are abundant in writers and artists. Benjamin Haydon—friend of John Keats, and a painter who eventually killed himself—once wrote exuberantly in his journal that "I have been like a man with air balloons under his armpits and ether in his soul,"[44] and Theodore Roethke captured the mystical merging of identities and experiences so common to the manic experience:

> For no reason I started to feel very good. Suddenly I knew how to enter into the life of everything around me. I knew how it felt to be a tree, a blade of grass, even a rabbit. I didn't sleep much. I just walked around with this wonderful feeling. One day I was passing a diner and all of a sudden I knew what it felt like to be a lion. I went into the diner and said to the counter-man, "Bring me a steak. Don't cook it. Just bring it." So he brought me this raw steak and I started eating it. The other customers made like they were revolted, watch-ing me. And I began to see that maybe it *was* a little strange. So I went to the Dean [at the university where Roethke taught] and said, "I feel too good. Get me down off this." So they put me into the tubs.[45]

William Meredith, in describing one of Robert Lowell's many manic attacks, related the psychotic grandiosity of Lowell's think-ing and actions:

No one predicts how long it will be before the drugs take hold &
[Lowell] begins to be himself again. Meanwhile he writes and revises
translations furiously and with a kind [of] crooked brilliance, and
talks about himself in connection with Achilles, Alexander, Hart
Crane, Hitler, and Christ, and breaks your heart.[46]

   Manic and hypomanic thought are flighty and leap from topic
to topic; in milder manic states the pattern of association between
ideas is usually clear, but, as the mania increases in severity, thinking becomes fragmented and often psychotic. Paranoid, religious,
and grandiose delusions are common, as are illusions and hallucinations. Lowell, for example, wrote about one of his manic experiences:

> Seven years ago I had an attack of pathological enthusiasm. The night
> before I was locked up I ran about the streets of Bloomington Indiana
> crying out against devils and homosexuals. I believed I could stop cars
> and paralyze their forces by merely standing in the middle of the high-
> way with my arms outspread. . . . Bloomington stood for Joyce's hero
> and Christian regeneration. Indiana stood for the evil, unexorcised,
> aboriginal Indians. I suspected I was a reincarnation of the Holy
> Ghost, and had become homicidally hallucinated. To have known the
> glory, violence and banality of such an experience is corrupting.[47]

Another side of mania—its dendritic, branching-out quality—was
described by John Ruskin:

> I roll on like a ball, with this exception, that contrary to the usual laws
> of motion I have no friction to contend with in my mind, and of course
> have some difficulty in stopping myself when there is nothing else to
> stop me. . . . I am almost sick and giddy with the quantity of things
> in my head—trains of thought beginning and branching to infinity,
> crossing each other, and all tempting and wanting to be worked out.[48]

Leonard Woolf noted the deteriorating quality of Virginia Woolf's
thinking and speech as her illness worsened; her speech, like
Ruskin's thought, went on seemingly without stop:

> She talked almost without stopping for two or three days, paying no
> attention to anyone in the room or anything said to her. For about a
> day what she said was coherent; the sentences meant something,

though it was nearly all wildly insane. Then gradually it became completely incoherent, a mere jumble of dissociated words.[49]

One of the best descriptions of the far-ranging, intoxicating, and leapfrogging nature of manic thought and conversation is given by Saul Bellow in *Humboldt's Gift*, a novel based in part on the manic and chaotic lives of poets Delmore Schwartz and John Berryman:

> Now a word about Humboldt's conversation. What was the poet's conversation actually like?
> He wore the look of a balanced thinker when he began, but he was not the picture of sanity. I myself loved to talk and kept up with him as long as I could. For a while it was a double concerto, but presently I was fiddled and trumpeted off the stage. Reasoning, formulating, debating, making discoveries Humboldt's voice rose, choked, rose again . . . he passed from statement to recitative, from recitative he soared into aria, and behind him played an orchestra of intimations, virtues, love of his art, veneration of its great men—but also of suspicion and skulduggery. Before your eyes the man recited and sang himself in and out of madness.
> He started by talking about the place of art and culture in the first Stevenson administration. . . . From this Humboldt turned to Roosevelt's sex life . . . he moved easily from the tabloids to General Rommel and from Rommel to John Donne and T. S. Eliot. About Eliot he seemed to know strange facts no one else had ever heard. He was filled with gossip and hallucination as well as literary theory. Distortion was inherent, yes, in all poetry. But which came first? And this rained down on me . . . chorus girls, prostitution and religion, old money, new money, gentlemen's clubs, Back Bay, Newport, Washington Square, Henry Adams, Henry James, Henry Ford, Saint John of the Cross, Dante, Ezra Pound, Dostoevski, Marilyn Monroe and Joe DiMaggio, Gertrude Stein and Alice, Freud and Ferenczi.[50]

As with all signs and symptoms of manic-depressive illness, including those of thought, perceptual and sensory changes vary in degree and kind. Mild increases in the awareness of objects that actually exist in an individual's environment—the "hyperacusis" so frequently a part of hypomania and mania—can progress to total disarray of the senses; this, in turn, can result in visual, auditory, and olfactory hallucinations (sensory experiences not based on existing physical phenomena). At the milder end of the continuum of perceptual change, Poe gave a fictional account of moods "of the keenest appetency":

> Not long ago, about the closing in of an evening in autumn, I sat at the large bow window of the D—— Coffee-House in London. For some months I had been ill in health, but was now convalescent, and, with returning strength, found myself in one of those happy moods which are so precisely the converse of *ennui*—moods of the keenest appetency, when the film from the mental vision departs . . . and the intellect, electrified, surpasses as greatly its everyday condition, as does the vivid yet candid reason of Leibnitz, the mad and flimsy rhetoric of Gorgias. Merely to breathe was enjoyment; and I derived positive pleasure even from many of the legitimate sources of pain.[51]

John Ruskin wrote of his own experiences with what he called the "conditions of spectral vision and audit" belonging to "certain states of brain excitement":

> I saw the stars rushing at each other—and thought the lamps of London were gliding through the night into a World Collision. . . . Nothing was more notable to me through the illness than the general exaltation of the nerves of sight and hearing, and their power of making colour and sound harmonious as well as intense—with altern- ation of faintness and horror of course. But I learned so much about the nature of Phantasy and Phantasm—it would have been totally inconceivable to me without seeing, how the unreal and real could be mixed.[52]

Among the particularly dramatic and extreme clinical features of acute mania are its associated frenetic, seemingly aimless, and violent actions. Bizarre, driven, paranoid, and impulsive patterns of behavior are common; irrational financial activities, including massive overspending and unwise investments, often occur. The idiosyncratically meaningful, often wildly funny purchases that manics can make are wonderfully captured in a recent novel by Jonathan Carroll:

> There was no screech of tires, screams, or thunderous crash when my mind went flying over the cliff into madness, as I gather is true in

many cases. Besides, we've all seen too many bad movies where
characters scratch their faces or make hyena sounds to indicate
they've gone nuts.

Not me. One minute I was famous, successful, self-assured
Harry Radcliffe in the trick store, looking for inspiration in a favorite
spot. The next, I was quietly but very seriously mad, walking out of
that shop with two hundred and fifty yellow pencil sharpeners. I
don't know how other people go insane, but my way was at least
novel.

Melrose Avenue is not a good place to lose your mind. The
stores on the street are full of lunatic desires and are only too happy
to let you have them if you can pay. I could.

Anyone want an African gray parrot named Noodle Koofty? I
named him in the ride back to Santa Barbara. He sat silently in a
giant black cage in the back of my Mercedes station wagon, surrounded by objects I can only cringe at when I think of them now:
three colorful garden dwarves about three feet high, each holding a
gold hitching ring; five Conway Twitty albums that cost twenty dollars each because they were "classics"; three identical Sam the Sham
and the Pharaohs albums, "classics" as well, twenty-five dollars a
piece; a box of bathroom tiles with a revolting peach motif; a wall-size
poster of a chacma baboon in the same pose as Rodin's *The Thinker*
. . . other things too, but you get the drift.[53]

Mania also tends to bring with it indefatigability, a markedly
decreased need for sleep, and the aggressive pursuing of human
contact. The emotional consequences of such behaviors can be
devastating. In portions of two letters to T. S. Eliot, Robert Lowell
wrote of his embarrassment following different manic episodes:

[June 1961] The whole business has been very bruising, and it is
fierce facing the pain I have caused, and humiliating [to] think that
it has all happened before and that control and self-knowledge come
so slowly, if at all.[54]

[March 1964] I want to apologize for plaguing you with so many
telephone calls last November and December. When the "enthusiasm" is coming on me it is accompanied by a feverish reaching to my
friends. After it's over I wince and wither.[55]

The aftermath of mania is usually depression—Lowell once
described mania as "a magical orange grove in a nightmare"[56]—and

indeed, as we shall see, mania and depression are frequently min-
gled together or alternate one to the other in an ongoing process of
changing vitalities, a process finding its counterpart in the natural
world, as described by Delmore Schwartz:

The river was opulence, radiance, sparkle, and shine, a rippling radiance dancing light's dances;
And the birds flew, soared, darted, perched, perched and whistled,
dipped or ascended
Like a ballet of black flutes, an erratic and scattered metamorphosis
of the villages of stillness into the variety of flying:
The birds were as a transformation of trunk and branch and twig into
the elation which is the energy's celebration and consummation!

—It was difficult, then, to believe—how difficult it was and how painful it was to believe in the reality of winter,
Beholding so many supple somersaults of energy and deathless feats
of superexuberant vitality, all self-delighting,
Arising, waving, flying, glittering, and glistening as if in irresistible
eagerness,

Seeking with serene belief and undivided certainty, love's miracles,
tender, or thrashing, or thrashing towards tenderness boldly.
It was necessary to think of pine and fir,
Of holly, ivy, barberry bush and icicle, of frozen ground,
And of wooden tree, white or wet and drained,
And of the blackened or stiffened arms of elm, oak and maple
To remember, even a little, that existence was not forever
May and the beginning of summer:
It was only possible to forget the presence of the present's green and
gold and white flags of flowering May's victory, summer's ascend-
ancy and sovereignty,
By thinking of how all arise and aspire to the nature of fire, to the
flame-like climbing of vine and leaf and flower,
And calling to mind how all things must suffer and die in growth and
birth,
To be reborn, again and again and again, to be transformed all over
again.[57]

Although much of our discussion of mania and depression has
emphasized the differences between the two clinical states, it is
important to note that the oscillation into, out of, and within the

various forms and states of the disease is, in its own right, a hall-mark of manic-depressive illness. Manic and depressive symptom patterns clearly have a polar quality, but the overlapping, transi-tional, and fluctuating aspects are enormously important in de-scribing and understanding the illness as a whole. Professor Emil Kraepelin, who more than anyone defined and described manic-depressive illness, wrote:

> The delimitation of the individual clinical forms of the malady is in many respects wholly artificial and arbitrary. Observation not only reveals the occurrence of gradual transitions between all the various states, but it also shows that within the shortest space of time the same morbid case may pass through most manifold transformations.[58]

More recently, in the 1950s, Dr. John Campbell emphasized this fundamentally dynamic nature of manic-depressive illness by com-paring the illness with a movie:

> The fluidity, change, and movement of the emotions, as they occur in the ever-changing cyclothymic process, may be compared to the pictures of a cinema, as contrasted with a "still" photograph. Indeed, the psychiatrist, observing a manic-depressive patient for the first time, or as he undergoes one of the many undulations in mood, from melancholia to euphoria or from hypomania to a depression, is re-minded of the experience of entering a movie during the middle of the story. No matter where one takes up the plot, the story tends to swing around again to the point where it started. The examiner may observe the manic-depressive patient first in a manic reaction, later in a depression, but eventually, if followed long enough, in another manic reaction. Like the movie, which is a continuous but constantly changing process, the cyclothymic process is also continuous even though for the moment the observer is attracted by the immediate cross-section view. This conception of change, or constant undulation of the emotions, is much more accurate than a static appraisal.[59]

The link between mania and depression had been noted for centuries.[60] As early as the second century A.D., for example, Aretaeus of Cappadocia observed that "melancholia is without any doubt the beginning and even part of the disorder called mania";[61] so too, Alexander of Tralles (c. 575) wrote that individuals tended to have cycles of mania and melancholia, and that "mania is nothing else but melancholia in a more intense form."[62] By the sixteenth century Jason Pratensis had concluded that "most physicians associate mania and melancholia (truly dreadful diseases) as one disorder";[63] he, like most others, distinguished mania from melancholia by "degree and manifestation" only. Alternating and interwoven patterns of mania and depression were well described by seventeenth-century writers, and Michel Foucault gives a vivid summary of the work of one of them, Dr. Thomas Willis:

> In the melancholic . . . the spirits were somber and dim; they cast their shadows over the images of things and formed a kind of dark tide; in the maniac, on the contrary, the spirits seethed in a perpetual ferment; they were carried by an irregular movement, constantly repeated; a movement that eroded and consumed, and even without fever, sent out its heat. Between mania and melancholia, the affinity is evident: not the affinity of symptoms linked in experience, but the affinity—more powerful and so much more evident in the landscapes of the imagination—that unites in the same fire both smoke and flame.[64]

By the eighteenth and nineteenth centuries, most medical writers thought of mania as an extreme form of melancholia. Richard Mead wrote in 1751:

> Medical writers distinguish two kinds of Madness, and describe them both as a constant disorder of the mind without any considerable fever; but with this difference, that the one is attended with audaciousness and fury, the other with sadness and fear: and that they call mania, this melancholy. But these generally differ in degree only. For melancholy very frequently changes, sooner or later, into maniacal madness; and, when the fury is abated, the sadness generally returns heavier than before.[65]

Doctors Jean Pierre Falret and Jules Baillarger, in the mid-nineteenth century, formally posited that mania and depression could represent different manifestations of a single illness. Falret noted the strong depressive quality often occurring before, during, and after manic episodes, as well as *melancholie anxieuse*, "characterized by constant pacing and inner turmoil, which incapacitates these patients so they cannot concentrate, and this state sometimes ends up as manic agitation."[66] Kraepelin, in his 1921 classic textbook about manic-depressive illness, described mixed states, in which depressive and manic symptoms coexist; he conceptualized these mixed states as primarily transitional phenomena—that is, they tended to occur when an individual was going into or out of a depressive or manic state.[67] Such states, as we shall see later, represent an important link between manic-depressive illness, artistic temperament, creativity, and the rhythms and temperament of the natural world. Unfortunately, they also are closely associated with the damaging and killing sides of manic-depressive illness: alcoholism, drug abuse, and suicide.

"But I am constitutionally sensitive—nervous in a very unusual degree. I became insane, with long periods of horrible sanity," wrote Poe. "During these fits of absolute unconsciousness I drank, God knows how much or how long. As a matter of course, my enemies referred the insanity to the drink rather than the drink to the insanity."[68] For many Poe personifies the stereotype of the alcoholic writer; it is rare to find a discussion of alcohol and writers without reference to him, or to Fitzgerald, Hemingway, Tennessee Williams, Berryman, or Lowell. And yet all suffered from depressive or manic-depressive illness as well, raising complicated questions about whether the melancholic muse is also a "thirsty muse"[69]—that is, whether alcohol and other drugs are used by writers and artists to alleviate painful depressions and agitated manic states; whether they are responsible for changes in mood; whether they are used to provoke or recapture freer, less inhibited states of mind and emotion; or whether some combination of all of these obtains. One Poe biographer wrote: "We know now that what made Poe write was what made him drink: alcohol and literature were the two safety valves of a mind that eventually tore itself apart,"[70] and W. R. Bett, writing in the 1950s, said:

> Poe's indulgence . . . was one of the methods by which he fought the intolerable morbidity of his manic-depressive state of mind and sought a temporary forgetfulness of the misfortunes and setbacks to which he seemed predestined. Had this been his only weapon to relieve the depressions that overtook him, he would, like thousands of others similarly affected, have lived his life unknown and gone unsung by posterity. But he had a second weapon—his pen.[71]

Indeed, Poe himself described some of this "intolerable morbidity"; he also described why on one occasion he reached out to laudanum in a desperate, suicidal attempt to escape from his psychological pain:

> You saw, you *felt* the agony of grief with which I bade you farewell—You remember my expressions of gloom—of a dreadful horrible foreboding of ill—Indeed—*indeed* it seemed to me that death approached me even then, & that I was involved in the shadow which went before him. . . . I remember nothing distinctly, from that moment until I found myself in Providence—I went to bed & wept through a long, long, hideous night of despair—When the day broke, I arose & endeavored to quiet my mind by a rapid walk in the cold, keen air—but all *would* not do—the demon tormented me still. Finally I procured two ounces of laudanum. . . . I am so *ill*—so terribly, hopelessly ILL in body and mind, that I feel I CANNOT live . . . until I subdue this fearful agitation, which if continued, will either destroy my life or, drive me hopelessly mad.[72]

Inordinately sensitive to his moods, Poe was also aware of their cyclic and alternating nature. In a letter to poet James Russell Lowell, whose own temperament was deeply moody, he wrote:

> I can feel for the "constitutional indolence" of which you complain—for it is one of my own besetting sins. I am excessively slothful, and wonderfully industrious—by fits. There are epochs when any kind of mental exercise is torture, and when nothing yields me pleasure but solitary communion with the "mountains & the woods"—the "altars" of Byron. I have thus rambled and dreamed away whole months, and awake, at last, to a sort of mania for composition. Then I scribble all day, and read all night, so long as the disease endures.[73]

Poe was scarcely alone in suffering from both manic-depressive illness and alcohol and drug abuse. Studies are quite consistent in finding elevated rates of alcohol and drug abuse in individuals with manic-depressive illness;[74] conversely, there is a significantly higher percentage of bipolar patients in populations of alcoholics and drug abusers.[75] The largest and best-designed investigation to date has been the Epidemiologic Catchment Area (ECA) study, a large survey conducted by the National Institute of Mental Health in five major American population centers (New Haven, Baltimore, St. Louis, Los Angeles, and Piedmont County, North Carolina). The study found an exceedingly high lifetime prevalence rate, 46 percent, for alcohol abuse and dependence in patients with manic-depressive illness; the figures for unipolar depressed patients and the general population were 21 and 13 percent respectively.[76] A related study found that mania was strongly associated with alcoholism but major depression was not.[77] Although it is perhaps more intuitive to link increased alcohol use with the depressed phase of manic-depressive illness, evidence suggests that increased alcohol consumption is actually more frequently associated with hypomania, mania, and the mixed or transitional states. Indeed, manic-depressive patients who increase their alcohol consumption generally do so during the manic phase.[78] For Robert Lowell the combination of alcohol and mania often proved an especially disinhibiting one. Here he is described by the congressional representative who accompanied him on a cultural exchange program to South America:

When we got to Argentina, it was six double vodka martinis before lunch. And he made me drink with him. We went to lunch at the presidential palace, the Casa Rosada, and Cal [Robert Lowell] promptly insulted the general, who was in fact about to be president of Argentina, and started one of the many diplomatic rumpuses he caused on that trip. There was the American cultural attaché, whose name I cannot remember, and Cal was sitting at this lunch in a very loud checked sports coat and open shirt, and all the generals were there, very uptight and distinguished. And there was this wonderful opening scene when Cal was introduced to the cultural attaché and talked to him for about three minutes. The guy was an absolute idiot and asked stupid questions and obviously didn't know who Cal was. So Cal turned on him and said, "You're the cultural attaché?" "Yep, sure am." And Cal said, "How can you be the cultural attaché? You're illiterate." That's how the lunch started, and it went on from there. After the lunch, Cal started his tour of the equestrian statues, undressing[,] and climbing the statues. He insisted on being taken to every statue in B.A.—well, we didn't do every one, thank God. And he'd stop the car and start clambering up and sit next to the general on top of the statue.[79]

Excesses of all kinds characterize mania, and intemperate drinking may be just one aspect of this general pattern; however, self-medication of painful or uncomfortable mood states no doubt accounts for some of the association as well. To an extent, alcohol does provide relief from the irritability, restlessness, and agitation associated with mania; not surprisingly, alcohol use often increases dramatically during mixed states as well. Unfortunately, however, alcohol and drug abuse often worsens the overall course of manic-depressive illness, occasionally precipitates the disease in vulnerable individuals, and frequently undermines the effects of treatment.[80]

Other drugs, such as cocaine and opium, are also abused by individuals who have manic-depressive illness.[81] The findings from the ECA study show that the lifetime prevalence rate of drug abuse in bipolar patients is 41 percent; this is far higher than in unipolar depressed patients or the general population (18 and 6 percent, respectively).[82] Conversely, the rates of bipolar illness among cocaine and opiate abusers are several times higher than in the general population.[83] The selection of drugs for self-medication tends to depend upon the predominant nature of the symptoms an individual experiences; sedative drugs such as alcohol and opiates are generally preferred by those patients who have agitated and perturbed forms of depression, or irritable and highly uncomfortable manias. The use of cocaine and other stimulants by individuals with manic-depressive illness is more complicated; for example, there is evidence that most patients report using cocaine, primarily when hypomanic or manic, in order to enhance or induce the euphoric moods associated with these states.[84] One group of clinical investigators has reported that the majority of their bipolar and cyclothymic patients who abused cocaine stated that they were not self-medicating their depressions; rather, they were attempting to lengthen or intensify the euphoric effects of mild mania.[85]

The coexistence of alcoholism, drug abuse, and manic-depressive illness is more common than not; approximately 60 percent of patients with bipolar illness have a history of some kind of substance abuse or dependence.[86] These problems, not surprisingly, are common in writers and artists with manic-depressive illness as well; the consequences are often devastating. Samuel

Taylor Coleridge, for one, described his struggles with laudanum to a friend:

> No sixty hours *have yet passed* without my having taking [taken?] Laudanum—tho' for the last week comparatively trifling doses. I have full belief, that your *anxiety* will not need to be extended beyond the first week: and for the first week I shall not, I *must not be permitted* to leave your House, unless I should walk out with you.— Delicately or indelicately, this *must* be done: and both the Servant and the young Man must receive absolute commands from you on no account to fetch any thing for me. The stimulus of Conversation suspends the terror that haunts my mind; but when I am alone, the horrors, I have suffered from Laudanum, the degradation, the blighted Utility, almost overwhelm me—.[87]

One and one-half centuries later, American poet John Berryman wrote graphically about his destructive relationship with alcohol:

> Social drinking until 1947 during a long & terrible love affair, my first infidelity to my wife after 5 years of marriage. My mistress drank heavily & I drank w. her. Guilt, murderous & suicidal. Hallucinations one day walking home. Heard voices. 7 years of psychoanalysis & group therapy in N.Y. Walked up & down drunk on a foot-wide parapet 8 stories high. Passes at women drunk, often successful. Wife left me after 11 years of marriage bec. of drinking. Despair, heavy drinking alone, jobless, penniless, in N.Y. Lost when blacked-out the most important professional letter I have ever received. Seduced students drunk. Made homosexual advances drunk, 4 or 5 times. Antabuse once for a few days, agony on floor after a beer. Quarrel w. landlord drunk at midnight over the key to my apartment, he called police, spent the night in jail, news somehow reached press & radio, forced to resign. Two months of intense self-analysis-dream-interpretation etc. Remarried. My chairman told me I had called up a student drunk at midnight & threatened to kill her. Wife left me bec. of drinking. Gave a public lecture drunk. Drunk in Calcutta, wandered streets lost all night, unable to remember my address. Married present wife 8 yrs ago. Many barbiturates & tranquilizers off & on over last 10 yrs. Many hospitalizations. Many alibis for drinking, lying abt. it. Severe memory-loss, memory distortions. DT's once in Abbott, lasted hours. Quart of whisky a day for months in Dublin working hard on a long poem. Dry 4 months 2 years ago. Wife hiding bottles, myself hiding bottles.[88]

The ultimate self-destruction by alcohol, however, was personified by the life and death of the wildly mercurial Welsh poet Dylan Thomas:

> Dylan was now having blackouts at frequent intervals. On more than one occasion he had been warned by his doctor that he must go on a regime of complete abstinence from alcohol if he was to survive. . . . Dylan seemed exhausted, self-preoccupied, and morbidly depressed. He went out alone, and an hour and a half later returned to announce, "I've had eighteen straight whiskeys. I think that's the record." [Shortly afterwards] he died.[89]

In addition to drinking and using drugs to excess, individuals with depressive and manic-depressive illness are also far more likely to commit suicide than individuals in any other psychiatric or medical risk group. The mortality rate for untreated manic-depressive illness is higher than it is for many types of heart disease and cancer. Kraepelin described the grim, virtually incomprehensible level of anguish and desperation experienced by many of his patients:

> The patients, therefore, often try to starve themselves, to hang themselves, to cut their arteries; they beg that they may be burned, buried alive, driven out into the woods and there allowed to die. . . . One of my patients struck his neck so often on the edge of a chisel fixed on the ground that all the soft parts were cut through to the vertebrae.[90]

A recent review of thirty studies found that, on the average, one-fifth of manic-depressive patients die by suicide. From a slightly different perspective, at least two-thirds of those people who commit suicide have been found to have suffered from depressive or manic-depressive illness.[91] In an extensive clinical investigation carried out in Sweden, suicide was almost eighty times more likely among patients with depressive illness—unipolar or bipolar—than in those individuals with no psychiatric disorder,[92] and, in a recent study of risk factors among adolescents who had died by suicide, four factors accounted for more than 80 percent of the suicides: a diagnosis of bipolar manic-depressive illness, coexisting alcohol or drug abuse, lack of prior treatment, and the availability of firearms. Of these the diagnosis of manic-depressive illness contributed the most to the prediction.[93] Suicide, for many who suffer from untreated manic-depressive illness, is as much "wired" into the disease as myocardial infarction is for those who have occluded coronary arteries. Because suicide appears more volitional, some- how more existentially caused, and more tied to external circum- stance than it often actually is, the seriousness of manic-depressive illness as a potentially lethal medical condition is frequently over- looked. (A partial listing of artists, writers, and composers who attempted or committed suicide is given in Appendix B.) In his suicide note American artist Ralph Barton predicted that those he left behind would be tempted to read into his death all manner of explanation while constantly overlooking the crucial one, his men- tal illness:

> Everyone who has known me and who hears of this will have a
> different hypothesis to offer to explain why I did it. Practically all of
> these hypotheses will be dramatic—and completely wrong. Any sane
> doctor knows that the reasons for suicide are invariably psycho-
> pathological. Difficulties in life merely precipitate the event—and
> the true suicide type manufactures his own difficulties. I have had
> few real difficulties. I have had, on the contrary, an exceptionally
> glamorous life—as lives go. And I have had more than my share of
> affection and appreciation. The most charming, intelligent, and im-
> portant people I have known have liked me—and the list of my
> enemies is very flattering to me. I have always had excellent health.
> But, since my early childhood, I have suffered with a melancholia
> which, in the past five years, has begun to show definite symptoms
> of manic-depressive insanity. It has prevented my getting anything
> like the full value out of my talents, and, for the past three years, has
> made work a torture to do at all. It has made it impossible for me to
> enjoy the simple pleasures of life that seem to get other people
> through. I have run from wife to wife, from house to house, and from
> country to country, in a ridiculous effort to escape from myself. In
> doing so, I am very much afraid that I have spread a good deal of
> unhappiness among the people who have loved me.[94]

Studies of attempted suicide in bipolar patients show that between one-fourth and one-half attempt suicide at least once.[95] In the largest epidemiological survey to date (more than twenty thou- sand participants), the lifetime rate for attempted suicide in indi-

viduals with no history of mental disorder was 1 percent; for those
with major depressive illness it was 18 percent, and for those suffering from manic-depressive illness it was 24 percent.[96] Novelist
Graham Greene, by his own account a manic-depressive, openly
discussed his suicidal behavior while an undergraduate at Oxford;
one of his friends, Lord Tranmire, told Greene's biographer: "We
were very worried over his attempts at Russian roulette. And in the
end we made him promise he would never do it with more than
two shots out of the five chambers."[97] Greene himself described
his first attempt:

> I slipped a bullet into a chamber and, holding the revolver behind
> my back, spun the chambers round. . . . I put the muzzle of the
> revolver into my right ear and pulled the trigger. There was a minute
> click, and looking down at the chamber I could see that the charge
> had moved into the firing position. I was out by one.[98]

Lord Byron thought seriously about suicide as well, although
his droll wit often masked the depth of his true suffering (his severe, often agitated melancholias are discussed further in chapter
5). In a letter to his friend and fellow poet Thomas Moore, Byron
wrote, "I should, many a good day, have blown my brains out, but
for the recollection that it would have given pleasure to my mother-
in-law; and, even *then*, if I could have been certain to haunt her—
but I won't dwell upon these trifling family matters."[99] Robert
Lowell, who in one poem used Byronic wit to describe the ambiguities and ambivalences attendant upon suicide—"A doubtful suicide should choose the ocean,/Who knows, he might reach the
other side?"[100]—wrote more tellingly in another:

> Do I deserve credit
> for not having tried suicide—
> or am I afraid
> the exotic act
> will make me blunder,
>
> not knowing error
> is remedied by practice,
> as our first home-photographs,
> headless, half-headed, tilting
> extinguished by a flashbulb?[101]

People who commit suicide generally communicate their intentions to others; in a study of 134 suicides, fully two-thirds of the manic-depressive patients had communicated their suicidal ideas, most frequently through a direct and specific statement of the intent to commit suicide.[102] Men and women did not differ significantly in their frequency of suicidal communication, and the communications were repeated and expressed to a number of different people; rarely were these communications perceived as "manipulative" or "playing on the emotions of others." No one committed suicide while manic; all were judged to have been depressed at the time of death. In *Darkness Visible* novelist William Styron wrote about the inescapability of his suicidal depression:

> The pain is unrelenting, and what makes the condition intolerable is the foreknowledge that no remedy will come—not in a day, an hour, a month, or a minute. If there is mild relief, one knows that it is only temporary; more pain will follow. It is hopelessness even more than pain that crushes the soul. So the decision-making of daily life involves not, as in normal affairs, shifting from one annoying situation to another less annoying—or from discomfort to relative comfort, or from boredom to activity—but moving from pain to pain. One does not abandon, even briefly, one's bed of nails, but is attached to it wherever one goes.[103]

And Leo Tolstoy described his weariness with life, his melancholy, and his suicidal obsessions, all of which existed within the framework of a seemingly complete and happy existence:

> The thought of suicide came to me as naturally then as the thought of improving life had come to me before. This thought was such a temptation that I had to use cunning against myself in order not to go through with it too hastily. I did not want to be in a hurry only because I wanted to use all my strength to untangle my thoughts. If I could not get them untangled, I told myself, I could always go ahead with it. And there I was, a fortunate man, carrying a rope from my room, where I was alone every night as I undressed, so that I would not hang myself from the beam between the closets. And I quit going hunting with a gun, so that I would not be too easily tempted to rid myself of life. I myself did not know what I wanted. I was afraid of life, I struggled to get rid of it, and yet I hoped for something from it.

And this was happening to me at a time when, from all indications, I should have been considered a completely happy man; this was when I was not yet fifty years old. I had a good, loving, and beloved wife, fine children, and a large estate that was growing and expanding without any effort on my part. More than ever before I was respected by friends and acquaintances, praised by strangers, and I could claim a certain renown without really deluding myself.[104]

Poet and critic A. Alvarez, in his book *The Savage God*, vividly portrayed the despair, violence and highly individualistic motives involved in suicide. In citing Italian writer Cesare Pavese—who once wrote that "no one ever lacks a good reason for suicide"[105] and who subsequently did commit suicide—Alvarez emphasized the limits to knowing the mind of any truly suicidal person. While it is important to avoid a sweepingly nihilistic notion of such limits, it also remains essential to recognize the ultimate inaccessibility of the many complex and idiosyncratic emotional states that usually accompany suicide:

It goes without saying that external misery has relatively little to do with suicide. . . . Suicide often seems to the outsider a supremely motiveless perversity, performed, as Montesquieu complained, "most unaccountably . . . in the very bosom of happiness," and for reasons which seem trivial or even imperceptible . . . At best they assuage the guilt of the survivors, soothe the tidy-minded and encourage the sociologists in their endless search for convincing categories and theories. The real motives . . . belong to the internal world, devious, contradictory, labyrinthine, and mostly out of sight.[106]

In the same book Alvarez also described the sterile and cold world of suicidal depression; like Hugo Wolf he drew the contrast between the normal and the depressed worlds, portraying an abyss that cannot be spanned:

A suicidal depression is a kind of spiritual winter, frozen, sterile, unmoving. The richer, softer and more delectable nature becomes, the deeper that internal winter seems, and the wider and more intolerable the abyss which separates the inner world from the outer. Thus suicide becomes a natural reaction to an unnatural condition.

Perhaps this is why, for the depressed, Christmas is so hard to bear. In theory it is an oasis of warmth and light in an unforgiving season, like a lighted window in a storm. For those who have to stay outside, it accentuates, like spring, the disjunction between public warmth and festivity, and cold, private despair.[107]

Suicidal thoughts and attempts, as well as suicide itself, are particularly common in mixed states. In one study conducted in the 1930s, Jameison found that mixed states were the most dangerous clinical phase of illness. In his study of one hundred suicides, half of whom had manic-depressive psychosis, he noted that the combination of depressive symptoms, mental alertness, and tense, apprehensive, and restless behavior was especially lethal; many other studies have found this as well.[108] Mixed states represent a critical combination of depressed feelings and thoughts combined with an exceptionally perturbed, agitated, and unpleasant physical state; usually accompanied by a heightened energy level and increased impulsivity, mixed states are far too often lethal to those who experience them. Percy Bysshe Shelley's melancholic states were made even more unbearable by wild agitation, insomnia, confusion, visions, obsessions, and thoughts of suicide. Themes of madness, despair, and suicide can be found in many of his poems:

> Then would I stretch my languid frame
> Beneath the wild wood's gloomiest shade,
> And try to quench the ceaseless flame
> That on my withered vitals preyed;
> Would close mine eyes and dream I were
> On some remote and friendless plain,
> And long to leave existence there,
> If with it I might leave the pain
> That with a finger cold and lean
> Wrote madness on my withering mien.[109]

That such a final, tragic, and awful thing as suicide can exist in the midst of remarkable beauty is one of the vastly contradictory and paradoxical aspects of life and art. The extraordinary and seemingly counterintuitive level of control in many of van Gogh's last canvases, completed just before his suicide, finds a comparable calm and lyricism in lines by Russian poet Vladimir Mayakovsky who, like van Gogh, committed suicide when he was in his mid-thirties:

> It's after one.
>   You must have gone to bed.
> The Milky Way runs like a silvery river through the night.
> I'm in no hurry
>   and with lightning telegrams
> there's no need to wake and worry you.
> As they say
>   the incident is closed
> The love boat
>   has smashed against convention
> Now you and I are through
>   No need then
> To count over mutual hurts, harms, and slights.
> Just see how quiet the world is!
> Night has laid a heavy tax of stars upon the sky.
> In hours like these you get up and you speak
> To the ages, to history, and to the universe.[110]

Mayakovsky's biographer Edward Brown notes "he included four lines from this poem in his suicide note, with the change of "you" to "life."[111]

The clinical reality of manic-depressive illness is far more lethal and infinitely more complex than the current psychiatric nomenclature, *bipolar disorder*, would suggest. Cycles of fluctuating moods and energy levels serve as a background to constantly changing thoughts, behaviors, and feelings. The illness encompasses the extremes of human experience: Thinking can range from florid psychosis, or "madness," to patterns of unusually clear, fast and creative associations, to retardation so profound that no meaningful mental activity can occur. Behavior can be frenzied, expansive, bizarre, and seductive, or it can be seclusive, sluggish, and dangerously suicidal. Moods may swing erratically between euphoria and despair or irritability and desperation. The rapid oscillations and combinations of such extremes result in an intricately textured clinical picture: Manic patients, for example, are depressed and irritable as often as they are euphoric; the highs associated with

mania are generally only pleasant and productive during the earlier, milder stages. Lowell's description of the "glory, violence and
banality" of mania is compelling; so, too, is Bryon's portrayal of "an
awful chaos":

> This should have been a noble creature: he
> Hath all the energy which would have made
> A goodly frame of glorious elements,
> Had they been wisely mingled; as it is,
> It is an awful chaos—light and darkness—
> And mind and dust—and passions and pure thoughts,
> Mix'd, and contending without end or order,
> All dormant or destructive[112]

   We turn from describing this "awful chaos" to the controver-
sies and arguments surrounding the idea of a link between certain
types of "madness" and artistic genius. In particular, we focus on
the accumulating, and surprisingly consistent, recent evidence suggesting that it is manic-depressive illness and its related temperaments that are most closely allied to creativity in the arts.

3.
COULD
IT BE
MADNESS–THIS?

Controversy and Evidence

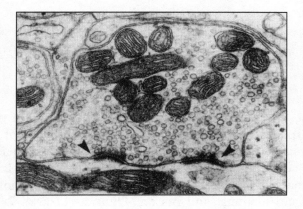

[Emily Dickinson] was not an alcoholic, she was not abusive, she was not neurotic, she did not commit suicide. Neurotic people or alcoholics who go through life make better copy, and people talk about them, tell anecdotes about them. The quiet people just do their work.

—JOYCE CAROL OATES[1]

And Something's odd—within—
That person that I was—
And this One—do not feel the same—
Could it be Madness—this?

—EMILY DICKINSON[2]

Chemical Synapse: The Unbridged Junction
(Courtesy of J. E. Heuser and T. S. Reese)

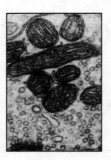

A possible link between madness and genius is one of the oldest and most persistent of cultural notions; it is also one of the most controversial. An intimate relationship between the ancient gods, madness, and the creators was described in pre-Grecian myths, most dramatically in the Dionysian struggles between violence and creation, and madness and reason. Dionysus, son of Zeus and a mortal mother, was afflicted with madness while young and episodically subject to both great ecstasies and suffering. As the god of wine, and perhaps hallucinogenic mushrooms as well,[3] Dionysus induced frenzied ecstasies, madness, and savage brutality in those around him. The rituals of worship set up in his honor came to symbolize the emergence of new life and creation from chaos, brutality, and destruction. Renewed vitality, restored sanity, gifts of prophecy, and creative inspiration often followed the violent, Dionysian blood feasts (which frequently involved the dismemberment of both animals and humans). Significantly, much of the greatest poetry in Greece was written for Dionysus. These rituals of ecstatic worship, frenetic dance and violent death, were cyclic in nature and tied to the seasons, representing the recurrent themes of death and rebirth. We shall see later how these seasonal and regenerational themes represent ties between the nature of manic-depressive illness and creativity.

By the time of Plato and Socrates, common lore held that priests and poets communicated with the gods through inspired "madness" and sacred enthusiasms. Divine madness and inspiration were thought obtainable only during particular states of mind, such as loss of consciousness, affliction with illness, madness, or states of "possession." Socrates, in his speech on divine madness in *Phaedrus,* said:

> Madness, provided it comes as the gift of heaven, is the channel by which we receive the greatest blessings. . . . the men of old who gave things their names saw no disgrace or reproach in madness; otherwise they would not have connected it with the name of the noblest of all arts, the art of discerning the future, and called it the manic art. . . . So, according to the evidence provided by our ancestors, madness is a nobler thing than sober sense . . . madness comes from God, whereas sober sense is merely human.[4]

He then went on to discuss artistic "madness," or possession by the Muses: "If a man comes to the door of poetry untouched by the madness of the Muses, believing that technique alone will make him a good poet, he and his sane compositions never reach perfection, but are utterly eclipsed by the performances of the inspired madman."[5] Madness, as used by Plato and Socrates, encompassed a wide range of states of thought and emotion, not just psychosis, but the emphasis clearly was upon a profoundly altered state of consciousness and feeling. Later Aristotle focused more specifically on the relationship between melancholia, madness, and inspiration. "Why is it," he asked, "that all men who are outstanding in philosophy, poetry or the arts are melancholic?" "The same is true of Ajax and Bellerophontes," Aristotle went on, "the former went completely insane. . . . And many other heroes suffered in the same way as these. In later times also there have been Empedocles, Plato, Socrates and many other well-known men. The same is true of most of those who have handled poetry."[6]

During the Renaissance there was a renewed interest in the relationship between genius, melancholia, and madness. A stronger distinction was made between sane melancholics of high achievement and individuals whose insanity prevented them from using their ability. The eighteenth century witnessed a sharp change in attitude; balance and rational thought, rather than "inspiration" and emotional extremes, were seen as the primary components of genius. This comparatively brief period, which associated moderation with genius, was almost completely reversed by the nineteenth-century Romantics, who once again emphasized not only the melancholic side, but also the more spontaneous, inspired, and swept-by-the-muses qualities of genius. William Wordsworth, for example, in writing about Thomas Chatterton— the brilliant eighteenth-century poet who committed suicide at the age of seventeen—described the fate of poets:

> By our own spirits are we deified:
> We Poets in our youth begin in gladness;
> But thereof come in the end despondency and madness.[7]

Lord Byron, the personification of anguished, volatile intensity within the group of Romantic poets, described a turmoil of emotional life in words that captured the brooding frenzy of the "poetic genius":

> Yet must I think less wildly:—I *have* thought
> Too long and darkly, till my brain became,
> In its own eddy boiling and o'erwrought,
> A whirling gulf of phantasy and flame:
> And thus, untaught in youth my heart to tame,
> My springs of life were poison'd.[8]

In 1812, the same year that the first two cantos of Byron's *Childe Harold's Pilgrimage* were published, Professor Benjamin Rush of the University of Pennsylvania wrote the first major psychiatric treatise in the United States. In it he recorded his observations about the relationship between certain kinds of mania, mental acuity, and artistic talent; like Byron and many other nineteenth-century writers, he used metaphors of upheaval derived from the natural world:

From a part of the brain preternaturally elevated, but not diseased, the mind sometimes discovers not only unusual strength and acuteness, but certain talents it never exhibited before. . . . Talents for eloquence, poetry, music and painting, and uncommon ingenuity in several of the mechanical arts, are often involved in this state of madness. . . . The disease which thus evolves these new and wonderful talents and operations of the mind may be compared to an earthquake, which by convulsing the upper strata of our globe, throws upon its surface precious and splendid fossils, the existence of which was unknown to the proprietors of the soil in which they were buried.[9]

Several European scholars—Dr. Jacques-Joseph Moreau in France, and Professors Cesare Lombroso in Italy and Karl August Möbius in Germany—also wrote extensively about the relationship between mental illness and genius.[10]

An ironic exception to these nineteenth-century writers who were emphasizing the mysterious, irrational, and overwhelming forces that gave rise to genius was the essayist Charles Lamb; confined at one time to a private asylum for what now would almost certainly be called manic-depressive illness, he was also the close companion to a sister intermittently insane with manic-depressive psychosis. In *The Sanity of True Genius* he argued for a balance of faculties, much as the eighteenth-century writers had done:

So far from the position holding true, that great wit (or genius, in our modern way of speaking), has a necessary alliance with insanity, the greatest wits, on the contrary, will ever be found in the sanest writers. It is impossible for the mind to conceive a mad Shakespeare. The greatness of wit, by which the poetic talent is here chiefly to be understood, manifests itself in the admirable balance of all faculties. Madness is the disproportionate straining or excess of any one of them. . . . The ground of the mistake is, that men, finding in the raptures of the higher poetry a condition of exaltation, to which they have no parallel in their own experience, besides the spurious resemblance of it in dreams and fevers, impute a state of dreaminess and fever to the poet. But the true poet dreams being awake. He is not possessed by his subject, but has dominion over it.[11]

Privately, however, in a letter to Samuel Taylor Coleridge, Lamb described the intoxicating, exalted side to his own delusional break-

down: "While it lasted I had many many hours of pure happiness. . . . Dream not of having tasted all the grandeur and wildness
of Fancy, till you have gone mad."[12]

The late nineteenth and early twentieth centuries saw a moderation of earlier views, in part due to the inevitable swing away
from any extreme—in this case that of the Romantics—and in part
to the subduing, occasionally stultifying influences of academic
psychology and psychiatry. Psychologist William James and clinical
psychiatrist and scholar Emil Kraepelin, both writing early in the
twentieth century, emphasized the positive features associated
with certain kinds of madness and speculated about how these
features might, in some instances, combine with other talents to
produce an extraordinarily creative or accomplished person. Also
accented, however, were the debilitating extremes of psychiatric
illness (psychosis or morbid depression, for example) in contrast to
the milder manic states and the more reflective, philosophical melancholias. These scholars underscored the need for sustained attention, discipline, and balance in the truly imaginative individual.
This more moderate view has characterized most twentieth-
century thinking about the relationship between psychopathology
and genius. James, as we shall see in chapter 6, was himself no
stranger to melancholia and disturbing mood swings, and he wrote
insightfully about the potential value of combining a fiery, unstable
temperament with intellect:

> The psychopathic temperament [by which he meant "borderline in-
> sanity, insane temperament, loss of mental balance"], whatever be
> the intellect with which it finds itself paired, often brings with it
> ardor and excitability of character. . . . His conceptions tend to pass
> immediately into belief and action . . . when a superior intellect and
> a psychopathic temperament coalesce—as in the endless permuta-
> tions and combinations of human faculty, they are bound to coalesce
> often enough—in the same individual, we have the best possible
> condition for the kind of effective genius that gets into the biograph-
> ical dictionaries. Such men do not remain mere critics and under-
> standers with their intellect. Their ideas possess them, they inflict
> them, for better or worse, upon their companions or their age.[13]

Kraepelin, like Benjamin Rush a century earlier, linked increased
artistic productivity more specifically to manic-depressive illness:

The volitional excitement which accompanies the disease may under certain circumstances set free powers which otherwise are constrained by all kinds of inhibition. Artistic activity namely may, by the untroubled surrender to momentary fancies or moods, and especially poetical activity by the facilitation of linguistic expression, experience a certain furtherance.[14]

By the 1940s Dr. A. Myerson and R. D. Boyle, clinicians at Boston's McLean Hospital, reiterated James's basic position but, as Kraepelin and Rush had done, they focused on manic-depressive illness. In discussing affective psychosis in socially prominent families they concluded:

It does not necessarily follow that the individuals who appear in these records were great because they had mental disease, although that proposition might be maintained with considerable cogency and relevance. It may be that the situation is more aptly expressed as follows. The manic drive in its controlled form and phase is of value *only* if joined to ability. A feebleminded person of hypomanic temperament would simply be one who carried on more activity at a feebleminded level, and this is true also of mediocrity, so the bulk of manic-depressive temperaments are of no special value to the world, and certainly not of distinguished value. If, however, the hypomanic temperament is joined to high ability, an independent characteristic, then the combination may well be more effective than the union of high ability with normal temperament and drive might be.[15]

Not surprisingly, twentieth-century literary and art scholars also have approached the subject of the relationship between psychiatric illness and genius. Lionel Trilling, in his well-known essay on art and neurosis, and Rudolf and Margot Wittkower, in *Born Under Saturn*, acknowledge the extent to which artistic genius and "madness" have been, and continue to be, linked by society. Trilling notes that the conception of the artist as mentally ill "is indeed one of the characteristic notions of our culture,"[16] and the Wittkowers caution that "the notion of the mad artist is a historical reality and that by brushing it aside as mistaken, one denies the existence of a generic and deeply significant symbol."[17] They also emphasize, as many had before them, the important distinction between "positive" and "negative" melancholia (consistent with their reiteration of the Platonic distinction between clinical insanity, which is detrimental to and at cross-purposes with true artistic achievement, and "the sacred madness of enthusiasm and inspiration"). While granting that the poet may be "uniquely neurotic," Trilling also emphasizes the essential point (to which we return later) that "the one part of [the poet or artist] that is healthy, by any conceivable definition of health, is that which gives him the power to conceive, to plan, to work, and to bring his work to a conclusion."[18] In short, he stresses the indisputable roles of discipline, rationality, and sustained effort in the execution of lasting works of art and literature.

The controversy over a link between melancholia, manic-depressive illness, and the artistic temperament continues well into the current era. In the remainder of this chapter we review the biographical and scientific evidence supporting a link between the extremes of mood and artistic imagination, as well as the arguments against it.

There are several ways to examine the relationship between mood disorders, or affective illness, and artistic creativity. Biographical studies focus on life-study investigations of prominent writers, artists, and composers. Research in the late nineteenth and early twentieth centuries, for example, provided anecdotal but suggestive evidence of significantly increased rates of mood disorders and suicide in eminent writers and artists and their first-degree relatives.[19] Recently, more systematic biographical research has given strong support to a much higher rate of mood disorders in artistic populations than could be expected from chance alone. Diagnostic and psychological studies of living writers and artists, conducted during the past twenty years, give more scientifically meaningful estimates of the rates and types of psychopathology in groups of artists and writers. Finally, studies of creative and related achievement in affectively ill patients provide corroborating evidence from a different perspective, as do family studies of psychopathology and creative accomplishment. We shall examine, in turn, the findings from each of these types of investigations.

There are, of course, many problems in studying the relationship between mood disorders and artistic achievement. Biographical studies—while intrinsically fascinating and irreplaceable, deeply instructive sources of information about moods, their extremes, and their roles in the lives of artists—are fraught with difficulties. Writers and artists, however brutally honest they may be in some of their self-assessments, are frequently blinded and biased as well. The reliability of their letters, journals, and memoirs can be limited because they are written from a single perspective or fully mindful of future biographers and posterity. Biographers, too, write with strong slants and under the influence of prevailing or idiosyncratic viewpoints. Historical context and existing social customs also determine which behaviors are culled out or emphasized for comment. As noted earlier, certain lifestyles provide cover for deviant and bizarre behavior, and the arts, especially, have long given latitude to extremes in behavior and mood. The assumption that within artistic circles madness, melancholy, and suicide are somehow normal is prevalent, making it difficult at times to ferret out truth from expectation.

Biographical or posthumous research carries with it other problems as well.[20] Any historical perspective necessarily dictates that a listing of highly accomplished, affectively ill individuals (see Appendix B, for example) will be only a partial one—illustrative but by no means definitive. Always, in the analysis of individual lives, problems arise. It is fairly easy to identify any number of major nineteenth-century British or American poets who were manic-depressive, for example, but it is more difficult to determine what proportion of the total pool of "great poets" they represent. (In many instances, of course, the individuals under study are sufficiently important to be interesting in their own right, independent of any general grouping.) Also, more detailed information exists for some individuals than for others (for example, those more in the public eye, those existing in relatively recent times, or those writing more extensively about themselves). Anthony Storr put it well: "The more we know about anyone, the easier it becomes to discern neurotic traits, mood disorders and other aspects of character which, when emphatically present, we call neurotic. The famous and successful are usually less able to conceal whatever vagaries of character they may possess because biographers or Ph.D. students will not let them rest in peace."[21]

The tendency for highly accomplished individuals to be, almost by definition, inordinately productive and energetic creates problems of another sort—a bias toward the underdiagnosis of the manic side of manic-depressive illness. Biographical studies indicate that writers, artists, and composers often describe in great detail their periods of melancholy or depression, but that other aspects of mood swings, such as hypomania, and even at times overt psychosis, are subsumed under "eccentricity," "creative inspiration," or "artistic temperament." Thus many individuals with clear histories of profound or debilitating depressions are labeled "melancholic" rather than manic-depressive, despite their episodic (and often seasonal) histories of extremely high energy, irritability, enthusiasm, and increased productivity levels (periods often also accompanied by costly lapses in financial, social, and sexual judgment). Paradoxically, the more chronically hypomanic the individual, the more noticeable and relatively pathological the depression will appear. Diagnostic biases in the opposite direction also occur. Some researchers have tended to overdiagnose manic-depressive illness because they observe patterns of behavior common to both hypomania and normal accomplishment (for example, enthusiasm, high energy, and the ability to function with little sleep) and then label as manic-depressive anyone displaying these "symptoms."

Despite the difficulties in doing diagnostic studies based on biographical material, valid and highly useful research can be done by using in a systematic way what is known about manic-depressive illness: its symptomatic presentation (for example, pronounced changes in mood, energy, sleep, thinking, and behavior), associated behavior patterns (such as alcohol and drug abuse, pathological gambling, pronounced and repeated financial reversals, and chaotic interpersonal relationships), suicide (70 to 90 percent of all suicides are associated with manic-depressive or depressive illness; therefore, if an individual has committed suicide, it is almost always the case that a mood disorder was at least contributory),[22] its natural course (an episodic, cyclic course of symptoms, with normal functioning in between; usual onset of symptoms in the late teens or early twenties, with temperamental signs often exhibited much earlier; seasonal aspects to the mood and energy changes; and, if untreated, a worsening of the illness over time), and, very important, a family history, especially in first-degree relatives (parents, siblings, or children), of depression, mania, psychosis, or suicide. Other psychiatric and medical conditions that can have similar symptoms (for example, thyroid and other metabolic disturbances, drug-induced states, organic brain syndromes, or complex partial seizures and related epileptic conditions) need to be considered, and ruled out, as well. Making a retrospective diagnosis is, in many ways, like putting together the pieces of an elaborate psychological puzzle or solving a mystery by a complicated but careful marshaling of elements of evidence. Biographical diagnoses must ultimately, of course, be more tentative than diagnoses made on living individuals, but they *can* be done, reliably and responsibly, and with an appreciation of the complexities that go into anyone's life, most especially the life of an artist. (Ultimately it should prove possible to extract DNA from hair or tissue samples and make more definitive posthumous diagnoses.)

Several case-history studies of psychopathology in eminent writers and artists were conducted during the late nineteenth and early twentieth centuries—for example, those done by Drs. Francis Galton, Cesare Lombroso, J. F. Nisbet, and Havelock Ellis— but it is only more recently that systematic biographical research has been carried out.[23] Dr. Adele Juda, who in 1949 studied 113 German artists, writers, architects, and composers, was one of the first to undertake an extensive, in-depth investigation of both artists and their relatives.[24] Her research was hampered somewhat by ambiguous inclusionary criteria (that is, how the subjects were chosen) as well as inadequate diagnostic methods (a common problem in psychiatric research prior to the development of standardized diagnostic criteria in the early 1970s), which led to an inevitable confusion between schizophrenia and manic-depressive illness. (Although some confusion still remains, it is much less of a problem than it used to be. Most clinicians are now aware that psychotic features such as flagrant paranoia, severe cognitive disorganization, delusions, and hallucinations—once thought by some psychiatrists to be more characteristic of schizophrenia—are in fact relatively common in manic-depressive illness. The latter can usually be distinguished from schizophrenia by a family history of depression, manic-depressive illness, or suicide, a lifetime course of manic and depressive episodes interspersed with long periods of normal thinking and behavior, and generally healthier personality and social functioning prior to the onset of the illness. Bizarre behavior, once thought to be much more characteristic of schizophrenia, is now recognized as a frequent component of mania as well. Many artists and writers described by some earlier biographers as schizophrenic—for example, Ruskin, Schumann, Strindberg, Woolf, Pound, Poe, Artaud, Dadd, and van Gogh—would not be classified as such today.)

Juda's study remains an important one, however, both for its scope (more than 5,000 individuals were interviewed during the course of seventeen years) and its attempt to bring rigor to a highly subjective field. Juda found that although two-thirds of the 113 artists and writers were "psychically normal," there were more suicides and "insane and neurotic" individuals in the artistic group than could be expected in the general population. The highest rates of psychiatric abnormality were found in the poets (50 percent) and musicians (38 percent); lower rates were found in painters (20 percent), sculptors (18 percent), and architects (17 percent). The brothers, sisters, and children of those in the artistic group were much more likely to be cyclothymic, commit suicide, or suffer from manic-depressive illness than were individuals in the general population; psychosis was far more common in the grandchildren of the artistic group as well.

In another biographical study Dr. Colin Martindale examined the lives of twenty-one eminent English poets (born between 1670 and 1809) and twenty-one eminent French poets (born between 1770 and 1909).[25] More than one-half (55 percent) of the English poets and 40 percent of the French had a history of significant psychopathology (for example, "nervous breakdowns," suicide, or alcoholism), and fully one in seven poets had been institutionalized in an asylum or had suffered from severe "recurring and unmistakable symptoms" such as hallucinations or delusions. Combining the expected general population rates for the two major psychoses, schizophrenia and manic-depressive illness, yields a combined rate of only 2 percent; because, as we shall see, virtually all of the psychosis in creative individuals is manic-depressive rather than schizophrenic in nature, an expected base rate of 1 percent is probably a more appropriate comparison. Whichever figure is used, the expected rate is far less than that shown by the poets in Martindale's sample. Other researchers, including Dr. W. H. Trethowan, who looked at the lives of sixty composers, and Dr. Joseph Schildkraut A. J. Hirshfeld, and J. M. Murphy, who studied fifteen visual artists from the abstract expressionists of the New York School,[26] have found that approximately one-half of their subjects suffered from depressive or manic-depressive illness. Trethowan found that approximately one-half of the composers had a "melancholic temperament," and that mood disorders were "easily the commonest and most important of psychiatric illnesses."[27] This represents an almost tenfold increase in affective illness over what could be expected by chance alone. That 40 percent of the artists in the Schildkraut study actually received psychiatric treatment is significant as well, as research indicates that only one person in three with affective illness seeks help for it. Likewise, the suicide rate among the artists (two out of fifteen) is at least thirteen times the general rate; it is considerably higher (another 13 percent) if single-vehicle car accidents are thought of, at least in some instances, as suicide equivalents.

Dr. Arnold Ludwig's recent study of individuals, biographies of whom had been reviewed in the *New York Times Book Review* over a thirty-year period (1960 to 1990), is impressive for both its scope and careful methodology.[28] Consistent with Juda's findings in German artists and mine in British writers and artists (discussed in the following paragraphs), Ludwig found that the highest rates of mania, psychosis, and psychiatric hospitalizations were in poets; most significantly, a staggering 18 percent of the poets had committed suicide. Composers also showed high rates of psychosis and depression. Overall, when Ludwig compared individuals in the creative arts with those in other professions (such as businessmen, scientists, and public officials), he found that the artistic group showed two to three times the rate of psychosis, suicide attempts, mood disorders, and substance abuse. The rate of forced psychiatric hospitalization in the artists, writers, and composers was six to seven times that of the nonartistic group.

To study the occurrence of mood disorders and suicide in a consecutive sample of poets born within a hundred-year period, I examined autobiographical, biographical, and medical records (where available) for all major British and Irish poets born between 1705 and 1805.[29,30] There was within this group, as might be expected, a wide range of biographical, medical, and family history information available. For some, such as Lord Byron, both the quantity and quality of the material was excellent; for others—such as Robert Fergusson, John Bampfylde, and William Collins—the information, especially of a psychiatric nature, was far less complete. The available letters, books, and medical records were examined for symptoms of depression, mania, hypomania, and mixed states; seasonal or other patterns in moods, behavior, and productivity; the nature of the course of the illness (for example, age of onset, duration, and patterns of recurrence over time); and evidence of other psychiatric or medical illnesses (for example, syphilis) that might confound the diagnostic picture. A strong emphasis was placed upon both the severity and the recurrence of symptoms; in all cases it was the *patterning* of mood, cognitive, energy, sleep, and behavioral symptoms that formed the focus of study. The family histories of the poets, although more difficult to ascertain, were similarly analyzed. The results are summarized in table 3–1.

It can be seen that a strikingly high rate of mood disorders, suicide, and institutionalization occurred within this group of poets and their families. Six (William Collins, Christopher Smart, William Cowper, Robert Fergusson, John Codrington Bampfylde, and John Clare) were committed to lunatic asylums or madhouses, a rate easily twenty times that of the general population living during the same time period.[31] Two others (Thomas Chatterton and Thomas Lovell Beddoes) committed suicide. More than one-half of the poets showed strong evidence of mood disorders. Thirteen, or more than one out of three of the poets, seem likely to have suffered from manic-depressive illness (Christopher Smart, William Cowper, George Darley, Robert Fergusson, Thomas Chatterton, William Blake, Samuel Taylor Coleridge, George Gordon, Lord Byron, Percy Bysshe Shelley, John Clare, Hartley Coleridge, Thomas Lovell Beddoes, and James Clarence Mangan). Of these thirteen poets, the majority exhibited psychotic symptoms at one time or another, two committed suicide, and four were committed to asylums. William Collins and John Codrington Bampfylde, who also were committed to asylums, were probably manic-depressive as well, but only the melancholic side of Collins's illness is unequivocably documented and few details are available about the nature of Bampfylde's problems. Six poets—Oliver Goldsmith, Robert Burns, Walter Savage Landor, Thomas Campbell, John

TABLE 3–1.
MOOD DISORDERS AND SUICIDE IN BRITISH AND IRISH POETS BORN 1705–1805

	Manic-Depressive Illness					
	Recurrent Depression	Depressive Illness	Psychotic Features	Confined to Asylum	Suicide	Comments
Samuel Johnson 1709–84	■					Severe recurrent melancholia. Perceived himself as intermittently mad and had a terror of insanity. First severe breakdown at 20, lasting more than 2 years. Experienced tics, obsessions, and phobias as well. Felt he had inherited his "vile melancholy" from his father.
Thomas Gray 1716–71	■					"Habitual melancholy" and attacks of depression which grew more frequent over time. Father "subject to intermittent fits of insanity," extravagant, alcoholic, and violent.
William Collins 1721–59		◨	■	■		Psychotic melancholia and possible mania. First complete breakdown at 29. Confined to lunatic asylum; "accustomed to rave much and make great moanings." Dissipation, intemperance, and excess while undergraduate at Cambridge. Little known about family history.
Christopher Smart 1722–71		■	■	■		Ecstatic, grandiose, and religious mania. First confined to asylum in his early thirties, but financial extravagance, instability, and dissipation apparent while an undergraduate at Cambridge. Spent several years in "madhouse" on "incurable ward."

Key: ■ Definite/ Probable   ◨ Possible   ▨ Probable bipolar II or cyclothymia

NOTE: Quotations are taken from medical, autobiographical, and biographical materials; see text note 29 of this chapter.

	Recurrent Depression	Manic-Depressive Illness	Psychotic Features	Confined to Asylum	Suicide	Comments
Joseph Warton 1722–1800						No indication of a significant mood disorder.
Oliver Goldsmith 1730–74		▨				Violent temper, fitfully melancholic, financially extravagant, compulsive gambler. Increasingly irritable, melancholic, and subject to "violent alternations of mood" as he grew older. Little known about family history except that the Goldsmiths were perceived as "strange" and "eccentric."
William Cowper 1731–1800		■	■	■		Recurrent psychotic melancholia and repeated suicide attempts. Delusions and hallucinations. First signs of mental instability while in his twenties; confined to asylum in his early thirties. Family history of melancholia.
James Macpherson 1736–96						No indication of a significant mood disorder.
Robert Fergusson 1750–74		■	■	■		Cyclothymic temperament progressed to psychotic melancholia and then maniacal excitement (possibly exacerbated by head trauma). Died "furiously insane," at age 24, in the Edinburgh Bedlam.

	Recurrent Depression	Manic-Depressive Illness	Psychotic Features	Confined to Asylum	Suicide	Comments
Thomas Chatterton 1752–70		■			■	Committed suicide at age 17. Extremely moody even as a child. Subject to severe melancholia as well as periods of frenzied energies, occasionally incoherent enthusiasms, and extreme grandiosity. "Wild" fluctuations in mood. Sister confined to an asylum, and niece suffered from unspecified psychiatric condition.
John Bampfylde 1754–96				■		Confinement in private "madhouse" for 20 years. "Fell into dissipation" after Cambridge studies. Little known about the nature of his psychiatric problems. "A disposition to insanity in the family," including a sister who became insane.
George Crabbe 1754–1832	■					By age 24 he described an "annual woe and dread," and he suffered throughout his life from fits of depression. Daily opium use (initially prescribed for tic douloureux) for more than 40 years. Father, described as "a man of imperious temper and violent passions," became increasingly and more irrationally violent as he became older.

	Recurrent Depression	Manic-Depressive Illness	Psychotic Features	Confined to Asylum	Suicide	Comments
William Blake 1757–1827		■	■			Hallucinations and delusions from an early age. Periods of exaltation and grandiosity, as well as periods that he described as "a deep pit of melancholy—melancholy without any real reason." Excessive irritability and attacks of rage, suspiciousness, and paranoia. Little information about family history although one brother, who spoke of visions of Moses and Abraham, was described as a "bit mad."
Robert Burns 1759–96		▨				Severe recurrent, often seasonal, melancholia (described by Burns as "the miseries of a diseased nervous system" and a "deep incurable taint which poisons my existence"). Mercurial, agitated, and volatile temperament. Both parents described as "subject to strong passions," fiery, and irascible.
Joanna Baillie 1762–1851						No indication of a significant mood disorder.
William Lisle Bowles 1762–1850						No indication of a significant mood disorder.
Samuel Rogers 1763–1855						No indication of a significant mood disorder.

	Recurrent Depression	Manic-Depressive Illness	Psychotic Features	Confined to Asylum	Suicide	Comments
William Wordsworth 1770–1850	◩					Self-described as "of a moody and violent temper." Subject to hypochondriacal aches and pains. Described by some biographers as suffering from severe depressions "to the verge of a mental breakdown," but their nature and severity are unclear. Sister's "insanity" appears to have been due to senile dementia rather than to a psychiatric illness.
Sir Walter Scott 1771–1832	◩					At various times described himself as suffering from a "disposition to causeless alarm—much lassitude—and decay of vigor and intellect," a *morbus eruditorum*, and a "black dog" of melancholy.
Samuel Taylor Coleridge 1772–1834		■				Extended and recurrent melancholia. Mercurial, restless, extravagant, grandiose, and agitated. Fitful enthusiasms and despairs. Opiate addiction. Visionary states. Family history of affective illness and suicide.
Robert Southey 1774–1843						Described as unduly excitable, with a history of "nervous fever" and an unbalanced state of "nerves"; there is, however, little indication of recurrent mood disorder of any significant severity. Senility during last years of life.

	Recurrent Depression	Manic-Depressive Illness	Psychotic Features	Confined to Asylum	Suicide	Comments
Walter Savage Landor 1775–1864		▨				Violent, restless, and unstable temperament. Litigious and impulsive. "Very much disposed" to melancholy. Expelled from both Rugby and Oxford. Thought by others to have had "at least a touch of insanity." "Ungovernable temper" and financially extravagant.
Thomas Campbell 1777–1844		▨				Recurrent and severe melancholia, "aggravated fits of despondency." First attack when 18. Violently irritable, financially extravagant, and "alternately excited and depressed within short periods of time." Insanity in his and his wife's families. Son placed in asylum suffering from melancholia, "capricious fits of temper," paranoia, and "leap-frog play of thoughts."
Thomas Moore 1779–1852						No indication of a significant mood disorder.
Leigh Hunt 1784–1859	■					Autobiography describes a "nervous condition," a "melancholy state," which lasted, the first time, for several months. "I experienced it twice afterwards, each time more painfully than before, and for a much longer period . . . for upwards of four years, without intermission, and above six years in all."

	Recurrent Depression	Manic-Depressive Illness	Psychotic Features	Confined to Asylum	Suicide	Comments
Thomas Love Peacock 1785–1866						No indication of a significant mood disorder.
George Gordon, Lord Byron 1788–1824		■				Recurrent, often agitated, melancholia. Volatile temperament with occasional "paroxysms of rage." Mercurial and extravagant; worsening depressions over time. Strong family history of mental instability and suicide.
Percy Bysshe Shelley 1792–1822		■	■			Recurrent, agitated, and occasionally suicidal melancholia. "Hysterical attacks" followed by periods of listlessness; often seasonal. Ecstatic episodes and "violent paroxysms of rage." Self-described as "tormented by visions," the psychiatric nature of which remains unclear. Probable transient delusions. Intermittent laudanum use for "nerves."
John Clare 1793–1864		■	■	■		Spent 25 years in insane asylum. Long periods of inertia and melancholia interspersed with episodes of frenzied, violent, and extravagant activity. Hallucinations, as well as delusions of persecution and grandeur. Cause of madness listed as "hereditary" by asylum physician.

	Recurrent Depression	Manic-Depressive Illness	Psychotic Features	Confined to Asylum	Suicide	Comments
John Keats 1795–1821		▨				"Violent and ungovernable as a child"; described by brother as nervous, "morbid," and suffering from "many a bitter fit of hypochondriasm" [melancholy]; periods of depression often followed by periods of intense activity and "exhilaration." Described himself as having a "horrid Morbidity of Temperament." Rapidly shifting moods predated symptoms and diagnosis of tuberculosis.
George Darley 1795–1846		■				Recurrent, occasionally suicidal melancholia. Increasing periods of depression and social withdrawal. Described extreme mood swings, ranging from "causeless and unreasonable" periods of "frolic, extravagance, and insane" actions, to "crazed" periods of despair.
Hartley Coleridge 1796–1849		■	◹			Recurrent melancholia; severe mood swings alternating between "depression and extravagant hilarity." Lifelong struggles with alcoholism, "heavings of agony," and "paroxysms of rage." Expelled from Oxford for dissipation. Eccentric and visionary. Under conservatorship toward end of life. Insanity on both sides of his family.

	Recurrent Depression	Manic-Depressive Illness	Psychotic Features	Confined to Asylum	Suicide	Comments
Thomas Hood 1799–1845	■					Periods of morbidity, melancholia, and lethargy, but diagnosis complicated by severe, recurrent physical illness (probably pulmonary edema; possibly syphilis or tuberculosis).
Thomas Lovell Beddoes 1803–49		■			■	Committed suicide at 45 after at least one earlier attempt. Volatile, extravagant, eccentric, and subject to severe recurrent melancholia. Father, also a physician, was highly eccentric and of an "extremely ardent" temperament.
Robert Stephen Hawker 1803–75		▨	■			Fits of depression throughout his life. Deep depression and "brain fever" after wife's death; possibly psychotic. Volatile, extravagant, and eccentric. Intermittent opium habit. Physician had "never encountered in all his practice so excitable a tissue as that which held [his] Brain." "My Grandfather and Father," Hawker wrote, "were both of the same excitable temperament."
James Clarence Mangan 1803–49		■	■			Recurrent and prolonged psychotic depressions. Hallucinations, agitation, "great overcurtaining gloom." Extreme eccentricity: "with one voice they all proclaimed me mad." Probable opiate abuse. Father described as extravagant, financially dissolute, and of "quick and irascible temper."

Keats, and Robert Stephen Hawker—probably had milder forms of manic-depressive illness (cyclothymia or bipolar II disorder), although Keats and Burns died before it became clear what the ultimate severity and course of their mood disorders would have been. Samuel Johnson, Thomas Gray, George Crabbe, and Leigh Hunt suffered from recurrent depression. A comparison with rates of manic-depressive illness in the general population (1 percent), cyclothymia (1 to 2 percent), and major depressive disorder (5 percent) shows that these British poets were thirty times more likely to suffer from manic-depressive illness, ten to twenty times more likely to be cyclothymic or to have other milder forms of manic-depressive illness, more than five times as likely to commit suicide, and at least twenty times more likely to have been committed to an asylum or madhouse. These rates, while markedly elevated, are consistent with findings from the other biographical studies that we have reviewed; they are also consistent with results from more recent studies of living writers and artists that are discussed later in this chapter. The genetic nature of mood disorders is underscored by the family histories in many of the poets of depression, mania, suicide, violence, or insanity (for example, in the families of Byron, Gray, Cowper, Chatterton, Bampfylde, the Coleridges, and Campbell; and, suggestively, in the families of Johnson, Crabbe, Blake, Clare, Beddoes, and Mangan). Not without reason did Robert Burns write: "The fates and character of the rhyming tribe often employ my thoughts when I am disposed to be melancholy. There is not, among all the martyrologies that ever were penned, so rueful a narrative as the lives of the poets."[32]

Biographical studies such as the ones we have been discussing provide one kind of evidence, persuasive in its own right, about the link between mood disorders and artistic creativity. Modern studies of living writers and artists give a different perspective; their findings are, however, quite consistent with those obtained through the case-history, or biographical, methods. Dr. Nancy Andreasen and her colleagues at the University of Iowa were the first to undertake scientific diagnostic inquiries into the relationship between creativity and psychopathology in living writers.[33] Their studies, using structured interviews, systematic psychiatric diagnostic criteria, and matched control groups, represented a marked methodological improvement over prior anecdotally based research, as well as over the earlier studies that failed to distinguish adequately between types of psychopathology (especially manic-depressive illness and schizophrenia). The size of the sample of writers was relatively small (thirty), and the writers were at varying levels of creative achievement (all were participants in the University of Iowa Writers' Workshop, one of the most prestigious in the nation; some were nationally acclaimed but others were graduate students or teaching fellows not yet at the level of national or international recognition). Andreasen notes that because she studied only writers, her results cannot be generalized to other groups of creative individuals, such as philosophers, scientists, or musicians. Although this is true, and writers may be disproportionately likely to have affective disorders, the homogeneity of her sample is certainly valuable in its own right.

The results of the Iowa research are summarized in table 3–2. Clearly the writers demonstrated an extraordinarily high rate of affective illness. Fully 80 percent of the study sample met formal diagnostic criteria for a major mood disorder. In contrast, 30 percent of the control sample (individuals whose professional work fell outside the arts but who were matched for age, education, and sex)

TABLE 3–2.
LIFETIME PREVALENCE OF MENTAL ILLNESS
IN WRITERS AND CONTROL SUBJECTS

RDC Diagnosis[a]	Writers (N = 30) %	Controls (N = 30) %	p
Any affective disorder	80	30	.001
Any bipolar disorder	43	10	.01
Bipolar I	13	0	NS
Bipolar II	30	10	NS
Major depression	37	17	NS
Schizophrenia	0	0	NS
Alcoholism	30	7	.05
Drug abuse	7	7	NS
Suicide	7	0	NS

[a] RDC = Research Diagnostic Criteria (standardized diagnostic criteria for psychiatric illness).

SOURCE: Adapted from N. C. Andreasen, Creativity and mental illness: Prevalence rates in writers and their first-degree relatives, *American Journal of Psychiatry* 144 (1987): 1288–1292. Copyright 1992, American Psychiatric Association. Reprinted by permission. [a] RDC = Research Diagnostic Criteria (standardized diagnostic criteria for psychiatric illness).

met the same criteria. The statistical difference between these two rates is highly significant, $p < .001$; that is, the odds of this difference occurring by chance alone are less than one in a thousand. Although the lifetime prevalence of mood disorders in the control group is much less than in the group of writers, it still represents a rate much greater than could be expected in the general population (5 to 8 percent). It is unclear whether this is due to an overrepresentation of affective illness in the sample (for example, it could reflect the tendency, discussed later, for individuals who are better educated and from the upper social classes to suffer disproportionately from manic-depressive illness) or because the diagnostic criteria were overinclusive for both the creative and control groups. Of particular interest, almost one-half the creative writers met the diagnostic criteria for full-blown manic-depressive illness, bipolar I, or its milder variant, bipolar II (major depressive illness with a history of hypomania). Over one-third of the writers had experienced at least one episode of major depressive illness, and two-thirds of the ill writers had received psychiatric treatment. The writers' suicide rate was also greatly in excess of the general population's. Indeed, all five of the suicides that were reported occurred in either the writers or their first-degree relatives; none occurred in the control group. None of the writers or control subjects met the diagnostic criteria for schizophrenia; this is scarcely surprising, given the generally disorganizing and dementing quality of the illness, but it is significant in light of earlier claims that schizophrenia and creativity were closely allied. In fact, Dr. Andreasen, a prominent schizophrenia researcher, went into her study of writers in the belief that she would find a correlation between schizophrenia and creativity, not between mood disorders and creativity.

Other studies of living writers and artists have also found a greatly elevated rate of mood disorders in the artistically gifted, thus confirming the work of Dr. Andreasen and her colleagues. University of Tennessee psychiatrist Dr. Hagop Akiskal and his wife Kareen, for example, have recently completed extensive psychiatric interviews of twenty award-winning European writers, poets, painters, and sculptors.[34] Their study, which has not yet been published, found that recurrent cyclothymic or hypomanic tendencies occurred in nearly two-thirds of their subjects; all told, 50 percent of the writers and artists had suffered from a major depressive episode. Preliminary data from another study by the Akiskals (done in collaboration with Dr. David Evans of Memphis State University), show similar findings in blues musicians.[35]

Several years ago, while on sabbatical leave at St. George's Medical School in London and the University of Oxford, I studied a group of forty-seven eminent British writers and artists.[36] I was interested in looking at rates of treatment for mood disorders within these groups, as well as seasonal patterns of moods and productivity, the nature of intensely creative episodes, the similarities between such episodes and hypomania, and the perceived role of very intense moods in the work of the writers and artists. The poets, playwrights, novelists, biographers, and artists in my study were selected on the basis of their having won at least one of several major prestigious prizes or awards in their fields. All the painters and sculptors, for example, were either Royal Academicians or Associates of the Royal Academy, honors established by King George III in 1768 and held at any given time by a limited number of British painters, sculptors, engravers, and architects. Literary prizes used as selection criteria included the Queen's Gold Medal for Poetry, and the Hawthornden, Booker, and James Tait Black Memorial prizes. Significantly, nine of the eighteen poets already were represented in *The Oxford Book of Twentieth-Century English Verse*. Of the eight playwrights, six were winners of the New York Drama Critics Award or the Evening Standard (London) Drama Award; several had won both, had won one of these awards more than once, or had also received Tony awards. Participants in the study were British, Irish, or citizens of the British Commonwealth. Almost all (87 percent) were men; their average age was fifty-three; and approximately three-fourths were Protestant. There were no significant religious differences between the subgroups, except that the poets were disproportionately Protestant (94 percent) and the novelists were disproportionately Catholic or agnostic (50 percent).

The focus of the study was on the role of moods in the creative process, not on psychopathology; this fact was made clear to all potential subjects in order to minimize the possibility that individuals with mood disorders would be more likely to participate. Although my study required a considerable amount of time and effort

on the part of highly successful and busy individuals, the rate of
acceptance was surprisingly high, more than matching the standards for rates of response for such types of research. All the writers and artists were asked detailed questions about any history of
treatment for depressive or manic-depressive illness; seasonal or
diurnal patterns, if any, in their moods and productivity; behavioral, cognitive, and mood correlates of their periods of most creative work; and their perceptions of the role of very intense moods
in their work. Specific psychiatric diagnostic criteria were not used
in this study, as the aim was to determine the actual rates of
treatment; this is a more stringent criterion of illness severity than
whether or not an individual meets the diagnostic criteria for mood
disorders.[37]

A very high percentage of the writers and artists, 38 percent,
had been treated for a mood disorder (see figure 3–1). Of those
treated, three-fourths had been given antidepressants or lithium or
had been hospitalized. Poets were the most likely to have required
medication for their depression (33 percent) and were the only
ones to have required medical intervention (hospitalization, electroconvulsive therapy, lithium) for mania. Fully one-half of the
poets had been treated with drugs, psychotherapy, and/or hospitalization for mood disorders. The playwrights had the highest total
rate of treatment for depression (63 percent), but a relatively large
percentage of those treated, more than half, had been treated with
psychotherapy alone. It is unclear whether this was due to a difference in the severity of illness or to treatment preference.

With the exception of the poets, the artists and writers reported being treated for depression only, not mania or hypomania;
the design of the study did not allow systematic diagnostic inquiry
into the frequency of mild manic or hypomanic episodes. Approximately one-third of the writers and artists reported histories of
severe mood swings that were essentially cyclothymic in nature.
One out of four reported having experienced extended elated mood
states. Novelists and poets more frequently reported the prolonged
elated states; playwrights and artists, on the other hand, more often reported severe mood swings. The relatively low rate of
treatment for affective illness in those individuals in the predominantly nonverbal fields (painting and sculpture) is interesting,
and it may be that they are less inclined than writers to seek

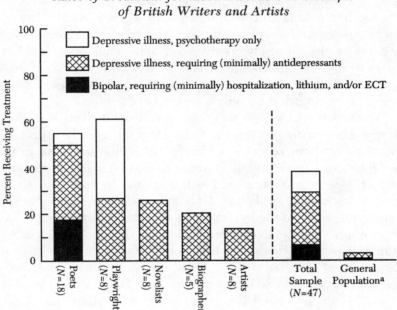

Figure 3–1.
Rates of Treatment for Mood Disorders in a Sample
of British Writers and Artists

ᵃ *The percentages for the general population are based on Epidemiologic Catchment Area
data. They indicate that less than one third of those individuals with bipolar or unipolar
illness receive treatment in any 6-month period.*

Source: From K. R. Jamison, Mood disorders and patterns of creativity in British writers
and artists, *Psychiatry* 52 (1989): 125–134.

psychiatric help. The total number of painters and sculptors in
my study is small, however, and it is difficult to generalize from
preliminary findings.

Virtually all the creative writers and artists (89 percent) said
they had experienced intense, highly productive, and creative episodes. This included all of the poets, novelists, and artists, and all
but one of the playwrights. Only one of the five biographers, however, reported experiencing such episodes. The most frequent duration of these episodes was two weeks, with half of them lasting
between one and four weeks. These "intensely creative" episodes
were characterized by pronounced increases in enthusiasm, energy, self-confidence, speed of mental association, fluency of

thoughts and elevated mood, and a strong sense of well-being (see figure 3–2). A comparison of these changes with the DSM-III criteria for hypomania (see chapters 2 and 4), reveals that mood, energy, and cognitive symptoms show the greatest degree of overlap between the intensely creative and hypomanic episodes. Several of the more behavioral changes typically associated with hypomania (hypersexuality, talkativeness, increased spending of money) were reported by only a minority of subjects.

The artists and writers were also asked about changes in sleep and mood occurring just prior to these intensely creative episodes. Almost all of them reported a clearly noticeable decrease in the need for sleep. Twenty-eight percent described waking spontaneously at 3:00 or 4:00 A.M. and being unable to return to sleep. Mood changes were profound. One-half reported a sharp increase in mood just prior to the beginning of an intensely creative period. For example, one person described feeling "excited, anticipatory, energetic," while others said they were "elated," "euphoric," or "ecstatic"; yet another said, "I have a fever to write, and throw myself energetically into new projects." The fact that the elevation in mood often preceded the creative periods rather than being entirely a result of them is important in understanding the relationship between moods and the creative process. We return to this point in chapter 4. Pronounced psychological discomfort preceded the creative episodes of another 28 percent of the artists and writers. Some described themselves as "more anxious"; one wrote that he felt he was "near suicide," and yet another that he had a sense of "fearfulness" and a "general mood of distress and slight paranoia." Finally, approximately one-fourth (22 percent) of the sample reported mixed mood changes and physical restlessness; for example, one described a "mixture of elation together with some gloominess, feeling of isolation, sexual pressure, fast emotional responses"; several noted "restlessness"; another wrote of a "low ebb bordering on despair often precedes good phase when work will flow almost as though one is a medium, rather than an originator," and several others observed feeling "restless and dissatisfied." When the subjects were asked specifically about the importance of very intense moods in the development and execution of their work, nine out of ten stated that such moods were either integral and necessary (60 percent), or very important (30

Figure 3–2.
Mood, Cognitive, and Behavioral Changes Reported During Intense Creative Episodes

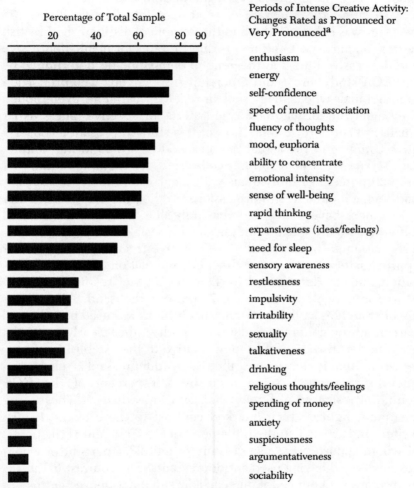

Percentage of Total Sample

20 40 60 80 90

Periods of Intense Creative Activity:
Changes Rated as Pronounced or
Very Pronounced[a]

enthusiasm

energy

self-confidence

speed of mental association

fluency of thoughts

mood, euphoria

ability to concentrate

emotional intensity

sense of well-being

rapid thinking

expansiveness (ideas/feelings)

need for sleep

sensory awareness

restlessness

impulsivity

irritability

sexuality

talkativeness

drinking

religious thoughts/feelings

spending of money

anxiety

suspiciousness

argumentativeness

sociability

[a]*Need for sleep decreased; all the others increased.*

SOURCE: From K. R. Jamison, Mood disorders and patterns of creativity in British writers and artists, *Psychiatry* 52 (1989): 125–134.

percent). Consistent with their higher rate of medical treatment for mood disorders, more poets than any other group regarded these moods as essential to what they did and how they did it.

In summary, the rate of treatment for affective illness (38 percent) was extremely high in this sample of distinguished British writers and artists. Lifetime prevalence rates for manic-depressive and depressive illness in the general population (as determined by the ECA study) are 1 and 5 percent respectively. The proportion of individuals who actually seek or receive treatment, even though they meet the formal diagnostic criteria for affective illness, is far smaller. Therefore, the findings of this study represent a conservative estimate of the actual rate of mood disorders in the sample. Dr. Myrna Weissman and her colleagues, for example, found that only 20 percent of individuals with a current psychiatric disorder had seen a mental health professional in the previous year;[38] other researchers have concluded that only one-third of affectively ill patients actually make a mental health visit of any kind.[39] Similarly, although lithium is the presumptive treatment of choice for approximately 1 percent of the adult population, the actual utilization rate, as determined by Drs. R. G. McCreadie and D. P. Morrison in Scotland, is only 0.77 per one thousand.[40] Dr. Javier Escobar and his associates found that lithium was used by only 0.15 percent of the general population.[41] Both studies clearly indicate a gross underutilization of lithium relative to the established prevalence of manic-depressive illness. Antidepressants, more frequently prescribed, were used by 2.5 percent of the ECA community sample of fifteen thousand individuals.[42] These drug treatment figures are in marked contrast to those of the British writers and artists I studied, 6.4 percent (16.7 percent of the poets) of whom reported the use of lithium, and 23.4 percent of whom acknowledged having used antidepressants. The contrast in rates is even more pronounced if one considers that antidepressant use in general is far more common in women than men,[43] yet the sample of writers and artists was predominantly male.

The British study revealed many overlapping mood, cognitive, and behavioral (especially sleep) changes between hypomania and intense creative states, despite the fact that questions regarding one state were asked independently of those regarding the other and in a manner designed to minimize possible effects of suggestion. Cognitive and mood changes shared far more overlap than behavioral ones, indicating that the milder forms of hypomania may represent the more productive phases of affective illness. The affective continuum that ranges from normal states through hypomania and then mania is very important, but poorly understood. It remains unclear whether the overlap in cognitive and mood changes represents etiologically related syndromes or phenomenologically similar but causally unrelated patterns of expression. It also remains unclear the extent to which writers and artists are simply more sensitive than the general population to their own mood states, and therefore more able—and perhaps also more willing—to articulate and report them.

Dr. Ruth Richards and her colleagues at Harvard used a very different research design to study the relationship between creativity and psychopathology.[44] They hypothesized that a genetic vulnerability to manic-depressive illness would be accompanied by a predisposition to creativity, which, according to this hypothesis, might be more prominent among close relatives of manic-depressive patients than among the patients themselves. Such a compensatory advantage, they speculated, would be roughly analogous to the resistance of malaria found among unaffected carriers of the gene for sickle-cell anemia. To test their hypothesis, Richards and her associates selected seventeen manic-depressive and sixteen cyclothymic patients, along with eleven of their normal first-degree relatives, using criteria that would ensure inclusions of a spectrum of disorders. These patients and their relatives were compared with fifteen normal control subjects, and eighteen controls who had a psychiatric diagnosis, but no personal or family history of major affective disorder, cyclothymia, schizoaffective disorder, schizophrenia, or suicide. Unlike other studies, which limited the definition of creativity only to significant, socially recognized accomplishment in the arts or sciences, this one attempted to measure the disposition toward originality manifested in a wide range of everyday endeavors. These investigators administered the Lifetime Creativity Scales, a previously validated instrument that assesses the quality and quantity of creative involvement in both work and leisure activities.

Richards and her colleagues found significantly higher combined creativity scores among the manic-depressive and cyclothymic patients, and their normal first-degree relatives, than among the control subjects. The normal-index relatives showed suggestively higher creativity than did the manic-depressive patients, and the cyclothymic patients were close to the normal relatives. The authors concluded:

> Overall peak creativity may be enhanced, on the average, in subjects showing milder and, perhaps, subclinical expressions of potential bipolar liability (i.e., the cyclothymes and normal first-degree relatives) compared either with individuals who carry no bipolar liability (control subjects) or individuals with more severe manifestations of bipolar liability (manic-depressives). . . . There may be a positive compensatory advantage . . . to genes associated with greater liability for bipolar disorder. The possibility that normal relatives of manic-depressives and cyclothymes have heightened creativity may have been overlooked because of a medical-model orientation that focused on dysfunction rather than positive characteristics of individuals. Such a compensatory advantage among the relatives of a disorder affecting at least 1% of the population could affect a relatively large group of people.[45]

Somewhat related, though as yet still preliminary, research has also found an unusually high incidence of special abilities (for example, outstanding artistic, language, and mathematical abilities) in a sample of children with manic-depressive illness.[46] Two British studies, one of architecture students and the other of chemistry students, found that higher academic and creative performance was associated with greater psychological disturbance and an increased use of mental health facilities.[47] Neither study, however, specified diagnosis or types of psychopathology.

Further support for a link between creativity and mood disorders comes from several family studies. Dr. Andreasen, in her study of writers from the University of Iowa Writers' Workshop, also investigated the family histories of the writers and the control subjects. Consistent with the higher rate of mood disorders in the writers, her findings showed that mood disorders in first-degree relatives (parents and siblings), summarized in table 3–3, was much higher for the writers than the controls. The overall rate for any type of psychiatric disorder was also much higher in the relatives of the writers than in the controls. Additionally, more first-degree

TABLE 3–3.
MENTAL ILLNESS IN FIRST-DEGREE RELATIVES OF THIRTY WRITERS AND THIRTY CONTROL SUBJECTS

Family History RDC Diagnosis	ALL RELATIVES			PARENTS			SIBLINGS		
	Of Writers (N=116) %	Of Controls (N=121) %	p	Of Writers (N=60) %	Of Controls (N=60) %	p	Of Writers (N=56) %	Of Controls (N=121) %	p
Any affective disorder	18	2	.001	7	2	.001	20	3	.01
Bipolar disorder	3	0	.056	2	0	NS	5	0	NS
Major depression	15	2	.01	5	2	.05	14	3	.05
Alcoholism	7	6	NS	8	7	NS	5	5	NS
Suicide	3	0	NS	3	0	NS	2	0	NS
Any illness	42	8	.0001	42	8	.00003	43	8	.001

SOURCE: Adapted from N. C. Andreasen, Creativity and mental illness: Prevalence rates in writers and their first-degree relatives, *American Journal of Psychiatry*, 144 (1987): 1288–1292. Copyright 1992, American Psychiatric Association. Reprinted by permission.

relatives of writers (20 percent) showed histories of creative accomplishment than did relatives of the controls (8 percent). The
fact that creativity and mental illness overlapped much more in the
relatives of the writers than in the relatives of the controls led
Andreasen to suggest a general familial association between creativity and affective disorders:

> It is perhaps noteworthy that the types of creativity observed in the
> relatives of the writers were far broader than literary creativity. Some
> relatives of creative writers were indeed also in literary fields, but
> many were creative in other areas, such as art, music, dance, or
> mathematics. This suggests that whatever is transmitted within fam-
> ilies is a general factor that predisposes to creativity, rather than a
> specific giftedness in verbal areas. Further, whenever traits are trans-
> mitted familially, it is of interest to determine whether the transmis-
> sion is due to social learning and modeling or to more purely genetic
> factors. While family studies cannot disentangle this issue to the
> same extent that adoption studies can, the variability in creativity in
> these families does suggest the possibility of some form of genetic
> transmission. If social learning were the sole factor involved, one
> would expect a preponderance of literary creativity in the families of
> writers.[48]

The familial association between mental illness and creativity
has been found in many other studies as well.[49] Early, far-less-
systematic investigations by C. Lombroso, F. Galton, and W.
Lange-Eichbaum, for example, strongly suggested that both psychopathology and creative accomplishment permeated the family
histories of eminent writers, composers, and artists. Likewise, the
pedigrees of several writers and composers presented later in the
book—for example, those of Byron, Schumann, Woolf, Mary Shelley, Tennyson, and the Jameses—also support a pronounced pattern of coexisting mood disorders and creative abilities, at least in
certain highly accomplished families. Juda's research findings,
which were discussed earlier, are consistent with a familial association between mental illness and creativity as well. More recently
Dr. Jon Karlsson, at the Institute of Genetics in Iceland, has shown
that the first-degree relatives of psychotic patients, as well as the
patients themselves, are far more likely than the general population to be eminent across many fields of artistic and intellectual

endeavor.[50] He also found that there was a significantly increased risk of mental illness in distinguished Icelandic scholars and their relatives. Although Karlsson has posited a familial relationship between schizophrenia and creativity, several researchers have pointed out that his data actually show a very strong relationship between mood disorders, especially manic-depressive illness, and creativity.[51]

These studies demonstrate that creativity and mental illness, especially mood disorders, tend to aggregate in certain families and not in others, but they do not decisively show that genetic factors are operating; that is, they show a family association but not necessarily that the characteristics under discussion are heritable. It could be, for example, that the family and its environment are exerting the primary influence, rather than the genetic inheritance itself. Dr. Thomas McNeil, using an adopted-offspring research design, attempted to clarify this nature-versus-nurture problem.[52] All of McNeil's subjects were adults who had been adopted shortly after birth and were part of a larger Danish psychiatric genetics study. They were classified as being "high creative" (most of the individuals in this group had achieved national prominence in the arts), "above average," or "low creative"; their rates of mental illness were then compared with those found in their biological and adoptive parents. These results are summarized in table 3–4. The rates of mental illness were highest in the "high" creative group and in their biological parents. The rates of psychopathology in the adoptive parents did not vary significantly from one level of adop-

TABLE 3–4.
RATES OF MENTAL ILLNESS IN ADOPTEES AND THEIR
BIOLOGICAL AND ADOPTIVE PARENTS

Adoptee Group	Adoptee %	Biological Parents %	Adoptive Parents %
High creative	30	27.7	5.3
Above average	10	8.3	5.0
Low creative	0	12.1	5.1

SOURCE: Adapted from data in T. F. McNeil, Prebirth and postbirth influence on the relationship between creative ability and recorded mental illness, *Journal of Personality*, 39 (1971): 391–406.

tee creativity to another. Although the size of the sample was necessarily small, and the type of psychopathology not rigorously ascertained, the study is both an interesting and an important one; its significance lies in the reasons given by Dr. McNeil in his summary remarks:

> Mental illness rates in the adoptees were positively and significantly related to their creative ability level, substantiating the hypothesized relationship between creative ability and mental illness. The mental illness rates of the biological parents were positively and significantly related to the creative ability of the adoptees. Mental illness rates among the adoptive parents and the adoptive and biological siblings were independent of the adoptees' creative ability level. The data were interpreted as evidence for the influence of prebirth factors on the relationship between creative ability and mental illness. No evidence of family-related postbirth influence was found.[53]

Studies of social class and manic-depressive illness provide yet another perspective on the relationship between intellectual abilities, personality characteristics, and manic-depressive illness. In a recent review of more than thirty studies of social class and manic-depressive illness, Dr. Frederick Goodwin and I found that, despite many methodological problems and incongruities—including a time span of more than seven decades, a vast range in the size of the samples surveyed (from twenty to forty-seven thousand), and a wide diversity of countries and cultures in which the studies were conducted—approximately three-fourths of the research reports showed a positive correlation between manic-depressive illness and the professional or upper classes.[54] Dr. Bagley, who carried out an earlier review of the literature, concluded from his extensive investigations:

> The studies reviewed suggest that there is some support for the view that some types of "depression" and upper class economic position are related. This finding seems to hold in several cultures, and in different points in time in the present century. . . . The definition of depression has often been unclear in many studies, but there is some evidence that the finding may apply to "psychotic" rather than "neurotic" depression, and to the classic manic depressive psychoses in particular.[55]

The same writer also compared the distribution of occupational positions in the adult English population at large with those among all fifteen hundred patients who had new episodes of mood disorders over a three-year period in England. Using a sophisticated diagnostic system for affective illness, he distinguished six major categories. Only in the category that we would term bipolar manic-depressive illness was there any significant difference in distribution across occupational classes. In this group of patients, members of the professional and managerial classes were significantly overrepresented. Several studies carried out during the past two decades have confirmed Dr. Bagley's findings. A well-designed study carried out in Sweden, for example, found a highly significant overrepresentation of manic-depressive patients in the upper social and educational classes;[56] so too did a large community sample study of residents of New Haven, Connecticut.[57] Yet other research, conducted in Jerusalem and drawn from Jewish first admissions to psychiatric hospitals, found that affective illness in general was correlated with higher social class.[58] Although the study did not distinguish the bipolar from unipolar patients, almost one-half of the patients in the affectively ill sample were bipolar manic-depressives.

Two major types of arguments have been advanced to explain the greater incidence of manic-depressive illness in the professional and upper social classes. First, some authors suggest that a relationship exists between certain personality and behavioral correlates of affective (primarily bipolar) illness and a rise in social position.[59] In fact, many features of hypomania—such as outgoingness, increased energy, intensified sexuality, increased risk-taking, persuasiveness, self-confidence, and heightened productivity—have been linked with increased achievement and accomplishments. The second hypothesis posits that manic-depressive illness is secondary to the stresses of being in, or moving into, the upper social classes. This hypothesis is rather implausible because it assumes that, compared with lower classes, there is a special kind of stress associated with being in the upper social classes, one capable of precipitating major psychotic episodes. Further, it ignores genetic factors and evidence suggesting that parental social class is often elevated as well.

Despite the inevitable methodological problems that exist in

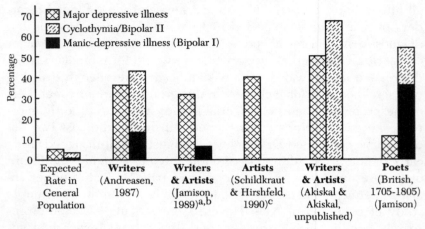

Figure 3–3.
Mood Disorders in Writers and Artists

[a]Treatment rate (estimated to be one-third of the rate of illness).
[b]Bipolar II and cyclothymia rates not ascertained.
[c]Bipolar I, bipolar II, and cyclothymia rates not ascertained.

all the studies discussed so far—the small number of individuals studied, types or lack of control groups, variable diagnostic and selection criteria, and flawed measurement techniques—there is an impressive consistency across the findings. Many lines of evidence point to a strong relationship between mood disorders and achievement, especially artistic achievement. Biographical studies, as well as investigations conducted on living writers and artists, show a remarkable and consistent increase in rates of suicide, depression and manic-depressive illness in these highly creative groups. Figures 3–3 and 3–4 summarize these findings in a visual way (see Appendix B as well). It can be seen that artistic groups, when compared with the expected rates for suicide and mood disorders in the general population,[60] demonstrate up to 18 times the suicide rate, eight to ten times the rate of major depressive illness (indeed, because the ECA study found that major depression was more than twice as common in women, 7 percent, as in men, 2.6 percent, the rates of depression in the primarily male samples represented in figure 3–3 are even more striking), and ten to forty times the rate of manic-depressive illness and its milder

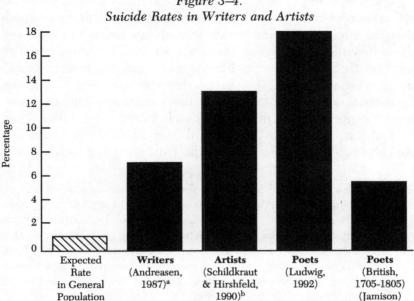

Figure 3–4.
Suicide Rates in Writers and Artists

[a]Suicide rate at time of study completion.
[b]Two other artists died individually in single car accidents.

variants. (Although only 6.4 percent of the writers and artists in my 1989 study are represented in figure 3–3 as having bipolar I illness, this is a spuriously low estimate; all of them had received medical intervention for mania, and epidemiological research indicates that only one person in three who meets the diagnostic criteria for manic-depressive illness actually seeks and receives treatment for it).[61] Findings from other types of studies also point to a strong association between mood disorders and creativity. Manic-depressive patients, cyclothymics, and their first-degree relatives show higher levels of creativity than normal individuals, for example, and both creativity and affective illness have been found to coexist at higher rates than expected in the first-degree relatives of writer and artists.

Given the historical as well as modern research support for a strong relationship between mood disorders and artistic creativity—"that fine madness" described centuries ago—why does such heated controversy continue? Putting aside for the moment Joyce

Carol Oates's very legitimate concerns about the necessity for normal and quiet creative lives, as well as her more than understand-
able resentment of reductionist stereotypes about neurotic and
abusive writers, the major resistance to an association between
psychopathology, or mental illness, and creativity seems to focus
on a few central points. The first is that many writers, artists, and
composers are, or were, perfectly sane; therefore, the argument
goes, the presumption of a strong link between mental illness and
creativity is, on the face of it, absurd. Harold Nicolson, in discussing the health of writers, makes the extreme point rather dryly:

> The theory that there exists some special connexion between literary
> genius and mental derangement is one which, to my mind, has been
> seriously exaggerated. It is true that a few creative writers have in
> their later years become demonstrably insane; it is also true that
> almost all creative writers have at some moments of their lives been
> panic-stricken by the conviction that their imagination was getting
> the better of their reason; but it is not in the least true that *all*
> creative writers have been mad *all* the time.[62]

But of course no one would argue that all writers or artists, or even
most of them, are actually mad; and, equally obviously, no one
would seriously argue that even one, much less all creative writers
had been mad all the time. But the fact that there is only a partial
correlation does not mean that there is no correlation at all. Clearly
there are many artists, writers, and composers who are perfectly
normal from a psychiatric point of view. The argument here is not
that such people do not exist, for they obviously do. Rather, the
argument is that a much-higher-than-expected rate of manic-
depressive illness, depression, and suicide exists in exceptionally
creative writers and artists. It is this discrepant rate that is of
interest and that ultimately needs to be explained.

Another argument set forth against an association between
"madness" and artistic creativity is that a bit of madness and turmoil is part and parcel of the artistic temperament, and that artists
are just more sensitive to life and the experiences of life than are
other people. This is almost certainly true, and it would be foolish
to diagnose psychopathology where none or little exists. Such an
argument, however, begs the issue. It is precisely this overlap

between the artistic and manic-depressive temperaments that we are interested in looking at. In this context Dr. William Frosch makes an important point in emphasizing that distinctions should be made between analogous and homologous behaviors; that is, those behaviors that look the same in mood disorders and in the personalities of artists—for example, intensity of moods or the capacity to experience strong feelings—may not in fact be the same.[63]

Nicolson, like Frosch, makes compelling arguments—although one might disagree with their conclusions—for restraint in diagnosing psychopathology in the artistically creative. For example, he defends Shelley from charges of insanity by arguing that Shelley was perceived as mad simply because he was different, and objects strenuously to the fact that Shelley's schoolmates at Eton described him as "Mad Shelley": "The facility with which English schoolboys attribute insanity to anyone who is not perfectly attuned to their own herd behaviour has always struck me as curious and distressing."[64] This is certainly a legitimate, and common, complaint that can also be leveled against biographers, psychologists, and psychiatrists who equate differentness with psychopathology. But Nicolson then goes on to engage in another common, but far more questionable, biographical practice: He attempts to make many of Shelley's odd behaviors seem much more normal than in fact they probably were. "It is customary," writes Nicolson in discussing Shelley's hallucinations, "for very gifted writers to see spectres and to hear voices calling."[65] This surely is open to debate, and certainly Shelley's friends found his behavior—as did he himself—both odd and very disturbing. Nicolson then gives an example of one of Shelley's many rather strange perceptual experiences: "Shelley saw a baby rise from the sea and clap its hands at him . . . it is clear from the writings of his friends that these sounds and visions were of not infrequent occurrence."[66] "And yet," he goes on to say, Shelley "was certainly not mad."[67] Similarly Nicolson gives Cowper, who not only attempted suicide repeatedly, but also spent a distressingly long period of time in an insane asylum, a relatively clean bill of psychiatric health (especially in light of his well-documented bouts of madness):

> Twice in his life he almost succeeded in hanging himself and now was only saved by chance. Yet although Cowper had twice to be put in

confinement, or at least under supervision, he enjoyed long inter-
ludes of perfect sanity, during which he composed much excellent
poetry and was happy in a quiet tea-party sort of way. It cannot be
said that Cowper was ever a demented maniac: the worst that can be
said of him was that he was sometimes sadly confused in the head.[68]

Perhaps the most heated debate about what constitutes madness in artists has occurred in the context of discussions of the life
and work of William Blake. Biographers and critics have debated
endlessly about whether Blake was or was not mad, was or was not
a visionary, and was or was not a mystic. Some have argued that he
was indisputably insane; many others have vehemently denied it.
No one doubts that he was subject to extraordinary visions from the
time he was very young, or that he had wild changes in mood from
states of highly energetic exhilaration to prolonged and severe periods of despondency. What really is at question is the meaning
that should be attached to these visions and moods. For those who
"defend" Blake against charges of insanity, much of the concern
seems to stem from assumptions that "mad" is somehow "bad,"
that madness is a fixed condition with no periods of rational thought
or experience, that great art cannot come from madness and, therefore, great artists cannot have been mad. Much of the rather heated
defense also seems to come from the notion that labeling Blake
mad, or even partially so, derives from an inability to comprehend
his work's subtleties and complexities. Scholar S. Foster Damon,
for example, dismisses the notion of Blake's madness by saying, "It
would be cruel to print even the names of those . . . critics who
have frankly pronounced Blake mad because they could not understand him,"[69] and distinguished critic Northrop Frye asserts,
"A modern writer on Blake is not required to discuss his sanity, for
which I am grateful: I could not do so without being haunted by
one of his own epigrams: 'The Man who pretends to be a modest
enquirer into the truth of a self evident thing is a Knave.' "[70]
English poet Algernon Charles Swinburne also attempted to defend Blake's sanity but, as Dr. Hubert Norman has pointed out, he
got a bit lost along the way:

It will be obvious that Blake's mental condition during the period of
his stay at Felpham was one of marked instability. Even those who

resent the ascription to him of the term "insane" admit this. "By the sounding shore," says Gilchrist, "visionary conversations were held with many a majestic shadow from the past—Moses and the Prophets, Homer, Dante, Milton." Swinburne says "that too much of Blake's written work while at Felpham is wanting in executive quality, and even in decent coherence of verbal dress, is undeniable"; and adds that "everything now written in the fitful impatient intervals of the day's work bears the stamp of an over-heated brain, and of nerves too intensely strung." Swinburne has, however, his own method of accounting for this. It was due to the "sudden country life, the taste and savour of the sea," which "touch sharply and irritate deliciously the more susceptible and intricate organs of mind and nature. How far such passive capacity of excitement differs from insanity; how in effect a temperament so sensuous, so receptive, and so passionate, is further off from any risk of turning unsound than hardier natures carrying heavier weight and tougher in the nerves, need scarcely be indicated." What does scarcely need to be indicated, after reading such passages as these, is that Swinburne was little competent to give a reasoned opinion on the matter of Blake's mental unsoundness. Only prejudice could have allowed him to draw such a conclusion from the evidence which he himself gives. The last part of the passage quoted is perilously like nonsense.[71]

Dr. Norman is not the only one to question the assumption of Blake's sanity. Max Byrd writes:

Admirers of Blake are always expressing surprise that he should have been called mad by anyone—"The legends of Blake's 'madness' never seem to cease, despite all scholarly rebuttal," complains Harold Bloom. Such puzzlement is unrealistic. The legends of Blake's madness persist because he wrote poetry that describes Milton entering his left foot, because he claimed to speak daily and hourly with the spirit of his dead brother and with other spirits, because he wrote long incomprehensible poems about unheard-of beings with names like Enitharmon and Golgonooza. In almost any age of human history such a man would have seemed insane. . . . What is striking in a way about Blake's career is not that so many people considered him insane but that so many people did not.[72]

A position perhaps somewhere in between the two absolutes of sane and insane, of manifest genius and rank incomprehensibility, is a presumptive diagnosis of manic-depressive illness. This would account not only for Blake's visionary and psychotic states, but for his forays into and out of the rather more prosaically rational world as well. The evidence that Blake suffered from manic-depressive illness is actually quite strong, as Norman argued compellingly more than seventy-five years ago.

> It is difficult to realise how any unprejudiced person who considers the evidence in Blake's case can arrive at any other conclusion than that he exhibited mental disorder. . . . Though the prevailing state with Blake was one of exaltation and belief in his own capabilities, there were also periods of extreme depression, and the condition may, with little doubt, be classified as one of maniacal-depressive insanity. The fluctuations in his mental condition were so marked as to be in themselves sufficient evidence of marked nervous instability, and these alternations were so pronounced as to be inconsistent with the normal periodicity which is to be noticed in those whose sanity is not impugned. When, too, we find that in addition to these alternations there is evidence of diminished control—as shown in undue excitability and impulsive violence, of hallucinations of sight and hearing, and of delusions of persecution—there is no doubt that the boundary which separates sanity from insanity has been crossed. Those who protest against this plain statement do not seem to realise that they do Blake less than justice. They would hold him responsible for all his vagaries rather than allow a verdict of *non compos*. Chiefly this is so in order that the vague, mystical element in his work may be imputed to some vague supra- or extra-natural power instead of to the disorderly functioning of unstable nerve-tissue, or to misunderstood organic reflexes. These nervous disorders are obscure enough even when they are considered apart from the veiling mystery in which so many love to hide them; it is not, therefore, necessary to invoke occult powers, and by so doing to render the subject nebulous and impenetrable. Still less is it wise to place behind the disease of insanity a Mumbo-Jumbo, which has to be invoked, or a Raw-head and Bloody-bones, which has to be exorcised.[73]

Suggesting the diagnosis of manic-depressive illness for Blake does not detract from the complexity of his life; it may, however, add a different kind of understanding to it. Likewise, it does not render his work any the less extraordinary, or make him any less a great visionary or prophet.[74] Seeing Blake as someone who suffered from an occasionally problematic illness—a constitutional predisposition shared in common with many other artists, writers, and composers—may not explain all or even most of who he was. But, surely, it does explain some.

What is to be made of this tendency to deny a link between psychopathology and genius, to regard bizarre—and occasionally dangerous—behavior as somehow normal if it occurs in writers and artists? Is it simply an admirable tolerance for deviant and eccentric behavior if it occurs in individuals who are, by definition, already far from the normal temperamental and intellectual standards of human society? Or does it reflect a belief that artists may just be fulfilling society's and their own expectations that they ought to act the part of the "tormented genius"? Do the strains and anxieties of being an artist somehow create a special type of melancholy and oddness? These possibilities, while no doubt true to a certain extent, tend to disregard the possibility that individuals with temperaments liable to emotional extremes may be more likely to choose artistic careers, thereby increasing the chances of an interaction between a biological vulnerability and psychological stress. Likewise, they do not take into account the fact that the artists and writers under discussion here generally have shown emotional instability prior to the onset of their artistic careers and manifested a severity of psychiatric symptoms, an age of onset, and a pattern of mood disturbances highly characteristic of manic-depressive illness; they also have had greatly increased rates of depression, manic-depressive illness, and suicide in their first-degree relatives.

Most of the controversy surrounding the "mad genius" versus "healthy artist" debate, however, arises from confusion about what is actually meant by "madness," as well as from a fundamental lack of understanding about the nature of manic-depressive illness.[75] These two issues—controversy over the meaning of "madness" and confusion about the nature of one of the major "madnesses" (that is, manic-depressive illness)—are inevitably and closely bound together. Dr. William Ober, in his essay "Madness and Poetry: A Note On Collins, Cowper, and Smart," makes the point that:

Plato distinguished clearly between prophetic insights and intuitive insights into the nature of reality. He distrusted the latter as being nonrational, but his use of the term mania does not necessarily imply irrationality or psychosis. Even today, in English usage, mania encompasses a wide range of attitudes and behavior, from folly through uncontrollable impulses to overt psychosis; it is not a restrictive term.[76]

Any attempt to arbitrarily polarize thought, behavior, and emotion into clear-cut "sanity" or "insanity" is destined to fail; it defies common sense and it is contrary to what we know about the infinite varieties and gradations of disease in general and psychiatric illness in particular. "Madness," in fact, occurs only in the extreme forms of mania and depression; most people who have manic-depressive illness never become psychotic. Those who do lose their reason— are deluded, hallucinate, or act in particularly strange and bizarre ways—are irrational for limited periods of time only, and are otherwise well able to think clearly and act rationally. Manic-depressive illness, unlike schizophrenia or Alzheimer's disease, is not a dementing illness. It may on occasion result in episodes of acute psychosis and flagrant irrationality, but these bouts of madness are almost always temporary and seldom progress to chronic insanity. Yet the assumption that psychosis is an all-or-nothing sort of phenomenon, and that it is stable in its instability, leads to tremendous confusion: Van Gogh, it is said, could not have been mad, as his paintings reflect lucidity of the highest order. Lucidity, however, is not incompatible with occasional bouts of madness, just as extended periods of normal physical health are not incompatible with occasional bouts of hypertension, diabetic crisis, hyperthyroidism, or any other kind of acute exacerbation of underlying metabolic disease. John Ruskin, for one, has described the transitions between psychological health and "morbid inflammation of the brain":

> For a physician's estimate of it, I can only refer them to my physicians. But there were some conditions of it which I knew better than they could: namely, first, the precise and sharp distinction between the state of morbid inflammation of brain which gave rise to false visions, (whether in sleep, or trance, or waking, in broad daylight, with perfect knowledge of the real things in the room, while yet I saw

others that were not there), and the not morbid, however dangerous, states of more or less excited temper, & too much quickened thought, which gradually led up to the illness, accelerating in action during the eight or ten days preceding the actual giving way of the brain . . . & yet, up to the transitional moment of first hallucination entirely healthy, & in the full sense of the word "sane"; just as the natural inflammation of a healing wound in flesh is sane, up to the transitional edge where it may pass at a crisis into morbific, or even mortified substance.[77]

There is a great deal of evidence to suggest that, compared to "normal" individuals, artists, writers, and creative people in general, are both psychologically "sicker"—that is, they score higher on a wide variety of measures of psychopathology—and psychologically healthier (for example, they show quite elevated scores on measures of self-confidence and ego strength).[78] Manic-depressive illness is an inherited vulnerability to a disease that can manifest itself in a wide range of fluctuating emotional states, behaviors, thinking patterns and styles, and energy levels. Heightened passions and partial derangement of the senses tend to come and go, as Byron so drolly described: "I can never get people to understand that poetry is the expression of *excited passion*, and that there is no such thing as a life of passion any more than a continuous earthquake, or an eternal fever. Besides, who would ever *shave* themselves in such a state?"[79] The temperaments associated with manic-depressive illness are also part of the affective continuum, forming in turn a natural bridge between a virulently psychotic illness on the one hand and the moody, artistic temperaments on the other. The relationship between the manic-depressive and artistic temperaments is discussed at length in the next chapter.

Finally, many critics who are opposed to the idea that psychopathology is linked to artistic ability express concern that labeling artists as mentally ill ignores the enormous discipline, will, and rationality that are essential to truly creative work.[80] In speaking of Goethe, for example, Thomas Carlyle wrote:

This man rules, and is not ruled. The stern and fiery energies of a most passionate soul lie silent in the centre of his being; a trembling sensibility has been inured to stand, without flinching or murmur, the sharpest trials. Nothing onward, nothing inward, shall agitate or

control him. The brightest and most capricious fancy, the most piercing and inquisitive intellect, the wildest and deepest imagination; the
highest thrills of joy, the bitterest pangs of sorrow: all these are his,
he is not theirs.[81]

This emphasis on the need for control calls to mind the ancient
admonition of Longinus, who argued that "sublime impulses are
exposed to greater dangers when they are left to themselves without the ballast and stability of knowledge; they need the curb as
often as the spur."[82] Poets, while beholden to the spur, have also
been mindful of a need for the curb. John Keats, in response to a
poem sent to him by Shelley, wrote:

> You I am sure will forgive me for sincerely remarking that you might
> curb your magnanimity and be more of an artist, and "load every rift"
> of your subject with ore. The thought of such discipline must fall like
> cold chains upon you, who perhaps never sat with your wings furl'd
> for six Months together. And is this not extraordina[r]y talk for the
> writer of Endymion? whose mind was like a pack of scattered
> cards—[83]

Coleridge, no stranger to the idea of scattered thoughts and un-
furled wings, also underscored the absolute necessity for order and
reason. "Poetry," he wrote, "even that of the loftiest, and seemingly, that of the wildest odes, [has] a logic of its own as severe as
that of science; and more difficult, because more subtle, more
complex, and dependent on more and more fugitive causes. In the
truly great poets . . . there is a reason assignable, not only for
every word, but for the position of every word."[84]

The need for clear and logical thought is obvious but, as we
discussed earlier, clarity and logic are perfectly compatible with
the ebbings and flowings of manic-depressive illness and its associated temperaments. Indeed, whether out of a need to impose
order upon a chaotic internal universe, or for other as yet unex-
plained reasons, many individuals with manic-depressive illness
are inclined to be unusually obsessive and highly organized.[85] And,
while many ideas may be generated during mildly manic states,
much of the structuring, editing, and fine-tuning of artistic work is
carried out during normal or mildly depressed periods. Seamus

Heaney described Robert Lowell's extraordinary ability to forge the raw material of his mind and emotions into finished art. Lowell, he wrote:

> had in awesome abundance the poet's first gift for surrender to those energies of language that heave to the fore matter that will not be otherwise summoned, or that might be otherwise suppressed. Under the ray of his concentration, the molten stuff of the psyche ran hot and unstanched. But its final form was as much beaten as poured, the cooling ingot was assiduously hammered. A fully human and relentless intelligence was at work upon the pleasuring quick of the creative act. He was and will remain a pattern for poets in this amphibiousness, this ability to plunge into his amphibiousness, this ability to plunge into the downward reptilian welter of the individual self and yet raise himself with whatever knowledge he gained there out on the hard ledges of the historical present.[86]

The molten and amphibious nature of artistic imagination represents not only a crucial element in creativity but an important link between the manic-depressive and artistic temperaments as well. It is to the links between mood, temperament, and thought that we turn next.

4.
THEIR LIFE
A STORM
WHEREON
THEY RIDE

Temperament and Imagination

Their breath is agitation, and their life
A storm whereon they ride, to sink at last,
And yet so nurs'd and bigotted to strife,
That should their days, surviving perils past,
Melt to calm twilight, they feel overcast
With sorrow and supineness, and so die;
Even as a flame unfed, which runs to waste
With its own flickering, or a sword laid by
Which eats into itself, and rusts ingloriously.

—GEORGE GORDON, LORD BYRON[1]

Cloud Study. John Constable, 1821
(Yale Center for British Art, Paul Mellon Collection)

The fact that manic-depressive illness really comprises a range of temperaments, behaviors, and patterns of thought (with occasional episodes of psychosis in some individuals) has led, as we have seen, to much of the controversy—and confusion—surrounding the needlessly polarized "mad genius" versus "psychologically healthy artist" debate. We have also seen that there is a greatly increased rate of depression, manic-depressive illness, and suicide in eminent writers and artists. Why should this be so? Is it only a coincidence? Do artists create in spite of their often-debilitating problems with moods? Or, as we will argue here, is there something about the experience of prolonged periods of melancholia—broken at times by episodes of manic intensity and expansiveness—that leads to a different kind of insight, compassion, and expression of the human condition? In this chapter we explore those aspects of manic-depressive illness that might—under some circumstances—add depth, fire, and understanding to artistic imagination.

Profound changes in mood, thinking, personality, and behavior can occur during all phases of manic-depressive illness. Even during normal states many individuals with the illness, or who have a cyclothymic temperament, will experience striking fluctuations in the intensity of their perceptions and feelings. All these changes have potentially important effects on personality and thought, but perhaps most relevant to the discussion of artistic creativity are those changes that occur during the milder manic, or hypomanic, states. Even the most casual review of the diagnostic criteria for hypomania, given in Appendix A, suggests a *prima facie* case for a connection between hypomania and intellectual or artistic achievement. There is perhaps some truth in the glib question that often arises during clinical teaching situations: Who would *not* want an illness that has among its symptoms elevated and expansive mood, inflated self-esteem, abundance of energy, less need for sleep, intensified sexuality, and—most germane to our argument here—"sharpened and unusually creative thinking" and "increased productivity"? The very fact that these two seemingly "soft" or subjective symptoms have been agreed upon by a group of data-based, research psychiatrists as part of the diagnostic criteria for hypomania is remarkable in its own right. Among other things, it speaks to the seriousness with which the association between mild mania and creativity has been taken by even some of the more rigorous clinical scientists within the field of academic psychiatry.

In looking at changes associated with extreme mood states that might be related to artistic creativity, especially changes in emotion and thinking, it is perhaps helpful to first discuss the pivotal issue of "inspiration." Earlier we looked at both ancient and modern speculations about the relationship between imagination, divine inspiration, and "madness." The notion of a special access to a power beyond what is ordinarily known to an individual or his society has extended across many different kinds of inspired states: the warlike, the druidic, the mystical, and the poetic. Attributions of inspiration once made to the gods or the muses have been transformed, during the twentieth century, into the rather more prosaic formulations of "primary process," "pre-logical thought," and "bisociative thinking." Arthur Koestler, who coined the latter phrase in his landmark book *The Act of Creation*, described the importance of combining both rational and irrational sources in the creative process:

> We have seen that the creative act always involves a regression to earlier, more primitive levels in the mental hierarchy, while other processes continue simultaneously on the rational surface—a condi-

tion that reminds one of a skin-diver with a breathing-tube. (Need-less to say, the exercise has its dangers: skin-divers are prone to fall victims to the 'rapture of the deep' and tear their breathing-tubes off—the *reculer sans sauter* of William Blake and so many oth-ers. . . .) The capacity to regress, more or less at will, to the games of the underground, without losing contact with the surface, seems to be the essence of the poetic, and of any other form of creativity. 'God guard me from those thoughts men think / In the mind alone, / He that sings a lasting song / Thinks in a marrow bone' (Yeats).[2]

From virtually all perspectives—early Greek philosopher to twentieth-century specialist—there is agreement that artistic cre-ativity and inspiration involve, indeed require, a dipping into pre-rational or irrational sources while maintaining ongoing contact with reality and "life at the surface." The degree to which individ-uals can, or desire to, "summon up the depths" is among the more fascinating individual differences. Many highly creative and accom-plished writers, composers, and artists function essentially within the rational world, without losing access to their psychic "under-ground." Others, the subject of this book, are likewise privy to their unconscious streams of thought, but they must contend with unusually tumultuous and unpredictable emotions as well. The integration of these deeper, truly irrational sources with more log-ical processes can be a tortuous task, but, if successful, the result-ing work often bears a unique stamp, a "touch of fire," for what it has been through.

Artists and writers, like other individuals, vary enormously not only in their capacity to experience but also to tolerate ex-tremes of emotions and to live on close terms with darker forces. Yeats described this in his essay "A Remonstrance with Scotsmen for Having Soured the Dispositions of Their Ghosts and Faeries":

> You have discovered the faeries to be pagan and wicked. You would like to have them all up before the magistrate. In Ireland warlike mortals have gone amongst them, and helped them in their battles, and they in turn have taught men great skill with herbs, and per-mitted some few to hear their tunes. Carolan slept upon a faery rath. Ever after their tunes ran in his head, and made him the great musician he was. . . . You—you will make no terms with the spirits of fire and earth and air and water. You have made the Darkness your enemy. We—we exchange civilities with the world beyond.[3]

No one understands what gives some people access to these "world[s] beyond," or why—once in contact with such worlds— some art derived from them should be so rich and vital and some so uninspired. One thing seems reasonably clear, however. Many of the changes in mood, thinking, and perception that characterize the mildly manic states—restlessness, ebullience, expansiveness, irritability, grandiosity, quickened and more finely tuned senses, intensity of emotional experiences, diversity of thought, and rapid- ity of associational processes—are highly characteristic of creative thought as well. Before we turn to the importance of mood changes in the creative process, we first look at those cognitive aspects of hypomania that might benefit imaginative thought.

Two aspects of thinking in particular are pronounced in both creative and hypomanic thought: fluency, rapidity, and flexibility of thought on the one hand, and the ability to combine ideas or categories of thought in order to form new and original connections on the other. The importance of rapid, fluid, and divergent thought in the creative process has been described by most psychologists and writers who have studied human imagination. The increase in the speed of thinking may exert its influence in different ways. Speed per se, that is, the quantity of thoughts and associations produced in a given period of time, may be enhanced. The in- creased quantity and speed of thoughts may exert an effect on the qualitative aspects of thought as well; that is, the sheer volume of thought can produce unique ideas and associations. Indeed, Sir Walter Scott, when discussing Byron's mind, commented: "The wheels of a machine to play rapidly must not fit with the utmost exactness else the attrition diminishes the Impetus."[4] The quick- ness and fire of Byron's mind were not lost on others who knew him. One friend wrote: "The mind of Lord Byron was like a vol- cano, full of fire and wealth, sometimes calm, often dazzling and playful, but ever threatening. It ran swift as the lightning from one subject to another, and occasionally burst forth in passionate throes of intellect, nearly allied to madness."[5] Byron's mistress, Teresa Guiccioli, noted: "New and striking thoughts followed from him in rapid succession, and the flame of his genius lighted up as if winged with wildfire."[6]

Psychologist J. P. Guilford, who carried out a long series of systematic psychological studies into the nature of creativity, found that several factors were involved in creative thinking; many of these, as we shall see, relate directly to the cognitive changes that take place during mild manias as well. Fluency of thinking, as defined by Guilford, is made up of several related and empirically derived concepts, measured by specific tasks: word fluency, the ability to produce words each, for example, containing a specific letter or combination of letters; associational fluency, the production of as many synonyms as possible for a given word in a limited amount of time; expressional fluency, the production and rapid juxtaposition of phrases or sentences; and ideational fluency, the ability to produce ideas to fulfill certain requirements in a limited amount of time. In addition to fluency of thinking, Guilford developed two other important concepts for the study of creative thought: spontaneous flexibility, the ability and disposition to produce a great variety of ideas, with freedom to switch from category to category; and adaptive flexibility, the ability to come up with unusual types of solutions to set problems. Guilford concluded that creative individuals were also far more likely to exhibit "divergent" rather than "convergent" thinking:

> In tests of convergent thinking there is almost always one conclusion or answer that is regarded as unique, and thinking is to be channeled or controlled in the direction of that answer. . . . In divergent thinking, on the other hand, there is much searching about or going off in various directions. This is most obviously seen when there is no unique conclusion. Divergent thinking . . . is characterized . . . as being less goal-bound. There is freedom to go off in different directions. . . . Rejecting the old solution and striking out in some direction is necessary, and the resourceful organism will more probably succeed.[7]

The importance of divergent thinking in the creative process, although not without controversy, has been corroborated by the work of many other researchers, including Frank Barron in the United States and Liam Hudson in England.[8]

Early clinical researchers noted the tendency of their manic patients to exhibit many characteristics of divergent and fluid thought. Kraepelin commented on the fact that manic thought showed "heightened distractibility," a "tendency to diffusiveness," and "a spinning out the circle of ideas stimulated and jumping off to others."[9] Swiss psychiatrist Eugen Bleuler concurred, and further drew the parallels between manic and artistic thought:

> The *thinking* of the manic is flighty. He jumps by by-paths from one subject to another, and cannot adhere to anything. With this the ideas run along very easily and involuntarily, even so freely that it may be felt as unpleasant by the patient. . . .
>
> Because of the more rapid flow of ideas, and especially because of the falling off of inhibitions, artistic activities are facilitated even though something worth while is produced only in very mild cases and when the patient is otherwise talented in this direction. The heightened sensibilities naturally have the effect of furthering this.[10]

More recently, several researchers have shown that manic patients, unlike normal individuals or schizophrenics, tend to exhibit pronounced combinatory thinking. Characterized by the merging of "percepts, ideas, or images in an incongruous fashion,"[11] the ideas formed in this way become "loosely strung together and extravagantly combined and elaborated."[12] Drs. Nancy Andreasen and Pauline Powers of the University of Iowa compared manic patients, schizophrenics, and writers from the University of Iowa Writers' Workshop on measures of conceptual overinclusiveness (the tendency to combine test objects into categories in a way that tends to "blur, broaden, or shift conceptual boundaries").[13] The authors' hypothesis that creative writers might show thinking styles similar to those seen in schizophrenics was found to be without grounds; instead, they observed that the writers showed conceptual styles quite like those of the manic patients: "Both writers and manics tend to sort in large groups, change dimensions while in the process of sorting, arbitrarily change starting points, or use vague distantly related concepts as categorizing principles."[14] They differed primarily in the degree of control they were able to exert over their patterns of thought, with the writers able to carry out "controlled flights of fancy during the process of sorting, while the manics tend to sort many objects for bizarre or personalized reasons."[15] Moreover, people who have strong emotional responses in general (who also tend to score higher on measures of being at risk for developing manic-depressive illness) tend to have more elaborate and generalizing cognitive operations.[16] More recently Dr. David Shuldberg has found that several hypomanic traits contribute to performance on tests measuring creativity; of particular relevance here he found that creative cognition is far more similar to hypomanic flight of ideas than it is to the loose associations that are characteristic of schizophrenia.[17] Other studies have found that rhymes, punning, and sound associations increase during mania, and many patients spontaneously start writing poetry while manic (often without any previous interest in either reading or writing poetry).[18] Likewise, in studies of word-associational patterns, researchers have found that the number of original responses to a word-association task (in which an individual is asked to give as many associations as possible to a particular word) increase threefold during mania; the number of statistically common, or predictable, responses falls by approximately one-third.[19] Hypomania also has been found to increase intellectual functioning on the Wechsler Adult Intelligence Scale.[20] Recent studies show that a strongly positive, or "up," mood facilitates creative problem solving;[21] relatedly, the majority of the British writers and artists in my study reported pronounced elevations in mood just prior to their periods of intensive creative activity.[22] Drs. Ruth Richards and Dennis Kinney of Harvard University found that the overwhelming majority of manic-depressives in their investigation reported being in a mildly or very elevated mood when experiencing their greatest periods of creativity. Several features that were closely tied to elevated mood states in their subjects clearly overlapped those found in the British writers and artists; these included increased speed of associations, ease of thinking, new ideas, and expansiveness.[23] Although the tendency has been to assume that creative periods lead to "high" or elevated moods and that noncreative periods lead to depressed ones, these studies suggest that the reverse may be true. It may be that elevations in mood such as those caused by hypomania result in more creative thought; likewise, depressed mood and thinking may well lead to periods relatively bereft of creative work.

In all these aspects of creative thought the elements of fluidity and flexibility of cognitive processing are pronounced. Clearly the mere quickening and opening up of thought in an otherwise unimaginative person will not result in creative achievement. If, however, a highly imaginative person's thinking processes are hastened and loosened by mild manic states, it is likely that a distinctive quality will be added to the creative process. The grandiosity of spirit and vision so characteristic of mania, coupled with manic drive and intensity, can add an expansiveness and boldness as well. Under unusual circumstances—and circumstances under which genius is bred are by definition unusual—this can result in a formidable combination of imagination, adventurousness, and a restless, quick, and vastly associative mind. No one better personifies the wide-ranging, expansive, wandering, and dendritic possibilities of the human mind than Samuel Taylor Coleridge.

Coleridge, whose life is further discussed in chapter 6, came to his imaginative life with turmoil and fire in his genes and a love for "the Vast" in his blood. "His mind was clothed with wings,"[24] wrote William Hazlitt, and Coleridge himself said: "My thoughts bustle along like a Surinam toad, with little toads sprouting out of back, side, and belly, vegetating while it crawls."[25] Thomas Carlyle described the intense, grandiose, and charismatic quality to Coleridge's far-ranging conversational style:

> I have heard Coleridge talk, with eager musical energy, two stricken hours, his face radiant and moist, and communicate no meaning whatsoever to any individual of his hearers,—certain of whom, I for one, still kept eagerly listening in hope; the most had long before given up, and formed (if the room were large enough) secondary humming groups of their own. He began anywhere: you put some question to him, made some suggestive observation: instead of answering this, or decidedly setting out towards answer of it, he would accumulate formidable apparatus, logical swim-bladders, transcendental life-preservers and other precautionary and vehiculatory gear, for setting out; perhaps did at last get under way,—but was swiftly solicited, turned aside by the glance of some radiant new game on this hand or that, into new courses; and ever into new; and before long into all the Universe, where it was uncertain what game you would catch, or whether any.[26]

John Keats, in a letter to his brother, wrote about his experiences after meeting Coleridge for the first time:

> —I walked with him a[t] his alderman-after-dinner pace for near two Miles I suppose. In those two Miles he broached a thousand things—

let me see if I can give you a list—Nightingales, Poetry—on Poetical
sensation—Metaphysics—Different genera and species of Dreams—
Nightmare—a dream accompanied by a sense of touch—single and
double touch—A dream related—First and second consciousness—
. . . Monsters—the Kraken—Mermaids—southey [sic] believes in
them—southeys [sic] belief too much diluted—A Ghost story—Good
morning—I heard his voice as he came towards me—I heard it as he
moved away—I had heard it all the interval—if it may be called so.[27]

Coleridge's wide-ranging, not to say cosmic, interests, tied together by seemingly infinite associative strands, formed the essence of his imaginative style. One scholar has given an illustrative
road map to Coleridge's mind and works:

But the road, as we shall actually travel it, leads through half the
lands and all the seven seas of the globe. For we shall meet on the
way with as strange a concourse as ever haunted the slopes of Par-
nassus—with alligators and albatrosses and auroras and Anti-
chthones; with biscuit-worms, bubbles of ice, bassoons, and breezes;
with candles, and Cain, and the Corpo Santo; Dioclesian, king of
Syria, and the dæmons of the elements; earthquakes, and the Eu-
phrates; frost-needles, and fog-smoke, and phosphorescent light;
gooseberries, and the Gordonia lasianthus; haloes and hurricanes;
lightnings and Laplanders; meteors, and the Old Man of the Mountain, and stars behind the moon; nightmares, and the sources of the
Nile; footless birds of Paradise, and the observatory at Pekin; swoons,
and spectres, and slimy seas; wefts, and water-snakes, and the Wandering Jew. Beside that compendious cross-section of chaos, nightmares are methodical. Yet of such is the kingdom of poetry. And in
that paradox lies the warrant of our pilgrimage.[28]

In order for far-flung or chaotic thoughts to be transformed
into works of art, original and meaningful connections (linkings, in
the Aristotelian sense of "dissimilarity with similarity") must be
made. Here again grandiosity and a related cosmic sense often
combine with acute observational powers to make otherwise un-
imaginable emotional and intellectual leaps. The effects of such
visionary and expansive states can be discerned not only in the
work of Coleridge, but in the writings of Poe, Smart, Blake,
Melville, Ruskin, and many others as well. Ruskin—whose ideas

and interests, like Coleridge's, spanned virtually every aspect of human knowledge but whose mind also occasionally strayed over the boundaries of the profound into utter manic madness—wrote in *Modern Painters* about the dynamic and complex interaction that takes place between the observer and observed during the process of imaginative, combining thought:

> A powerfully imaginative mind seizes and combines at the same instant, not only two, but all the important ideas of its poem or picture; and while it works with any one of them, it is at the same instant working with and modifying all in their relations to it, never losing sight of their bearings on each other; as the motion of a snake's body goes through all parts at once, and its volition acts at the same instant in coils that go contrary ways. [29]

This elaborate relationship between observations and the connections made between them is vividly portrayed by Olof Lagencrantz in his biography of August Strindberg:

> One brilliant observation followed another; Strindberg's intuitive awareness that everything is infinitely interconnected fired its lightning bolts into the great chaos—the starting-point of it all. Strindberg's imagination had gained a new resilience, a new confidence in his ability to see correspondences and parallels between different areas of knowledge. He connected all the kingdoms of nature, but never in a generalizing, pantheistic way: the connections are palpable, concrete. The kingfisher, he claimed, had evolved the brightly coloured, scale-like feathers on its neck and wings by spending many hours sitting and staring down into the water at its prey—the fishes. The mackerel's moiré back reflected wave motions in water, to the extent that one could copy and present them as waves on a canvas. The hoar-frost crystals on trees and blades of grass resembled caterpillars, roses and cauliflower heads: the observation is presented as evidence for a connection between the organic and the inorganic world. The pattern on the wings of the death's-head moth was generated by the fact that the insect frequented sites of execution and graveyards, where it laid its eggs in corpses. The forms of plant-life recur in metals. The sunflower reflects the image of the sun with its disc, rays and spots. Flowers and animals mistake themselves for one another and exchange forms. [30]

Strindberg (who, as we shall see, was not the only member of his family to suffer from manic-depressive psychosis) showed an extraordinary range of scientific interests. His biographer Michael Meyer provides an excellent example of the grandiosity of ideas floridly outpacing any realistic expectation of their execution:

> The range of his scientific explorations is remarkable. "When the moment comes that people take my research seriously," he wrote on 22 March to Birger Mörner, "found a Free Laboratory for me! All I need: a big cottage outside Stockholm, with cheap apparatus. . . . There I would concentrate on completing the inventions which I have half ready: e.g., colour photography. The telescope. Air electricity as motor power. Iodine from coal. Phosphorus from sulphur. Sulphuric acid from alum slate. Nickel plating without nickel (transmutation of metals). New ideas in iron and steel metallurgy, Etc. etc." To this list, writing six days later to Hedlund, he added: "To make silk from a liquid without silkworms. To transmute cotton thread into silk. To transmute linen thread into silk."[31]

Making connections between opposites, crucial to the creative process, is in many respects a specialized case of making connections in general, of seeing resemblances between previously unassociated conditions or objects. We will discuss this later in the context of possible artistic advantages to be gained from the coexistence of opposite emotional states such as mania and depression, the importance of their contrasting and fluctuating natures, and the need to come to terms with such wildly disparate perceptions, experiences, and aspects of personality.

The neurochemical and anatomical processes responsible for the cognitive changes occurring during both pathological and highly creative states are poorly understood. It will remain for molecular biology, neuropsychology, and the new neuroimaging techniques to provide us with a more sophisticated understanding of the underlying changes in thought and behavior that are enhanced, left unaffected, or impaired by shifting patterns of mood. The neuroimaging techniques—positron emission tomography (PET), magnetic resonance imaging (especially the newly developing fast MRI technologies), brain electrical activity mapping (BEAM), regional cerebral blood-flow studies (rCBF), single photon emission-computed tomography (SPECT), and magnetoencephalography (MEG)—have, in the past few years, already provided unprecedented insights into many aspects of higher cerebral functioning, including vision, memory, learning, hearing, and speech.[32] Neuropsychological studies of differences in cognitive abilities and deficits between those individuals with and without depressive or manic-depressive illness have also proven to be of interest.[33]

Characteristics of a noncognitive nature also link the manic side of manic-depressive illness with artistic temperament and imagination. Many of these are related to the fiery side of the manic temperament, and, when coupled with an otherwise imaginative, observant, and (ultimately) disciplined mind, they can result in literary, musical, and artistic works of singular power. The sheer force of life, the voltage, can be staggering in mania, and it often singes if not scorches the ideas that come in its wake, leaving them altered in lasting ways. Ruskin portrayed the role of force and fire in the action of elemental, instinctive genius:

Such is always the mode in which the highest imaginative faculty seizes its materials. It never stops at crusts or ashes, or outward images of any kind; it ploughs them all aside, and plunges into the very central fiery heart; nothing else will content its spirituality; whatever semblances and various outward shows and phases its subject may possess go for nothing; it gets within all fence, cuts down to the root, and drinks the very vital sap of that it deals with: once therein, it is at liberty to throw up what new shoots it will, so always that the true juice and sap be in them, and to prune and twist them at its pleasure, and bring them to fairer fruit than grew on the old tree; but all this pruning and twisting is work that it likes not, and often does ill; its function and gift are the getting at the root, its nature and dignity depend on its holding things always by the heart. Take its hand from off the beating of that, and it will prophesy no longer; it looks not in the eyes, it judges not by the voice, it describes not by outward features; all that it affirms, judges, or describes, it affirms, from within.[34]

The abandonment of normal judgment and restraint that is seen in the uninhibited, reckless, and violent behavior so central to mania, and in some drug- and alcohol-induced states as well, compels movement. Combined with the sheer disruption of senses and intellect that also occurs during mania, such movement can be—in those with artistic imagination and the capacity later to take more rational advantage of such experience—a form of forced voyage and exploration. The poet, wrote Rimbaud:

> makes himself a *seer* by a long, gigantic and rational *derangement* of *all the senses*. All forms of love, suffering, and madness. He searches himself. He exhausts all poisons in himself and keeps only their quintessences. . . . He reaches the unknown, and when, bewildered, he ends by losing the intelligence of his visions, he has seen them. Let him die as he leaps through unheard of and unnamable things: other horrible workers will come; they will begin from the horizons where the other one collapsed![35]

The boldness of temperament needed for original work was stressed in a different sort of way by Keats: "That which is creative must create itself—In Endymion, I leaped headlong into the Sea, and thereby have become better acquainted with the Soundings, the quicksands, & the rocks, than if I had stayed upon the green shore, and piped a silly pipe, and took tea & comfortable advice.—I was never afraid of failure; for I would sooner fail than not to be among the greatest."[36] High energy levels and boldness are clearly essential to virtually all creative endeavors; they tend to be characteristic of manic-depressive temperaments as well.[37]

Learning through intense, extreme, and often painful experiences, and using what has been learned to add meaning and depth to creative work, is probably the most widely accepted and written-about aspect of the relationship between melancholy, madness, and the artistic experience. John Berryman—poet, contemporary of Robert Lowell and Theodore Roethke, and, like them, a manic-depressive—eventually committed suicide, as his father and aunt had done before him. Disinclined to understatement, he described the role of ordeal in his artistic work:

> I do strongly feel that among the greatest pieces of luck for high achievement is ordeal. Certain great artists can make out without it,

Titian and others, but mostly you need ordeal. My idea is this: The artist is extremely lucky who is presented with the worst possible ordeal which will not actually kill him. At that point, he's in business. Beethoven's deafness, Goya's deafness, Milton's blindness, that kind of thing. And I think that what happens in my poetic work in the future will probably largely depend not on my sitting calmly on my ass as I think, "Hmm, hmm, a long poem again? Hmm," but on being knocked in the face, and thrown flat, and given cancer, and all kinds of other things short of senile dementia. At that point, I'm out, but short of that, I don't know. I hope to be nearly crucified.[38]

Roethke also wrote about adversity, focusing on the vision given by darkness and despair: "In a dark time, the eye begins to see," he wrote, and then continued:

> What's madness but nobility of soul
> At odds with circumstance? The day's on fire!
> I know the purity of pure despair,
> My shadow pinned against a sweating wall.
> That place among the rocks—is it a cave,
> Or winding path? The edge is what I have.[39]

More than a century earlier, Shelley had addressed a similar theme in *Julian and Maddalo*, an autobiographical poem about—among other things—madness, Byron, and himself:

> The colours of his mind seemed yet unworn;
> For the wild language of his grief was high
> Such as in measure were called poetry;
> And I remember one remark which then
> Maddalo made. He said: "Most wretched men
> Are cradled into poetry by wrong,
> They learn in suffering what they teach in song."[40]

Keats agreed. "Do you not see how necessary a World of Pains and troubles is to school an Intelligence and make it a soul? A Place where the heart must feel and suffer in a thousand diverse ways!"[41] Koestler, in *The Act of Creation*, discussed the central importance to the creative act of the archetypal "Night Journey," during which the artist-hero suffers overwhelming experiences, or a spiritual crisis, that convulses the deepest foundations of his being: 'He embarks on the Night Journey, is suddenly transferred to the Tragic Plane—from which he emerges purified, enriched by new insight, regenerated on a higher level of integration."[42] This is, of course, a variation on the ancient theme of "the suffered is the learned," of insight gained through trial and anguish. The dive, or journey underground, by definition provides a remarkable intensity and range of experience for those who take it; conversely, those who have intense emotions, moods, and sensitivities are probably much more likely to take the journey.

A passionate emotional makeup is thought by many to be an integral part of the artistic temperament. American essayist and poet George Edward Woodberry, for example, wrote:

> The sign of the poet, then, is that by passion he enters into life more than other men. That is his gift—the power to live. . . . [Poets] have been singularly creatures of passion. They lived before they sang. Emotion is the condition of their existence; passion is the element of their being; and, moreover, the intensifying power of such a state of passion must also be remembered, for emotion of itself naturally heightens all the faculties, and genius burns the brighter in its own flames.[43]

Poe, who in his nonfiction had written somewhat convincingly about the role of rationality in art, described in his fiction the importance of exalted moods, madness, and passion in those who would penetrate "into the vast ocean":

> I am come of a race noted for vigor of fancy and ardor of passion. Men have called me mad; but the question is not yet settled, whether madness is or is not the loftiest intelligence—whether much that is glorious—whether all that is profound—does not spring from disease of thought—from *moods* of mind exalted at the expense of the general intellect. They who dream by day are cognizant of many things which escape those who dream only by night. In their grey visions they obtain glimpses of eternity. . . . They penetrate, however rudderless or compassless, into the vast ocean of the "light ineffable."[44]

Artistic expression can be the beneficiary of either visionary and ecstatic or painful, frightening, and melancholic experiences. Even more important, however, it can derive great strength from the struggle to come to terms with such emotional extremes, and from the attempt to derive from them some redemptive value. "The more I am spent, ill, a broken pitcher," wrote van Gogh, "by so much more am I an artist—a creative artist . . . this green shoot springing from the roots of the old felled trunk, these are such abstract things that a kind of melancholy remains within us when we think that one could have created life at less cost than creating art."[45] Changes or extremes in mood and experience alone do not guarantee good art, of course. If, however, like the changes in thought discussed earlier, they are coupled with imagination and discipline, the possibilities for creating lasting and sustaining art may be greatly enhanced.

Profound melancholy or the suffering of psychosis can fundamentally change an individual's expectations and beliefs about the nature, duration, and meaning of life, the nature of man, and the fragility and resilience of the human spirit. Many writers, artists, and composers have described the impact of their long periods of depression, how they have struggled or dealt with them, and how they have used them in their work. The influence of pain's dominion fills novels, canvases, and musical scores; there is no shortage of portrayals. Poet Anne Sexton, for one, described the importance of using pain in her work: "I, myself, alternate between hiding behind my own hands, protecting myself anyway possible, and this other, this seeing ouching other. I guess I mean that creative people must not avoid the pain that they get dealt. . . . Hurt must be examined like a plague."[46] Robert Lowell, who wrote about depression: "I don't think it is a visitation of the angels but a weakening in the blood,"[47] also said:

> Depression's no gift from the Muse. At worst, I do nothing. But often I've written, and wrote one whole book—*For the Union Dead*—about witheredness. . . . Most of the best poems, the most personal, are gathered crumbs from the lost cake. I had better moods, but the book is lemony, soured, and dry, the drought I had touched with my own hands. That, too, may be poetry—on sufferance.[48]

Lowell wrote tellingly about "seeing too much and feeling it/with one skin-layer missing."[49] And Woolf, like Roethke, felt and used the double edge of emotion she experienced in her depressions: "But it is always a question whether I wish to avoid these glooms. . . . These 9 weeks give one a plunge into deep waters; which is a little alarming, but full of interest. . . . There is an edge to it which I feel is of great importance. . . . One goes down into the well & nothing protects one from the assault of truth."[50]

It seems counterintuitive that melancholy could be associated with artistic inspiration and productivity; the milder manic states and their fiery energies would seem, at first thought, to be more obviously linked. The extreme pain of the deeper melancholias, and the gentler, more reflective and solitary sides of the milder ones, can be extremely important in the creative process, however. Hypomania and mania often generate ideas and associations, propel contact with life and other people, induce frenzied energies and enthusiasms, and cast an ecstatic, rather cosmic hue over life. Melancholy, on the other hand, tends to force a slower pace, cools the ardor, and puts into perspective the thoughts, observations, and feelings generated during more enthusiastic moments. Mild depression can act as ballast; it can also serve a critical editorial role for work produced in more fevered states. Depression prunes and sculpts; it also ruminates and ponders and, ultimately, subdues and focuses thought. It allows structuring, at a detailed level, of the more expansive patterns woven during hypomania.

The slightly melancholic perspective is meaningful in its own right. The sensitivity and compassion afforded by depression are, for the most part, absent in the unbridled self-assurance and hectic pace of hypomania. The tendency to gaze inward, to ask why and of what avail, is, on the other hand, deeply embedded in the depressive view:

> In their milder forms, one is almost inclined to say that some of the insight manifested in the writings of people in what might be called the morbid state of mind, so far as depression is concerned, springs from the fact that they become self-searching, brood on the meaning of life—a brooding in which the healthy mind indulges only occasionally and even then only when thrown back on itself. United with

this ability, this brooding may produce poetic, philosophic and religious insight and manifest itself in words which influence the minds
and the life goals of posterity.[51]

Recent research has shown that observations and beliefs produced during mildly depressed states are actually closer to "reality" than are normal mood states,[52] underscoring the pervasiveness
of denial in everyday life and giving credence to T. S. Eliot's view
that "Human kind cannot bear very much reality."[53] Grief and
depression often bring with them, for good or ill, the heart of life:
the *Inferno*, "like Plato's cave, is the place where all men come to
know themselves."[54] "In these flashing revelations of grief's wonderful fire," wrote Melville, "we see all things as they are; and
though, when the electric element is gone, the shadows once more
descend, and the false outlines of objects again return; yet not with
their former power to deceive."[55] Depression forces a view on
reality, usually neither sought nor welcome, that looks out onto the
fleeting nature of life, its decaying core, the finality of death, and
the finite role played by man in the history of the universe. Not
surprisingly, Tennyson's great muses were astronomy and geology;
and thoughts of death, so often the companion of melancholy, have
been muse to countless composers, artists, and writers. Indeed, for
Keats, death was "Life's high meed":

> Heart! Thou and I are here sad and alone;
>   I say, why did I laugh? O mortal pain!
> O Darkness! Darkness! ever must I moan,
>   To question Heaven and Hell and Heart in vain.
> Why did I laugh? I know this Being's lease,
>   My fancy to its utmost blisses spreads;
> Yet could I on this very midnight cease,
>   And the world's gaudy ensigns see in shreds;
> Verse, Fame, and Beauty are intense indeed,
> But Death intenser—Death is Life's high meed.[56]

Melancholy itself often acts as a bittersweet potion and muse, adding a tincture of sadness and wistfulness to the creative process.
"Yet naught did my despair/But sweeten the strange sweetness,"[57]
wrote English poet Edward Thomas. Although subject to paralyz-

ing and suicidal depressions, he often declared his reliance upon the gentler side of melancholy:

> And yet I still am half in love with pain,
> With what is imperfect, with both tears and mirth,
> With things that have an end, with life and earth,
> And this moon that leaves me dark within the door.[58]

Likewise, Edgar Allan Poe wrote:

> And by a strange alchemy of brain
> His pleasure always turn'd to pain—
> His naivete to wild desire—
> His wit to love—his wine to fire—
> And so, being young and dipt in folly
> I fell in love with melancholy.[59]

And Alfred Tennyson, too, cast a partially covetous eye on melancholy:

> O Sorrow, wilt thou live with me
>   No casual mistress, but a wife,
>   My bosom-friend and half of life;
> As I confess it needs must be?
>
> O Sorrow, wilt thou rule my blood,
>   Be sometimes lovely like a bride,
>   And put thy harsher moods aside,
> If thou wilt have me wise and good.[60]

The use of the mild melancholic states to recall earlier and more painful times, but at a distance, can allow a measured tapping into deeper emotional pools, as well as a more controlled access to the back rooms of the unconscious mind. An artist certainly need not go through all extremes of all moods and all experience, but it is undeniable that familiarity with sadness and the pain of melancholy—as well as with the ecstatic, often violent energies of the manic states—can add a singular truth and power to artistic expression. To the extent that an artist survives, describes, and then transforms psychological pain into an experience with more universal meaning, his or her own journey becomes one that others can, thus better protected, take.

Biographer Leon Edel, in a lecture given before the American Psychiatric Association, carefully shied away from speculations about the genesis of melancholia, or "tristimania," in writers and artists; he did, however, powerfully argue for melancholia's crucial role in the arts. "Within the harmony and beauty of most transcendent works," he said, "I see a particular sadness. We might say it is simply the sadness of life, but it is a sadness that somehow becomes a generating motor, a link in the chain of power that makes the artist persist, even when he had lived an experience, to transform it within his medium."[61] Later in the talk he expanded on his belief: "I take it as a postulate, even an axiom, that by the time the creating personality has acquired his adult being, a great fund of melancholy has been accumulated. It clamors for release. We can hear it in all acuteness in Schubert and Schumann; it sounded for us in the cosmic cadences of Beethoven; it comes at us from almost every page of poetry."[62]

But, as Randall Jarrell reminds us, sometimes the darkness is only darkness:

I see at last that all the knowledge

I wrung from the darkness—that the darkness flung me—
Is worthless as ignorance: nothing comes from nothing,
The darkness from the darkness. Pain comes from the darkness
And we call it wisdom. It is pain.[63]

"No one has ever written, painted, sculpted, modeled, built, or invented except literally to get out of hell,"[64] wrote poet Antonin Artaud, who spend years in psychiatric wards for his recurrent bouts of insanity. His view—that art first heals the artist and subsequently helps heal others—is an ancient one, inextricably bound to the belief that "madness" and the arts are causally linked. In recent times Dr. Anthony Storr has articulated this position persuasively and eloquently in his book *The Dynamics of Creation*, citing the many instances of writers and artists who have used their work to save not only their souls, but their minds as well.[65] "A part,

then, of what Henry James called the madness of art," said Leon
Edel, "resides in the artist's search for some exit from the labyrinth
of the imprisoned and despairing self—the verbal structure, the
philter, the anodyne, that will somehow provide escape and sur-
cease."[66] Writers and artists themselves have been particularly
forceful about the relief that their work can bring. "Poetry led me
by the hand out of madness,"[67] wrote Anne Sexton; and, although
this was only partially true, poetry's extraordinary role in her life
has been well documented by biographer Diane Wood Middlebrook.[68] For many artists, writing or painting or composing has
provided an escape from their turmoils and melancholy. Cowper,
who, like Artaud and Sexton was institutionalized for his psychosis,
wrote that a "Dejection of Spirits, which I suppose may have prevented many a man from becoming an Author, made me one. I find
constant employment necessary, and therefore take care to be constantly employ'd. Manual occupations do not engage the mind
sufficiently, as I know by experience, having tried many. But Composition, especially of verse, absorbs it wholly."[69] Berlioz turned to
music for consolation, and for control of his often-overwhelming
mood swings:

> Sometimes I can scarcely endure this mental or physical pain (I can't
> separate the two), especially on fine summer days when I'm in an
> open space like the Tuileries Garden, alone. Oh then . . . I could
> well believe there is a violent "expansive force" within me. I see that
> wide horizon and the sun, and I suffer so much, so much, that if I did
> not take a grip of myself I should shout and roll on the ground. I have
> found only one way of completely satisfying this immense *appetite
> for emotion*, and that is music. Without it I am certain I could not go
> on living.[70]

Berlioz's temperamental soul mate in poetry, Lord Byron, described—in appropriately volcanic terms—the mind-saving role of
poetry: "It is the lava of the imagination whose eruption prevents
an earth-quake—they say Poets never or rarely go *mad* . . . but are
generally so near it—that I cannot help thinking rhyme is so far
useful in anticipating & preventing the disorder."[71] Eliot, who
wrote *The Wasteland* while recovering from a nervous breakdown,
remarked: "Poetry is not a turning loose of emotion, but an escape

from emotion, it is not the expression of personality, but an escape from personality. But, of course, only those who have personality and emotions know what it means to want to escape from these things."[72]

Creative work can act not only as a means of escape from pain, but also as a way of structuring chaotic emotions and thoughts, numbing pain through abstraction and the rigors of disciplined thought, and creating a distance from the source of despair. John Donne and Alfred, Lord Tennyson, although writing centuries apart, described in very similar terms the relief provided by the practice and structuring of their art. Donne stressed, however ironically, the taming of grief through its fettering in verse:

> Then as the earths inward narrow crooked lanes
>   Do purge sea waters fretfule salt away,
>   I thought, if I could draw my paines
>   Through Rimes vexation, I should them allay.
>   Griefe brought to numbers cannot be so fierce,
>   For, he tames it, that fetters it in verse.[73]

Tennyson focused on the opiate-like relief brought about by the writing of verse itself:

> But, for the unquiet heart and brain,
>   A use in measured language lies;
>   The sad mechanic exercise,
> Like dull narcotics, numbing pain.
>
> In words, like weeds, I'll wrap me o'er,
>   Like coarsest clothes against the cold:
>   But that large grief which these enfold
> Is given in outline and no more.[74]

Twentieth-century poet Lowell also wrote of wrapping himself in words for protection: "I am writing my autobiography literally to "pass the time." I almost doubt if the time would pass at all otherwise. However, I also hope the result will supply me with swaddling clothes, with a sort of immense bandage of grace and ambergris for my hurt nerves."[75] Years later, near the end of his life, he inquired tellingly in a poem, "Is getting well ever an art, / or art a way to get well?"[76]

Clearly the pain experienced by writers and artists is not always the result of a pathological state of madness or melancholy. Often it is the ordinary, as well as the universal, in life's experiences that combines with an unusually sensitive temperament (cyclothymic or otherwise) to produce a heightened sense of vulnerability, awareness, pain, and futility. Novelist Graham Greene, by his own account a manic-depressive and subject to extended periods of suicidal depression, said that "Writing is a form of therapy. Sometimes I wonder how all those who do not write, compose or paint can manage to escape the madness, the melancholia, the panic fear which is inherent in the human situation."[77] The elemental human desire to add meaning and permanence to life—to avoid the fate rendered by Dante as "no more memorial / Than foam in water or smoke upon the wind"[78]—takes on additional depth and urgency for those who have intense moods and brooding dispositions. The act of creating becomes, as Byron described it, essential in its own right:

> 'Tis to create, and in creating live
> A being more intense, that we endow
> With form our fancy, gaining as we give
> The life we image, even as I do now.
> What am I? Nothing; but not so art thou,
> Soul of my thought! with whom I traverse earth,
> Invisible but gazing, as I glow
> Mix'd with thy spirit, blending with thy birth,
> And feeling still with thee in my crush'd feeling's dearth.[79]

If the experience of pain—as well as its re-creation and conveyance, its control and transformation—is such an important, not to say integral, part of the artistic experience, what effect might the amelioration or treatment of it have on the creation of literature, art, and music? If, as Edel says, "Out of world-sadness, out of tristimania, immortal and durable things are brought into being,"[80] then what would fuel the artist who was cured of his anguish? "The world," wrote Nathaniel Hawthorne, "owes all its onward impulses to men ill at ease. The happy man inevitably confines himself within ancient limits."[81] Do modern psychiatric treatments and future gene therapies risk confining artists to "ancient limits"? This is a highly controversial but fundamental issue, and one to which we return in the final chapter. We end this section by simply noting Paul Celan's words: "Wherever one went the world was blooming. And yet despair gave birth to poetry."[82]

In addition to the changes in mood and thought that are brought about by mania and depression (and the experiences—both good and bad—gleaned from the pain intrinsic to melancholia), the less dramatic, day-to-day aspects of the manic-depressive temperament can provide artistic advantage as well. For individuals who live with moods that change often and intensely, life is a tempestuous experience. The manic-depressive, or cyclothymic, temperament, carries with it the capacity to react strongly and quickly; it is, in a biological sense, an alert and excitable system. It responds to the world with a wide range of emotional, perceptual, intellectual, behavioral, and energy changes, and it creates around itself both the possibilities and chaos afforded by altered experiences and fluctuating tempos. In a sense depression is a view of the world through a glass darkly, and mania is a shattered pattern of views seen through a prism or kaleidoscope: often brilliant but generally fractured. Where depression questions, ruminates, and is tentative, mania answers with vigor and certainty. The constant transitions in and out of these constricted and then expansive thoughts, subdued and then violent responses, grim and then ebullient moods, withdrawn from and then involving relationships, cold and then fiery states—and the rapidity and fluidity of moves across and into such contrasting experiences—can be painful and confusing. Such chaos, in those able ultimately to transcend it or shape it to their will, can, however, result in an artistically useful comfort with transitions, an ease with ambiguities and with life on the edge, and an intuitive awareness of the coexisting and oppositional forces at work in the world. The weaving together of these contrasting experiences from a core and rhythmic brokenness is one that is crucial to both the artistic and manic-depressive experience.

The cyclothymic lack of fixedness, a "delicate compass-needle

so easily set ajar,"[83] resembles nothing so much as the poetic concepts of *mobilité* and chameleon selves: "Mobilité," wrote Byron,
is "an excessive susceptibility of immediate impressions—at the
same time without *losing* the past; and is, though sometimes apparently useful to the possessor, a most painful and unhappy attribute."[84] In his poem *Don Juan*, Byron drew the distinction
between a seeming "want of heart," or inconstancy, and an attribute of a highly responsive and impressionable temperament:

> So well she acted, all and every part
>   By turns—with that vivacious versatility,
> Which many people take for want of heart.
>   They err—'tis merely what is called mobility,
> A thing of temperament and not of art,
>   Though seeming so, from its supposed facility;
> And false—though true; for surely they're sincerest,
> Who are strongly acted on by what is nearest.[85]

The amphibious, mercurial, many-personed, and highly responsive nature of both the artistic and manic-depressive temperaments
is at the core of what they are all about. Not without reason does
the word "chameleon" permeate the descriptions of the artistic
personality. Biographer Richard Holmes, for example, said of Coleridge that he had "essentially a chameleon gift, a gift for fluent
adaptation and vivid response,"[86] and Virginia Woolf wrote "You
know how chameleon I am in my changes—leopard one day, all
violet spots; mouse today."[87] Keats, too, drew upon the chameleonic metaphor, remarking: "What shocks the virtuous philosopher
delights the chameleon poet,"[88] and Shelley believed: "Poets, the
best of them, are a very chameleonic race."[89] Implicit to both
chameleonic and manic-depressive temperaments is the coexistence, within one body or mind, of multiple selves. The nature
of double or dual personalities has a long history, of course, in
both literature and medicine. The depiction of a warring within
of different minds, personalities, emotions, and values reached
its height in the nineteenth century; the arbitrary and shifting
borders between the rational and irrational, the inhibited and
uninhibited, were captured particularly well by Robert Louis
Stevenson in *Dr. Jekyll and Mr. Hyde:*

Man is not truly one but truly two. . . . I learned to recognize the thorough and primitive duality of man; I saw that, of the two natures that contended in the field of my consciousness, even if I could rightly be said to be either, it was only because I was radically both. . . . I had learned to dwell with pleasure, as a beloved day-dream, on the thought of the separation of these elements. If each, I told myself, could be housed in separate identities, life would be relieved of all that was unbearable. . . . It was the curse of mankind that these incongruous faggots were thus bound together—that in the agonised womb of consciousness, these polar twins should be continuously struggling.[90]

Extreme changes in mood exaggerate the normal tendency to have conflicting, or polar, selves; the undulating, rhythmic, and transitional moods so characteristic of manic-depressive illness and its temperaments can also blend, or harness, seemingly contradictory moods, observations, and perceptions. Yet, ultimately, these fluxes and yokings may more accurately reflect the changes, ambiguities, and linked oppositions that truly exist both in man and the natural world. The "consistent attitude toward life," may not, as Professor Jerome McGann points out, be as finally perceptive as an ability to live with, and portray, constant change.[91]

Such clinical characteristics as changes in mood, thinking, energy, and behavior are, as we saw earlier, usually opposite in mania and depression. This is also true for linguistic and artistic patterns. Manic patients, for example, tend not only to speak more, and more rapidly, but also to use more colorful and powerful speech, including more action verbs and adjectives.[92] Artistic expression also changes across mood states.[93] Manic patients tend to use vivid and highly contrasting colors; depressed patients, on the other hand, use primarily black and cold darker colors (when the depression begins to clear, the palette tends to lighten accordingly). The content of manic paintings tends to be more sexual, filled with motion and bright portrayals of natural phenomena such as fires, waterfalls, and landscapes; in contrast, paintings done during the depressed phase tend to show a paucity of ideas, a lack of motion, and themes of death and decay. Manic paintings, usually produced rapidly and impulsively, often have an agitated or swirling quality to them; paintings produced by depressed patients are relatively barren, painted slowly, and exhibit less imagination. The contrasting natures of the elated and depressive states provide, for those with artistic or literary ability, a rich variety of experiences and sensations from which to create. The explicit use of intense and opposite mood states was particularly pronounced in the Romantic poets and composers. In his preface to the *Davidsbündlertänze*, a piano work illustrating the contrasting sides of his temperament through abrupt alterations of mood and tempo, Robert Schumann wrote that "Joy and sorrow are inseparable all through life,"[94] echoing William Blake's words:

> Joy & Woe are woven fine,
> A clothing for the Soul divine;
> Under every grief & pine
> Runs a joy with silken twine.[95]

Samuel Clemens, who described his own "periodical and sudden changes of mood . . . from deep melancholy to half-insane tempests and cyclones,"[96] observed that the "secret source of humor is not joy but sorrow,"[97] reiterating years later that "there is no humor in heaven."[98] The simultaneous existence and shared residence of such opposite moods and feelings is well-illustrated by Franz Schubert's assertion that whenever he sat down to write songs of love he wrote songs of pain, and whenever he sat down to write songs of pain he wrote songs of love. Virginia Woolf, in *A Room of One's Own*, observed: "The beauty of the world . . . has two edges, one of laughter, one of anguish, cutting the heart asunder."[99] The ability to reconcile such opposite states, whether they are of mood, thought, or vitality, is a critical part of any creative act.[100] Thomas Moore, himself a poet, described this ability in his friend Byron:

> It must be perceived by all endowed with quick powers of association how constantly, when any particular thought or sentiment presents itself to their minds, its very opposite, at the same moment, springs up there also; if anything sublime occurs, its neighbour, the ridiculous, is by its side; across a bright view of the present or the future, a dark one throws its shadow; and, even in questions respecting morals and conduct, all the reasonings and consequences that may suggest themselves on the side of one of two opposite courses will, in

such minds, be instantly confronted by an array just as cogent on the other. A mind of this structure,—and such, more or less, are all those in which the reasoning is made subservient to the imaginative faculty,—though enabled, by such rapid powers of association, to multiply its resources without end, has need of the constant exercise of a controlling judgment to keep its perceptions pure and undisturbed between the contrasts it thus simultaneously calls up.[101]

The cyclic and contrasting nature of manic-depressive illness is perhaps its most defining clinical feature. The recurrent and opposite patterns so characteristic of the disease and its associated temperaments provide further possible connections between mood disorders and creative work. Likewise, the ebbing and flowing and seasonal quality to artistic "inspiration," the centrality of light, and the core themes of seasonal regeneration and life and death that are such part and parcel of artistic expression, bear inescapable resemblance to the rhythmic changes of light and dark and the turning of the seasons so central to the natural world. Indeed, a strong argument can be made that the periodicities of the natural world—as well as its great beholdenness to light, its chaos, perturbances, agitations, and violence, its fluctuations, shadows, edges, and upheavals—that all of these find their analogue in the periodicities and patterns intrinsic to the artistic and the manic-depressive temperaments. "The laws of nature he knows," wrote John Ruskin about the imaginative artist; he knows them because "They are his own nature."[102] The artist, I believe, is closer to the fundamental pulse of life because his or her daily and yearly rhythms are more similar to those of the natural world. The brinks, borders, and edges of nature—twilight and dawn in the course of a day, the equinoctial edges of autumn and spring during the course of a year—may actually be experienced quite differently by those who are artistic and/or cyclothymic by temperament. In fact there is an accumulation of evidence to suggest that those who have manic-depressive illness or a cyclothymic temperament show an elevated responsiveness and sensitivity to changes in light; there is also strong evidence that mood disorders have a pronounced seasonal component.

Life is partitioned by time—years, months, days, minutes—into events that tend to recur at regular intervals, a periodicity as evident in the behavior of protozoa and jellyfish as in the sleeping habits and other patterns of human behavior. Biological functioning is organized into periods linked to the rotations of the earth around the sun and of the moon around the earth. Although biological rhythms cycle in synchrony with these celestial rhythms, they are clearly regulated by endogenous processes. These innate rhythms probably evolved as adaptations to rhythmic fluctuations in Earth's lighting, heat, and humidity, and perhaps Earth's electromagnetic fields as well. Such evolutionary explanations for the origins of biological rhythms are controversial, but there is little disagreement that such oscillatory processes serve to regulate life on the cellular, biochemical, physiological, and probably psychological levels as well.

Rhythmic patterns and disturbances in manic-depressive illness are clinically apparent in many ways: diurnal variations in mood, pervasive disruptions in sleep, and seasonal recurrences of episodes. The illness is itself an important kind of rhythm. Daily oscillations in mood are a common feature of mood disorders and have been noted clinically for centuries. British psychiatrists W. Mayer-Gross, E. Slater, and M. Roth have described the diurnal pattern commonly observed in depressed patients:

> An important and significant symptom of the endogenous depression—but also of mania—is the *daily fluctuation* of mood and of the total state. Improvements of all symptoms usually occurs towards evening, the retardation and depressive mood particularly showing a change for the better. In the morning, however, the patient wakes direct from sleep into his characteristic sombre mood or is normal for a few minutes, before, as he says, the depression comes down "like a cloud."[103]

The very cyclicity of manic-depressive illness constitutes a type of rhythm. The episodic nature of the illness, together with its circadian disturbances, probably indicate malfunctions in a master biological clock. Findings from experimental treatments, such as altering sleep and light patterns in patients with depression and mania, point in the same direction. Drs. Thomas Wehr and Frederick Goodwin of the National Institute of Mental Health note: "Because of its inherent cyclicity, the illness itself is a kind of abnormal biological rhythm spanning weeks, months, or years. Circadian rhythms are implicated in some of the symptoms of depression, such as early awakening and diurnal variation in mood. The possible importance of the circadian system in its pathogenesis is suggested by the capacity of experimental alterations in the timing of sleep and wakefulness to alter clinical state."[104] Biological rhythms range in frequency from milliseconds to months or years. Most rhythmic disturbances identified in the symptoms of manic-depressive illness occur over the course of a day—that is, they are circadian rhythms—and are most apparent in the daily rest-activity cycle. The episodic recurrences of the illness, on the other hand, are usually infradian, oscillating over periods of months or years. Episodic mania and depression may also reflect disturbances in ultradian rhythms, those that oscillate more than once a day, which are common at the cellular level and in hormone secretion, as well as in such autonomic functions as circulation, blood pressure, respiration, heart rate, and in the cycles of sleep.

More than two thousand years ago Hippocrates observed that mania and melancholia were more likely to occur in the spring and autumn,[105] and Posidonius, in the fourth century A.D., noted that mania tended to occur most frequently in the summer months.[106] Toward the end of the eighteenth century, French psychiatrist Phillipe Pinel described seasonal patterns in intermittent insanity;[107] more recently, Kraepelin, writing about manic-depressive illness earlier in this century, described his clinical experience with seasonal patterns of mood: "Repeatedly I saw in these cases moodiness set in in autumn and pass over in spring: 'when the sap shoots in the trees,' to excitement, corresponding in a certain sense to the emotional changes which come over even healthy individuals at the changes of the seasons."[108] Modern research bears out these early observations. I recently reviewed the scientific literature for seasonal patterns in mania, depression, and suicide (see figures 4–1 and 4–2). The review of studies of seasonal patterns for peak months of occurrence for episodes of mania and depression indicates that there is a consistency of findings despite the methodological problems intrinsic to such research.[109] Two broad peaks are evident in the seasonal incidence of major depressive episodes:

Figure 4–1.
Seasonal Variations in Peak Occurrences of Mania and Depression

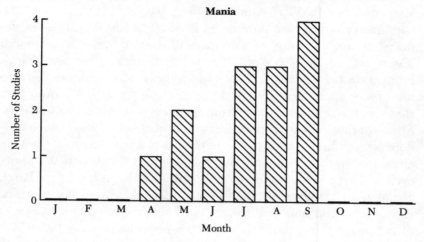

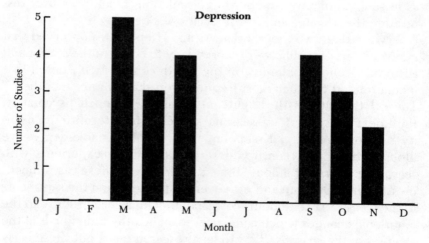

SOURCE: Based on review of studies of peak months for the onset of episodes and/or hospitalizations, in F. K. Goodwin and K. R. Jamison, *Manic-Depressive Illness* (New York: Oxford University Press, 1990).

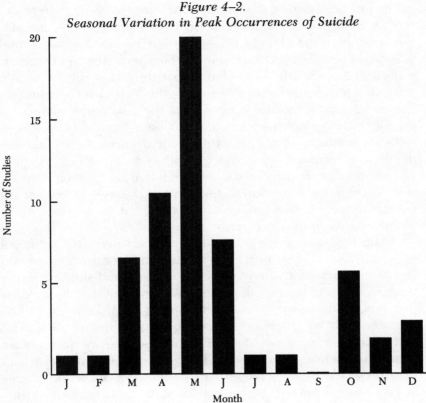

Figure 4–2.
Seasonal Variation in Peak Occurrences of Suicide

SOURCE: Based on review of studies of monthly peak occurrences of suicide, in F. K. Goodwin and K. R. Jamison, *Manic-Depressive Illness* (New York: Oxford University Press, 1990).

spring (March, April, May) and autumn (September, October, and November). The data on mania are somewhat more scarce, but the peak incidences clearly occur in the summer months, as well as in the early fall. Studies show significant correlations of hospital admissions for mania with monthly total hours of sunshine and average monthly day length; results are inconsistent with respect to environmental temperature. Seasonal patterns in suicide (see figure 4–2) generally parallel those for depression in that they show a large peak in the spring (especially in May). The second suicide peak in October may reflect an increase not only in depressive episodes but also in bipolar depressions following the increase in

manic episodes during the summer months; that is, it may represent suicidal postmanic depressions. Consistent with the assumption that patterns of light are important in mood changes and
suicide, two studies carried out in the Southern Hemisphere (Australia and New South Wales) found that the seasonality of suicide
was consistent with the pattern seen in the Northern Hemisphere;
that is, peaks of suicide occurred in the Australian months of
spring.[110] It is important to note that both figures 4–1 and 4–2
reflect a *summary* of studies of peak occurrences; thus, although
depressive episodes and suicides certainly occur in July, August,
and September, few of the studies found that the *peak* months for
their occurrence were during that time. Likewise, mania not infrequently occurs in October and March, but these are not the
months of maximum occurrence across studies.

The light-dark cycle is, for our purposes here, the principal
seasonal variable of interest. The overall length of the photoperiod
has two extremes (it is longest in the summer and shortest in the
winter), whereas the rate of change in the ratio of light to dark has
two peaks, one in late winter–early spring, and the other in late
summer–early fall (these peaks occur because of the elliptical orbit
of the earth around the sun). Thus, if manic-depressive patients are
abnormally sensitive to seasonal light changes, one would expect
that this would be reflected either by opposite behavioral patterns
at the two extremes (winter and summer) or behavioral disturbances in early spring or early fall, reflecting the period of rapidly
increasing light and rapidly decreasing light, respectively. Research findings show that patients with manic-depressive illness
do, in fact, have an increased sensitivity to light.[111] This increased
sensitivity is found in both the ill and well states and has also been
found in children who have not yet shown symptoms of manic-
depressive illness but who are at increased risk for it because either
one or both parents has the disease.[112] This suggests that increased
sensitivity to light may be part of the genetic vulnerability to manic-
depressive illness and that abnormal light sensitivity in manic-
depressive patients is probably not simply a result of the illness but
may be more causally linked.

Seasonal variations in mood and behavior appear to be common in the general population as well as in individuals with mood
disorders. Dr. S. Kasper and his associates have found that at least

90 percent of the general population experiences some degree of seasonal variation in mood.[113] Dr. M. R. Eastwood and his colleagues compared the infradian rhythms of mood, sleep, anxiety, and energy over a period of fourteen months in thirty patients with mood disorders (twenty-five of whom had manic-depressive illness) with those of thirty-four healthy control subjects matched for age and sex. They found that the majority of patients, and many of the healthy subjects, had infradian rhythms in mood, energy, and sleep; about half of these were seasonal:

> The principal difference between patients and control subjects is the amplitude of cycles, and hence, affective symptoms may be considered a variant of normal hedonic states. . . . Affective symptoms seem to be universal, with a periodic component that differs in degree rather than kind; the pattern of cycles for ill persons is defined by amplitude. This makes affective disorder akin to hypertension and diabetes, wherein a physiological variable shades into a pathological variant.[114]

Eastwood's group hypothesized that, because half the rhythms were seasonal, "some infradian mood cycles may be driven or timed by meteorologic factors." They further suggested that a "familial tendency toward depression may be the factor that determines the amplitude of the cycle." In addition to the many biological variables that show seasonal patterns in fluctuation,[115] recent studies show that certain cognitive abilities in men, such as spatial-reasoning skills, are enhanced in the spring. This is assumed to be due to the seasonal changes in testosterone levels.[116] In the current psychiatric literature, recognition of a syndrome characterized by the regular appearance of depressive, manic, or hypomanic episodes at certain seasons of the year came less than a decade ago, when Dr. Norman Rosenthal and his colleagues, who were studying recurrent winter depressions (which were often followed by summer hypomanias), published the original diagnostic criteria for seasonal affective disorder.[117] Because 50 to 60 percent of patients who have seasonal affective disorder also have at least one first-degree relative with depressive or manic-depressive illness, it is probably part of the general spectrum of major mood disorders that includes manic-depressive illness.

———————

Clearly, everyone experiences seasons and patterns of light; just as clearly, everyone experiences seasons and patterns of light quite differently. Individuals who have manic-depressive or artistic temperaments may share an uncommon sensitivity to seasonal fluctuations in light as well as pronounced changes in mood as a result of those fluctuations. Whether these similarities are due to the same biological process is unclear, although other similarities between the cyclothymic and artistic temperaments—as well as the greatly increased rate of manic-depressive and depressive illness in writers and artists—make it likely that similar biological mechanisms may be operating. In any event, the inexorable changing of light patterns, the passing of seasons, is one of the great and ancient themes of both life and art. Among the many poets particularly sensitive to these shifts was Delmore Schwartz, who—in addition to the other complexities of his life and mind—was a manic-depressive:

As I looked, the poplar rose in the shining air
Like a slender throat,
And there was an exaltation of flowers,
The surf of apple tree delicately foaming.

All winter, the trees had been
Silent soldiers, a vigil of woods,
Their hidden feelings
Scrawled and became
Scores of black vines,
Barbed wire sharp against the ice-white sky.
Who could believe then
In the green, glittering vividness of full-leafed summer?
Who will be able to believe, when winter again begins
After the autumn burns down again, and the day is ashen,
And all returns to winter and winter's ashes,
Wet, white, ice, wooden, dulled and dead, brittle or frozen,
Who will believe or feel in mind and heart
The reality of the spring and of birth,

In the green warm opulence of summer, and the inexhaustible vitality
        and immortality of the earth?[118]

The progression of seasons is among the most commonly used metaphors in art, signifying—among many other things— the passage of time, extremes and contrasts in the natural world, the cyclicity of life, the inevitability of death, belief in rebirth, and the impermanence, as well as the stages, of human life. So, too, seasons have become metaphorical for life, and for the creative process itself: its barren winters and hoped-for springs, and its mixed and disturbing seasons, so beautifully captured by T. S. Eliot in "Little Gidding":

> When the short day is brightest, with frost and fire,
> The brief sun flames the ice, on pond and ditches,
> In windless cold that is the heart's heat,
> Reflecting in a watery mirror
> A glare that is blindness in the early afternoon.
> And glow more intense than blaze of branch, or brazier,
> Stirs the dumb spirit: no wind, but pentecostal fire
> In the dark time of the year. Between melting and freezing
> The soul's sap quivers. There is no earth smell
> Or smell of living thing. This is the spring time
> But not in time's covenant.[119]

Relatively little systematic research has looked into the relationship between changes in mood, including actual episodes of mania or depression, seasonal patterns, and changes in artistic productivity. The work that has been done shows a tendency for artistic productivity to increase during spring and autumn, but there is clearly a wide variability across artists and writers. Italian psychiatrist Cesare Lombroso, working toward the end of the nineteenth century, dated the production of hundreds of poems, novels, paintings, and musical compositions.[120] Despite many methodological problems in Lombroso's work, it is both intrinsically interesting as well as the first to attempt a systematic look at seasonal patterns in creativity. I have plotted Lombroso's findings in figure 4–3, and it can be seen that he found peaks of productivity in the late spring and early fall. A few years ago I studied seasonal patterns of mood and productivity in forty-seven of Britain's leading writers and artists (the details of the study are given in chapter 3).[121] Mood and productivity ratings were obtained for a thirty-six-month period, and these were then analyzed

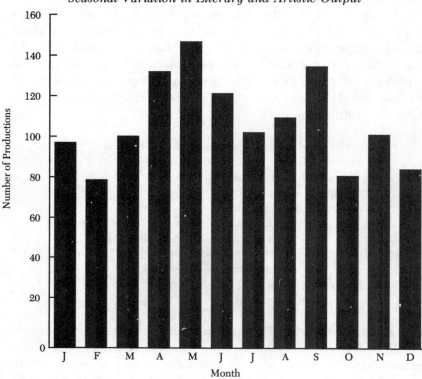

Figure 4–3.
Seasonal Variation in Literary and Artistic Output

SOURCE: Based on data in Cesare Lombroso, *Pensiero e meteore, Biblioteca scientifica internazionale*, vol. 16 (Milan: Dumonlard, 1872); *L'Homme de Génie* (Paris: Alcon, 1889).

separately for those artists and writers who had been treated for depression or manic-depressive illness and those without a history of treatment for mood disorders; these results are shown in figures 4–4 and 4–5, respectively. Productivity in both groups showed a tendency to peak in the fall or late fall and in May. The two groups differed, however, in the relationship shown between moods and productivity. Those artists and writers with a history of treatment showed inversely related curves for summer productivity and moods, whereas those in the group with no history of treatment showed mood and productivity curves that more

Figure 4–4.
Mean Mood and Productivity Ratings (for Thirty-six Months) in British
Writers and Artists with a History of Treatment for Depression or
Manic-Depressive Illness

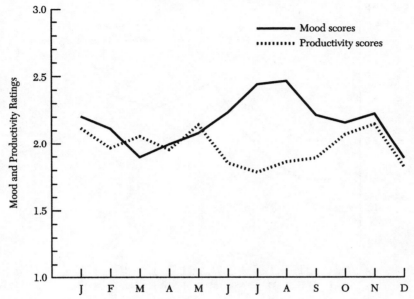

SOURCE: From K. R. Jamison, Mood disorders and patterns of creativity in British writers and artists, *Psychiatry,* 52(1989):125–134.

closely corresponded with one another. In the group with a history of psychiatric treatment, the peaks for productivity precede and follow the mood peak by three to four months. There are several possible explanations for this. Elevated mood, when associated with elevated productivity, is less likely to lead to the seeking out of treatment than low productivity associated with a high (or any other kind of mood). The elevated mood of the treatment group also probably reflects more true hypomania (that is, greater distractibility, irritability, increases in seeking out of other people, and alcohol abuse) than does just an expansive, elevated, and creative mood; this might well lead to less productivity in the acute phase. In the group with no history of treatment, the periods of increased mood and productivity may

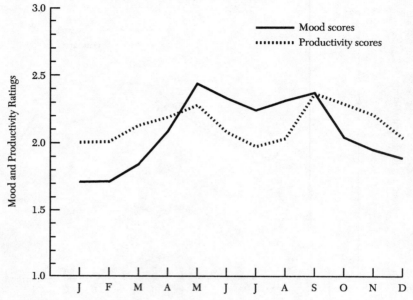

Figure 4–5.
Mean Mood and Productivity Ratings (for Thirty-six Months) in British Writers and Artists with No History of Treatment for Depression or Manic-Depressive Illness

SOURCE: From K. R. Jamison, Mood disorders and patterns of creativity in British writers and artists, *Psychiatry*, 52(1989):125–134.

represent a milder form of hypomania (or simply an intensification of normal mood), with cognitive and mood changes only. These milder states may result in simultaneous peaks for mood and productivity. Within the total sample, playwrights showed the least seasonal fluctuation in their productivity and had no discernible monthly peaks. Poets, novelists, and visual artists, on the other hand, showed pronounced seasonal patterns. The poets and novelists reported that their greatest artistic productivity occurred during September, October, and November; the painters and sculptors exhibited not only the fall peak (although September and October only) but one in the spring (April, May, and June) as well.

Every artist and writer has his or her own pattern of moods and creative energies; some will have reasonably little variation in how and when they produce what they do, and some will have wide seasonal or other swings in their productivity: months or years when they produce next to nothing and then weeks or months during which they are phenomenally active. English poet John Clare, for example, wrote that "the Muse is a fickle Hussey with me she sometimes stilts me up to Madness & then leaves me as a beggar by the way side with no more life than whats mortal & that nearly extinguished by mellancholy forbodings."[122] Here we briefly look at seasonal patterns of productivity in the work of Vincent van Gogh and Robert Schumann's lifelong productivity patterns.

Vincent van Gogh has been diagnosed as having had virtually every illness known to man, and then some. Diagnoses have included, among many others, epilepsy, schizophrenia, absinthe poisoning, porphyria, and Ménière's disease. Dr. Richard Wyatt, Chief of Neuropsychiatry at the National Institute of Mental Health, and I have argued elsewhere that there is compelling evidence for a diagnosis of manic-depressive illness.[123] The evidence includes the nature of van Gogh's psychiatric symptoms (extreme mood changes, including long periods of depression and extended episodes of highly active, volatile and excited states, altered sleep patterns, hyperreligiosity, extreme irritability, visual and auditory hallucinations, violence, agitation, and alcohol abuse), the age of onset of his symptoms (late adolescence, early twenties), his premorbid personality, the cyclic nature of his attacks, which were interspersed with long periods of highly lucid functioning, the lack of intellectual deterioration over time, the increasing severity of his mood swings, the seasonal exacerbations in his symptoms, and his quite remarkable family history of suicide and psychiatric illness. (This is documented more extensively in chapter 6. His brother Theo suffered from recurrent depressions and became psychotic at the end of his life; his sister Wilhelmina spent forty years in an insane asylum with a "chronic psychosis," and his younger brother Cor committed suicide.)[124] Although the overlap between manic-depressive illness and complex partial seizures (temporal lobe epilepsy) is an interesting

one—and it is of no little interest that the director of the asylum
at St. Rémy diagnosed van Gogh as suffering from both epilepsy
and "acute mania with hallucinations of sight and hearing"[125]—
van Gogh's symptoms, the natural course of his illness, and his
family psychiatric illness are completely consistent with a diagnosis of manic-depressive illness. Arguments against a diagnosis
of Ménière's disease or porphyria in van Gogh are presented
elsewhere and discussed more extensively in the endnotes for
this chapter.[126] Using what is known about the dating of van
Gogh's artwork (which is considerable, due to van Gogh's extensive documentation in his correspondence),[127] we have illustrated
in figure 4–6 the total number of paintings, watercolors, and
drawings done by van Gogh during different months of the year.
The summer peak in productivity is consistent with what we
know about his own description of his frenzied moods and energy
during those months of the year, as well as with a perhaps natural tendency to paint more in the longer, warmer, drier days of
summer. Perhaps more interesting, however, is his pattern of
productivity during the winter and late fall. From his letters it
appears that van Gogh had relatively more "pure" depressive episodes during November and February, and more "mixed" depressive episodes during December and January. The increased
agitation of these mixed states may well have resulted in both
more energy, and more motivation, to paint. Van Gogh was the
first to appreciate the episodic nature of his psychotic illness, his
moods, and his artistic productivity:

> If the emotions are sometimes so strong that one works without
> knowing one works, when sometimes the strokes come with a con-
> tinuity and a coherence like words in a speech or a letter, then one
> must remember that it has not always been so, and that in time to
> come there will again be hard days, empty of inspiration.
>   So one must strike while the iron is hot, and put the forged bars
> on one side.[128]

The springtime peak of productivity that is shown in the works
of many writers and artists, as well as by those in both Lombroso's
study and my own, fits with popular conceptions about the blos-

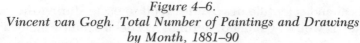

Figure 4–6.
Vincent van Gogh. Total Number of Paintings and Drawings
by Month, 1881–90

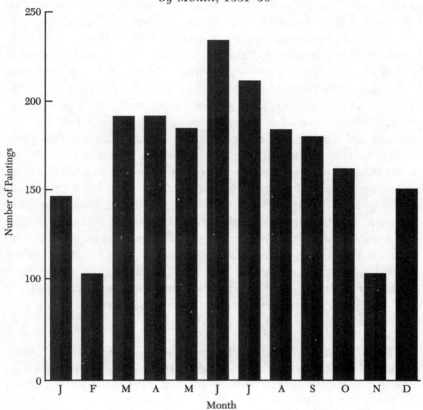

SOURCE: Adapted from work summarized in K. R. Jamison and R. J. Wyatt, Van Gogh: Meniere's disease? Epilepsy? Psychosis?, *Journal of the American Medical Association,* 264 (1991): 723–724. Copyright © 1991 American Medical Association.

soming forth of life during springtime. But how do these findings make sense in light of the striking peaks for severe depressive episodes, and suicide itself, during these same months? And why should so many artists and writers have another peak of productivity during the autumn months? (This is shown in the works of many writers, as well as in the findings from both Lombroso's and my studies. Interestingly, there is some evidence that major mathematical and scientific discoveries tend to occur during the spring and fall as well.)[129] Indeed, autumn has been seen by many artists as their most inspiring season. John Clare wrote, for example, that "the muses always pay their visits more frequent [*sic*] at that season,"[130] and Rosamond Harding quotes Robert Burns as saying, "Autumn is my most propitious season, and I make more verses in it than all year else"; likewise, George Crabbe declared: "Autumn is the most favourable season of the year for poetical composition."[131] One likely explanation for these equinoctial patterns in productivity is that it is the *rate* of change of light that is most pronounced during these times, and it is also during these two seasons of spring and autumn that there is a significant overlap in peaks for not only depressive but manic episodes as well (this can be seen clearly in figure 4–1).[132] Mixed states, where manic energies and perturbance combine with melancholic mood, are more common during transitions into and out of mania and depression, and it may well be, as with van Gogh's fluctuations in productivity during the winter months, that these mixed states (or their milder equivalents in those who do not have a mood disorder)—these periods of maximum change, contrast, and transition—are, in their own way, highly conducive to creative work. Lucretius wrote centuries ago:

> It is in autumn that the starlit dome of heaven throughout its breadth and the whole earth are most often rocked by thunderbolts, and again when the flowery season of spring is waxing. In cold weather there is a scarcity of fire, and in hot weather of winds, and then, too, the clouds are not so thick. So it is in weather between these extremes that the various causes of the thunderbolt all conspire. Then the year's turning tide mingles cold and heat, which are both needed to forge a thunderbolt within a cold. Then there may be a clash of opposites, and the air tormented by fire and wind may surge in tumultuous upheaval. . . . These then are the year's crises.[133]

British psychiatrists Slater and Meyer undertook a fascinating analysis of Robert Schumann's compositional patterns and his manic-depressive illness, not by months of the year but over the course of the composer's lifetime.[134] Schumann, as we shall see later, suffered from episodic depressions and manias throughout most of his adult life. As he grew older, the more melancholic and taciturn side of his temperament became more prominent, no doubt a cumulative consequence of the relentless and devastating depressions he had been through. Figure 4–7 presents Schumann's works by year, as well as his most clinically significant episodes of depression and mania. The quantitative relationship between his mood states and his creative output is quite striking: When most depressed he produced least, and when hypomanic he produced at a remarkable level. The fluctuations in his musical productivity over the years were extreme. The relationship of his mood states to the quality of his productions is somewhat unclear, although both the quality and quantity of his work, as well as his psychological health, deteriorated in the final years of his life.

Not all writers, artists, or composers will show significant seasonal or lifetime patterns of creative work; certainly not all of them will show clear peaks of productivity in the spring and fall. But many do, and these ebbings and flowings provide a fascinating link with the natural world on the one hand, and the ancient, persistent notions about a "divine madness," on the other. Gaelic poet Sorley MacLean has written about life's fallow and then fertile times in "Glen Eyre," a poem from his collection *Spring Tide and Neap Tide:*

> My life running to the seas
> through heather, bracken and bad grass,
> on its fanked eerie course,
> like the mean and shallow stream
> that was taking its meagre way through a green patch
> to the sea in the Kyle.
>
> But again and again a spring tide came
> to put beauty on the river foot,
> to fill its destination with richness,
> and sea-trout and white-bellied salmon came
> to taste the water of the high hills
> with flood-tide in Inver Eyre.[135]

No one better illustrates these tidal fluctuations in life, the dynamics of temperament, and the fiery intricacies of "that fine

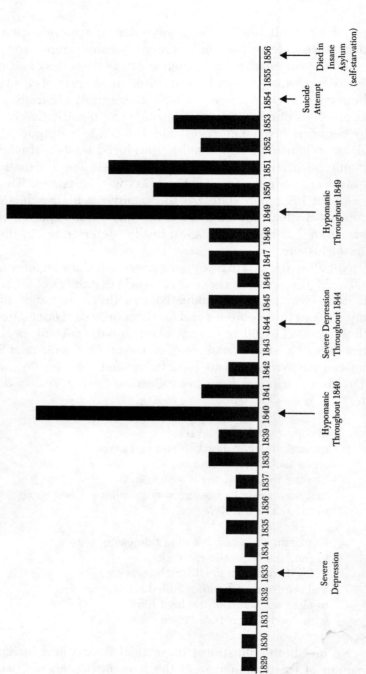

Figure 4–7.
Robert Schumann's Work: Number of Compositions by Year

SOURCE: Adapted from E. Slater and A. Meyer. Contributions to a pathography of the musicians: Robert Schumann, *Confinia Psychiatrica*, 2(1959):65–94. Reprinted by permission of Karger, Basel, Switzerland.

madness" than the poet to whose life we turn next: George Gordon, Lord Byron. It was he who had written the lines so important to Robert Schumann and so finally descriptive of them both:

> Look on me! there is an order
> Of mortals on the earth, who do become
> Old in their youth, and die ere middle age,
> Without the violence of warlike death;
> Some perishing of pleasure—some of study—
> Some worn with toil—some of mere weariness—
> Some of disease—and some insanity—
> And some of withered, or of broken hearts.[136]

5.
THE MIND'S CANKER IN ITS SAVAGE MOOD

George Gordon, Lord Byron

. . . the mind's canker in its savage mood,
When the impatient thirst of light and air
Parches the heart; and the abhorred grate,
Marring the sunbeams with its hideous
    shade,
Works through the throbbing eyeball to
    to the brain
With a hot sense of heaviness and pain.

—GEORGE GORDON, LORD BYRON[1]

George Gordon, Lord Byron. Alain Moreau
(Based on an original drawing by G. H. Harlow, 1821)

"Lord Byron," declared the poet's tutor at Cambridge, "is a young man of *tumultuous passions*,"[2] thus summing up succinctly the views of Byron's friends, enemies, and Byron himself. Fiery, fitful, and often high-spirited, with a temperament he described as "naturally burning,"[3] Byron was by all means inflammable, his bold and expansive moods yoked to a restless, pervasive, and virulent melancholy. Notoriously a study in contrasts, Byron, with his divided and mercurial temperament, resembled less a cohesive personality than a field of tectonic plates clashing and grating against one another. "There is a war," he wrote, "a chaos of the mind,/ When all its elements convulsed—combined—/Lie dark and jarring with perturbed force."[4] For virtually all his life, Byron engaged in such a war—a consuming civil war within his own mind, which, then convulsing outward, at times was waged as an anything but civil war on the people and world around him. From these wars came much of what made Byron who he was. "His very defects," observed his close friend and fellow poet Moore, "were among the elements of his greatness," and it was "out of the struggle between the good and evil principles of his nature that his mighty genius drew its strength."[5] Byron was the first to recognize the importance of his unsettled, impetuous, and romantic temperament. In 1813 he wrote to his future wife, Annabella Milbanke: "—You don't like my 'restless' doctrines—I should be very sorry if *you* did—but I can't *stagnate* nevertheless—if I must sail let it be on the ocean no matter how stormy—anything but a dull cruise on a level lake without ever losing sight of the same insipid shores by which it is surrounded.—"[6]

The conflicting factions of his temperament, interlaced with and beholden to his constantly shifting moods, gave rise to the sense that Byron housed within himself a veritable city of selves. One of his physicians described this mutability:

> Those only, who lived for some time with him, could believe that a man's temper, Proteus like, was capable of assuming so many shapes. It may literally be said, that at different hours of the day he metamorphosed himself into four or more individuals, each possessed of the most opposite qualities; for, in every change, his natural impetuosity made him fly into the furthermost extremes. In the course of the day he might become the most morose, and the most gay; the most melancholy, and the most frolicsome . . . the most gentle being in existence, and the most irascible.[7]

Byron himself, who had written in *Don Juan* that "I almost think that the same skin/For one without—has two or three within,"[8] remarked to his friend Lady Blessington, "I am so changeable, being every thing by turns and nothing long,—I am such a strange *mélange* of good and evil, that it would be difficult to describe me."[9] She clearly concurred:

> I am sure, that if ten individuals undertook the task of describing Byron, no two, of the ten, would agree in their verdict respecting him, or convey any portrait that resembled the other, and yet the description of each might be correct, according to his or her received opinion; but the truth is, the chameleon-like character or manner of Byron renders it difficult to portray him.[10]

Byron's chameleonlike qualities, along with the widely disparate aspects of his personality, were critical to the moody, contrasting, and Romantic casting of his poetry: Man was "half dust, half

deity, alike unfit/To sink or soar,"[11] a "mix'd essence,"[12] a "conflict
of elements."[13] Melancholic, although often sardonic, mixtures of
emotions—foreboding, aloneness, regret, and a dark sense of lost
destiny and ill-used passions—are woven throughout Byron's most
autobiographical poems, especially *Childe Harold's Pilgrimage*,
Lara, and *Manfred*. Perturbed and constant motion, coupled with
a brooding awareness of life's impermanence, also mark the transient and often bleak nature of Byron's work.

The emphasis on shifting essences, uncertainty, and fiercely
contrasting opposite states was, of course, neither new nor unique
to Byron. He and the other Romantic poets, however, took the
ideas and emotions to a particularly intense extreme. Shelley's
belief that poetry "marries exultation and horror, grief and pleasure, eternity and change,"[14] and that it "subdues to union, under
its light yoke, all irreconcilable things,"[15] was in sympathy not only
with the views of Byron but those of Keats as well. "*Negative
capability*," wrote Keats, exists "when a man is capable of being in
uncertainties, Mysteries, doubts, without any irritable reaching
out after fact & reason."[16] The "poetical Character," he said:

> has no self—it is every thing and nothing—It has no character—it
> enjoys light and shade; it lives in gusto, be it foul or fair, high or low,
> rich or poor, mean or elevated—It has as much delight in conceiving
> an Iago as an Imogen. What shocks the virtuous philosop[h]er, de-
> lights the camelion Poet. It does no harm from its relish of the dark
> side of things any more than from its taste for the bright one; because
> they both end in speculation.[17]

This mobility and mutability of temperament so intrinsic to
the creative process was discussed at some length in the last
chapter. Here our focus is on the intensity, changeability, and
complexity of Byron's temperament, its relationship to his manic-
depressive illness, and Byron's quite extraordinary ability to harness and then transform the "storms whereon he rode."[18] Many of
Byron's critics have assumed that much of what he wrote about—
especially his tortured emotional states—was melodramatic, self-
dramatizing, and posturing. It is the contention here that Byron in
fact exerted a quite remarkable degree of control over a troubled,
often painful existence, and that he showed an uncommonly ex-

pressive style, wit, and courage in playing out the constitutional cards he was dealt.

"There are some natures that have a predisposition to grief, as others have to disease," remarked Byron:

> The causes that have made me wretched would probably not have discomposed, or, at least, more than discomposed, another. We are all differently organized; and that I feel *acutely* is no more my fault (though it is my misfortune) than that another feels not, is his. We did not make ourselves, and if the elements of unhappiness abound more in the nature of one man than another, he is but the more entitled to our pity and our forebearance.[19]

Byron suffered greatly from his "predisposition to grief," and often feared that he was going mad. He wrote and talked about suicide and actively engaged in a life-style likely to bring about an early death; from a medical point of view, his symptoms, family psychiatric history, and the course of his illness clearly fit the pattern of manic-depressive illness.

Symptoms consistent with mania, depression, and mixed states are evident in the descriptions of Byron given by his physicians, friends, and Byron himself. His mood fluctuations were extreme, ranging from the suicidally melancholic to the irritable, volatile, violent, and expansive. Symptoms of depression included ennui, despair, lethargy, and sleeplessness. He thought of suicide and discussed it with others, to the extent that his friends and wife were at times concerned that he would take his own life. To a degree he saw his involvement with the Greek independence cause as a probable road to death, and it is likely that had he not died in Greece he would have killed himself in another way. His erratic financial behavior was in a class by itself, and—taken together with his episodic promiscuity, violent rages, impetuousness, restlessness, risk taking, poor judgment, and extreme irritability—it constitutes a classic presentation of manic behavior. Although there is no clear evidence that Byron suffered from either hallucinations or delusions, these are not a necessary component for the diagnosis of mania. Byron's irritability and rage often existed within the context of a melancholic mood, which is consistent with the diagnosis of mixed states (coexisting symptoms of mania and depression).

The clinical hallmark of manic-depressive illness is its recurrent, episodic nature.[20] Byron had this in an almost textbook manner, showing frequent and pronounced fluctuations in mood, energy, sleep patterns, sexual behavior, alcohol and other drug use, and weight (Byron also exhibited extremes in dieting, obsession with his weight, eccentric eating patterns, and excessive use of epsom salts). Although these changes in mood and behavior were dramatic and disruptive when they occurred, it is important to note that Byron was clinically normal most of the time; this, too, is highly characteristic of manic-depressive illness. An inordinate amount of confusion about whether someone does or does not have manic-depressive illness stems from the popular misconception that irrationality of mood and reason are stable rather than fluctuating features of the disease. Some assume that because an individual such as Byron was sane and in impressive control of his reason most of the time, that he could not have been "mad" or have suffered from a major mental illness. Lucidity and normal functioning are, however, perfectly consistent with—indeed, characteristic of—the phasic nature of manic-depressive illness. This is in contrast to schizophrenia, which is usually a chronic and relatively unrelenting illness characterized by, among other things, an inability to reason clearly.

The diagnosis of manic-depressive illness in Lord Byron is given further support by other aspects of the natural course of his illness. Byron first wrote about his melancholic moods while still a schoolboy at Harrow; this is consistent with what is well known about manic-depressive illness, that its first symptoms tend to occur in adolescence or early adulthood.[21] It is not uncommon for the underlying mobility of temperament to be apparent even earlier, and this also was the case with Byron. Manic-depressive illness is frequently seasonal as well, with depressive episodes more common in the winter months and around the time of the vernal and autumnal equinoxes, and mania more common in the summer.[22] In addition to experiencing "September melancholias," which he described to his mistress Teresa Guiccioli, Byron appears to have had a tendency toward both winter depressions and mixed states. August, for Byron, was often a time of extreme irritability, wrathfulness, and irrationality. In manic-depressive illness such states frequently are followed by depressive ones, and this would be consistent with Byron's observations that Septembers "kill with their sadness." Mood disorders, in addition to exhibiting seasonal patterns, frequently show pronounced diurnal rhythms as well. Byron described the most common form of this, being depressed in the morning and showing improved mood and increased energy as the day progressed. Yet another feature of the natural course of the disease, and probably the most important, is that manic-depressive and recurrent depressive illness, left untreated (or inadequately treated), often worsen over time; that is, the episodes of mania, depression, and mixed states tend to occur more frequently, be more severe, or last longer.[23] This was true for Byron.

Finally, and especially compelling in a genetic illness, Byron had a family history remarkable for its suicide (in itself more likely to be associated with manic-depressive illness than with any other condition), violence, irrationality, financial extravagance, and recurrent melancholia. All these are common features of manic-depressive illness. Byron himself was the first to believe in the constitutional basis of his illness and temperament: "It is ridiculous," he remarked to Lady Blessington, "to say that we do not inherit our passions, as well as . . . any other disorder,"[24] and to Teresa Guiccioli he wrote, "My melancholy is something temperamental, inherited."[25] To his publisher John Murray, he stated, "I am not sure that long life is desirable for one of my temper & constitutional depression of Spirits."[26] Lady Byron, who ultimately sued Byron for separation on the grounds that he was insane, wrote: "The day after my marriage he said, 'You were determined not to marry a man in whose family there was insanity.' . . .—'You have done very well indeed,' or some ironical expression to that effect, followed by the information that his maternal grandfather had committed suicide, and a Cousin . . . had been mad, & set fire to a house."[27]

Lord Byron's morbidly excitable temperament was indeed an almost inevitable inheritance, far more so than that of his title and properties. For the latter he was obliged to the quirk of the early death of more probable heirs; for the former, he was the recipient of genes passed down inexorably by generations of violent, reckless, suicidal, and occasionally insane ancestors. In 1880 one of Byron's biographers noted: "Never was poet born to so much illustrious, and to so much bad blood,"[28] a sentiment shared by Byron scholar Leslie Marchand. "The Byrons," declared Marchand, "seem to have grown more irresponsible with each generation, until the summit of social irregularity is reached in the character and conduct of the great-uncle and the father of the poet, if not indeed in the poet himself."[29] Byron's maternal side, the Gordons of Gight, displayed, he wrote, "a startling record of violence rare even in the annals of Scottish lairds," presenting "a spectacle of unrestrained barbarity."[30]

Certainly, the Byrons were an ancient and notorious family in England—among other things, by the mid-seventeenth century, it was being written, "Is't not enough the Byrons all excell,/As much in loving, as in fighting well?"[31] In the late seventeenth century, Margaret Fitzwilliam, wife of Sir John Byron and mother of the first and second Lords Byron, "went out of her mind and never recovered her reason."[32] Lady Margaret was described as a woman of "rare talent and beauty, skilled in the composition of music and poetry,"[33] and it was said that "her ravings were more delightful then [sic] other women's most rationall conversations."[34] From its description, and because the breakdown occurred following childbirth, it is possible that what she experienced was manic-depressive psychosis. The genes, however, do not appear to have been passed on down through the branch of the family tree leading directly to George Gordon Byron, the poet. The true dissipation, eccentricity, financial chaos, and wildness of temperament appear to have been brought into the bloodlines at a quite specific point in the eighteenth century. In 1720 William, the fourth Lord Byron, an amateur artist who had studied under the Flemish painter Peter Tillemans, married for a third time. It was this wife, Frances, daughter of Lord Berkeley and great-grandmother of the poet, who seems to have been largely responsible for bringing the "taint of blood" into the Byron line.[35] She and the fourth Lord Byron had five children who survived into adulthood. The eldest, Isabella, who showed strong interests in art and literature, had "many money difficulties,"[36] was "distinguished for eccentricity of manners,"[37] and exhibited "peculiar conduct"[38] which "excited comment even in that golden age of eccentrics."[39] The youngest child,

George, showed "neither marked eccentricity nor blameless respectability,"[40] and Richard, the next youngest, was a clergyman and amateur artist hallmarked by his "undeviating respectability."[41] In striking contrast to the younger Byrons, however, was the eldest son and heir to the title, William, who became the fifth Lord Byron. Known as the Wicked Lord, he was renowned for his extravagances, strange behavior, and violent temper. In 1795, after a relatively minor dispute, Byron killed his cousin and was brought to trial in the House of Lords. He was found guilty of manslaughter but acquitted of murder and allowed to return to Newstead Abbey, the Byron family seat in Nottinghamshire. Like his grandnephew the poet, the fifth Lord Byron was easily inflamed. Enraged at his son, who—having inherited his father's financial irresponsibility but not his willingness to marry for money—eloped with his cousin (he, like several other Byrons, married first cousins, thus hopelessly muddling the attribution of inheritance patterns, or acquired traits), the Wicked Lord did everything possible to insure that little of worth passed on to his heirs. His singularity of purpose and peculiarity of style were described by biographer André Maurois:

> He paid his gambling debts with the oaks of the park, felling five thousand pounds' worth and stripping his marvelous forest nearly bare of timber. . . . As a finishing touch in the spoliation of his son, Lord Byron killed two thousand seven hundred head of deer in the park, and granted a twenty-one years' lease of the Rochdale estate, where coal-seams had just been discovered, at the ridiculous rental of sixty pounds a year.
>
> His pleasures were those of a mischievous child. He would go down in the dark and open sluice-gates on the streams in order to damage the cotton mills; he emptied his neighbours' ponds; and on the edge of his own lake he had two small stone forts constructed, with a fleet of toy ships which he used sometimes to launch. He would spend whole days directing naval battles between the vessels and the forts; they fired on each other with miniature cannon. Lord Byron crouched in one of the forts, while his manservant, Joe Murray, lay stretched in a boat commanding the fleet. Sometimes, again, his lordship would lie on the stone flags of the Abbey kitchen and amuse himself by staging races of cockroaches up and down his own body, flipping the insects with straws when they were sluggish.[42]

The Wicked Lord, in fact, outlived both his son and his grandson; when he died in 1798 he passed on not only his title to his grand-nephew, the future poet, but his financial shambles as well.

John ("Foulweather Jack") Byron, the fifth lord's brother and George Gordon's grandfather, became a vice admiral in the British Navy and wrote one of the classic books about shipwreck; portions of his adventures, in altered form, found their way years later into Byron's great poem *Don Juan*. Although little has been written about any emotional difficulties Admiral Byron might have experienced, a suggestive comment about a possible "breakdown" has been made by Byron genealogist Violet Walker. She notes that Byron declined, for "health reasons," an appointment as second in command in North America during the War of Independence, and a few years later was the subject of a concerned letter written by a fellow officer; included in the latter's report was the observation: "Since I wrote to your Lordship concerning Mr. Byron, I learn that this unfortunate man was struck with disorder and disease that deprived him of his reason."[43] Admiral Byron, like his nephew, had married a first cousin; of particular interest here, she was the daughter of the sister of Frances, Lady Byron, the wife of the fourth Lord Byron and the one thought responsible for inserting the "family madness" into the Byron line. Sophia Trevanion, Admiral Byron's wife and therefore the poet's paternal grandmother, appears to have had a rather vivacious and mercurial temperament herself. Dr. Johnson wrote, after meeting her, "Poor Mrs. Byron is a feeler,"[44] and her friends "all agreed that she had too much sensibility, was very much up and down;"[45] she was, as A. L. Rowse said about both her and her famous grandson, a "true Celt."[46]

In 1756 the first son of these two cousins (Sophia Trevanion and Admiral Byron), Byron's father, was born. John ("Mad Jack") Byron soon made the gambling debts, financial mayhem, and overall level of dissipation of his uncle the Wicked Lord seem subdued by comparison. Charming, good-looking, and ebullient, he served briefly in America with the Coldstream Guards before returning to the social whirl of London. There he met the wife of the future Duke of Leeds, and an heiress in her own right. After a scandalous affair and her subsequent divorce, they married, moved to France, and had several children. The only child to survive infancy, Augusta, was the poet's half-sister and great love. (In the Byron tradition, Augusta married their first cousin, George Leigh, who went on to have massive financial problems and gambling debts of his own; two of their three sons and two of their daughters had severe financial difficulties as well.[47] [In addition, at least one of their children, described as "mentally unbalanced," had to be removed from their home and taken care of elsewhere.]) When his wife died, Mad Jack, after accumulating even more debts, returned to England and married yet another heiress—this one Scottish—Catherine Gordon of Gight. He made rapid headway in spending this second fortune as well; eventually, a few years after the birth of their son, George Gordon, he moved back to France to avoid his creditors. He died young, dissolute, alcoholic, a victim of "his restless moods, his sensual appetites, his wild gaieties and glooms,"[49] and a probable suicide.[50]

Byron's heritage from his mother's family was far more fierce, colorful, and dangerously unstable than the one from the spendthrift, now and again rather eccentric Byrons:

> The first laird of Gight, Sir William Gordon, had been the son of the Earl of Huntly and Annabella Stuart, sister of King James the Second. But although the family history opened thus royally, a more tragic sequence of events could hardly be imagined. William Gordon was drowned, Alexander Gordon murdered. John Gordon hanged for the killing of Lord Moray in 1592, another John Gordon hanged in 1634 for the assassination of Wallenstein—it seemed as if a Gordon of Gight had been strung up on every branch of their family tree. . . . The sixth laird, a conscious evildoer, used to say: "I can tak' no rest. I know I will die upon a scaffold. There is an evil turn in my hand."[51]

Several generations later, Alexander Gordon, the eleventh laird and great-grandfather of Byron, died in a midwinter drowning that was almost certainly a suicide. Marchand quotes one skeptical response to a contemporary newspaper article (which had reported that the death was due to drowning while bathing): "Scotsmen in 1760 had not become slaves to the tub so much as to induce them to bathe in ice-covered rivers in the depths of winter."[52] Alexander Gordon's son, the twelfth laird, George Gordon, also drowned; his death was probably a suicide as well.[53] Years later his grandson the poet in describing the constitutional basis for his own melancholy, wrote:

> You know—or you do *not* know—that my maternal Grandfather (a very clever man & amiable I am told) was strongly suspected of Suicide—(he was found drowned in the Avon at Bath) and that another very near relative of the same branch—took poison—& was merely saved by antidotes.—For the first of these events—there was no apparent cause—as he was rich, respected,—& of considerable intellectual resources—hardly forty years of age—& not at all addicted to any unhinging vice.—It was however but a strong suspicion—owing to the manner of his death—& to his melancholy temper.[54]

Predictably, Byron's mother was left not altogether untouched by the Gordon inheritance; described as a woman "full of the most passionate extremes,"[55] she was easily excited to rage and subject to wildly swinging changes of mood. During his adolescence Byron often confided in his half-sister Augusta about his mother's violent moods and unpredictable behavior: "My mother has lately behaved to me in such an eccentric manner,"[56] he wrote while still a student at Harrow, adding several days later, "Her temper is so variable, and when inflamed, so furious, that I dread our meeting . . . she flies into a fit of phrenzy."[57] "Her method is so violent, so capricious," he continued, with traces of the wit that was to characterize so much of his writing and speech as he grew older, "that the patience of Job, the versatility of a member of the House of Commons could not support it."[58] The following year brought a continuation of Byron's outcries about his mother's behavior and temperament: "She is as I have before declared certainly mad . . . her conduct is a . . . compound of derangement and Folly";[59] she was, he complained, his "tormentor" whose "*diabolical* disposition . . . seems to increase with age, and to acquire new force with Time."[60] The combination of Byron's temperament with his mother's must have been an incendiary one, and Thomas Moore recounts: "It is told, as a curious proof of their opinion of each other's violence, that, after parting one evening in a tempest . . . they were known each to go privately that night to the apothecary's inquiring anxiously whether the one had been to purchase poison, and cautioning the vender of drugs not to attend to such an application, if made."[61]

The mingling of the Byron and Gordon bloodlines was bound to raise the temperature of the already fiery gene pools. As we shall see, Byron was the most immediate beneficiary of this coalescence but inevitably the effects extended to Byron's descendants as well. Allegra, his illegitimate daughter with Claire Clairmont (stepsister of Mary Shelley), died when she was only five years old and was therefore far too young to show definitive signs of either the Gordon-Byron temperament or any kind of serious mood disorder. It is suggestive, however, that Shelley quoted Byron as saying that his daughter's temper was "violent and imperious,"[62] and Shelley himself noted that "she has a contemplative seriousness which mixed with her excessive vivacity . . . has a very peculiar effect in a child."[63] In a letter to his sister, Byron observed that Allegra had "a devil of a spirit but that is Papa's."[64] Assessments of Allegra's temperament must, due to her early death, remain highly speculative. Much more is known about Byron's one legitimate child, however. Ada Byron, later to become Ada, Countess of Lovelace, inherited from her mother—whom Byron early in their relationship had dubbed the "Princess of Parallelograms"—remarkable mathematical abilities. Described by eminent mathematician Augustus De Morgan as having the potential to become "an original mathematical investigator, perhaps of first rate eminence,"[65] Ada worked on Charles Babbage's calculating machine and earned for herself the designation of being the first computer programmer. (In 1980 the United States Department of Defense honored her contributions by naming its computer programming language ADA.[66])

From her father Ada inherited a mercurial temperament that swung precipitously from the ecstatic and grandiose to the melancholic. She also acquired the Byron proclivities for gambling and financial chaos; at one point, convinced she had invented an infallible system for betting on horses, she suffered such severe losses that she was forced to pawn the Lovelace family jewels. It was her temperament, however, by which she was most particularly her father's daughter. Indeed, Byron, who although in exile followed her childhood as closely as he could, noted not long before he died that a description he had received of her disposition and tendencies "very nearly resembles that of my *own* at a similar age—except that I was much more impetuous."[67] Earlier, in his inimitable manner, he had summed up his notion of the more diversified headwaters of Ada's temperament:

> Her temper is said to be extremely violent.—Is it so?—It is not unlikely considering her parentage.—My temper is what it is—as you may perhaps divine—and my Lady's was a nice little sullen nucleus of concentrated Savageness to mould my daughter upon,—to say nothing of her two Grandmothers—both of whom, to my knowledge were as pretty specimens of female Spirit—as you might wish to see on a Summer's day.[68]

Ada, like her father, was episodically charged with an *"awful energy & power"* and a vastly confident "exhilaration of spirit";[69] her grandiosity, occasionally delusional in degree, rivaled the cosmic sweep of Poe and Melville. One of her biographers quotes Ada, who had outlined her plans for taking on "the mysteries of the universe, in a way no purely mortal lips or brains could do":[70]

> I intended to incorporate with one department of my labours a complete reduction to a system, of the principles & methods of *discovery*, elucidating the same with examples. I am already noting down a list of discoveries hitherto made, in order myself to examine into their *history, origin, & progress*. One first & main point, *whenever & wherever* I introduce the subject, will be to *define & to classify* all that is to be legitimately included under the term *discovery*. Here will be a fine field for my *clear, logical & accurate*, mind, to work its powers upon; & to develop its *metaphysical* genius, which is not least amongst its qualifications and characteristics.[71]

No wonder that Ada wrote elsewhere that "there is in my nervous system such utter want of *all* ballast & steadiness that I cannot regard my life or powers as other than precarious."[72] The lack of ballast was reflected also in her grandiose belief that she was "simply the *instrument* for the divine purpose to act on *& thro'*. . . . Like the Prophets of old, I shall *speak the voice* I am inspired with. I may be the Deborah, the Elijah of Science."[73] Doris Langley Moore points out that Ada's swings from "transcendent elation" to "despair" were often only weeks, rather than months or years apart.[74] These rapid cycling mood swings were quite similar, in many respects, to those experienced by her father. Her writing during her melancholic moods occasionally bears an uncanny resemblance to his as well. In a letter to her mother she wrote:

> I must refer you to Dr. Locock as to my present condition, for I am WHOLLY *unable* to write. . . . He will tell you how shattered & done for I at length am. Pray don't be angry with me for *what I can't do*. As long as I had *fever* I could *write*, & had almost preternatural power. Now, this is all over. . . .
> The least exertion, either mental or bodily, has effects now that I never knew before. And *repose* is absolutely necessary.
> . . . . Every power, mental & bodily, seems worn out.[75]

Ada, like her father and his father before him, died at the age of thirty-six:

> The child of love,—though born in bitterness,
> And nurtured in convulsion,—of thy sire
> These were the elements,—and thine no less.[76]

Manic-depressive illness is the only medical diagnosis that could reasonably account for Byron's singular family history of suicide, tempestuous moods, violent melancholy, and erratic behavior—to say nothing of Byron's own symptoms and the worsening course of his depressions and rages. A few months before he died Byron had a convulsive attack of some kind ("Epileptic—Paralytic—or Apoplectic is not yet decided by the two medical men who attend me"),[77] and this, in conjunction with Byron's violent rages, has been used as an argument that he may have suffered from an epileptic or seizure disorder.[78] The attack was, however, the first in his life ("This is the first attack that I have had of this kind to the best of my belief. I never heard that any of my family were liable to the same—though my mother was subject to *hysterical* affections")[79] and almost certainly related to the final illness that caused his death. The diagnosis of a seizure disorder, such as temporal lobe epilepsy (or, complex partial seizures), would not account for Byron's pronounced family history of suicide and psychiatric illness, nor would it be the most explanatory diagnosis for

George Gordon, Lord Byron
Partial Family History

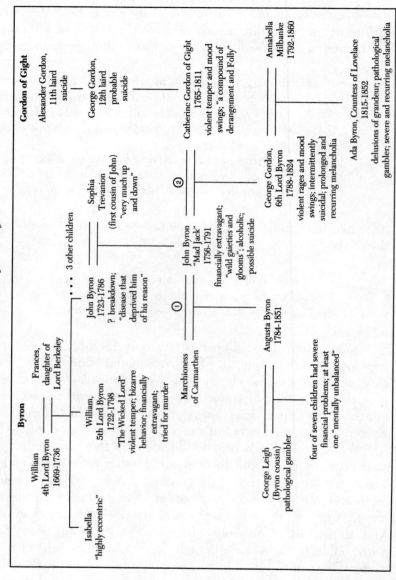

Byron

William
4th Lord Byron
1669-1736

Frances,
daughter of
Lord Berkeley

Isabella
"highly eccentric"

William,
5th Lord Byron
1722-1798
"The Wicked Lord"
violent temper; bizarre
behavior; financially
extravagant;
tried for murder

• • • 3 other children

John Byron
1723-1786
? breakdown;
"disease that
deprived him
of his reason"

Sophia
Trevanion
(first cousin of John)
"very much up
and down"

John Byron
"Mad Jack"
1756-1791
financially extravagant;
"wild gaieties and
glooms"; alcoholic;
possible suicide

① Marchioness
of Carmarthen

Augusta Byron
1784-1851

George Leigh
(Byron cousin)
pathological gambler

four of seven children had severe
financial problems; at least
one "mentally unbalanced"

Gordon of Gight

Alexander Gordon,
11th laird
suicide

George Gordon,
12th laird
probable suicide

Catherine Gordon of Gight
1765-1811
violent temper and mood
swings; "a compound of
derangement and Folly"

②

George Gordon,
6th Lord Byron
1788-1824
violent rages and mood
swings; intermittently
suicidal; prolonged and
recurring melancholia

Annabella
Milbanke
1792-1860

Ada Byron, Countess of Lovelace
1815-1852
delusions of grandeur; pathological
gambler; severe and recurring melancholia

his history of mood swings and the other symptoms so characteristic of manic-depressive illness.

The severity and pattern of Byron's moods, and their devastating effect upon his life, form part of the argument for a diagnosis
of manic-depressive illness rather than cyclothymic temperament alone. Yet Byron's temperament, coupled with his poetic
genius, made him who he was. Byron is perhaps alone among
English writers in having a particular kind of temperament and
personal style named for him. The "Byronic" has come to mean the
theatrical, Romantic, brooding, mock heroic, posturing, cynical,
passionate, or sardonic. Unfortunately, these epithets suggest an
exaggerated or even insincere quality, and in doing so tend to
minimize the degree of genuine suffering that Byron experienced;
such a characterization also overlooks the extraordinary intellectual
and emotional discipline he exerted over a kind of pain that brings
most who experience it to their knees.

Byron's fiery and melancholic temperament at times crossed
over the fine line that separates illness from health. (This is analogous to many other medical conditions—for example, diabetes,
thyroid disease, and hypertension—in which the underlying predisposition flares up, from time to time, into acute disease. Such
exacerbations of ongoing metabolic and other states may be temporary and ultimately self-correcting, representing only short-term
discomfort and possible danger, or they may be progressive and life
threatening. But they can also be both, and manic-depressive illness tends to fit this latter description.) In Byron's case aspects of
his underlying temperament often worsened into periods of painful
melancholia and disruptive, perturbed mental states; by the end of
his life these periods of emotional distress began to outweigh periods of health. His temperament also, however, made him exquisitely responsive to virtually everything in his physical and
psychological world; it gave to him much of his great capacity for
passion and understanding, as well as for suffering.

George Gordon Byron was born in London in 1788, shortly after
his parents' return from France, where "Mad Jack" Byron had
taken refuge from his creditors. Before young Byron was two, the

family moved to Aberdeen, where he and his mother stayed until
he inherited his great-uncle's title and properties at the age of ten.
"Mad Jack," in the meantime, had returned to France and died
before Byron was three. It seems clear that Byron's temperament
as a child was father to his temperament as a man. His friend
Moore wrote that "as a child his temper was violent, or rather
sullenly passionate";[80] his was, he said, an "uncontrollable spirit."[81]
His schoolmasters in Aberdeen described him as "lively, warm-
hearted, and high-spirited . . . passionate and resentful, but affec-
tionate and companionable . . . to a remarkable degree venturous
and fearless."[82]

Byron wrote later in his life: "I differed not at all from other
children, being neither tall nor short, dull nor witty . . . but rather
lively—except in my sullen moods, and then I was always a
devil."[83] Describing himself when he was about ten years old, he
said: "They once (in one of my silent rages) wrenched a knife from
me, which I had snatched from [the] table . . . and applied to my
breast."[84] By all accounts Byron also manifested early a desire and
ability for deeply held friendships. Moore said: "Of all the qualities, indeed, of his nature, affectionateness seems to have been the
most ardent and deep,"[85] and his closest friend, John Cam Hobhouse, wrote in his journal:

> No man ever lived who had such devoted friends. His power of
> attaching those about him to his person was such as no one I ever
> knew possessed. No human being could approach him without being
> sensible of this magical influence. There was something command-
> ing, but not overawing in his manner. He was neither grave nor gay
> out of place, and he seemed always made for that company in which
> he happened to find himself. There was a mildness and yet a decision
> in his mode of conversing, and even in his address, which are seldom
> united in the same person. He appeared exceedingly free, open, and
> unreserved to everybody.[86]

Most of the qualities in his temperament that made Byron who he
was—volatility, contradictoriness, and intensity of emotions; generosity of impulse and money; caustic and occasionally bitter wit,
usually followed by regret and softened by compassion; and a
straightforwardness and honesty in dealing with emotional mat-

ters—had been set in place by the time he was sixteen years old. He possessed, through his experience and understanding, a piercing insight into the human condition and a broad understanding of the things that make human nature so especially human—love, envy, disappointment, aspiration, sex, revenge, vulnerability, and man's uneasy awareness of his own mortality.

Byron's proneness to melancholy was evident even when he was a schoolboy; while at Harrow, for example, he wrote to his sister of being "peevish and fretful,"[87] thanking her for a letter that "acted as a cordial on my drooping spirits and for a while dispelled the gloom."[88] A year later he described his "idle disposition," "very bad spirits," and then continued, "I never was in such low spirits in my life."[89] His constitutional melancholy was joined by painful self-consciousness about having been born lame. To Byron, taunted about it as a child in Scotland and then as a student in England, his deformity remained a source of bitterness and unhappiness throughout his life. Two examples of this, given by his friend Moore, are particularly poignant:

> Seeing an unfortunate woman lying on the steps of a door, Lord Byron, with some expression of compassion, offered her a few shillings; but, instead of accepting them, she violently pushed away his hand, and, starting up with a yell of laughter, began to mimic the lameness of his gait. He did not utter a word; but "I could feel," said Mr. Bailey, "his arm trembling within mine, as we left her."[90]

> In coming out, one night, from a hall, with Mr. Rogers, as they were on their way to the carriage, one of the link-boys ran on before Lord Byron, crying, "This way, my lord." "He seems to know you," said Mr. Rogers. "Know me!" answered Lord Byron, with some degree of bitterness in his tone; "every one knows me—I am deformed."[91]

Byron took on and transformed his personal anguish; the following passage from his drama *The Deformed Transformed* captures the belief that disadvantage and pain—both psychological and physical—often fuel action and drive excellence:

. . . . Deformity is daring.
It is its essence to o'ertake mankind
By heart and soul, and make itself the equal—

Aye, the superior of the rest. There is
A spur in its halt movements, to become
All that others cannot.[92]

In October 1805 Byron arrived at Trinity College, Cambridge, where, if he "ever attended a lecture," wrote one biographer, "he found it too dull to mention."[93] He did, however, read a great deal, write poetry, make friends, and lead an intermittently dissolute life. "I have been extravagant,"[94] he wrote Augusta in December of his first year, an understated confession if ever there was one. His personal generosity, as well as his other intemperate financial ways, led him inevitably to moneylenders and an ever-increasing indebtedness (by January 1808 he had accrued debts of £3,000; by the end of that year he owed £12,000; and by the time of his marriage in 1815 he was at least £30,000 in debt).[95] During the following years at Cambridge and in London these extravagances fitted into a larger pattern of frenzied activity and excesses of all kinds; this pattern, skeined with melancholy, was particularly pronounced in the winter and spring. In January 1806 he wrote Augusta that her attempts to "reanimate" his spirits would, "I am afraid, fail in their effort,"[96] and by the end of that year and into the beginning of 1807, Byron was in the throes of "alternate moods of depression, ambition, and reckless indulgence."[97] His letters to his sister and friends throughout his Cambridge and early London years confirm this. In February he wrote to a close friend from Harrow days, "I have recovered every thing but my spirits, which are subject to depression"[98]; two months later he wrote to another friend, "Nature stampt me in the Die of *Indifference*. I consider myself as destined never to be happy, although in some instances fortunate. I am an isolated Being on the Earth, without a Tie to attach me to life."[99]

Life never remained entirely bleak for Byron, however. In fall 1807, having been told that regulations would not allow him to keep his dog at Cambridge, he acquired a tame bear—there being no rule forbidding bears—and housed it in the turret of his college rooms. His pleasure in the bear, which he walked through the streets of Cambridge, was obvious: "I have got a new friend, the finest in the world, a *tame bear*, when I brought him here, they asked me what I meant to do with him, and my reply was 'he should *sit for a Fellowship. . . .'* This answer delighted them not."[100] Byron and the bear, when later reunited at Newstead Abbey, would occasionally swim together in a vault leading to the graves of the monks who had previously inhabited the Byron ancestral home; along with other animals, the bear was kept in the family chapel, a thirteenth-century converted Chapter House. Byron had inherited his father's love for animals—in addition, as Doris Langley Moore has pointed out, to their shared capacity for incurring debt, as well as probable incest with their respective sisters[101]—and eventually developed a menagerie that, by the time he went into exile years later, was the subject of Shelley's bemused comments:

> Lord B's establishment consists, besides servants, of ten horses, eight enormous dogs, three monkeys, five cats, an eagle, a crow, and a falcon; and all these, except the horses, walk about the house, which every now and then resounds with their unarbitrated quarrels, as if they were the masters of it . . . [later] I find that my enumeration of the animals in this Circean Palace was defective, and that in a material point. I have just met on the grand staircase five peacocks, two guinea hens, and an Egyptian crane. [102]

By January 1808 Byron was living in London and writing to a friend that others thought of him as "the votary of Licentiousness, and the Disciple of Infidelity";[103] typically, however, the rest of the letter was filled with discussion about poetry and literary critics. Just after his twentieth birthday in the same month, Byron wrote that he was "buried in an abyss of Sensuality," "given to Harlots," and in a "state of Concubinage."[104] His immersion in drinking, gambling, and women was not without its expected toll:

> My dear Hobhouse,—The Game is almost up, for these last five days I have been confined to my room, Laudanum is my sole support, and even Pearson wears a woeful visage as he prescribes, however I am now *better* and I trust my hour is not yet arrived.—I began to apprehend a complete Bankruptcy of Constitution, and on disclosing the mode of my Life for these last two years (of which my residence at Cambridge constituted the most sober part) my [Surgeon] pronounced another quarter would have settled my earthly accounts, and left the worms but a scant repast.—[105]

In July 1809, Byron left England for a two-year "Grand Tour" of Portugal, Spain, Gibraltar, Malta, Greece, and Turkey. His high spirits and aggressive enjoyment of life continued to be mixed with periods of melancholy. In May 1810 he resolved to adopt a new life: "I am tolerably sick of vice which I have tried in its agreeable varieties, and mean on my return to cut all dissolute acquaintance, leave off wine and 'carnal company' "; he meant, he said, to keep to "politics and Decorum."[106] Intermittently he was "vastly happy and childish,"[107] having a "most social & fantastical"[108] winter in Athens, and enjoying excellent health. His inevitable melancholy caught up with him again in late 1810, however, and he wrote from Greece with blackish humor: "I have nothing more to hope, and may begin to consider the most eligible way of walking out of it [life], probably I may find in England somebody inclined to save me the trouble. . . . I wish I could find some of Socrates's Hemlock."[109] In May of the following year he wrote: "At twenty three the best of life is over and its bitters double. . . . I am sick at heart. . . . I have outlived all my appetites and most of my vanities,"[110] and the next month he explained to a friend the morbidity at the heart of his seeming levity: "I am so out of Spirits, & hopes, & humour, & pocket, & health, that you must bear with my merriment, my only resource against a Calenture."[111] As usual the low spirits were preceded and followed by high ones, for Byron's enthusiasms and excesses were part breeding ground for, and part distraction from, his brooding seasons; ultimately, of course, the ennui and vivacity were inextricably bound to one another, not entirely opposite sides to the same temperamental coin.

When Byron returned to England in July 1811 he brought with him the first two cantos of *Childe Harold's Pilgrimage*, the largely autobiographical[112] poem that was to make him famous, as well as a typically intriguing collection of acquisitions, including additions to his menagerie. He catalogued a few of these purchases: "Four ancient Athenian skulls, dug out of Sarcophagi—a phial of Attic Hemlock—four live Tortoises—a Greyhound . . . two live Greek Servants."[113] Already depressed prior to his return to England, within a few months of being back, Byron experienced the deaths of his mother, two close friends, and his "violent, though *pure*"[114] love from his Cambridge days, John Edleston. The combination of his naturally melancholic temperament with the losses of these deaths sent him into a deep depression; he drafted a will, adding twice for emphasis that he wished neither ceremony nor burial service and desired to be buried with his "faithful dog," who was not to be removed from their shared vault. His dark mood was strangely mixed, however, "for though I feel tolerably miserable, yet I am at the same time subject to a kind of hysterical merriment, or rather laughter without merriment, which I can neither account for nor conquer."[115] He remained depressed for several months and wrote to a friend about his state of mind:

> I am growing *nervous* (how you will laugh!)—but it is true,—really, wretchedly, ridiculously, fine–ladically *nervous*. . . . I can neither read, write, or amuse myself, or any one else. My days are listless, and my nights restless. . . . I don't know that I sha'n't end with insanity, for I find a want of method in arranging my thoughts that perplexes me strangely.[116]

To another friend he wrote a few days later, "I am very low-spirited on many accounts. . . . I am indeed very wretched. . . . all places are alike, I cannot live under my present feelings, I have lost my appetite, my rest, & can neither read write or act in comfort—"[117]

Byron's spirits revived gradually, and in February 1812 he delivered his maiden speech, the first of three speeches he was to give, in the House of Lords. It was fiery—"perhaps a little theatrical,"[118] by his own account—and one that reportedly "kept the House in a roar of laughter."[119] A few days later his brooding poem *Childe Harold's Pilgrimage* was published; he awoke one morning, he reported drolly, and found himself famous. Byron became, almost overnight, the focus of London society. The Duchess of Devonshire wrote that *Childe Harold* "is on every table, and himself courted, visited, flattered and praised whenever he appears. . . . He is really the only topic of conversation—the men jealous of him, the women of each other."[120] Lady Caroline Lamb, wife of the future prime minister (Lord Melbourne), dashed in her journal after meeting him that Byron was "mad—bad—and dangerous to know,"[121] giving more credence to the notion that the similar are inclined toward their own. Although their temperaments were likewise overwrought and volatile, their characters were in fact quite different. Byron was ultimately a highly disciplined if yet emotional man, and he was used to keeping his tempestuous moods under relatively tight control; Lady Caroline Lamb either would not or could not do the same, and after several turbulent months of passionate attraction on both sides, and then dreadful, acrimonious public scenes—including knife slashing (on her part) and verbal slashing (on his)—Byron ended the relationship. He had written to her that:

> People talk as if there were no other pair of absurdities in London.— It is hard to bear all this without cause, but worse to give cause for it.— Our folly has had the effect of a fault.— I conformed and could conform, if you would lend your aid, but I can't bear to see you look unhappy. . . . We must make an effort, this dream this delirium of two months must pass away."[122]

Although there continued to be some contact and correspondence, the affair was, for all intents and purposes, over; she continued to request time, meetings, and commitment but Byron remained resolute that the damage was long past repairing. Despite the public embarrassment, he held himself singularly accountable for his own actions, as he was to do years later following the far greater hurts and damages he experienced due to his wife's behavior. In a letter to his closest confidante, Lady Melbourne (who was also Caroline Lamb's mother-in-law and the aunt of Byron's wife-to-be), he wrote that Caroline "never did nor can deserve a single reproach which must not fall with double justice & truth upon myself, who am much much more to blame in every respect, nor shall I in the least hesitate in declaring this to any of her family."[123]

Byron's spirits continued to fluctuate over the months to follow. January 1813 found him "exceedingly wearied"[124] and irritable, November with a "mind in fermentation,"[125] and by the end of the year he was again feeling depressed and aimless:

> I am *ennuyé* beyond my usual tense of that yawning verb, which I am always conjugating; and I don't find that society much mends the matter. I am too lazy to shoot myself—and it would annoy Augusta . . . but it would be a good thing for George [Byron's first cousin and successor to his title], on the other side, and no bad one for me; but I won't be tempted.[126]

By the end of the same month, however, he was working at break-
neck speed on a new poem, *The Corsair*, writing more than two
hundred lines a day; when published a few months later, it sold ten
thousand copies on the first day of publication and twenty-five
thousand copies within one month. Yet he wrote on February 27,
"I am not well; and yet I look in good health. At times, I fear, 'I am
not in my perfect mind;'—and yet my heart and head have stood
many a crash, and what should ail them now? They prey upon
themselves, and I am sick—sick—'. . . why should a cat, a rat, a
dog have life—and *thou* no life at all?' "[127] Although the quality of
his life may have been in question to Byron, it was not strictly the
case that he had no life at all: In addition to affairs with Lady Oxford
and Lady Frances Webster, he had become involved in the most
emotionally binding and scandalous relationship of his life, an affair
with his half-sister Augusta:

> I say 'tis blood—my blood! the pure warm stream
> Which ran in the veins of my fathers, and in ours
> When we were in our youth, and had one heart,
> And loved each other as we should not love. . . .
>
> .   .   .   .
>
> She was like me in lineaments—her eyes,
> Her hair, her features, all, to the very tone
> Even of her voice, they said were like to mine;
> But soften'd all, and temper'd into beauty;
> She had the same lone thoughts and wanderings[128]

They traveled together in the summer and fall of 1813 and then
spent part of the early winter of 1814 together in Newstead Abbey.
She became pregnant, but it remains unclear whether Byron or
Augusta's husband was the father of the child (in any event Byron
was godfather).

    In April 1814 Byron wrote to Lady Melbourne that he had
called in a physician for himself and that he "puts so many questions to me about *my mind* and the state of it—that I begin to think
he half suspects my senses—he asked me—how I felt 'when anything weighed upon my mind—' and I answered him by a question
why he should suppose that anything did?—I was laughing & sit-

ting quietly in my chair the whole time of his visit—& yet he thinks me horribly restless—and irritable—and talks about my having lived *excessively* 'out of all compass.' "[129] The following month Byron described feeling a deep indifference to life and most sensations, "the same indifference which has frozen over the 'Black Sea' of almost all my passions."[130] Continuing in the same letter to Moore, he wrote, "It is that very indifference which makes me so uncertain and apparently capricious. It is not eagerness of new pursuits, but that nothing impresses me sufficiently to *fix;* neither do I feel disgusted, but simply indifferent to almost all excitements."[131] He was again reporting to Moore in August that he felt "quite enervated and indifferent";[132] during the same period of time, in a rage, he threw a bottle of ink out the window. Increasingly convinced that his only "salvation" in life was to marry, he proposed late that summer to Annabella Milbanke, an unlikely and unfortunate choice: Prophetically, Byron was to write of his "Princess of Parallelograms" that "Her proceedings are quite rectangular, or rather we are two parallel lines prolonged to infinity side by side but never to meet."[133] To all intents and purposes humorless, she was also cool, cerebral, morally superior, and in almost every possible respect opposite in temperament from her husband-to-be. She was, as biographer Doris Langley Moore has pointed out, "a conspicuously frigid type . . . perhaps no young woman ever lived whose writings show so intense a preoccupation with her own rectitude."[134] Annabella had, however, shown not inconsiderable, if somewhat smug, insight into Byron's character and temperament in her "Character of Lord Byron," written not long after she first met him. "The passions have been his guide from childhood," she wrote, "and have exercised a tyrannical power over his very superior Intellect"; there was, however, "a chivalrous generosity in his ideas of love & friendship, and selfishness is totally absent from his character." She then went on to describe his mercurial temperament and his inconsistency of mind and mood:

> When indignation takes possession of his mind—and it is easily excited—his disposition becomes malevolent. He hates with the bitterest contempt. But as soon as he has indulged those feelings, he regains the humanity which he had lost—from the immediate impulse of provocation—and repents deeply. So that his mind is con-

tinually making the most sudden transitions—from good to evil, from evil to good. A state of such perpetual tumult must be attended with the misery of restless inconsistency. He laments his want of tranquillity and speaks of the power of application to composing studies, as a blessing placed beyond his attainment, which he regrets.[135]

She concluded, with unintended irony, "He is inclined to open his heart unreservedly to those whom he believes *good.*"

In the midst of much melancholy and ambivalence, Byron—in part "to repair the ravages of myself & prodigal ancestry"[136]—married Annabella Milbanke in January 1815. Despite his resentments, reservations, and savage mood, Byron was able to maintain some of his customary wit. His friend John Cam Hobhouse, serving as best man and well aware that Byron was at least thirty thousand pounds in debt, described the marriage ceremony: "Miss M. was as firm as a rock and during the whole ceremony looked steadily at Byron—she repeated the words audibly & well. B[yron] hitched at first when he said, 'I George Gordon' and when he came to the words, 'with all my worldly goods I thee endow' looked at me with half a smile."[137] By every account available the year of married life to follow was a nightmare for both parties, seared with the absolute ferocity of Byron's moods and Lady Byron's inability to deal with them (Professor Marchand notes that "Byron's valet, Fletcher, who had seen his master in all of his moods and had by then been witness to his relations with dozens of women of all kinds, remarked with naïve wisdom: 'It is very odd, but I never yet knew a lady that could not manage my Lord, *except* my Lady.' "[138]) Byron's rages and periods of morbid depression were clearly frightening to Lady Byron, and excessive drinking and discussions of other women only exacerbated the situation:

> He had for many months professed his intention of giving himself up either to women or drinking, and had asked me to sanction these courses, adding however that he should pursue them whether I gave him leave or not. Accordingly for about three months before my confinement he was accustomed to drink Brandy & other liquors to intoxication, which caused him to commit many outrageous acts, as breaking & burning several valuable articles, and brought on paroxysms of rage or frenzy—not only terrifying but dangerous to me in my then situation [her pregnancy]—[139]

Lady Byron also reported her concerns that Byron might kill himself: "He used to get up almost every night, and walk up & down the long Gallery in a state of horror & agitation which led me to apprehend he would realize his repeated threats of Suicide."[140] On another occasion she noted, "He then had his loaded pistols & dagger (which are always by his bedside at night) on the table through the day, and frequently intimated a design of Suicide. Once he seized the dagger, & ran with it to his own room, the door of which I heard him lock."[141] Not only Annabella was concerned that Byron might take his own life. Augusta, in a letter to Annabella, wrote:

> I have before told you of *his hints* of self destruction. The night before last, I went as usual to his room to light his Candles & seeing a Draught on the chimney piece which looked *fermenting*, I said "What is this." "My Draught, to be sure—what did you think it was? Laudanum?" I replied jokingly that I was not even *thinking* of Laudanum & the truth—that I thought the Draught spoilt, which caused my inquiry. He immediately looked very dark & black (in the old way) & said "I have plenty of Laudanum—& shall use it." Upon my laughing & trying to turn off the subject he only repeated in the most awful manner *his most solemn determination* on the subject.[142]

The winter of 1815 appears to have been filled with violent rages and dark moods, but the spring and summer brought some relief, despite unremitting financial problems. By August, however, Byron's moods again had become wild and unpredictable, and in October "he became the victim again of sleepless nights and nervous fears."[143] His drinking and rages became even worse, his behavior "increasingly erratic," and by the end of the year Lady Byron was convinced that he was insane. She called in a consulting physician who could not give a "decided opinion"; neither he nor Lady Byron's own doctor could agree that Byron was definitely insane (he had "nothing like a settled lunacy")[144] and so Lady Byron was left to conclude that, if not the first part of Lady Caroline's jottings—that is, mad—then Byron must instead be bad (the "dangerous to know" was a given). Later Byron was to write to this point in *Don Juan:*

> Don Jóse and the Donna Inez led
>   For some time an unhappy sort of life,

Wishing each other, not divorced, but dead.
   They lived respectably as man and wife,
Their conduct was exceedingly well-bred,
   And gave no outward signs of inward strife,
Until at length the smother'd fire broke out,
And put the business past all kind of doubt.

For Inez call'd some druggists and physicians,
   And tried to prove her loving lord was *mad*,
But as he had some lucid intermissions,
   She next decided he was only *bad*;
Yet when they ask'd her for her depositions,
   No sort of explanation could be had,
Save that her duty both to man and God
Required this conduct—which seem'd very odd.[145]

In December 1815 their daughter was born; in January of the
following year Byron and his wife separated. He never saw Lady
Byron or his daughter again. Augusta described her brother's de-
meanor shortly after the separation:

He staid at home last night & was tolerably quiet, tho singing wildly
& irritable. He gave me an opportunity of saying much more of
derangement, & took it very quietly. He said "Oh don't say so or talk
of it because of my Will"—told me about Grandfather's end & his
Mother always perceiving a resemblance between them—talked quietly & rationally abt it, but seemed rather alarmed at the thought.[146]

Byron's depression grew worse, deepening to the extent that
his friend Hobhouse thought it worse than at any time since he had
known Byron. In a letter to his father-in-law, written early in
February, Byron discussed his own perspective on his temperament and marriage:

During the last year I have had to contend with distress without—&
disease within:—upon the former I have little to say—except that I
have endeavoured to remove it by every sacrifice in my power—&
the latter I should not mention if I had not recent & professional
authority for saying—that the disorder which I have to combat—
without much impairing my apparent health—is such as to induce a
morbid irritability of temper—which—without recurring to external
causes—may have rendered me little less disagreeable to others than

I am to myself.—I am however ignorant of any particular ill treatment which your daughter has encountered:—she may have seen me gloomy—& at times violent—but she knows the causes too well to attribute such inequalities of disposition to herself—or even to me—if all things be fairly considered. [147]

It soon became clear that there was to be no reconciliation with his wife, and that the thickening rumors of incest, insanity, perversion, and violence were to provide no opportunity for even a semblance of a livable existence in England. Accordingly, Byron made plans to go abroad. Before doing so, however—and despite staggering debts requiring the forced auction even of his books—he ordered an inordinately lavish traveling coach modeled on Napoleon's; it cost five hundred pounds and was furnished with dining and sleeping facilities as well as a library. It turned out to be, in its own way, a bit like Byron: grand, Romantic, and liable to breakdowns. Byron and his companions, including his physician (the youngest graduate in the history of the University of Edinburgh medical school, he was himself no bastion of sanity and eventually went on to commit suicide), left London in April 1816. Byron left with bitterness and never saw England again:

I was accused of every monstrous vice by public rumor and private rancour; my name, which had been a knightly or a noble one since my fathers helped to conquer the kingdom for William the Norman, was tainted. I felt that, if what was whispered, and muttered, and murmured, was true, I was unfit for England; if false, England was unfit for me. . . . I recollect, some time after, Madame de Staël said to me in Switzerland, "You should not have warred with the world—it will not do—it is too strong always for any individual. " . . . I perfectly acquiesce in the truth of this remark; but the world has done me the honour to begin the war. [148]

Shortly after arriving in Europe, during repairs to the carriage—which had broken down for the third time, Byron began writing the third canto (his favorite, and the most personally revealing) of *Childe Harold's Pilgrimage.* When published later in the year, it caused Byron's great friend and supporter, Sir Walter Scott, to write:

I have just received *Childe Harold*, part 3rd. Lord Byron has more avowedly identified himself with his personage than upon former occasions, and in truth does not affect to separate them. It is wilder and less sweet, I think, than the first part, but contains even darker and more powerful pourings forth of the spirit which boils within him. I question whether there ever lived a man who, without looking abroad for subjects excepting as they produced an effect on himself, has contrived to render long poems turning almost entirely upon the feelings, character, and emotions of the author, so deeply interesting. We gaze on the powerful and ruined mind which he presents us, as on a shattered castle, within whose walls, once intended for nobler guests, sorcerers and wild demons are supposed to hold their Sabbaths. There is something dreadful in reflecting that one gifted so much above his fellow-creatures, should thus labour under some strange mental malady that destroys his peace of mind and happiness, altho' it cannot quench the fire of his genius. I fear the termination will be fatal in one way or other, for it seems impossible that human nature can support the constant working of an imagination so dark and so strong. Suicide or utter insanity is not unlikely to close the scene.[149]

A few weeks after beginning the third canto, in late May 1816, Byron met Percy Bysshe Shelley for the first time. The two poets rented villas near one another, not far from Geneva, and spent long days and evenings together talking, sailing, reading, and critiquing each other's poetry. Byron was "an exceedingly interesting person," wrote Shelley, but "mad as the winds."[150] Claire Clairmont, Mary Godwin's stepsister, with whom Byron had begun an affair just before leaving England, was also living with the Shelleys; when they returned to England in August she left with them, pregnant with Byron's child. The rest of 1816 passed uneventfully, at least by Byron standards. His friend Hobhouse, who visited in September, reported that Byron was "free from all offense, either to God, or man, or woman; no brandy; no very late hours. . . . Neither passion nor perverseness."[151] In the same month Byron began *Manfred*, in November he fell in love, and in December he described his recent times as among the "pleasantest" and "quietest" of any in his life.[152] To Augusta he wrote, in high spirits and humor, "At present I am better—thank Heaven above—& woman beneath."[153]

Moderation, of course, could last only so long, and by January and February 1817 Byron was ill from the dissipations of an increasingly reckless and promiscuous lifestyle. In March he wrote Moore that he had been plagued by sleeplessness and "half-delirium" for a week.[154] June and July found him again in good spirits, living near Venice and writing furiously (including the completion of more than 125 stanzas of the fourth canto of *Childe Harold*). Hobhouse, in October, noted that Byron was "well, and merry and happy."[155] Byron, never one to be paralyzed by convention, sent for his horses so that he could gallop them along the water. Marchand writes that "Byron's horses on the Lido became a byword in the city. When Henry Matthews, brother of Byron's Cambridge friend, visited Venice in 1819, he recorded: 'There are eight horses in Venice: four are of brass, over the gate of the cathedral; and the other four are alive in Lord Byron's stable.' "[156]

January and February 1818 brought with them the early-winter dissolution that had become an almost predictable pattern, dating back to his Cambridge and London days. In May he described "a world of other harlotry,"[157] and in June he moved into the Palazzo Mocenigo on the Grand Canal, where he was joined— rather improbably given the circumstances—by his infant daughter Allegra and her nurse. The following month Byron began writing *Don Juan,* and by August, according to Shelley, he had "changed into the liveliest and happiest looking man I ever met";[158] by December, however, Shelley had altered his view somewhat and, with clear disapproval, wrote that Byron "allows fathers and mothers to bargain with him for their daughters. . . . He associates with wretches . . . who do not scruple to avow practices which are not only not named, but I believe seldom even conceived in England."[159] Perhaps. In any event, Mary Shelley added her concerns to those of her husband by April of the following year (Byron, it must be admitted, had written to his publisher in February that his involvement in the dissipations of Carnival had resulted in his not going to bed until 7:00 or 8:00 A.M. for ten days in a row): "All goes on as badly with the noble poet as ever I fear—he is a lost man if he does not escape soon."[160] Byron, in the meantime, was in the midst of falling in love again—this time with the Countess Guiccioli, a nineteen-year-old girl married to a man in his late fifties. The relationship with Teresa Guiccioli was to prove a long and stable one, certainly as measured against the chaos of the rest of Byron's life. His moods, however, were becoming increasingly melancholic and disturbing to him. Writing to his publisher in London, Byron said, "I am out of sorts—out of nerves—and now and then—(I begin to fear) out of my senses,"[161] and in August he wrote to Hobhouse that he was writing "with ill health and worse nerves." He continued:

> I am so bilious—that I nearly lose my head—and so nervous that I cry for nothing—at least today I burst into tears all alone by myself over a cistern of Gold fishes—which are not pathetic animals. . . . I have been excited—and agitated and exhausted mentally and bodily all this summer—till I really sometimes begin to think not only "that I shall die at top first"—but that the moment is not very remote.—I have had no particular cause of grief—except the usual accompaniments of all unlawful passions.[162]

Byron's melancholy returned in January 1820 and January 1821, as well as intermittently throughout the year. In September he wrote to Teresa describing his depression and its seasonal turns: "This season kills me with sadness every year. You know my last year's melancholy—and when I have that disease of the Spirit—it is better for others that I should keep away. . . . Love me. My soul is like the leaves that fall in autumn—all yellow—*A cantata!*"[163] The next day he wrote her again: "As to my *sadness*—you know that it is in my character—particularly in certain seasons. It is truly a temperamental illness—which sometimes makes me fear the approach of madness—and for this reason, and at these times, I keep away from everyone."[164]

In January 1821 Byron wrote in his journal:

> What is the reason that I have been, all my lifetime, more or less *ennuyé*. . . . [I] presume that it is constitutional,—as well as the waking in low spirits, which I have invariably done for many years. Temperance and exercise, which I have practiced at times, and for a long time together vigorously and violently, made little or no difference. Violent passions did;—when under their immediate influence—it is odd, but—I was in agitated, but *not* in depressed spirits.[165]

The following month he noted again the tendency for his mood to be more despondent in the morning: "I have been considering what can be the reason why I always wake, at a certain hour in the morning, and always in very bad spirits—I may say, in actual despair and despondency, in all respects—even of that which pleased me over night. In about an hour or two, this goes off, and I compose either to sleep again, or, at least, to quiet."[166] In September, as in the preceding year, he was again despairing, describing "a mountain of lead upon my heart";[167] he also noted the worsening nature of his illness, writing that "I have found increasing upon me (without sufficient cause at times) the depression of Spirits (with few intervals) which I have some reason to believe constitutional or inherited."[168] In April 1822, Byron's young daughter Allegra died; he again wrote in his journal that his melancholy was becoming worse. In July Shelley drowned. Byron, who had for a long time been involved in various political causes, became deeply caught up in the Greek independence movement. Always an activist, and one who believed that "a man ought to do something more for mankind than write verses,"[169] he gave freely of his money, his efforts, and ultimately his life. The winter before Byron sailed for Greece, an English physician observed the poet's melancholy and reported that Byron had asked him, "Which is the best and quickest poison?"[170] His sudden and ungovernable rages, which had been part of his emotional makeup since childhood, and which had been especially pronounced during his year with Lady Byron, became more frequent and more furiously irrational. Moore noted that one of the grounds for the charges of insanity brought by Lady Byron against her husband, in addition to fears for her own safety, was the fact that Byron had taken an old watch that he loved and had had for years, and in "a fit of vexation and rage . . . furiously dashed this watch upon the hearth, and ground it to pieces among the ashes with the poker."[171] In the spring of 1823, not long before he sailed for Greece, Lady Blessington described a scene in which Byron had "betrayed such ungovernable rage, as to astonish all who were present." His appearance and conduct, she wrote:

> forcibly reminded me of the description of Rousseau: he declared himself the victim of persecution wherever he went; said that there was a confederacy to pursue and molest him, and uttered a thousand

extravagances, which proved that he was no longer master of himself. I now understood how likely his manner was, under any violent excitement, to give rise to the idea that he was deranged in his intellects. . . . The next day, when we met, Byron . . . asked me if I had not thought him mad the night before: "I assure you," said he, "I often think myself not in my right senses, and this is perhaps the only opinion I have in common with Lady Byron."[172]

Byron had earlier commented to her:

As long as I can remember anything, I recollect being subject to violent paroxysms of rage, so disproportioned to the cause, as to surprise me when they were over, and this still continues. I cannot coolly view anything that excites my feelings; and once the lurking devil in me is roused, I lose all command of myself. I do not recover a good fit of rage for days after: mind, I do not by this mean that the ill-humour continues, as, on the contrary, that quickly subsides, exhausted by its own violence; but it shakes me terribly, and leaves me low and nervous after.[173]

Byron sailed for Greece in July 1823, and in the following month he experienced an even more violent attack of irrationality and rage. One of his companions at the time described the onset of the episode: "He now vented his anger in sundry anathemata and imprecations, until he gradually lashed himself into one of those furious and ungovernable torrents of rage, to which at times he was liable; the paroxysm increased so as almost to divest him of reason."[174] Byron escaped into another room; the resulting scene is described by Marchand:

First the abbot [host for the evening's activity] and then Dr. Bruno attempted to soothe the angry lord, but both were forcibly ejected. "It appeared," Smith wrote, "that Lord Byron was seized with violent spasms in the stomach and liver, and his brain was excited to dangerous excess, so that he would not tolerate the presence of any person in his room. He refused all medicine, and stamped and tore all his clothes and bedding like a maniac. . . ." Trelawny entered next, "but soon returned, saying that it would require ten such as he to hold his lordship for a minute, adding that Lord Byron would not leave an unbroken article in the room." The Doctor asked Smith to get Byron to take a pill. Pushing past a barricade, Smith found Byron "half-undressed, standing in a far corner like a hunted animal at bay. As I looked determined to advance in spite of his imprecations of 'Baih! out, out of my sight! fiends, can I have no peace, no relief from this hell! Leave me, I say!' and he simply lifted the chair nearest to him, and hurled it direct at my head; I escaped as best I could."[175]

The remainder of 1823 and the beginning of 1824 were filled with political and military planning focused on the Greek freedom cause. On his birthday, January 22, 1824, Byron wrote one of his last poems:

On This Day I Complete My Thirty-Sixth Year

Missolonghi, Jan. 22nd, 1824

'Tis time this heart should be unmoved,
    Since others it hath ceased to move:
Yet though I cannot be beloved,
                Still let me love!

My days are in the yellow leaf;
    The flowers and fruits of Love are gone;
The worm—the canker, and the grief
                Are mine alone!

.   .   .   .

If thou regret'st thy Youth, *why live?*
    The land of honourable Death
Is here:—up to the Field, and give
                Away thy Breath!

Seek out—less often sought than found—
    A Soldier's Grave, for thee the best;
Then look around, and choose thy Ground,
                And take thy Rest![176]

Byron contracted a fever and died in April 1824, almost certainly a result not only of the illness but the medical treatment he received for it. He expressed repeatedly during the final days of his life a fear of going mad. To both his physician and servant he said: "I know that without sleep one must either die or go mad. I would sooner die a thousand times,"[177] and it was only by using his fear that he might lose his reason that his doctors were able to persuade Byron to be bled. "Do you suppose that I wish for life?" Byron asked his physician, "I have grown heartily sick of it, and shall welcome the hour I depart from it."[178] At another point he said, "Your efforts to preserve my life will be vain. Die I must: I feel it. Its loss I do not lament; for to terminate my wearisome existence I came to Greece."[179] Byron briefly recovered his mordant wit, however. A servant, told that his master was dying, said: "The Lord's will be done." "Yes," Byron replied, "not mine."[180]

Byron's body was returned to England. The scandal attached to Byron's life was such that the Dean of Westminster Abbey refused him burial there (he was buried near Newstead Abbey instead), and the aristocracy was unwilling to participate directly in the funeral procession. Instead they sent their carriages, a "very long train of splendid carriages [more than forty], all of which . . . were empty."[181] Finally, as recently as 1969, nearly a century and a half after Byron's death, C. Day Lewis, England's poet laureate, put a wreath of laurel and red roses on the white marble tablet newly laid for Byron in the Abbey floor. No doubt Byron would have been gratified, as he would have been vastly amused by the absurd delay and attendant moral outrages. It is also likely, however, that he would have appreciated the two lines chosen for his epitaph, taken from a stanza in *Childe Harold:*

> But I have lived, and have not lived in vain:
> My mind may lose its force, my blood its fire,
> And my frame perish even in conquering pain,
> *But there is that within me which shall tire*
> *Torture and Time, and breathe when I expire;*
> Something unearthly, which they deem not of,
> Like the remembered tone of a mute lyre,
> Shall on their softened spirits sink, and move
> In hearts all rocky now the late remorse of love.[182]

Byron's work was inextricably bound to his life. He has become truly mythic, and his life's story, like a Greek tragedy or a requiem mass, is written and rewritten, within a given form and with a certain ordering of elements: set pieces to be arranged, anecdotes to tell, fragments of poetry from which to choose and then to recite. Upon this framework the thoughts, theories, and speculations of each writer are woven, and into this framework each writer's feelings about Byron—and the human condition—are

Autograph page from stanza 9, canto III, of Byron's Don Juan
(reduced by one-third)

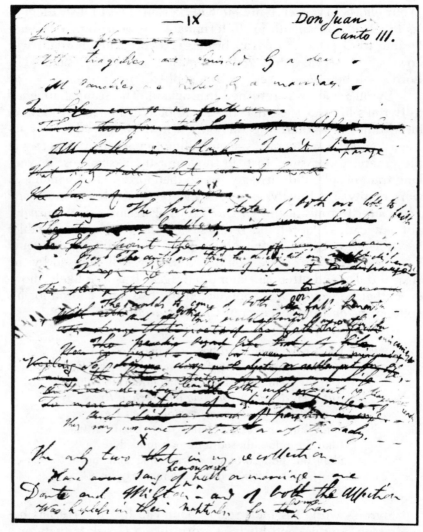

Reworking by Byron of stanza 9, canto III, from Don Juan
CANTO III, ST. 9

1 ~~Life is a play and men~~
  All tragedies are finished by a death,
2 All Comedies are ended by a marriage,
3 ~~For Life can go no further~~
  ~~These two form the last gasp of Passion's breath~~
4 ~~All further is a blank—I won't disparage~~
5 ~~That holy state—but certainly beneath~~
6 ~~The Sun—of human things~~
3 ~~These two are levellers, and human breath~~
    ~~So   These point the epigram of human breath,~~
    ~~Or any~~ The future states of both are left to faith,
4 ~~Though Life and love I like not to disparage~~
    ~~The~~ For authors ~~think~~ description might disparage
                   fear
5 ~~'Tis strange that poets never try to wreathe~~ [*sic?*]
    ~~With eith   'Tis strange that poets of the Catholic faith~~
6 ~~Neer go beyond—   and   but seem to dread miscarriage~~
7 ~~So dramas close with death or settlement for life~~
    ~~Veiling   Leaving the future states of Love and Life~~
    ~~The paradise beyond like that of life~~
8 ~~And neer describing either~~
    ~~To mere conjecture of a devil—and—or wife~~
    ~~And don't say much of paradise or wife~~
5 The worlds to come of both—~~&~~ or fall beneath,
6 And ~~all   both the worlds would blame them for miscarriage~~
    And them both worlds would punish their miscarriage—
7 ~~So leaving both with priest & prayerbook ready~~
    So leaving ~~Clerg both a~~ each their Priest and prayerbook ready,
8 They say no more of death or of the Lady.

SOURCE: Truman Guy Steffan. *Byron's Don Juan: The Making of a Masterpiece.* Austin: University of Texas Press, 1971, p. 345.

projected. Byron commands in death what he commanded in life: love, hate, respect, contempt, loyalty, and disdain—in short, controversy. Seldom, however, does Byron elicit indifference. In his own time, for example, *Blackwood's Edinburgh Magazine* published an article stating that he was "one of the most remarkable men to whom [England] has had the honour and disgrace of giving birth." "It appears," the authors wrote, "as if *this miserable man*, having exhausted every species of sensual gratification—having drained the cup of sin even to its bitterest dregs, were resolved to shew us that he is no longer a human being, even in his frailties; but *a cool unconcerned fiend*."[183] Byron fared even less well at the hands of William Hazlitt, a contemporary critic and essayist, who, while admitting that Byron was "never dull, or tedious,"[184] vehemently objected to the shadow Byron's temperament cast over his work, as well as his bent for making "man in his own image, woman after his own heart."[185] These criticisms were captured in a particularly good description of extreme Byronism:

> He hangs the cloud, the film of his existence over all outward things—sits in the centre of his thoughts, and enjoys dark night, bright day, the glitter and the gloom "in cell monastic"—we see the mournful pall, the crucifix, the death's heads, the faded chaplet of flowers, the gleaming tapers, the agonized growl of genius, the wasted form of beauty—but we are still imprisoned in a dungeon, a curtain intercepts our view, we do not breathe freely the air of nature or of our own thoughts.[186]

His influence on other writers and artists, however, was profoundly different. Tennyson related to William Allingham: "When I heard of his death . . . I went out to the back of the house and cut on a wall with my knife, 'Lord Byron is dead,' "[187] and Goethe acknowledged that "Byron alone I admit to a place by my side."[188] To John Ruskin "Byron wrote, as easily as a hawk flies";[189] "Byron," he said, "was to be my master in verse, as Turner in colour."[190] "Here at last," he continued, "I have found a man who spoke only of what he had seen, and known; and spoke without exaggeration, without mystery, without enmity, and without mercy."[191] More recently W. H. Auden stated his belief that, "Whatever its faults, *Don Juan* is the most original poem in English,"[192] and Byron was the only poet singled out for a separate chapter in Bertrand Russell's *History of Western Philosophy*. The list of writers, artists, and composers who were directly inspired by Byron's life and poetry is almost without peer; it includes Hector Berlioz, Alexander Pushkin, J. M. W. Turner, Robert Schumann, Victor Hugo, Alfred-Victor de Vigny, Alfred de Musset, Giuseppe Verdi, Gaetano Donizetti, Franz Liszt, Peter Ilich Tchaikovsky, Arnold Schoenberg, Gioacchino Rossini, Charles Baudelaire, and Virgil Thomson.[193] Not surprisingly, most of those influenced by Byron were themselves intensely emotional and inclined toward the Romantic.

Byron, for all his Romanticism, thought and wrote with remarkable clarity, maintaining an unrelenting grasp on the realities of both his own and human nature. His biographers have made this point repeatedly. Moore, who was also a close friend, noted: "Born with strong affections and ardent passions, the world had, from first to last, too firm a hold on his sympathies to let imagination altogether usurp the place of reason,"[194] and Leslie Marchand wrote that Byron was the "most completely realistic of all the romantics" because "he accepted the romantic urge as a part of human nature without pretending it was more than a dream."[195] In a related vein, but with a more interpersonal emphasis, Doris Langley Moore has made the point that Byron's "was a singularly reasonable mind";[196] this comes through again and again in his journals, what is known of his conversations, and most especially in his letters. A particularly impressive example is contained in a letter written by Byron to his wife several years after their separation. In it he asked that she review what he had written about her in his memoirs (which, unfortunately, were burned by his publisher and friends after he died):

I could wish you to see, read and mark any part or parts that do not appear to coincide with the truth.—The truth I have always stated—but there are two ways of looking at it—and your way may not be mine.—I have never revised the papers since they were written.—You may read them—and mark what you please. . . . You will find nothing to flatter you—nothing to lead you to the most remote supposition that we could ever have been—or be happy together.—But I do not choose to give to another generation statements which we cannot arise from the dust to prove or disprove—without letting you see fairly & fully what I look upon you to have been—and what I depict you as being.—If seeing this—you can detect what is false—or answer what is charged—do so—*your mark* shall not be erased.[197]

One of the many things that makes Byron so interesting is the sheer power of his life and emotions. To focus exclusively, or even largely, on his psychopathology—other than to use it to understand him and his work—would be to make a mockery of his complexity, imagination, and vast energies. His personal discipline was extraordinary; his technical discipline, although overshadowed by the more Romantic notion of effortless poetry written "as easily as the hawk flies" (and not helped by the fact that he seems to have published, with little discrimination, virtually everything he ever wrote) was also impressive. Byron's extensive reworking of a single stanza from *Don Juan*, for example, is shown here in its first draft and an accompanying diagrammatic outline. "His reason was punctuated, even disturbed, by passion," wrote Alan Bold. "But whatever he was in person he was not, as an artist, passion's slave. In the poetry Byron masks his passion and makes it into endurable art."[198] Byron himself wrote: "Yet, see, he mastereth himself, and makes/His torture tributary to his will."[199]

In the end Byron brought a deeply redemptive spirit to the problems of despair, ennui, uncertainty, and disillusionment. In writing about another, he more finally described himself:

> The apostle of affliction, he who threw
> Enchantment over passion, and from woe
> Wrung overwhelming eloquence, first drew
> The breath which made him wretched; yet he knew
> How to make madness beautiful, and cast
> O'er erring deeds and thoughts, a heavenly hue
> Of words.[200]

Byron's life and work were profoundly shaped by many things, not least of which were the traits passed on to him by his ancestors. He was not alone among writers and artists in having to play out the cards of a troubled inheritance.

6.
GENEALOGIES
OF THESE
HIGH MORTAL
MISERIES

The Inheritance of Manic-Depressive Illness

The most poisonous reptile of the marsh perpetuates his kind as inevitably as the sweetest songster of the grove; so, equally with every felicity, all miserable events do naturally beget their like. . . . To trail the genealogies of these high mortal miseries . . . we must needs give in to this: that the gods themselves are not for ever glad. The ineffaceable, sad birth-mark in the brow of man, is but the stamp of sorrow in the signers.

—HERMAN MELVILLE[1]

Tree and Cathedral Graveyard, St. Andrews, Scotland. Alain Moreau

Manic-depressive illness is a genetic disease, running strongly, not to say pervasively, in some families while absent in most. Robert Burton, as early as the seventeenth century, wrote unequivocally, "I need not therefore make any doubt of Melancholy, but that it is an hereditary disease,"[2] a view held by most medical observers long prior and long subsequent to his time. The inexorable passing on of madness from generation to generation is an ancient literary theme, as well as a traditional cultural and medical belief. Alfred, Lord Tennyson, who, as we shall see, had good reason to cast a brooding eye on his family's issue, spoke of a "taint of blood"; Lord Byron, of like vein but in a slightly different context, felt that "Some curse hangs over me and mine." And Edgar Allan Poe, of course, with a high sense of Gothic desolation and foreboding, described these family taints and curses in *The Fall of the House of Usher:*

> During the whole of a dull, dark, and soundless day in the autumn of the year, when the clouds hung oppressively low in the heavens, I had been passing alone, on horseback, through a singularly dreary

tract of country; and at length found myself, as the shades of the evening drew on, within view of the melancholy House of Usher. . . .

Its proprietor, Roderick Usher . . . spoke of acute bodily illness—of a mental disorder which oppressed him . . .

I was at once struck with an incoherence—an inconsistency . . . an excessive nervous agitation. . . . His action was alternately vivacious and sullen. His voice varied rapidly from a tremulous indecision (when the animal spirits seemed utterly in abeyance) to that species of energetic concision . . . which may be observed in the lost drunkard, or the irreclaimable eater of opium, during the periods of his most intense excitement. . . .

It was, he said, a constitutional and a family evil, and one for which he despaired to find a remedy—[3]

Modern medicine gives credence to these literary notions of familial madness; the genetic basis for manic-depressive illness is especially compelling, indeed almost incontrovertible.[4] Studies of identical and fraternal twins provide one strong source of evidence for the hereditability of manic-depressive illness. (Identical, or monozygotic, twins share the same genetic material whereas fraternal, or dizygotic, twins share only half their genes [in this, then, they are no different from other siblings]; in contrast, both types of twins share a generally similar environment.) If one twin has manic-depressive illness, the other is far more likely (70 to 100 percent) to have it if the twins are identical than if they are fraternal (approximately 20 percent).[5] These concordance rates (the likelihood of a second twin being affected) for bipolar illness are much higher than those for unipolar depressive illness.[6] In an attempt to determine the relative importance of genetic as opposed to environmental influences, a few adoption studies have been carried out. A review of a total of twelve pairs of monozygotic twins who were reared apart from the time of infancy—and in which at least one of the twins had been diagnosed as having manic-depressive illness—found that eight of the twelve pairs were concordant for the illness. This suggests the strong influence of genetic factors.[7]

In family studies of mood disorders, researchers look for familial patterns in occurrence of mania, depression, and suicide. The many studies of this nature that have been done are quite consistent in showing that manic-depressive illness is indeed familial; the rate of manic-depressive and depressive illness in first-degree relatives of patients (that is, parents, siblings, and children) is far higher than the rate found in relatives of control groups.[8] Individuals who have manic-depressive illness are quite likely to have both bipolar and unipolar relatives. There is also some evidence that bipolar II illness (major depressive illness with a history of hypomania rather than mania) "breeds true"; that is, there is an increased risk of bipolar II illness among relatives of bipolar II patients.[9] Based on an extensive study of affectively ill patients Dr. Elliot Gershon, chief of the Clinical Neurogenetics Branch of the National Institute of Mental Health, estimates that if one parent has manic-depressive illness and the other parent is unaffected the risk of affective illness in the child (either depressive or manic-depressive illness) is 28 percent. If, however, both parents have affective illness and one of them is bipolar, the risk of major depression or manic-depressive illness rises dramatically, to almost 75 percent.[10] There is a tendency for individuals with mood disorders to marry one another—"assortative mating"—and it has tremendous significance not only genetically but also psychologically for the children of such marriages.

A vigorous pursuit of the actual gene or genes responsible for manic-depressive illness is now underway. In 1987 a group of investigators studying an Amish community in Pennsylvania reported a link between a dominant gene they thought conferred a predisposition to manic-depressive illness and chromosome 11;[11] at roughly the same time another team of researchers, studying an Israeli population, reported possible linkage on the X chromosome.[12] Subsequent research has brought into question the validity of both the chromosome 11 and X chromosome findings,[13] but few scientists in the field doubt that the gene—or, far more likely, the genes—for manic-depressive illness will be found. Interestingly, a significant number of individuals who have the gene for manic-depressive illness, perhaps 20 or 30 percent, will never develop the disease. This so-called "incomplete penetrance," together with the tremendous range in the severity of the expression of the disease, raises central questions about the interactions between genetic predisposition, the physical and psychological environment (including stress, alcohol and other drugs, sleep loss, changing patterns of light, and psychological loss or trauma), and other protective or potentiating genes. Pat Conroy, in his novel *The Prince of Tides,* describes how the complexities of madness played themselves out in one family:

> I thought about how we had all arrived at this point in time, what benedictions and aggrievements each of us had carried from the island and how each of us had an indisputable and unchangeable role in our family's grotesque melodrama. From earliest childhood, Savannah had been chosen to bear the weight of the family's accumulated psychotic energy. Her luminous sensitivity left her open to the violence and disaffection of our household and we used her to store the bitterness of our mordant chronicle. I could see it now: One member of the family, by a process of artificial but deadly selection, is nominated to be the lunatic, and all neurosis, wildness, and displaced suffering settles like dust in the eaves and porches of that tenderest, most vulnerable psyche. Craziness attacks the softest eyes and hamstrings the gentlest flanks. When was Savannah chosen to be the crazy one? I thought. When was the decision made and was it by acclamation and had I, her twin, agreed to the decision? Had I played a part in stringing up the bleeding angels in her room and could I help cut those angels down?[14]

We next look at several writers, composers, and artists who were deeply affected by their "taint of blood." Apart from an individual's own history of recurrent, severe, and fluctuating mood states, the most useful information in making a diagnosis of mood disorders is a family history of manic-depressive illness, severe depressive illness, or suicide. The family histories of these creative individuals— histories of melancholia, mania, and suicide—not only provide diagnostic and psychological insights into the writers, artists, and composers under discussion, but they bring sharply into focus the implications that the genetic basis of manic-depressive illness has in the understanding of the disease, its treatment, and its role in society.

"Must I too creep to the hollow . . . ?"

ALFRED, LORD TENNYSON

I hate the dreadful hollow behind the little wood,
Its lips in the field above are dabbled with blood-red heath,
The red-ribb'd ledges drip with a silent horror of blood,
And Echo there, whatever is ask'd her, answers 'Death.'

For there in the ghastly pit long since a body was
    found,
His who had given me life—O father! O God! was it
    well?—
Mangled, and flatten'd, and crush'd, and dinted
    into the ground:
There yet lies the rock that fell with him when he fell.

.   .   .   .

What! am I raging alone as my father raged in his mood?
Must *I* too creep to the hollow and dash myself down
    and die
Rather than hold by the law that I made, nevermore
    to brood
On a horror of shatter'd limbs . . . ?

—ALFRED, LORD TENNYSON[15]

"Maud or the Madness," Tennyson wrote about the poem quoted above, "is a little Hamlet, the history of a morbid poetic soul . . . the heir of madness."[16] It was Tennyson's favorite poem; he would recite it over and over again—bleakly, tirelessly—to family and friends. Obsessed by the "black blood" of the Tennysons, he struggled throughout his life not only with fierce and recurrent depressions but with the fear of going mad as well. Even the most fleeting glance over the Tennyson bloodline makes clear how sane his fears of madness were. Melancholy, violence, and insanity can be traced at least as far back as the seventeenth-century branches of the Clayton and Tennyson families.[17] Both Alfred's father and grandfather had recurrent attacks of uncontrollable rage and depression, and at least one of his paternal aunts, probably both,

suffered from depressive illness. Tennyson's father's brother was described by Alfred's grandson, Sir Charles Tennyson, as also having inherited his father's melancholic "fretfulness and irritability."[18] But it was George Clayton Tennyson, father of the poet, who suffered most and caused the most suffering: "The black blood which flowed in the veins of all the Tennysons had in his case turned to bile."[19] Robert Bernard Martin, in his excellent biography of Alfred Tennyson, describes the elder Tennyson as having been "ungovernable" from an early age, "inconstant in mood," "vacillating between frenzy and lethargy," an alcohol abuser, and suffering from debilitating, black depressions.[20] Later in his life George Tennyson also experienced "fits," whose nature remains unclear. Interestingly, Alfred described having seizurelike trances but, although terrified of inheriting his father's "epilepsy," he was reassured by his physician that he did not in fact have the disease.

Eventually, George Tennyson (Alfred's father) became insane, endangering his own life as well as those of others. Professor Martin writes:

> He kept a large knife and a loaded gun in his room, and he was with difficulty persuaded not to fire the gun through the kitchen window. In his mania he often had his time confused and probably thought he was back in Cambridge as an undergraduate, firing through the chapel window of the college. . . . When he was persuaded to give up the gun, he said he would take the knife and kill Frederick [his son] by stabbing him in the jugular vein and the heart. "We may thank God that we do not live in a barbarous Country," said Frederick, "or we should have murdered each other before this."[21]

The troubled inheritance of the Tennysons seems to have taken its most virulent root in the males of the family: Alfred's father, grandfather, and two great-grandfathers, as well as all six of his brothers, suffered from insanity, severe melancholia, incendiary tempers, or manic-depressive illness. One of Alfred's brothers, Edward, was confined to an insane asylum for almost sixty years and eventually died from manic exhaustion. Another, Septimus, "the most morbid of all the Tennysons," was described by Alfred in a concerned letter written to their uncle: "I have very little doubt but that his mind will prove as deranged as Edward's . . . I have studied the minds of my own family—I know how delicately they

Alfred, Lord Tennyson
Partial Family History

Clayton

Tennyson

Christopher
1687–1737
imprisoned for
violence and death
threats

George
1694–1741

Ralph
"long been suffering a
despondency and had not
left his bed for two years"

Michael
1721–1796

William

David
d. 1765
"liable to violent
outbursts of passion";
declared insane

Christopher
"a mind on the
verge of
insanity"

Elizabeth

Mary
1753–1825

Anne

George
1750–1835
"choleric rages" and recurrent
melancholia; unpredictable temper;
"too susceptible of melancholy from
every passing cloud"

Charles (d'Eyncourt)
1784–1861
"inherited his father's instability and fretfulness"; spendthrift
tendencies; expansive, grandiose activities and interests

Elizabeth
b. 1776
recurrent bouts
of depression

Mary
b. 1777
"ferocious pessimism";
constant quarreling
and gloominess

■ (Bipolar) Manic-depressive illness

◐ Recurrent depressive illness

▨ Rage, unstable moods, and/or insanity

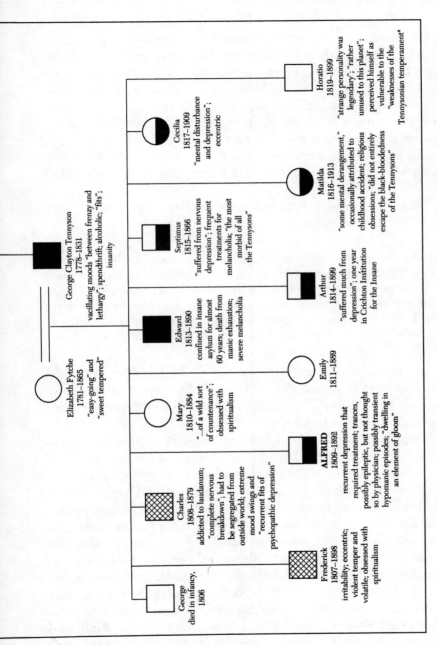

BIOGRAPHICAL SOURCES: Tennyson, 1897; Nicolson, 1947; Tennyson and Dyson, 1974; Martin, 1980; Tennyson, 1981. See text note 17.

George Clayton Tennyson
1778–1831
vacillating moods "between frenzy and lethargy"; spendthrift; alcoholic; "fits"; insanity

Elizabeth Fytche
1781–1865
"easy-going and sweet tempered"

George
died in infancy,
1806

Frederick
1807–1898
irritability; eccentric; violent temper and volatile; obsessed with spiritualism

Charles
1808–1879
addicted to laudanum; "complete nervous breakdown"; had to be segregated from outside world; extreme mood swings and "recurrent fits of psychopathic depression"

ALFRED
1809–1892
recurrent depression that required treatment; trances, possibly epileptic, but not thought so by physician; possibly transient hypomanic episodes; "dwelling in an element of gloom"

Mary
1810–1884
"...of a wild sort of countenance"; obsessed with spiritualism

Emily
1811–1889

Edward
1813–1890
confined in insane asylum for almost 60 years; death from manic exhaustion; severe melancholia

Arthur
1814–1889
"suffered much from depression"; one year in Crichton Institution for the Insane

Septimus
1815–1866
"suffered from nervous depression"; frequent treatments for melancholia; "the most morbid of all the Tennysons"

Matilda
1816–1913
"some mental derangement," occasionally attributed to childhood accident; religious obsessions; "did not entirely escape the black-bloodedness of the Tennysons"

Cecilia
1817–1909
"mental disturbance and depression"; eccentric

Horatio
1819–1899
"strange personality was legendary"; "rather unused to this planet"; perceived himself as vulnerable to the "weaknesses of the Tennysonian temperament"

are organized— . . . At present his symptoms are not unlike those with which poor Edward's unhappy derangement began—he is subject to fits of the most gloomy despondency."[22] And, very early on in Alfred's own life, in 1831, his closest friend Arthur Hallam, noting that Alfred's mind "certainly is in a distressing state," wrote: "Fare thee well. I hope you do fare well, and make head against 'despondency and madness.' "[23] Alfred's uncle Charles appears to have shared in the family temperament, as did Charles's son, George Hildeyard d'Eyncourt, and Julius, son of Alfred's eldest brother Frederick.

Alfred Tennyson's own two sons, Hallam and Lionel, were markedly different in temperament and interests:

> Hallam was to become a highly conventional man, obedient, careful, devoted to his parents almost beyond credibility. Lionel was far more interesting, with some poetic ability, a mercurial personality, a talent for getting into scrapes, and a charm that his elder brother never had. The headmaster of their first school correctly described them: 'Lionel the more brilliant, Hallam by far the more accurate.'[24]

Lionel, "the heir of the Tennyson's black blood,"[25] in turn had three sons, one of whom also "inherited the mental instability of Somersby and Tealby"[26] (the sixth generation of Tennyson men documented here to be affected).

Threaded in and around the Tennysonian temperament was an equally pervasive, similarly extraordinary, family bent and passion for poetry. Three of the Tennyson brothers together published a book of their poems prior to matriculating at Cambridge; as undergraduates they received the university's major literary prizes: Frederick, who went on to publish three volumes of verse, received the Cambridge prize for Greek odes; Charles, who also published several subsequent volumes of verse and who was regarded by both Coleridge and Wordsworth as the most promising of the Tennyson brothers, received the Cambridge prize for his English translation of the classics; and Alfred, who went on to write *In Memoriam, Tears, Idle Tears, Ulysses, Idylls of the King,* and *Maud,* received the University Prize for poetry. Arthur, Septimus, Edward, Mary, Cecilia, and Emily also wrote verse, and Emily's granddaughter became a poet and novelist. Horatio, the youngest of the Tennyson children, although displaying "no literary tastes whatsoever"[27] and who was wonderfully described by Edward FitzGerald as "rather unused to this planet,"[28] had a son with considerable literary ability. Alfred Tennyson's grandson noted:

> The Somersby Tennysons could never have arisen in any previous age and the likes of them are not likely to be seen again. They would all now presumably be classed as, in some degree, manic depressives; they all succumbed at some time or other and for varying periods to some form of religious obsession. . . . Though only three attempted to publish, all wrote verse and one feels that, given Alfred's concentration and stamina, all might have found honourable places in the roll of British poets. . . .
>
> Canon H. D. Rawnsley in 1892 asked the eighty-five-year-old Frederick Tennyson to which of their ancestors the poetic genius of the Somersby Tennysons could be attributed. Frederick replied from Jersey in a clear bold hand and in characteristically rotund, but slightly incorrect, phrases:
>
>> With respect to your query as to what fountain of inspiration the Tennysons are indebted, the Creator himself only could give a perfectly definitive answer. From many generations of ancestors posterity derives collective influences, and therefore it is difficult to assign to any single individual what may have been mingled in an accumulated form in the last inheritor.[29]

As for the poetic inheritance of Alfred Tennyson: He was, wrote T.S. Eliot—himself no stranger to melancholy—"not only a minor Virgil, he is also with Virgil as Dante saw him, a Virgil among the Shades, the saddest of all English poets."[30]

"The storm-tossed body and soul"

ROBERT SCHUMANN

And so it is throughout human life—the goal we have attained is no longer a goal, and we yearn, and strive, and aim ever higher and higher, until the eyes close in death, and the storm-tossed body and soul lie slumbering in the grave.

—ROBERT SCHUMANN[31]

The youngest of five children, German composer Robert Schumann was born one year after Alfred Tennyson, in 1810. A melancholic and restless streak appears to have come from both sides of his family. His father, August Schumann, was an author, translator, and publisher; from him Robert inherited an early and sustained passion for poetry and literature. Among the first to translate Lord Byron's poetry, including *Childe Harold's Pilgrimage*, into German, Schumann's father was of "exquisite sensibility"; his first reading of Edward Young's poetry "took so strong hold upon him that he believed himself near madness."[32] The elder Schumann was also an unsettled, anxious, ambitious, and deeply brooding man who reputedly had a nervous breakdown, from which he never fully recovered, in the year of Robert's birth. Like his son, August Schumann worked in phenomenal bursts of energy and productivity; during one eighteen-month period he wrote, among other things, seven novels. Robert's mother had recurrent attacks of depression, the dark moods of which were captured graphically in a letter he wrote to her in 1829: "Oh, mother, again you can't tear yourself away from the grandfather chair, you have been sitting there for two everlasting hours, saying not a word, singing a dead old song, stroking up and down the window with your hand."[33] Her morbid letters, he said, left a "dreadful discord" in his soul.[34]

Other members of his family also showed signs of the mental instability that was to haunt Schumann from the time he was eighteen until his death in an insane asylum at the age of forty-six. His sister committed suicide, as did a physician cousin on his father's side; one of Schumann's sons went insane in his early twenties and was confined to an asylum for thirty-one years; yet another became a morphine addict.[35]

Schumann himself was an intensely emotional man, soft-spoken, reflective, gentle, idealistic, absent- and dreamy-minded, and generous. He was well known, particularly during his days as a law student at the University of Leipzig, for his love of champagne and cigars, his financial extravagance, and his fervor for music and poetry. As early as his student years he began to experience the violent mood changes that characterized much of the rest of his life. When he was eighteen Schumann described the first episode of what he called madness: "My heart pounds sickeningly and I turn pale . . . often I feel as if I were dead . . . I seem to be losing my mind. I did have my mind but I thought I had lost it. I had actually gone mad."[36] The following year, 1829, found Schumann in a completely different state—ebullient, active, and highly productive: "But if you only knew how my mind is always working, and how my symphonies would have reached op. 100, if I had but written them down . . . sometimes I am so full of music, and so overflowing with melody, that I find it simply impossible to write down anything."[37]

Although one tends to associate Robert Schumann with melancholic thoughts and writings, there was clearly much of the joyous in him. During his twenties, at various times, he described those feelings: "I am so fresh in soul and spirit that life gushes and bubbles around me in a thousand springs. This is the work of divine fantasy and her magic wand";[38] and, after publishing his first composition, he wrote: "I doubt if being a bridegroom will be in the same class with these first joys of being a composer. The entire heavens of my heart are hung full of hopes and presentiments. As proudly as the doge of Venice once married the sea, I now, for the first time, marry the wide world."[39]

As music increasingly dominated his life, law school—ever an endurance and rarely actually attended—became intolerable. Schumann wrote: "Chilly jurisprudence, with its ice-cold definitions, would crush the life out of me from the onset. Medicine I will not, theology I cannot, study."[40] He finally received permission to study piano with Friedrich Wieck, father of Clara, the woman Schumann was eventually to marry after many years of separations and crises. Wieck's vitriolic opposition to their marriage was based in part on paternal jealousy and in part on his concerns about Schumann's reputation for heavy drinking and financial irresponsibility. Schumann wrote to Clara in 1837: "My interview with your father was terrible. He was frigid, hostile, confused, and contradictory at once. Truly his method of stabbing is original, for he drives in the hilt as well as the blade."[41]

They finally married in 1840, Schumann's great "year of song." He composed more than 130 songs during what was undoubtedly one of the most productive periods in the career of any composer in the history of music. By that time Schumann's highly disruptive and painful mood swings had become part of his life. In his work as founding editor and critic of the *Neue Leipziger Zeitschrift für*

Musik, Schumann introduced into his public writings two characters who represented the conflicting, but often complementary
sides of his stormy personality. Florestan was portrayed as impulsive, wildly energetic, impassioned, decisive, masculine, high-
spirited, and iconoclastic. Eusebius, in contrast, was the gentler,
more melancholic, pious, introspective, and inward-gazing part of
himself. Schumann's extraordinary ability to put his feelings into
his music was closely matched by his ability to express them in
words. In 1838 he described in a letter to Clara the terrors of his
emotional life five years earlier:

> As early as 1833 a certain melancholy made itself felt. . . . In the
> night between the 17th and 18th of October I was seized with the
> worst fear a man can have, the worst punishment Heaven can in-
> flict—the fear of losing one's reason. It took so strong a hold of me
> that consolation and prayer, defiance and derision, were equally
> powerless to subdue it. Terror drove me from place to place. My
> breath failed me as I pictured my brain paralyzed. Ah, Clara! no one
> knows the suffering, the sickness, the despair, except those so
> crushed. In my terrible agitation I went to a doctor and told him
> everything—how my senses often failed me so that I did not know
> which way to turn in my fright, how I could not be certain of not
> taking my own life when in this helpless condition.[42]

A diary entry in 1834 notes simply: "I was obsessed with the
thought of going mad."[43] Periods of remarkable creativity, productivity, and high spirits were woven into the otherwise frighteningly
sad fabric of Schumann's life. In 1841, Schumann's most important
year of symphonic composition, Clara wrote in her diary: "On
Tuesday Robert finished his symphony; so begun and ended in four
days."[44] Schumann himself described his work during this period:
"It was born in a fiery hour. . . . I wrote the Symphony in that
flush of Spring which carries a man away even in his old age and
comes over him anew every year."[45] But the fiery times for Schumann were always outweighed by the melancholic. In 1845 he
described his gradual recovery from yet another breakdown to his
friend and fellow composer, Felix Mendelssohn: "I have a great
deal to tell you—what a bad winter I have had; how a complete
nervous collapse, with an onslaught of terrifying thoughts in its
train brought me to the verge of despair, that the prospect is

pleasanter now, and music, too, is beginning again to sound within me, and I hope soon to be quite restored."[46]

The year 1849 was another one of extraordinary productivity for Schumann. *Manfred*, composed during this time, was based upon Byron's melancholic poem of the same name. Tellingly, Schumann wrote: "Never before have I devoted myself with such love and outlay of energy to any composition as that of *Manfred*."[47] Looking back over the year he wrote with awful prophecy of the tragic events to come: "I have been extremely busy this whole year. One has to work as long as the daylight is there."[48] During that same period of time he wrote with characteristic understatement and modesty: "I cannot see that there is anything remarkable about composing a symphony in a month. Handel wrote a complete oratorio in that time."[49]

For Schumann there was not much daylight left, and "with the shadow of his insanity already hanging over him [Tchaikovsky's description],"[50] he wrote in 1849:

> Lately I was looking for information about Düsseldorf in an old geography book, and there I found mentioned as noteworthy: "three convents and a lunatic asylum." To the first I have no objection if it must be so; but it was disagreeable to me to read the last. . . . I am obliged to avoid carefully all melancholy impressions of the kind. And if we musicians live so often, as you know we do, on sunny heights, the sadness of reality cuts all the deeper when it lies naked before our eyes.[51]

In 1854 his illness, perhaps complicated by general paresis (although recent evidence suggests Schumann may never have contracted syphilis),[52] became particularly virulent. His wife described in her diary what Schumann no longer was able to:

> In the night, not long after we had gone to bed, Robert got up and wrote down a melody which, he said, the angels had sung to him. Then he lay down again and talked deliriously the whole night, staring at the ceiling all the time. When morning came, the angels transformed themselves into devils and sang horrible music, telling him he was a sinner and that they were going to cast him into hell. He became hysterical, screaming in agony that they were pouncing

Robert Schumann
Partial Family History

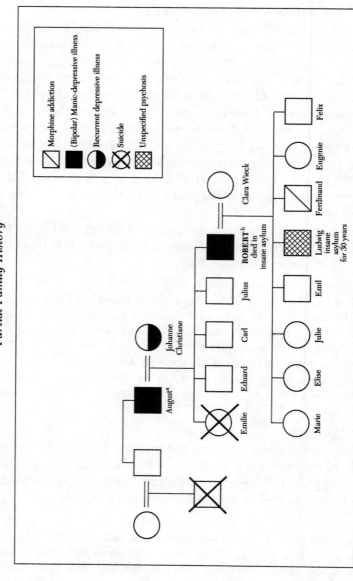

[a] Probable manic-depressive illness but information is limited.
[b] Self-starvation; intentionality unclear.

BIOGRAPHICAL SOURCES: Garrison, 1934; Slater and Meyer, 1959; Sadie (Ed.), 1980; Taylor, 1982; Ostwald, 1983, 1985; Reich, 1985. See text note 35.

on him like tigers and hyenas, and seizing him in their claws. The two doctors who came only just managed to control him.[53]

Clara wrote this description on February 10; for the next several days his moods continued to fluctuate wildly from one extreme to another. On February 27 Schumann rushed out of the house, sobbing and without an overcoat, and threw himself into the Rhine. He was rescued and placed in the insane asylum in Endenich, where—never having left it—he died of self-starvation in 1856.

Franz Liszt, having observed Schumann's struggles with his complicated and self-lacerating temperament, added his own poignant commentary:

No one can fail to recognize that instead of venturing, conquering, discovering, Schumann strove to reconcile his romantic personality, torn between joy and pain, and often driven by a dark urge towards the fantastic and the bizarre, with the modalities of classical form, whereas the clarity and symmetry of such forms lay beyond his characteristic spirit. . . . This struggle against his true nature must have caused him great suffering, and it has stained even his most beautiful pages with the blood that has flowed from the open wound.[54]

"A whiff of melancholy, things that sound a knell"

THE JAMES FAMILY

The natural inheritance of everyone who is capable of spiritual life is an unsubdued forest where the wolf howls and the obscene bird of night chatters.

—HENRY JAMES, SR.[55]

Unsuspectedly from the bottom of every fountain of pleasure . . . something bitter rises up: a touch of nausea, a falling dead of the delight, a whiff of melancholy, things that sound a knell, for

fugitive as they may be, they bring a feeling of coming from a
deeper region and often have an appalling convincingness.

—WILLIAM JAMES[56]

Experience is never limited, and it is never complete; it is an
immense sensibility, a kind of huge spiderweb of the finest silken
threads suspended in the chamber of consciousness, and catching
every airborne particle in its tissue.

—HENRY JAMES[57]

Henry James, Sr.—writer, theologian, and philosopher, as
well as father of the psychologist and the novelist—was born in
1811 to an enormously successful and cyclonically active businessman, William James, who had emigrated from Ireland and settled
in Albany. His grandson, novelist Henry James, recounts in his
autobiography:

> Our grandfather's energy, exercised in Albany from the great
> year 1789, appears promptly to have begun with his arrival there.
> "Everywhere we see his footsteps, turn where we may, and these are
> the results of his informing mind and his vast wealth. His plans of
> improvement embraced the entire city, and there is scarcely a street
> or a square which does not exhibit some mark of his hand or some
> proof of his opulence. With the exception of Mr. Astor," this delight-
> ful report [New York Evening Post, 1832] goes on to declare, "no
> other business man has acquired so great a fortune in this State
> [three million dollars]."[58]

This singular success, F. O. Matthiesen points out, was in bitter
contrast to the fate of Allan Melvill—another New York businessman who was to be father to a famous writer—who died bankrupt
and insane in the same year. Both men, however, were to pass on
their powerful temperaments to their sons.

By all accounts Henry James, Sr., was a roaming, restless,
idealistic, and evangelical man, an expansive enthusiast whose
"ballooning mind was filled with a heady cosmic gas that defied
condensation."[59] He was also a fiercely and affectionately involved
father who crisscrossed the Atlantic with his family in a frenetic
quest for an ideal and "sensuous" education for his children. Of

"high-strung sensibility,"[60] he wrote in his autobiography that his "earliest sensible foundations" were laid in a "horror of great darkness."[61] While still young he became addicted to alcohol and, during his early thirties, suffered from a nervous breakdown that lasted for more than two years:

> In a lightning-flash as it were—'fear came upon me, and trembling, which made all my bones to shake.' To all appearance it was a perfectly insane and abject terror, without ostensible cause, and only to be accounted for, to my perplexed imagination, by some damned shape squatting invisible to me within the precincts of the room, and raying out from his fetid personality influences fatal to life . . . this ghastly condition of mind continued with me, with gradually lengthening intervals of relief, for two years, and even longer.[62]

During this period of intense desolation, Henry James, Sr., like so many others of his era including the Tennysons, turned to the mystical writings of Emanuel Swedenborg, a Swedish scientist, philosopher, and theologian. Of similarly expansive mind and like temperament, he had himself experienced psychological crises of, to say the least, great mood and moment. Swedenborg was convinced that he had conversed with the inhabitants of all the planets (except Uranus and Neptune, which had not yet been discovered) and thought he could discern witches.[63] In 1886 British psychiatrist H. Maudsley described the controversy and impact of Swedenborg's (almost certainly manic) hallucinations on his religious followers, as well as on his dissenters:

> The visitation was the forerunner of an attack of acute mania—so overwhelming the pressure of supernatural influx upon the mental equilibrium of the natural man—which lasted for a few weeks; on recovery from which he was what he remained for the rest of his life—either, as his disciples think, a holy seer endowed with the faculty of conversing with spirits and angels in heaven and hell, and in whom the Lord Jesus Christ made His second coming for the institution of a new Church, described in the Revelation under the figure of the New Jerusalem; or, as those who are not disciples think, an interesting and harmless monomaniac, who, among many foolish sayings, said many wise and good things, attesting the wreck of a mind of large original endowment, intellectual and moral.[64]

Henry James, Sr., passed on his melancholic strain, as well as his vastness of spirit and energies, to at least four of his five children. William, the eldest, was, like his father before him, passionately committed to the problems of philosophy, religion, and psychology. Author most importantly of *The Principles of Psychology* and *The Varieties of Religious Experience*, William James as a young man had hoped to continue his studies of painting with John La Farge and William Morris Hunt in Newport. (A strong artistic streak in the James family was later remarked upon by Henry Junior, William's younger brother, the novelist: "No less than three of our father's children, with two of the grandsons to add to these, and with a collateral addendum representing seven, in all, of our grandfather's, William James', descendants in three generations, should have found the artistic career in general and the painter's trade in particular irresistibly solicit them.")[65] Instead, his father encouraged him toward a more scientific education; in 1869 he obtained his medical degree from Harvard, although he never practiced medicine. For several years prior to and following his graduation William suffered from severe "nervous instability" and depression. Described by his mother as possessing a "morbidly hopeless"[66] temperament he, by his own account, spent all of one winter "on the continual verge of suicide."[67] As Jacques Barzun has pointed out, James's "neurasthenia . . . was no temporary trouble of late adolescence. It was a deep-rooted depression which held up his choice of career till his mid-twenties, which he overcame in part by an heroic effort of will, and which periodically returned, though less crippling, throughout his life."[68]

Later in his life James was to incorporate into *The Varieties of Religious Experience* his own experience with dread and melancholy. In the original accounting, before he acknowledged that the passage was autobiographical, James wrote that "the worst kind of melancholy is that which takes the form of panic fear" and went on:

> Suddenly there fell upon me without any warning, just as if it came out of the darkness, a horrible fear of my own existence. Simultaneously there arose in my mind the image of an epileptic patient whom I had seen in the asylum, a black-haired youth with greenish skin, entirely idiotic, who used to sit all day on one of the benches, or rather shelves against the wall, with his knees drawn up against his

chin, and the coarse gray undershirt, which was his only garment, drawn over them inclosing his entire figure. He sat there like a sort of sculptured Egyptian cat or Peruvian mummy, moving nothing but his black eyes and looking absolutely non-human. This image and my fear entered into a species of combination with each other. *That shape am I*, I felt, potentially. Nothing that I possess can defend me against that fate, if the hour for it should strike for me as it struck for him. There was such a horror of him, and such a perception of my own merely momentary discrepancy from him, that it was if something hitherto solid within my breast gave way entirely, and I became a mass of quivering fear. After this the universe was changed for me altogether. . . . although the immediate feelings passed away, the experience has made me sympathetic with the morbid feelings of others ever since. It gradually faded, but for months I was unable to go out into the dark alone.[69]

William James's melancholia, interspersed with intense and ecstatic experiences as well, recurred throughout his life and caused him to seek, in Tennysonian manner, endless remedies, reliefs, and cures. His younger brother Henry, although less severely afflicted, showed similar tendencies. In a brief portrait of Henry, William wrote:

Harry is as nice and simple and amiable as he can be. He has covered himself, like some marine crustacean, with all sorts of material growths, rich sea-weeds and rigid barnacles and things, and lives hidden in the midst of his strange alien [English] manners and customs; but these are all but 'protective resemblances,' under which the same dear, old, good, innocent and at bottom very powerless-feeling Harry remains, caring for little but his writing, and full of dutifulness and affection for all gentle things.[70]

On the same day he also wrote, tellingly, that Henry was "a native of the James Family, and has no other country"; this was certainly true, in his common holdings of not only the Jamesian experience but the Jamesian temperament as well. Like William he suffered throughout his life from intermittent, often deep melancholy, "the black devils of nervousness, direst damndest demons."[71] Jean Strouse, biographer of their sister Alice, points out: "It did seem as though Henry and William were for years on opposite ends of a scale: when one was healthy and productive, the other floundered in illness and a sense of uselessness."[72] In his recent biography of the Jameses, R. W. B. Lewis quotes Henry's description of his "damnable nervous state." His "black depression—the blackness of darkness and the cruelest melancholia," Henry wrote, "were his 'chronic enemy and curse.' "[73] His friend, novelist Edith Wharton, described a particularly deep depression experienced by Henry in 1910 (during which time he was examined by the well-known physician Sir William Osler, who had attended William James on an earlier occasion):

> I sat down beside the sofa and for a terrible hour looked into the black depths over which he is hanging—the super-imposed "abysses" of all his fiction. I, who have always seen him so serene, so completely the master of his wonderful emotional instrument . . . so sensitive to human contacts and yet so *secure* from them; I could hardly believe it was the same James who cried out to me his fear, his despair, his craving for the "cessation of consciousness," and all his unspeakable loneliness and need of comfort, and inability to be comforted! "Not to wake—not to wake—" that was his refrain; "and then one *does* wake, and one looks again into the blackness of life, and everything ministers to it."[74]

Robertson James, the youngest of the four James brothers, was melancholic, restless, and irritably sensitive from the time he was very young. He appears to have been the one most clearly affected and debilitated by his temperament, a stormy and volatile one punctuated by wild mood swings. Robertson ("Bob") James, wrote F. O. Matthiesen: "seems to have been the most nakedly sensitive of the whole family. They spoke of the high-strung agitation and the morbid self-distrust that lurked behind his animation and his gift for talk."[75] He was artistically inclined—he wrote poetry, painted, and wished to be an architect—but, after serving with valor in the Civil War as a white officer in one of the black Massachusetts regiments (as had his older brother Wilkie, who was wounded fighting next to Colonel Robert Gould Shaw during his doomed attack on Fort Wagner, South Carolina), he became increasingly restless, erratic, and depressed. He had repeated nervous breakdowns—periods of violence and abusiveness followed by periods of morbid melancholy—which, combined with alcoholism, led to several extended periods of treatment in different asylums. His illness, unlike the lighter tincturing of moods and madness experienced by William and Henry, took a far greater toll on both his personal life and his work. His brother William wrote that Bob's "cure is hopeless, I think, his brain is getting more set in these irascible grooves. . . . The only manly and moral thing for a man in his plight is to kill himself,"[76] and Henry wrote of him: "There was much and of the most agitated and agitating—that he had been dipped as a boy into the sacred stream; to some effect which, thanks to two or three of his most saving and often so amusing sensibilities, the turbid sea of his life might never quite wash away."[77]

Alice, the youngest of the James children, shared the family ability for writing and its lively but melancholic temperament. She underwent extensive treatments for her "nervous attacks" and depressions, which, evident from a very early age, resulted in her first major breakdown when she was nineteen years old:

> I have passed thro' an infinite succession of conscious abandonments and in looking back now I see how it began in my childhood, altho' I wasn't conscious of the necessity until '67 or '68 when I broke down first, acutely, and had violent turns of hysteria. . . . Owing to some physical weakness, excess of nervous susceptibility, the moral power *pauses*, as it were for a moment, and refuses to maintain muscular sanity, worn out with the strain of its constabulary functions. As I used to sit immovable reading in the library with waves of violent inclination suddenly invading my muscles taking some one of their myriad forms such as throwing myself out of the window, or knocking off the head of the benignant pater as he sat with his silver locks, writing at his table, it used to seem to me that the only difference between me and the insane was that I had not only all the horrors and suffering of insanity but the duties of doctor, nurse, and strait-jacket imposed upon me, too.[78]

Although Alice wrote long and lucidly about her "breakdowns" (which were usually characterized by mixed symptoms of both mania and depression) and her preoccupations with suicide, she was by no means a predominantly morbid person. She had great vivacity, a fiery sense of life, and a stunning ability to reduce with scathing wit the lives and works of those less charged than she with *joie de vivre.* After finishing George Eliot's letters and journals, for example, she wrote in her diary:

> There is a faint spark of life and an occasional, remotely humorous touch in the last half. But what a monument of ponderous dreariness is the book! What a lifeless, diseased, self-conscious being she must have been! Not one burst of joy, not one ray of humour, not one living breath in one of her letters or journals. . . . Whether it is that her dank, moaning features haunt and pursue one thro' the book, or not, but she makes upon me the impression, morally and physically, of mildew, or some morbid growth—a fungus of a pendulous shape, or as of something damp to the touch.[79]

As one would expect, manic-depressive illness and its temperaments were not confined to the immediate family of Henry James, Senior. Jean Strouse describes the brothers of the senior James as "a roster of dissipation—aimlessness, alcoholism, uninteresting failures;"[80] his niece Katharine Barber James (daughter of Rev. William James, Henry Senior's older brother) spent a year, as a young woman, in an insane asylum. While there she fell in love with her physician, whom she later married, but she then spent the rest of her life in and out of psychiatric hospitals.

The James family represents an extraordinary example of the pervasiveness of a psychotic illness and its milder variants in a single, remarkable American pedigree.[81] In a study addressing the advisability of sterilizing individuals with manic-depressive illness, undertaken by the Committee on Heredity and Eugenics (a chilling context, and one to which we return in the final chapter) and published in 1941 in the *American Journal of Psychiatry,* Dr. Abraham Myerson and Rosalie Boyle reported on the strikingly high incidence of manic-depressive illness in certain socially prominent families. One thinly (not to say excruciatingly thinly) disguised "case history" clearly portrays the Jameses:

> Two generations before the patients at the McLean Hospital, an immigrant accumulated great wealth in America. He was a man of great drive and intelligence. His son was an intimate of the great literary men of America and England and well known in his own right as lecturer and man of ability. However, the history of his life shows that from time to time he had depressions, and on one occasion the

William & Henry James
Partial Family History

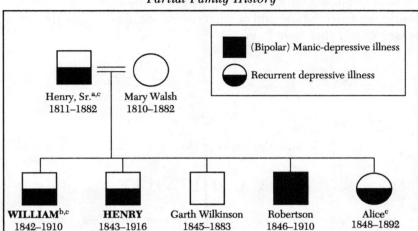

[a] *One of Henry, Sr.'s nieces was hospitalized repeatedly for psychosis.*
[b] *William James's only daughter, Margaret (Peggy), suffered several "breakdowns" from recurrent depression.*
[c] *Probable mixed and/or hypomanic states as well.*

BIOGRAPHICAL SOURCES: Matthiessen, 1947; Edel, 1969, 1985: Strouse, 1980; Maher, 1986; Myers, 1986; Lewis, 1991. See text note 81.

attack lasted two years. He suffered greatly and finally reached a religious philosophy which comforted him a good deal. In the third generation there appeared a patient at the McLean Hospital with manic-depressive psychosis. His two brothers achieved fame of a type which may be described as international in the highest sense of the word, since the writings of both of these men have been translated into all the languages. . . . In other words, although these men are dead and gone, they are still influential in the world of philosophy, psychology and literature. One of these men graphically describes his own mental periodic illness. On one occasion he was sick five years striving to recover some grip on life . . . he had other breakdowns and periods of nervous exhaustion. This man emphasized that there was no sharp line between healthy and unhappy minds and that people who had nervous burdens to carry, hereditary perhaps, could order their lives fruitfully and derive some gain from their degenerate sensitiveness.[82]

The authors then go on to ask a heart-stopping question: "Whom could we have sterilized in this family line to prevent the manic-depressive state and at what cost of social riches, in the truer sense, would this have been done?"

"Utter darkness is then his light"

HERMAN MELVILLE

The intensest light of reason and revelation combined, can not shed such blazonings upon the deeper truths in man, as will sometimes proceed from his own profoundest gloom. Utter darkness is then his light, and cat-like he distinctly sees all objects through a medium which is mere blindness to common vision. Wherefore have Gloom and Grief been celebrated of old as the selectest chamberlains to knowledge? Wherefore is it, that not to know Gloom and Grief is not to know aught that an heroic man should learn?[83]

—HERMAN MELVILLE

The death of businessman William James in 1832, as noted by his grandson Henry, was marked by extensive tributes to his financial acumen and his generous and energetic involvement with the city and people of Albany. No such tributes tolled the passing of Allan Melvill, father of novelist Herman, who died manic, insane, and bankrupt in the same year. Melville's brother-in-law, instead, described the awful circumstances of his final illness:

He was unwell. . . . But persisted in giving attention to his business—He devoted himself so closely and assiduously, as to produce a state of excitement, which in a great measure robbed him of his sleep. . . . The excitement could not be allayed and yesterday he occasionally manifested an alienation of mind. . . . today he presents the melancholy spectacle of a deranged mind.[84]

Allan's brother Thomas, who was with him during his "excited delirium," wrote of his own despair that, even if Allan survived, "in all human probability—he would live, a *Maniac!*"[85]

Allan Melvill (the spelling of the family name was changed in Herman's generation) was born in 1782, the son of Major Thomas Melvill, an activist in the Boston Tea Party and a man who was known for "cultivating his eccentricities"; his brother, like Allan, had debilitating financial problems and patterns of excess that eventually led to his being put in a debtor's prison. In 1814 Allan married Maria Gansevoort, who also suffered from "nerves," although on the melancholic rather than manic end of the mood continuum. Her husband wrote frequently and with great concern about her depressed spirits and at one point expressed his fears that she might not obtain "relief from mental excitement."[86] Of their children, Herman experienced clear and extended periods of both melancholy and manic excitement, although he never required hospitalization. His wife wrote often of her concerns about Herman's "severe nervous affections,"[87] his "constant working of the brain, and excitement of the imagination,"[88] and his being in "such a frightfully nervous state."[89] He talked of suicide to his friend Nathaniel Hawthorne, having "pretty much made up his mind to be annihilated."[90] He suffered from severe mood swings that ranged from expansive, energetic, and highly productive states to irascible, bitterly morbid, withdrawn, and listless periods in which little was done and he was obsessed with death and filled with pessimism. Like Ishmael, Melville would, now and again, take to the sea:

> It is a way I have of driving off the spleen, and regulating the circulation. Whenever I find myself growing grim about the mouth; whenever it is a damp, drizzly November in my soul; whenever I find myself involuntarily pausing before coffin warehouses, and bringing up the rear of every funeral I meet; and especially whenever my hypos get such an upper hand of me, that it requires a strong moral principle to prevent me from deliberately stepping into the street, and methodically knocking people's hats off—then, I account it high time to get to sea as soon as I can.[91]

Themes of madness, and its interlacings with visionary grandness, permeated Melville's writings in much the same way that his melancholic temperament wended its way in and around the lives of his fictional characters. He wrote to a friend:

> This going mad of a friend or acquaintance comes straight home to every man who feels his soul in him,—which but few men do. For in all of us lodges the same fuel to light the same fire. And he who has never felt, momentarily, what madness is has but a mouthful of brains. What sort of sensation permanent madness is may be very well imagined—just as we imagine how we felt when we were infants, tho' we cannot recall it. In both conditions we are irresponsible & riot like gods without fear of fate.—It is the climax of a mad night of revelry when the blood has been transmuted into brandy.—But if we prate much of this thing we shall be illustrating our own propositions.[92]

It was not only his own and his father's madness he had to fear. His older bother, Gansevoort Melville—a lawyer and political speaker known for his extravagances—died at the age of thirty: "almost manic and sometimes a little paranoid," "mad" for almost a month prior to his death; and, according to his physician, suffering from a disorder that was "in some degree connected with the brain, and a state of nervous derangement."[93] Although it is unclear what the immediate cause of death was (one biographer has suggested a brain tumor), his symptoms and family history were consistent with manic delirium. Before effective treatment became available, death from acute mania was not uncommon. Herman's younger brother Allan got easily and often into debt; his depressive temperament was a source of ongoing concern in the letters of both his sister and mother. Herman's cousin Henry, son of his father's brother Thomas, was declared legally insane, and Herman's own son Malcolm killed himself with a pistol at the age of eighteen. The coroner's initial verdict was suicide while "suffering from a temporary aberration of mind," although—presumably in deference to the family—the verdict was later changed to accidental death. It is difficult to reconcile the second opinion with the fact that Malcolm was found with his gun in his hand, alone, and with a bullet hole in the temple.

Throughout all his difficulties with his own moods, his work, his life, and his troubled family Melville displayed a remarkable, if occasional, vastness of spirit and grandiosity of scale; in his description of the fossil whale, for example, his "comprehensiveness of sweep" is truly Coleridgian:

> Give me a condor's quill! Give me Vesuvius' crater for an inkstand! Friends, hold my arms! For in the mere act of penning my thoughts of this Leviathan, they weary me, and make me faint with their outreaching comprehensiveness of sweep, as if to include the whole circle of the sciences, and all the generations of whales, and men, and mastodons, past, present, and to come, with all the revolving panoramas of empire on earth, and throughout the whole universe not excluding its suburbs.[94]

"Slow and slow that ship will go"

SAMUEL TAYLOR COLERIDGE

FIRST VOICE
But why drives on that ship so fast,
Without or wave or wind?

SECOND VOICE
The air is cut away before,
And closes from behind.

Fly, brother, fly! more high, more high!
Or we shall be belated:
For slow and slow that ship will go,
When the Mariner's trance is abated.

—SAMUEL TAYLOR COLERIDGE[95]

My nerves have more phases than the moon—*varium et mutibile semper femina:* I seem to be moon struck, and infected with her changeful disposition—but her changes are all lovely, mine all distressful.

—SARA COLERIDGE[96]

Samuel Taylor Coleridge—the most restless, unsettled, and dendritic of minds—was born in 1772, the youngest of ten children. His father, like those of Alfred Tennyson and William and Henry James, was both a cleric and writer. Also like the Tennyson and James families, the Coleridges were an accomplished clan—soldiers and scholars in Samuel's generation and, in the following, a "successful race of judges, bishops, and senior academics."[97] Moody and exquisitely suggestible from the earliest age, Coleridge described himself as a boy as "haunted by spectres"; a dreamer; one who was "fretful," "inordinately passionate"; and one who, from the time he was very young, possessed—like Melville, Blake, and Whitman—a cosmic temperament, a sympathy with "a love of the Great and the Whole." In a letter written to a friend, Coleridge recalled an early experience with his father:

> I remember, that at eight years old I walked with him one winter evening from a farmer's house, a mile from Ottery—& he told me the names of the stars—and how Jupiter was a thousand times larger than our world—and that the other twinkling stars were Suns that had worlds rolling round them—& when I came home, he shewed me how they rolled round. . . . my mind had been habituated *to the Vast*—& I never regarded *my senses* in any way as the criteria of my belief.[98]

This love for the "Vast," and easeful familiarity with the "Great and the Whole," formed the heart of Coleridge's thought, and its importance in his originality cannot be overstated. The expansiveness of his thinking and the often mystical quality of Coleridge's associational patterns, as well as other cognitive styles likewise associated with hypomanic and creative thought, were discussed earlier.

The tumultuous as well as visionary side of Coleridge's nature became more aggressively apparent as he grew older. He matriculated at Cambridge in 1791 and during his undergraduate years there accumulated massive debts; chaos, extravagance, and melancholy became normal, if aberrant, parts of his life. Biographer Richard Holmes writes:

> He began to live a kind of double life at Cambridge, his wild expenditure on books, drinking, violin lessons, theatre and whoring (he

later described this as the time of his "unchastities") alternating with
fits of suicidal gloom and remorse. . . .

The atmosphere was now subtly different from the scholarly
triumph of the previous year: there was much drinking and arguing
with Edward [his brother], much flirtation with local girls, and considerably more poetry. . . .

By the end of October [1793] his "Embarrassments" buzzed
round him "like a Nest of Hornets", and in November he gave up all
attempts to get his affairs under control. Instead he abandoned himself to a whirl of drunken socializing, alternating with grim solitary
resolutions to shoot himself as the final solution to bad debts, unre-
quited love, and academic disgrace.[99]

Early in December, during a time when he was, in his own
words, "a fool even to madness," he impulsively enlisted in the
British Army under an improvised name; it was a clearly disastrous
and irrational act, led up to by weeks of similarly erratic and unpredictable behavior. Within four months he was discharged: "The
Regimental Muster Roll recorded succinctly: 'discharged S. T.
Comberbache, Insane; 10 April 1794.' "[100] In a letter to his
brother, Coleridge recalled some of his mercurial experiences:

I laugh almost like an insane person when I cast my eye backward on
the prospect of my past two years—What a gloomy *Huddle* of eccentric Actions, and dim-discovered motives! To real Happiness I
bade adieu from the moment, I received my first Tutor's Bill—since
that time since that period my Mind has been irradiated by Bursts
only of Sunshine—at all other times gloomy with clouds, or turbulent
with tempests. Instead of manfully disclosing the disease, I con-
cealed it with a shameful Cowardice of sensibility, till it cankered my
very Heart . . . . How many and how many hours have I stolen from
the bitterness of Truth in these soul-enervating Reveries—in build-
ing magnificent Edifices of Happiness on some fleeting Shadow of
Reality! My Affairs became more and more involved—I fled to De-
bauchery—fled from silent and solitary Anguish to all the uproar of
senseless Mirth![101]

Most of the rest of Coleridge's life was marked by these periods of agitation, expansive but troubled restlessness, and "depression too dreadful to be described."[102] He was intermittently
addicted to laudanum, a tincture of opium, and he turned to the

drug frequently for relief from his mental perturbance and black
moods. In a letter written in response to chastisements about his
laudanum use, Coleridge wrote:

> The longer I abstained, the higher my spirits were, the keener my
> enjoyments—till the moment, the direful moment, arrived, when
> my pulse began to fluctuate, my Heart to palpitate, & such a dreadful
> *falling-abroad*, as it were, of my whole frame, such intolerable Rest-
> lessness & incipient Bewilderment, that in the last of my several
> attempts to abandon the dire poison, I exclaimed in agony, what I
> now repeat in seriousness & solemnity—"I am too poor to hazard
> this! Had I but a few hundred Pounds, but 200£, half to send to Mrs.
> Coleridge, & half to place myself in a private madhouse, where I
> could procure nothing but what a Physician thought proper, & where
> a medical attendant could be constantly with me for two or three
> months (in less than that time Life or Death would be determined)
> then there might be Hope. Now there is none!"—O God! how will-
> ingly would I place myself under Dr. Fox in his Establishment—for
> my Case is a species of madness, only that it is a derangement, an
> utter impotence of the *Volition*, & not of the intellectual Faculties—
> You bid me rouse myself—go, bid a man paralytic in both arms rub
> them briskly together, & that will cure him. Alas! (he would reply)
> that I cannot move my arms is my Complaint & my misery.[103]

Coleridge's letter, as we shall see, bears a more than slight family
resemblance to an essay on "Nervousness," written twenty years
later by his daughter Sara. Although manic-depressive illness and
its temperaments were not as pervasive in the Coleridge family as
they were in some other of the families under discussion, it is of
interest that Samuel Coleridge's father's father, described by the
poet as "half-poet and half-madman," went bankrupt; there was
also some indication that he drank heavily.[104] Francis, one of Coleridge's older brothers, committed suicide at the age of twenty-two,
and Hartley, eldest child of Samuel Taylor Coleridge and Sara
Fricker Coleridge (whose sister had to be committed to an asylum), had symptoms consistent with manic-depressive illness.[105]
But it was the younger Sara Coleridge who, in addition to being an
intriguing and talented person in her own right, was most like her
father in temperament. Born in 1802, she had published two books
by the time she was in her early twenties and was, as well, the
editor of her father's works. She suffered from severe depressions,

"recurrent hysteria," "nervous derangement," and, like her father, became a laudanum addict. With no little irony, she observed: "Every medical man speaks ill of the drug, prohibits it, & after trying in vain to give me sleep without it, ends with prescribing it himself."[106] Like many, she emphasized that "nervous sufferings" could not be understood by the inexperienced. In recounting her nighttime fears in childhood—"that hideous assemblage of horrors—the horse with eyes of flame!"—she noted that unlike other members of her family, who laughed at her terrors, her father alone understood: "He insisted that a lighted candle should be left in my room, in the interval between my retiring to bed and mamma's joining me. From that time forth my sufferings ceased."[107] Although her childhood fears subsided, she was mentally ill much of her adult life. Her biographer, Bradford Keyes Mudge, describes one long period of disturbance, classically melancholic in nature:

> And so Sara's nervous illness continued unabated for more than two years, from September 1832 to January 1835. Her worst period occurred during the first six months of 1833 when she gave herself up to opium and hysteria, throwing two "fits" a day, sleeping only every third night, and eating so little that her menstrual cycle stopped completely. . . . From all accounts, her "sad hysterical dejection" remained beyond the control of patient and doctors alike, an inexplicable and overpowering "weakness" that robbed her of all energy, all enthusiasm, all pleasure. . . . "O this dreadful restlessness of body—this deep dejection—nay, often blackening into despair!—I have a thousand strange bodily feelings—perpetually varying, yet ever most alarming and distressing; but even that is nothing to the despondency of mind."[108]

An astute, almost clinical, observer of her moods, Sara Coleridge described, counterintuitively and in detail, the relative independence of true melancholia from external events, and she noted that certain types of "hypochondria" (especially those of delusional proportion) and mania "may be two different species of the same genius [? genus]—but both are madness."[109] Commenting on the varieties of "nervous illness," and their beholdenness to the idiosyncrasies of the individuals they affect, she wrote: "Diseases are like tulips & auriculas which vary without limit according to unknown differences of soil & situation."[110] In "Nervousness," she wrote out her suggestions, as applicable today as then, for how physicians might best help their depressed patients:

> Sympathy is like rain on the brown grass. Mingle admonitions with sympathy according to the Lucretian prescription—let them feel that they are understood.
>
> To be a fully competent judge of the complaint, as to its trials & requisitions, you should have been within the charmed circle yourself. There is a sort of knowledge which experience only can give. . . .
>
> [Do] not wonder at the change in a nervous person & think it inconsistent.
>
> It is the capacity for comfort that is wanting.[111]

Sara Coleridge, wrote Virginia Woolf, was a "continuation" of her father's mind and temperament. Unfortunately, neither ever found much comfort from their grim, unsettled moods, but neither did they lose their grand and beautiful scale of the universe. Sara once said that her father was "almost always on the star-paved road, taking in the whole heavens in his circuit";[112] but as Woolf wrote, Sara herself was a "heaven-hunter, too."[113]

"I feel certain I am going mad again"

VIRGINIA WOOLF

Dearest,

I feel certain I am going mad again. I feel we can't go through another of those terrible times. And I shan't recover this time. I begin to hear voices, and I can't concentrate. So I am doing what seems the best thing to do. You have given me the greatest possible happiness. You have been in every way all that anyone could be. I don't think two people could have been happier till this terrible disease came. I can't fight any longer.

—VIRGINIA WOOLF[114]

In his recent book *The Flight of the Mind*, Dr. Thomas Caramagno documented in impressive detail the generations of depressive and manic-depressive illness in Virginia Woolf's family.[115] Her grandfather, mother, sister, brother, and niece all suffered from recurrent depressions, her father and another brother were cyclothymic, and her cousin James, who had been institutionalized for mania and depression, died of acute mania. Although James had suffered an earlier head trauma, the injury appears to have been of minimal severity and unlikely to have caused, though it may have triggered, the pattern of symptoms that occurred. Virginia herself was repeatedly treated and admitted to hospitals for psychotic manias and depressions and eventually committed suicide in 1941.[116]

"I am a porous vessel afloat on sensation," wrote Woolf, "a sensitive plate exposed to invisible rays . . . taking the breath of these voices in my sails and tacking this way and that through daily life as I yield to them."[117] With the breath of voices in her sails, Virginia Woolf lived her life as a journey from one great individual moment to the next. To an extraordinary degree she was able to transform from chaos into meaning her tumultuous thoughts and feelings. In her struggle to understand her "violent moods of the soul," she was able, as a consummate writer, to give eloquent voice to the fragmented and wildly opposing ways of perceiving that existed within her. Like many other mercurial writers, she learned to absorb what her fiery, violent, and desolate moods might teach. In their contrasts she saw different truths, and in seeking their reconciliation she imposed a kind of order and rhythm unique in literature.

Woolf's ability to express heightened moments of remembered intensity came in part, no doubt, from an exquisite sensitivity to the inconstancies and contrasts in her own psychological life. Like Edward Thomas, another writer of melancholic temperament, she sought always to catch the essence of such moments, whether bitter or sweet. What she took into prose he described in poetry:

> As for myself,
> Where first I met the bitter scent is lost.
> I, too, often shrivel the grey shreds,
> Sniff them and think and sniff again and try
> Once more to think what it is I am remembering,
> Always in vain. I cannot like the scent,
> Yet I would rather give up others more sweet,
> With no meaning, than this bitter one.[118]

By Woolf's willingness to examine the bitter as well as the transient she gave name, meaning, and memory to the ephemeral:

> "Stars, sun, moon," it seemed to say, "the daisy in the grass, fires,
> frost on the windowpane, my heart goes out to you. But," it always
> seemed to add, "you break, you pass, you go." And simultaneously
> it covered the intensity of both these states of mind with "I can't
> reach you—I can't get at you," spoken wistfully, frustratedly. And
> the stars faded, and the child went.[119]

Without question, much of Virginia Woolf's ability to describe
the transience and volatility of the natural world came from her
own rapid shifts of moods and thoughts. She believed unequivocally in the importance of melancholia and madness to her imaginative powers: "As an experience, madness is terrific I can assure
you, and not to be sniffed at; and in its lava I still find most of the
things I write about. It shoots out of one everything shaped, final,
not in mere driblets, as sanity does. And the six months—not
three—that I lay in bed taught me a good deal about what is called
oneself."[120]

Yet the illness that drove the lava also killed her. Unable to
live with the certainty that she was "going mad again," she wrote
a note to her husband, walked to the river, and drowned herself:

> We do not know our own souls, let alone the souls of others. Human
> beings do not go hand in hand the whole stretch of the way. There
> is a virgin forest in each; a snowfield where even the print of birds'
> feet is unknown. Here we go alone, and like it better so. Always to
> have sympathy, always to be accompanied, always to be understood
> would be intolerable. But in health the genial pretence must be kept
> up, and the effort renewed—to communicate, to civilise, to share, to
> cultivate the desert, to educate the native, to work together by day
> and by night to sport. In illness this make-believe ceases.[121]

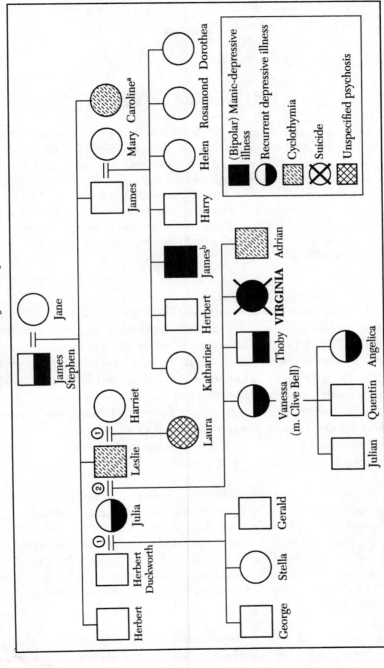

Virginia Woolf
Partial Family History

(Bipolar) Manic-depressive illness

Recurrent depressive illness

Cyclothymia

Suicide

Unspecified psychosis

[a] *Recurrent hypomania*
[b] *Death from mania*

BIOGRAPHICAL SOURCES: Woolf, 1964; Bell, 1972; Caramagno, 1992; See text note 116.
Pedigree drawn in collaboration with Dr. Caramagno and based largely on his research.

━━━━

"If you died you had done everything"

ERNEST HEMINGWAY

My father was a coward. He shot himself without necessity. At least I thought so. I had gone through it myself until I figured it in my head. I knew what it was to be a coward and what it was to cease being a coward. Now, truly, in actual danger I felt a clean feeling as in a shower. Of course it was easy now. That was because I no longer cared what happened. I knew it was better to live it so that if you died you had done everything that you could do about your work and your enjoyment of life up to that minute, reconciling the two, which is very difficult.

—ERNEST HEMINGWAY[122]

Ernest Hemingway's family—like those of Tennyson, Schumann, and Woolf—was filled with depressive and manic-depressive illness.[123] What is even more striking, however, is the unnerving number of suicides—four, in just two generations of the family: Hemingway's father, brother, sister, and Hemingway himself. Although not formally diagnosed as manic-depressive, Hemingway's father (physician Dr. Clarence Hemingway) clearly suffered from violent mood swings and erratic behavior. Hemingway's biographer Kenneth Lynn touches on the family reluctance to label Dr. Hemingway in this way:

> Thirty-four years after Dr. Hemingway took his father's ancient Smith & Wesson revolver from a drawer of his desk and fired a bullet into his head, his oldest daughter was still unwilling to talk about the possibility that for as long as she had known him he had been struggling with some form of manic-depressive illness—that his convulsive rages, feverish enthusiasms, and sporadic nervous collapses (which twice required "rest cures") were the contrasting part of a pattern.[124]

Similar rages, feverish enthusiasms, and morbid depressions—in addition to ceaseless frenetic, restless energies—haunted his son Ernest's life as well. In 1961, following a psychiatric hos-

Ernest Hemingway
Partial Family History

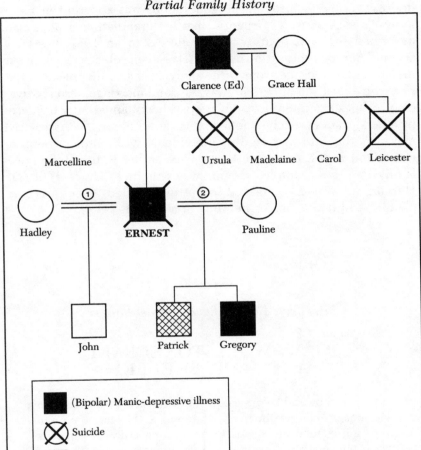

BIOGRAPHICAL SOURCES: Baker, 1980; Yalom and Yalom, 1971; Hendrickson, 1987; Lynn, 1987. See text note 123.

pitalization and electroconvulsive therapy for psychotic depression, "Hemingway . . . arose from his bed, went to the kitchen, got the key, opened the storeroom, selected a twelve-gauge, double-barreled English shotgun he had bought at Abercrombie & Fitch, pushed two shells into it, walked upstairs to the foyer, turned the gun against himself and fired."[125] The passing down of manic-depressive illness through the generations was apparent in Hemingway's sons as well. Gregory, like his grandfather a physician, described his own bouts with the illness in an 1987 interview: seven "nervous breakdowns," ninety-seven electroshock treatments, and wreckage from three marriages and divorces.[126] Patrick, the eldest son of Hemingway's second marriage, also received electroshock treatment for a severe psychosis, apparently triggered by a head trauma received following a car accident.[127] "Assortative mating," the intermarriage of individuals with similar temperaments and genes, may have taken place earlier in the Hemingway family line; for example, Hemingway's mother, Grace Hall (Dr. Hemingway's wife), suffered from unspecified "nervous complaints" and had a "major nervous breakdown."[128]

"I collected bones from charnel-houses"

MARY WOLLSTONECRAFT AND MARY SHELLEY

The grey cobweb-like appearance of the aged pines is a much finer image of decay; the fibres whitening as they lose their moisture, imprisoned life seems to be stealing away. I cannot tell why—but death, under every form, appears to me like something getting free.

—MARY WOLLSTONECRAFT[129]

I collected bones from charnel-houses and disturbed, with profane fingers, the tremendous secrets of the human frame.

—MARY SHELLEY[130]

Mary Wollstonecraft, early feminist and author of *A Vindication of the Rights of Woman*, was born in 1759 and died within a few months of the birth of her daughter, Mary Shelley, in 1797. An adventurous, forceful woman, she was subject to "terrible swings of mood, from hectic noisy enthusiasm to almost suicidal depression";[131] she in fact twice attempted suicide.[132] Her father was "unstable and drunken,"[133] her sister Eliza suffered a severe depression following childbirth, and her elder daughter, Fanny Imlay, committed suicide. Mary Wollstonecraft's only other child, her daughter Mary, was a writer and the second wife of Percy Bysshe Shelley. She, too, experienced long periods of "nervous depression" and severe mood swings. After putting together Shelley's papers and manuscripts in 1839 she suffered from a major "nervous illness." In March of that year she wrote: "Illness did ensue—what an illness—driving me to the verge of insanity—Often I felt the cord w^d snap and I should no longer be able to rule my though[t]s with fearful struggles—miserable relapses—After long repose, I became somewhat better."[134] In a letter to Leigh Hunt she described some of the fears and anguish she had experienced: "I really felt in danger of losing my senses. My physician ordered me opium. . . . it certainly strengthened my head, which had gone far astray—you . . . will understand the sort of unspeakable sensation of wildness and irritation."[135] Her depression during the last years of her life was more or less chronic, and in one of the final entries in her journal she recorded some of the toll it had taken: "My mind slumbers & my heart is dull—Is life quite over? Have the storms and wrecks of the last years destroyed my intellect, my imagination, my capacity of invention—What am I become?[136]

"That depression of mind which enchains the faculties"

SAMUEL JOHNSON AND JAMES BOSWELL

. . . that depression of mind which enchains the faculties without destroying them, and leaves reason the knowledge of right without the power of pursuing it.

—SAMUEL JOHNSON[137]

Burton's *Anatomy of Melancholy*, he said, was the only book that ever took him out of bed two hours sooner than he wished to rise.

—JAMES BOSWELL[138]

Samuel Johnson and James Boswell, two of the leading literary figures of the eighteenth century, both suffered from severe depression and both had it in their families. Their relationship, in its own rather odd way, represents a literary form of "assortative mating." Johnson had an almost obsessive fear of insanity and was, intermittently, suicidally depressed at different periods in his life. He had his first major breakdown, which lasted for two years, at the age of twenty; he remained "still in a rather shattered condition for at least another three years."[139] Dr. Roy Porter, who has put Johnson's illness in the broader and deeper context of his life and beliefs, describes this early episode:

> Kicking his heels at his parental home . . . after being forced by chill penury to quit Oxford, degreeless and careerless, Johnson sank into suicidal lethargy, "overwhelmed [Boswell put it] with an horrible hypochondria, with perpetual irritation, fretfulness and impatience; and with a dejection, gloom and despair, which made existence misery. From this dismal malady he never afterwards was perfectly relieved."[140]

He was convinced he had inherited his "vile melancholy"[141] from his father, a "morbid disposition both of Body and Mind,"[142] a "terrifying melancholy . . . which he was sometimes apprehensive bordered on insanity."[143] He was again severely afflicted by depression when he was in his early fifties, writing in 1761: "*My terrours and perplexities have so much increased,* that I am under great depression. . . . Almighty and merciful Father look down upon my misery with pity."[144]

James Boswell, his biographer, was more cyclothymic in nature: Alternatingly melancholic, euphoric, and irritable, he suffered from clear-cut depressions and hypomanias from adolescence onward.[145] Drs. William Ober and Henry Kranzler, as well as Boswell himself, noted the strongly hereditary side of Boswell's temperament: His brother became mentally ill while in his twenties and had to be confined to an asylum; his father's father had a "melancholic turn;" and his father's brother suffered from episodic depressions. One of Boswell's daughters also had manic illness.[146]

"The root of the evil"

VINCENT VAN GOGH

The root of the evil lies in the constitution itself, in the fatal weakening of families from generation to generation. . . . The root of the evil certainly lies there, and there's no cure for it.

—VINCENT VAN GOGH[147]

Vincent van Gogh's psychiatric diagnosis has been a subject of debate for a century; the argument that he suffered from manic-depressive illness, conceivably complicated by a complex partial seizure disorder, was made earlier. One strong piece of the evidence for the diagnosis of manic-depressive illness (the details of which were given in chapter 4) is van Gogh's striking family history of psychiatric disease, especially mood disorders and suicide. Theo, Vincent's younger brother, suffered from recurrent depressions and had a psychotic illness—which included delusions, hallucinations, and violence—at the end of his life. Van Gogh's biographer Marc Tralbaut has noted that "Vincent's and Theo's mental and physical disabilities were similar in every respect . . . the probability of hereditary influences seems to be overwhelming,"[148] and Jan Hulsker has written recently that Theo's life was "characterized by a melancholy that may have been even greater than his brother's,"[149] citing Vincent's and Theo's physician in Paris as saying that Theo's case was "far worse than Vincent's."[150]

Wilhelmina, their sister, suffered from a chronic psychotic illness and spent almost forty years in an insane asylum; Cornelius, their younger brother, committed suicide.[151] Dr. Peyron, Vincent's physician while he was in the asylum, noted that Vincent "told us that his mother's sister was epileptic, and that there were many cases in this family";[152] the distinction between epilepsy and manic-depressive illness was unclear in nineteenth-century France, and the two diagnoses often overlapped or were used interchangeably. Two of Vincent's uncles on his father's side of the family—Hein and Cent, both art dealers—suffered from unspecified recurrent illnesses. Interestingly, and consistent with the seasonal component of mood disorders, one van Gogh biographer observed that Cent was "forever disappearing to the South of France for the sunshine which helped lift him out of whatever it was that ailed him."[153]

It is not difficult to understand why Vincent would write to Theo: "[Our neurosis] . . . is also a fatal inheritance, since in civilization the weakness increases from generation to generation. If we want to face the real truth about our constitution, we must acknowledge that we belong to the number of those who suffer from a neurosis which already has its roots in the past."[154]

Other artists and writers who almost certainly suffered from manic-depressive or depressive illness, and had strong histories of severe mood disorders or suicide in their families include French painter Théodore Géricault,[155] Austrian composer Gustav Mahler,[156] American poets Robert Lowell,[157] John Berryman,[158] and Anne Sexton,[159] Swedish playwright August Strindberg,[160] Amer-

Vincent van Gogh
Partial Family History

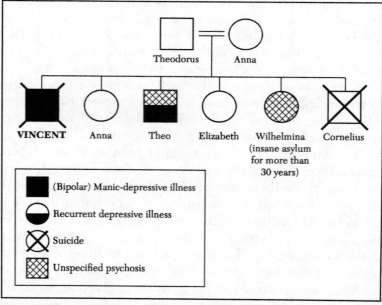

BIOGRAPHICAL SOURCES: Van Gogh, 1959; Tralbaut, 1969; Hulsker, 1990. See text notes 147–149.

ican dramatists Eugene O'Neill[161] and Tennessee Williams,[162] and French poet Victor Hugo.[163] The family histories of these artists are discussed briefly in the notes for this chapter. A listing of other affected families is given later in the text.

The families discussed in this chapter share in common certain themes of madness, suicide, destructive patterns of drug and alcohol use, and financial chaos; however, uncommon ability and originality are often present as well. Clearly not every family that shows signs of instability, eccentricity, moodiness, or alcoholism is affected by manic-depressive or depressive illness. Rather, a constellation or pattern of symptoms evolves that is characteristic of a highly genetic, relatively common, volatile, disruptive, and yet occasionally—and only partially—advantageous psychiatric disease. Because manic-depressive illness appears to be the most genetic of the major psychiatric illnesses, as well as the one most definitively linked to creativity, if a particular madness or "nervous affliction" runs throughout certain families—especially highly successful ones—the odds are very strong that it is manic-depressive illness.

Suicide runs in some of the literary and artistic families we have discussed—for example, the Hemingways, the Gordon-Byrons, and the Schumanns—but not in others. This is consistent with findings from genetic studies in general,[164] and from studies of the Pennsylvania Amish in particular. Investigation of their extensive pedigrees, which go back several centuries, shows that a few families with manic-depressive illness account for a very high proportion of the suicides.[165] The influence of intermarriage between individuals of similar temperaments and possibly similar genetic backgrounds, or assortative mating, can also be seen in some of the families discussed. In those families where mood disorders appear to have been inherited from both sides of the pedigree there is a higher incidence of manic-depressive and depressive illness in the offspring. The intermarriage of the Clayton and Tennyson lines, for example, seems to have resulted in an extraordinarily high rate of penetrance of the presumptive manic-depressive gene. Similarly, in Virginia Woolf's family, the offspring of her mother's first marriage (to Herbert Duckworth, who showed no evidence of having a mood disorder) were not affected by mental illness; however, when her mother, who suffered from recurrent depressions, married Leslie Stephen, who was cyclothymic, all four of their children suffered from significant mood disorders. Likewise, Stephen's daughter from his first marriage, who was mentally retarded, suffered from an unspecified psychosis that was characterized by intermittent rapid speaking, outbursts of rage, and "sluggishness." It is of significance here that her maternal grandmother, Isabella Thackeray (wife of the novelist), suffered from what almost certainly was manic-depressive illness. All these pedigrees demonstrate the wide range of expression of a genetic illness, from its milder forms, which can appear as temperaments, to the more psychotic and suicidal forms that appear as full-blown manic-depressive insanity.

Obviously, many other writers, artists, and composers had family members who suffered from manic-depressive illness or severe recurrent depressions, were declared insane and committed to asylums or hospitals, or committed suicide. Those with at least one seriously affected first-degree relative (often there were several) include Hans Christian Andersen, Konstantin Batyushkov, Arthur and E. F. Benson, Elizabeth Bishop, Aleksandr Blok, Charlotte and Emily Brontë, Anton Bruckner, Thomas Campbell, Thomas Chatterton, Samuel Clemens, John Sell Cotman, Gustave Courbet, Richard Dadd,[166] Isak Dinesen, Ernest Dowson, Thomas Eakins, Ralph Waldo Emerson, Edward FitzGerald, Robert Frost, Thomas Gainsborough, Johann Wolfgang Goethe, Nikolai Gogol, Kenneth Graham, Thomas Gray, Hermann Hesse, Charles Lamb, Louis MacNeice, John Martin, Marianne Moore, Edvard Munch, Francis Parkman, Walker Percy, Sylvia Plath, Jackson Pollock, Cole Porter, Edwin Arlington Robinson, Dante Gabriel Rossetti, Giocchino Rossini, John Ruskin, Alexander Scriabin, Robert Louis Stevenson, Peter Tchaikovsky, J.M.W. Turner, Walt Whitman, and Emile Zola. These findings are consistent with those of Drs. Andreasen, McNeil, Richards, and Karlsson (presented in chapter 3) showing that mental illness and creativity tend to aggregate in certain families and not in others.[167] The high rates of mood disorders and suicide in the literary and artistic families portrayed in this chapter are also consistent with studies showing greatly increased rates of manic-depressive and depressive illness in the first-degree relatives of individuals who have manic-depressive illness.[168]

It is important to emphasize, however, that many writers and artists have no family history of these illnesses, nor do they themselves suffer from depression or manic-depressive illness. This point is critical. The basic argument of this book is not that all writers and artists are depressed, suicidal, or manic. It is, rather, that a greatly disproportionate number of them are; that the manic-depressive and artistic temperaments are, in many ways, overlapping ones; and, that the two temperaments are causally related to one another. The genetic basis of manic-depressive illness provides not only one part of this argument, but also the constitutional core of a determining temperament, one providing in part the sealed orders with which so many sail:

> As a man-of-war that sails through the sea, so this earth that sails through the air. We mortals are all on board a fast-sailing, never-sinking, world-frigate, of which God was the shipwright; and she is but one craft in a Milky-Way fleet, of which God is the Lord High Admiral. The port we sail from is forever astern. And though far out of sight of land, for ages and ages we continue to sail with sealed orders, and our last destination remains a secret to ourselves and our officers; yet our final haven was predestinated ere we slipped from the stocks at Creation.
>
> Thus sailing with sealed orders, we ourselves are the repositories of the secret packet, whose mysterious contents we long to learn. There are no mysteries out of ourselves.
>
> —HERMAN MELVILLE[169]

7.
THIS NET THROWNE UPON THE HEAVENS

Medicine and the Arts

Of Meridians, and Parallels,
Man hath weav'd out a net, and this net throwne
Upon the Heavens, and now they are his owne.

—JOHN DONNE[1]

View Along the Axis of the βDNA Double Helix
(Courtesy of Dr. Robert Langridge, University of California, San Francisco
© Regents of the University of California)

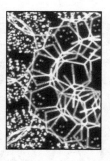

Occasionally an exhilarating and powerfully creative force, more often a destructive one, manic-depressive illness gives a touch of fire to many of those who experience it. The melancholic side of manic-depressive illness is a source of intolerable suffering, torporous decay, and death; scarely less damaging, mania in its extreme forms can be violently psychotic and life threatening. Yet there is strong scientific and biographical evidence linking manic-depressive illness and its related temperaments to artistic imagination and expression. Biographies of eminent poets, artists, and composers attest to the strikingly high rate of mood disorders and suicide—as well as institutionalization in asylums and psychiatric hospitals—in these individuals, and recent psychiatric and psychological studies of living artists and writers have further documented the link. Manic-depressive illness, then, is a very strange disease —one that confers advantage but often kills and destroys as it does so. Not surprisingly, the clinical, ethical, and philosophical issues surrounding such a paradoxically advantageous and yet destructive illness are often difficult.

From the perspectives of both the clinician and the artist, one of the most important of these issues is treatment. If manic-depressive illness and its associated temperaments are relatively common in artists, writers, and composers, and if the illness is, at least to some extent, an important part of what makes their work what it is, what are the implications of treating the underlying disease and its temperaments? Edward Thomas once wrote, "I wonder whether for a person like myself whose most intense moments were those of depression a cure that destroys the depression may not destroy the intensity—a *desperate* remedy?"[2]; and Edvard Munch, hospitalized on several occasions for his psychiatric illness, remarked, "A German once said to me: 'But you could rid yourself of many of your troubles.' To which I replied: 'They are part of me and my art. They are indistinguishable from me, and it would destroy my art. I want to keep those sufferings.' "[3] This is a common concern. Many artists and writers believe that turmoil, suffering, and extremes in emotional experience are integral not only to the human condition but to their abilities as artists. They fear that psychiatric treatment will transform them into normal, well-adjusted, dampened, and bloodless souls—unable, or unmotivated, to write, paint, or compose. These fears have greatly intensified as a result of the availability of a wide range of highly effective mood-stabilizing medications. Some concerns stem from a misunderstanding of the actions and side effects of these medications, while others are based on a romanticized notion of "madness" or psychopathology, a notion that does not take into account the severity and consequences of untreated manic-depressive illness. Some of the mistrust is well placed, however, and we deal with this issue first.

The short- and long-term effects on artistic creativity of the major drugs used in the treatment of manic-depressive illness (lithium, valproate, carbamazepine, the neuroleptics, and the antidepressants) remain unclear. We focus here on lithium because it is the most important and frequently prescribed drug for manic-depressive illness and cyclothymia, and because more is known about its effects on temperament and cognition, as well as its other side effects, than about any of the other medications used. It is noteworthy that even the early lithium researchers were aware of problems created by lithium's dampening effects on certain useful or enjoyable qualities of the illness and its associated temperaments (for example, decreasing or eliminating the "highs" of the milder manic states, or decreasing sexuality and energy levels), as well as by the untoward side-effects of lithium (occasional cognitive slowing and memory impairment). Mogens Schou, the Danish psychiatrist who, more than anyone else, is responsible for the tens of thousands of lives saved by lithium, was aware of and concerned about the drug's potential limitations. He noted that some patients on lithium reported feeling that life was flatter and more colorless than it had been before taking the medication.[4] Other researchers observed that patients occasionally felt less creative and productive, and that some of them missed their hypomanic periods.[5] Missing the highs of hypomania is, in fact, an important reason why many patients stop taking lithium against medical advice.[6]

Evidence for a strong effect of lithium on personality and temperament came from several sources: studies of lithium effects on normal subjects, *prima facie* evidence derived from both clinical and systematic observation of lithium's profound therapeutic effect on behavior, mood, and personality in affectively ill patients, and comparisons of personality studies completed in the prelithium era with those completed after lithium treatment became widespread.[7] The latter are quite consistent in showing that personality differences between manic-depressive patients and "normal" comparison groups pale considerably, and often entirely, once lithium is used effectively.[8] Several clinical researchers have also examined the effects of lithium on personality in normal subjects. Schou, the first to systematically describe the cognitive, behavioral, and personality effects of lithium in normal individuals, found that at relatively low blood levels lithium had minimal effects on medical-student volunteers. In three medical researchers taking lithium at higher levels, however, effects were more pronounced. They reported experiencing a decreased responsiveness to their environment, increased indifference and malaise, greater passivity, and cognitive changes:

> The subjective experience was primarily one of indifference and slight general malaise. This led to a certain passivity. . . . The subjective feeling of having been altered by the treatment was disproportionately strong in relation to objective behavioral changes. The subjects could engage in discussions and social activities but found it

difficult to comprehend and integrate more than a few elements of the situation. Intellectual initiative was diminished and there was a feeling of lowered ability to concentrate and memorize; but thought processes were unaffected, and the subjects could think logically and produce ideas.[9]

Dr. Lewis Judd and his colleagues at the University of California, San Diego, also studied the effects of lithium on normal male volunteers. They found that their subjects, in addition to reporting a mood-lowering effect of the drug, had less inclination and desire to "deal with the demands of the environment."[10] Likewise, Drs. D. Kropf and B. Müller-Oerlinghausen in Germany showed that normal men while on lithium had decreased social involvement, activity, and concentration, as well as increased boredom and lethargy.[11] Other studies of normal volunteers have also found a reduced sense of well-being, fewer social interactions, fatigue, lack of efficiency and initiative, and attenuated emotional responsiveness.[12] A few studies have examined personality and mood stabilization over time in lithium-treated, affectively ill patients. One investigation of twenty-eight manic-depressive patients found that lithium's most pronounced effects were in decreasing sociability, initiative, and impulsiveness;[13] others indicated that moods may become unusually stable in manic-depressive patients treated with lithium.[14] Like many effects of lithium, the extent of personality change or emotional dampening appears to be a function of the blood level of the drug. Kropf and Müller-Oerlinghausen found, for example, that patients on higher levels of lithium were less active, less obsessive, and less elated than those on lower levels, who showed proportionately more initiative and assertiveness, as well as greater sociability and sensitivity.[15] Unfortunately, those patients who were maintained at a reduced lithium level were also more likely to become manic or severely depressed again.

Since lithium's primary action is mediated through the central nervous system, it is not surprising that the drug can also cause cognitive impairments of varying types and degrees of severity. Indeed, mental slowing and impaired concentration are among the side effects of lithium treatment that patients report most frequently, and are most frequently implicated in an unwillingness to continue treatment.[16] It is important to keep in mind, however, that acute mania and depression also cause pronounced cognitive impairment and inability to function;[17] depression can contribute to the tendency to overreport side effects, as well, especially difficulties in memory and concentration.[18] Likewise, a recent review of twenty-five neuropsychological studies of patients with manic-depressive illness found a quite consistent pattern of right-hemispheric (or nondominant) impairment.[19] This type of impairment—associated with problems in perception, spatial relations, integration of holistic figures, and complex nonverbal tasks—was found not only in those individuals who had already experienced episodes of mania and depression but also in children of manic-depressive parents who were, subsequently, at a high risk for developing manic-depressive illness but had not yet been ill.[20] Clearly, preexisting cognitive differences, as well as impairment due to the acute effects of mania and depression, can make it difficult to sort out illness from treatment effects.

These and many other complex methodological problems have led to conflicting interpretations of the data from studies of lithium's cognitive effects in both animals and humans.[21] Some investigators have concluded that there is "no convincing proof that lithium causes memory disorder,"[22] while others have found strong evidence to the contrary.[23] In their review of lithium's effects on normal subjects, Dr. Judd and his colleagues concluded that lithium:

> often induces subjective feelings of cognitive slowing together with decreased ability to learn, concentrate and memorize. In addition, controlled studies have consistently described small but consistent performance decrements on various cognitive tests, including memory tests. The available data suggest that the slowing of performance is likely to be secondary to a slowing in rate of central information processing.[24]

Evidence for lithium's effects on long-term memory, associative processing, semantic reasoning, memory retrieval, and speed of cognitive and psychomotor performance comes, in fact, from many studies.[25] Results showing actual impairment in general intellectual functioning are less consistent, although certainly suggestive.[26] In most instances, the intellectual problems that occur in patients taking lithium are probably due to some combination of lithium side-effects and the underlying disease itself.

The specific effects of lithium on productivity and creativity are not clear. In 1971 Drs. P. Polatin and R. Fieve in New York described their clinical experience using lithium in creative individuals:

> In the creative individual who does his best work in the course of a hypomanic period, the complaint regarding the continued use of lithium carbonate is that it acts as a "brake." These patients report that lithium carbonate inhibits creativity so that the individual is unable to express himself, drive is diminished, and there is no incentive. These patients also indicate that when they are depressed, the symptoms are so demoralizing and so uncomfortable that they welcome the "mild high" when the depression disappears and prefer to settle for a cyclothymic life of highs and lows rather than an apathetic middle-of-the-road mood state achieved through the use of lithium carbonate.
>
> Their argument is that if lithium carbonate prevents the high and may possibly prevent the "low," they prefer not to take lithium carbonate, since never to have a high as a result of the drug seems equivalent to being deprived of an "addictive-like" pleasurable and productive state. Some of these patients are terrified of having a low again, but insist on taking their chances without lithium carbonate therapy, knowing that sooner or later they will be compensated by the high, even if they do go into a low state.[27]

This is a common, and almost certainly valid, clinical observation, and clinicians who treat artists and writers who suffer from manic-depressive illness would concur with several of its essential points. However, in the two studies that actually asked artists and writers about lithium's effect on their artistic productivity, the overwhelming majority indicated that their productivity while on lithium had either increased (57 percent) or remained the same (20 percent).[28] Approximately one-fourth (23 percent) reported a decrease in productivity, and a significant minority (17 percent) stated they had stopped lithium due to its adverse effects. Schou, the author of one of the two studies, emphasized the importance of individual differences in interpreting the findings. He noted that lithium might affect inspiration, the ability to execute ideas, or both. Likewise, artists and writers clearly vary in a number of important ways, including the severity and type of their illnesses, their degree of dependence upon manic periods for artistic inspiration, and individual sensitivities to the pharmacological action of lithium.[29]

Cognitive studies of particular relevance for artistic creativity conflict in their results. Judd and his associates found no effects of short-term lithium use on creativity in normal individuals;[30] a more recent study, however, found substantial detrimental effects of lithium on associational processing in patients with manic-depressive illness.[31] Differences between these and other results may be due in part to the fact that lithium's effect on cognition is almost certainly quite different in manic-depressives and normals.[32] Individual differences in clinical state, serum lithium levels, sensitivity to cognitive side effects, and the severity and type of affective illness also clearly affect the degree to which an individual will experience impairment in intellectual functioning, creativity, and productivity.

Although our discussion thus far has focused on the potential difficulties arising from treatment with lithium, three crucial and offsetting points need to be kept in mind. First, most individuals who are on lithium experience few significant side effects of any kind,[33] and fewer than one-third report significant negative changes in their intellectual functioning.[34] In the great majority of instances the effective treatments now available do not hinder creative ability. Indeed, competent treatment almost always results in longer periods of sustained productivity. A major concern, however, remains the study, public discussion, and aggressive development of treatments that will minimize the side effects that occur with the currently available medications.

Second, modern psychiatric treatment for manic-depressive illness is not limited to lithium alone. Two anticonvulsants, carbamazepine and valproate (valproic acid), have been effective in treating many patients who cannot tolerate or do not respond to lithium.[35] There is some anecdotal clinical evidence to suggest that cognitive side effects and emotional blunting may be less troublesome with valproate, or with a combination of valproate with a lower dose of lithium, than with standard lithium therapy alone. These clincial impressions, if confirmed by more systematic investigation, may prove invaluable to the minority of individuals who now suffer from their treatment as well as from their disease. Psychotherapy is also an important part of the treatment of manic-depressive illness. While there is no evidence that psychotherapy alone can effectively treat or prevent manic-depressive illness, evidence is accumulating to show that psychotherapy, in conjunction with medication, can reduce the risk of relapse.[36] Researchers at the University of California, Los Angeles demonstrated many years ago that a combination of psychotherapy, family education, and medication allowed clinicians to prescribe lower doses of antipsychotic medications for schizophrenic patients.[37] One of the ultimate goals of doing psychotherapy with manic-depressive patients might be to permit lower levels of lithium, thereby minimizing the cognitive, temperamental, and other side effects of the drug. Several studies now show that the lower doses of lithium currently used (compared with early clinical practice, in which the blood levels were, on the average, 30 percent higher) result in fewer and milder somatic side effects.[38] There is evidence that cognitive side effects are also tied to blood level,[39] and competent treatment of manic-depressive illness entails using the lowest possible level of lithium that is consistent with preventing recurrences of mania and depression. Intelligent timing of dosages is also important; for example, a single daily dose of lithium can result in fewer side effects than several doses taken throughout the day.[40] Recent studies, although quite preliminary, have found that side effects may be reduced even further in some individuals by administering 150 percent of the usual daily lithium dose every forty-eight hours instead of every twenty-four.[41] Interestingly, two of the patients in these particular studies were artists who had stopped painting during the course of regular lithium therapy but resumed once the two-day regimen was instituted. (These findings are preliminary, and any changes in lithium dosages should be carefully discussed within the context of a good clinical relationship.) The judicious use of adjunctive treatments (such as antidepressants, antipsychotic medications, electroconvulsive therapy, phototherapy, and sleep deprivation) can also be important in minimizing the adverse effects of treatment and maximizing the benefits. Likewise, the daily charting of moods in order to follow and utilize seasonal, diurnal, and other patterns of moods and productivity can be invaluable, recalling Emerson's remarks: "We are intent on Meteorology to find the law of the Variable Winds to the end that we may not get our hay wet. I also wish a Farmer's Almanac of the Mental Moods that I may farm my mind. There are undulations of power & imbecility & I lose days sitting at my table which I should gain to my body & mind if I knew beforehand that no thought would come that day."[42] Many artists and writers, once stabilized on lithium, opt for a low level of the drug in hopes of achieving a kind of controlled cyclothymia, willing to take the "undulations of power & imbecility" in exchange for periods of high enthusiasms and flowing thoughts. When it works this can be a good solution to a difficult problem; unfortunately, it is a strategy that carries with it an increased risk of depressive and manic relapses.[43] The attempt to balance the ebbings and flowings of imagination and temperament with the treatment for their extremes is captured by French poet Antonin Artaud, who spent many years of his life in a psychiatric hospital:

> DOCTOR—There's a point on which I would have liked to insist: it's concerning the importance of the thing on which your injections act; this kind of essential relaxation of my being, this lowering of my mental waterlevel which, as one might think, doesn't mean any diminution whatever of my morality (my moral soul) or even of my intelligence but, if you wish, only of my usable intellect, of my possibilities for thought, and which has more to do with the feeling I have of myself than what I show to others. . . .
>
> And now, Monsieur le Docteur, since you are quite aware of what in me is capable of being attacked (and healed by drugs). . . . I hope you have the know-how to give me the quantity of subtle liquids, of specious agents, of mental morphine which will uplift my abasement, balance what is crumbling, reunite what is separated, recompose what is destroyed.[44]

When discussing the very real problems associated with treating manic-depressive illness, it is most important to be acutely aware of the generally far worse, often fatal, consequences of not treating it. There can be no serious question that lithium and the anticonvulsants are enormously effective in treating manic-depressive illness and preventing suicide. The scientific literature to support their efficacy is compelling.[45] While it is true that lithium has side effects, it is also true that the illness for which it is prescribed is serious and life-threatening. In this sense lithium is no different in causing side effects (except that they are generally milder) from drugs used in the treatment of other potentially lethal illnesses such as cancer and heart disease. No one is creative when paralytically depressed, psychotic, institutionalized, in restraints, or dead because of suicide. While some writers and artists have emphasized the roles of angst, turmoil, and a mercurial temperament in their work, many have not. Robert Burns, for example, described the effect of his depression on his poetry: His body, he said, "was atacked by that most dreadful distemper, . . . a confirmed melancholy; in this wretched state, the recollection of which makes me yet shudder, I hung my harp on the willow trees, except in some lucid intervals."[46] And Robert Lowell, nearly two centuries later, wrote: "Mania is sickness for one's friends, depression for one's self. Both are chemical. In depression, one wakes, is happy for about two minutes, probably less, and fades into dread of the day. Nothing will happen, but you know twelve hours will pass before you are back in bed and sheltering your consciousness in dreams, or nothing. It isn't danger; it's not an accomplishment. I don't think it a visitation of the angels but a weakening in the blood."[47] The list of writers and artists who ended their lives by suicide is staggeringly long. Poets include Thomas Lovell Beddoes, John Berryman, Barcroft Boake, Paul Celan, Thomas Chatterton, Hart Crane, John Davidson, Tove Ditlevsen, Sergey Esenin, John Gould Fletcher, Adam Lindsay Gordon, Randall Jarrell,[48] Heinrich Von Kleist, Vachel Lindsay, Vladimir Mayakovsky, Cesare Pavese, Sylvia Plath, Anne Sexton, Sara Teasdale, and Marina Ivanovna Tsvetayeva. Other writers who committed suicide include Romain Gary, Ernest Hemingway, William Inge, Yukio Mishima, Gérard de Nerval, John Kennedy Toole, and Virginia Woolf. Among painters and sculptors who killed themselves were Ralph Barton, Francesco Bassano, Francesco Borromini, Vincent van Gogh, Arshile Gorky, Benjamin Haydon, Ernst Ludwig Kirchner, Wilhelm Lehmbruck, Jules Pascin, Mark Rothko, Nicolas de Staël, and Pietro Testa. (See Appendix B as well.) Almost all these individuals suffered from depressive or manic-depressive illness. We will never know what Thomas Chatterton and Virginia Woolf might have written or Vincent van Gogh painted had they lived rather than committing suicide. Van Gogh described this well: "If I could have worked without this accursed disease—what things I might have done. . . . following what the country said to me. But there, this journey is over and done with,"[49] and Robert Lowell's publisher, Robert Giroux, observed poignantly:

> Of all our conversations, I remember most vividly [Lowell's] words about the new drug, lithium carbonate, which had such good results [after almost twenty manic attacks and subsequent hospitalizations] and gave him reason to believe he was cured: "It's terrible, Bob, to think that all I've suffered, and all the suffering I've caused, might have arisen from the lack of a little salt in my brain."[50]

Suicide is not the only risk of not treating manic-depressive illness. In addition to the suffering caused by individual attacks of mania and depression, the natural course of the disease, left untreated, is to worsen over time (the attacks become more frequent and more severe). This pattern can be seen in the illnesses of many writers and artists, for example, Byron, Clare, Coleridge, van Gogh, Hopkins, Poe, Roethke, Ruskin, Schumann, and Woolf. Manic-depressive illness and cyclothymia not only worsen over time, they also become less responsive to medication the longer they remain untreated (perhaps because the biochemical and anatomical substrates change as a result of recurrent manic and depressive episodes).[51] Secondary problems are also created by the use of alcohol, laudanum, cocaine, nicotine, and the many other drugs that artists and writers have used over the centuries to medicate or induce the moods associated with manic-depressive illness. Clearly these drugs are less specific and less effective and cause many more adverse effects and complications (including worsening the nature and course of the illness; causing both short- and long-term damage to the brain and other parts of the nervous system; and compromising the functioning of the pulmonary and cardiovascular systems) than do the medications now available for treating the illness.

Artists and writers, like everyone else, ultimately decide for themselves whether or not, and how, to be treated. Fortunately they also tend to bring to their treatment decisions the same independence, imagination, skepticism, and willingness to take risks that characterize the rest of their lives and their work. Some end up choosing traditional medical treatment, others opt for idiosyncratic versions, and yet others choose no treatment at all, even mindful of the suffering they might experience. It is clear that, whatever else, depth and intensity of human feeling must be a part of creation in the arts. But modern medicine now allows relief of the extremes of despair, turmoil, and psychosis: It allows choices not previously available. Most of the writers, artists, and composers discussed in this book had no meaningful choice.

> The capacity to blunder slightly is the real marvel of DNA. Without this special attribute, we would still be anaerobic bacteria and there would be no music.
>
> —LEWIS THOMAS[52]

Very different issues of choice arise from the fact that manic-depressive illness is a genetic disease. These genetic issues are of considerably more long-term concern than the ones surrounding pharmacological treatments. Inevitably, given time and increasingly sophisticated research, the development of new drugs should make it possible to medicate individuals who have manic-depressive illness in such a way that the side effects are inconsequential and, it is to be hoped, in such a way that those aspects of temperament and cognition that are essential to the creative process will remain intact. The search for the gene, or genes, involved in manic-depressive illness raises far more difficult ethical problems, however;[53] these issues become particularly complicated because manic-depressive illness can confer advantages on both the individual and society. Although unusual as a disease that brings with it certain advantages, it is by no means alone. Carriers of the sickle-cell trait, for example, appear to have had relative immunity to certain types of malarial infections; in this context, David Suzuki and Peter Knudtson make the argument for a broad biological perspective when considering the notion of "defective genes":

> The story of sickle-cell anemia does underscore the striking capacity of a seemingly defective gene to simultaneously offer both advantages and disadvantages—depending on its quantities and surroundings. Moreover, there is growing evidence that natural selection

often routinely maintains a balance of such mutant DNA sequences in populations of many species. The problem is that we are blind to that fragile balance except in rare instances, such as sickle-cell anemia, where geneticists have managed to unravel the intricacies of gene action in relation to hereditary disease.

But how many other "defective" genes responsible for hereditary disorders might harbor some unseen evolutionary value? And, until we know enough about human genetics to begin to grasp their evolutionary roles, what price might we eventually pay if we overzealously try to "cure" these genetic abnormalities by ridding the human gene pool of these DNA sequences. . . ?[54]

Manic-depressive illness appears to convey its advantages not only through its relationship to the artistic temperament and imagination, but through its influence on many eminent scientists as well as business, religious, military, and political leaders.[55] Subtler effects that derive from its being a common illness with a wide range of temperamental and cognitive expression have yet to be assessed; indeed, few studies have examined the possible evolutionary reasons for the survival of *any* of the genes responsible for psychopathology, although some writers have suggested that schizophrenia, while devastating to those who suffer from it, might confer certain intellectual and temperamental advantages on first-degree relatives.[56] The complexities surrounding the search for the genes responsible for manic-depressive illness are enormous. It is highly unlikely, for example, that only one gene is involved and, even if an individual carries the gene (or genes), he or she may never become ill (likewise, he or she may or may not have the temperamental and cognitive characteristics associated with the illness). This suggests the likelihood of subtle, or not so subtle, interactions with the environment that might precipitate the first manic or depressive attack (for example, exposure to prolonged or significant changes in light, pronounced sleep reduction, drug or alcohol intake, childbirth) or the inheritance of other genes that might either trigger or protect against the disease. Physical and psychological factors also clearly play an important, although as yet unspecified role in the triggering and maintenance of, or protection against, the underlying genetic predisposition to manic-depressive illness. The complexity of locating the gene or genes underlying the inordinately broad range of temperamental, behavioral, and cognitive traits that constitute manic-depressive illness is beyond our current ability to imagine. Too, it is not unlikely that yet additional genetic, biochemical, and environmental factors may be at least in part responsible for both the illness and the cognitive and temperamental characteristics associated with artistic genius.

Several genetic issues are especially relevant to the diagnosis, treatment, and social policies surrounding manic-depressive illness; these include prenatal testing, abortion, forced sterilization, and gene therapy. Prenatal testing for manic-depressive illness and abortion based on a determination that a fetus is at risk for the disease may be choices that are available before the end of this century. The decision to abort any fetus obviously brings with it major ethical considerations—both for the parents involved and the society in which they live.[57] Treatable common diseases, such as manic-depressive illness—ones that almost certainly confer societal and individual advantage and that vary greatly in the nature of their expression and their severity—are particularly problematic. Dr. Francis Collins, the medical geneticist at the University of Michigan who was instrumental in finding the genes for cystic fibrosis and neurofibromatosis, was asked in an interview about prenatal testing for diseases that vary in severity or that first occur only later in life:

> This is where it gets muddy, and everyone is going to draw the line differently. Consider the situation with manic-depressive illness, a reasonably common disorder. It is clearly genetically influenced, though not in a simple way. Now, manic-depressive illness can be a terrible cross to bear. The swings into depression are awful, and the highs can be very destructive. Yet a substantial number of highly creative people have suffered from this disease. Suppose we find the gene responsible for manic depression. If every couple has a prenatal test to determine if a fetus is at risk for manic depression, and if every time the answer is yes that fetus is done away with, then we will have done something troubling, something with large consequences. Is this what we want to do?[58]

Several related issues about prenatal testing have been raised: for example, the unclear boundaries between pathological conditions and normal traits, the important distinction between medically treatable and nontreatable genetic defects, the wide spectrum of severity of defects, and the variable ages of onset of the diseases in question.[59] Larry Gostin, the director of the American Society of

Law and Medicine, has addressed some of the difficult issues involved in genetic testing:

> Complex and often pernicious mythologies emerge from public ignorance of genetically-based diagnostic and prognostic tests. The common belief is that genetic technologies generated from scientific assessment are always accurate, highly predictive and capable of identifying an individual's or offspring's inevitable pre-destination of future disability. The facts are diametrically opposed to this common belief. The results of genetic-based diagnosis and prognosis are uncertain for many reasons.
>
> Predicting the nature, severity and course of disease based upon a genetic marker is an additional difficulty. For most genetic diseases the onset date, severity of symptoms, and efficacy of treatment and management are highly variable. Some people remain virtually symptom free, while others progress to seriously disabling illness.[60]

Other scientists and ethicists have raised different concerns, including those of a more directly eugenic nature; for example, are there societal advantages to getting rid of certain genes altogether? On the other hand, might there be characteristics associated with a particular disease or trait that should be encouraged in the gene pool?[61] (It is of no little interest and irony that Francis Galton, a cousin of Charles Darwin and proponent of selective breeding in humans in order to obtain a "highly gifted race of man," was himself subject to "nervous breakdowns"; he was also appreciative of the "thin partitions" between greatness and psychopathology. Dr. Daniel Kevles, in his book *In the Name of Eugenics*, quotes Galton as saying that "men who leave their mark on the world are very often those who, being gifted and full of nervous power, are at the same time haunted and driven by a dominant idea, and are therefore within a measurable distance of insanity.")[62] Involuntarily sterilization, a hallmark of the eugenics movement, and mandatory abortion seem highly unlikely options in this day and age, but many provinces in China still have government policies requiring individuals who have hereditable mental illness (especially hereditary psychoses, which is of specific relevance to manic-depressive illness) to be sterilized; if pregnancy occurs, abortions are obligatory.[63] The historical precedent is chilling. Tens of thousands of mentally ill individuals, including many with manic-depressive illness, were sterilized or killed during the Third Reich, and many other thousands of psychiatric patients were sterilized earlier this century in the United States.[64] Ironically, one study carried out in Germany during the 1930s addressed the advisability of forced sterilization of individuals with manic-depressive illness. The author, who found that manic-depressive illness was greatly overrepresented in the professional and higher occupational classes, recommended against sterilization of these patients "especially if the patient does not have siblings who could transmit the positive aspects of the genetic heritage."[65] During the 1940s, in a study undertaken by the Committee on Heredity and Eugenics, researchers at the McLean Hospital in Boston studied the pedigrees of several socially prominent American families. They came to a similar conclusion:

> Perhaps the words of Bumke need to be taken into account before we embark too whole-heartedly on any sterilization program, "If we could extinguish the sufferers from manic-depressive psychosis from the world, we would at the same time deprive ourselves of an immeasurable amount of the accomplished and good, of color and warmth, of spirit and freshness." Finally, only dried up bureaucrats and schizophrenics would be left. Here I must say that I would rather accept into the bargain the diseased manic-depressives than to give up the healthy individuals of the same heredity cycle.[66]

Dr. John Robertson had written in like vein in his psychiatric study of Edgar Allan Poe twenty years earlier:

> The qualities of the mind, as well as their morbid reactions, are too delicate ever to be understood or scientifically prearranged. For the world this is fortunate, however high an inheritance tax the victims of heredity must pay. Eradicate the nervous diathesis, suppress the hot blood that results from the overclose mating of neurotics, or from that unstable nervous organization due to alcoholic inheritance, or even from insanity and the various forms of parental degeneracy, and we would have a race of stoics—men without imagination, individuals incapable of enthusiasms, brains without personality, souls without genius. . . . Who could, or would, breed for a hump-backed Pope, or a clubfooted Byron, a scrofulous Keats, or a soul-obsessed Poe? Nature has done fairly well by us.[67]

Debates about sterilization and forced abortion have been replaced, for the most part, by far more sophisticated debates about
prenatal testing, voluntary abortions based on the results from such
testing, and gene therapy. Many of the ethical problems remain
very much the same, however.

  Gene therapies comprise a variety of types of genetic manip-
ulation,[68] and all of them raise enormously complicated issues in
their own right.[69] The major ethical questions do not center primarily on the techniques designed to change the genetic code for
only one individual (for example, inserting normal genes into a
chromosome, removing defective genes, or using drugs that would
treat genetic illnesses by "turning off" certain genes or "turning
on" others). Even under those circumstances, however, one could
argue the advisability of changing genes that may be associated
with subtle cognitive and temperamental characteristics vital to the
well-being of society (including, for our discussion here, those related to the development of artistic imagination and expression).
Certainly it is unclear what the alleviation of highly intense emotional experiences—including ecstatic or visionary states, psychosis, severe melancholia, or other types of mental suffering—might
do to the ultimate nature of artistic expression as well as to the
motivations underlying the production of works of art. The primary
focus of ethical debate, however, is on those techniques that involve introducing genetically altered material into the reproductive cells (eggs and sperm), which could then be passed on to affect
future generations as well. This, as Joel Davis points out, "violates
the primary canon of human experimentation—the consent of the
subject. The individual who agrees to have his or her germ cells
changed can consent [depending upon the age of the individual, of
course]. *But that person's progeny are now committed to an ex-
periment to which they did not consent.*"[70] Society, as well as the
individual and his or her progeny, is bound to be deeply affected
by decisions such as these.

  Many of these ethical issues are being brought to the fore-
ground by the Human Genome Project, a vast fifteen-year program
established by the U.S. government in 1990 with the goal of identifying the exact location and function of all of the genes in the
human body. The potential benefits to health and basic science are
largely obvious; without question, individuals who have genetic

diseases—including those with manic-depressive illness—will gain immeasurably from the knowledge obtained about early identification and treatments, including the development of drugs that are based on an understanding of diseases at their molecular level. The mitigation of suffering and prevention of early death in those who have manic-depressive illness, or who are at risk for it, is a major public health priority. Although manic-depressive illness is much more common in writers and artists than in the general population, it would be irresponsible to romanticize an extremely painful, destructive, and lethal disease. Most people who suffer from manic-depressive and depressive illness are not unusually creative, and they reap few benefits from their experiences of mania and depression; even those who are highly creative usually seek relief from their suffering. Molecular biology research and the scientific advances ultimately provided by the mapping of the human genome have the potential to provide more specific, more effective, and less troubling treatments than now exist. Already, only two years after the Recombinant DNA Advisory Committee of the National Institutes of Health approved the first gene therapy trials in the United States, experimental treatment is being carried out in patients with cancer, diseases of the immune system, inherited high-cholesterol disorder, and other illnesses. Clinical trials have been proposed in several other countries as well and procedures viewed only a short time ago as radical and controversial are beginning to be used in medical research. The ethical ramifications of gene therapy and the Human Genome Project, however, are certainly far beyond our present capacity to comprehend. Because of the magnitude of potential social and ethical problems, 3 to 5 percent of the project's total budget (which is conservatively estimated at three billion dollars) has been set aside for studies of the social, ethical, and legal implications of genetic research. This is an unprecedented commitment to ethical studies and will almost certainly ensure that troubling issues such as those we have been discussing will be examined at length and with subtlety. But they need to be raised and vigorously debated. While it is inconceivable that there will be any simple answer, awareness of the problem is a beginning. Dr. James Watson, co-discoverer of the structure of DNA and the first director of the Human Genome Project, has made this point forcefully and repeatedly in his insistence on allocating massive resources to the study of ethical issues in genetic research:

> It would be naive to say that any of these answers are going to be simple. About all we can do is stimulate the discussion, and essentially lead the discussion instead of having it forced on us by people who say, "You don't know what you're doing." We have to be aware of the really terrible past of eugenics, where incomplete knowledge was used in a very cavalier and rather awful way, both here in the United States and in Germany. We have to reassure people that their own DNA is private and that no one else can get at it. We're going to have to pass laws to reassure them. [And] we don't want people rushing and passing laws without a lot of serious discussion first.[71]

Fortunately it seems more likely than not that the infinite varieties and complexities of life, with their infinite capacities for change, will be more rather than less recognized and appreciated as the genetic code begins to unwind:

> The real surprises, which set us back on our heels when they occur will always be the mutants. We have already had a few of these, sweeping across the field of human thought periodically, like comets. They have slightly different receptors for the information cascading in from other minds, and slightly different machinery for processing it, so that what comes out to rejoin the flow is novel, and filled with new sorts of meaning. Bach was able to do this, and what emerged in the current were primordia in music. In this sense, the Art of Fugue and the St. Matthew Passion were, for the evolving organism of human thought, feathered wings, apposing thumbs, new layers of frontal cortex.[72]

Finally, there must be serious concern about any attempt to reduce what is beautiful and original to a clinical syndrome, genetic flaw, or predictable temperament. It is frightening, and ultimately terribly boring, to think of anyone—certainly not only writers, artists, and musicians—in such a limited way. The fear that medicine and science will take away from the ineffability of it all, or detract from the mind's labyrinthian complexity, is as old as man's attempts to chart the movement of the stars. Even John Keats, who had studied to be a surgeon, felt that Newton's calculations would blanch the heavens of their glory. The natural sciences, he wrote, "will clip an Angel's wings,/Conquer all mysteries by rule and line,/Empty the haunted air, and gnomed mine—/Unweave a rainbow."[73] What remains troubling is whether we have diminished the most extraordinary among us—our writers, artists, and composers—by discussing them in terms of psychopathology or illnesses of mood. Do we—in our rush to diagnose, to heal, and perhaps even to alter their genes—compromise the respect we should feel for their differentness, independence, strength of mind, and individuality? Do we diminish artists if we conclude that they are far more likely than most people to suffer from recurrent attacks of mania and depression, experience volatility of temperament, lean toward the melancholic, and end their lives through suicide? I don't think so. Such statements seem to me to be fully warranted by what we now know; to deny them flies in the face of truth and risks unnecessary suffering, as well as not coming to terms with the important treatment and ethical issues that are raised by this complicated illness. American novelist Walker Percy, whose father and grandfather committed suicide and in whose family an unrelenting path of suicide, mania, and depression can be traced for at least two hundred years, wrote:

> Death in the form of death genes shall not prevail over me, for death genes are one thing but it is something else to name the death genes and know them and stand over against them and dare them. I am different from my death genes and therefore not subject to them. My father had the same death genes but he feared them and did not name them and thought he could roar out old Route 66 and stay ahead of them or grab me and be pals or play Brahms and keep them, the death genes, happy, so he fell prey to them.
>   Death in none of its guises shall prevail over me, because I know all the names of death.[74]

No one knows for certain where any of our knowledge—scientific or artistic—will take us, but that has always been so. Uncertainty, romantic imagination, and mystery tend to weave their way throughout both the scientific and artistic fields of thought and experience. Byron, the skeptical Romantic, gave testament to these common threads and uncommon voyages:

>   we must deem the mode
> In which Sir Isaac Newton could disclose
>   Through the then unpaved stars the turnpike road,
> A thing to counterbalance human woes;
>   For ever since immortal man hath glowed
> With all kinds of mechanics, and full soon
> Steam-engines will conduct him to the Moon.
>
> And wherefore this exordium?—Why, just now,
>   In taking up this paltry sheet of paper,
> My bosom underwent a glorious glow,
>   And my internal Spirit cut a caper:
> And though so much inferior, as I know,
>   To those who, by the dint of glass and vapour,
> Discover stars, and sail in the wind's eye,
> I wish to do so much by Poesy.
>
> In the Wind's Eye I have sailed, and sail; but for
>   The stars, I own my telescope is dim;
> But at the least I have shunned the common shore,
>   And leaving land far out of sight, would skim
> The Ocean of Eternity: the roar
>   Of breakers has not daunted my slight, trim
> But *still* sea-worthy skiff; and she may float
>   Where ships have foundered, as doth many a boat.[75]

The great imaginative artists have always sailed "in the wind's eye," and brought back with them words or sounds or images to "counterbalance human woes." That they themselves were subject to more than their fair share of these woes deserves our appreciation, understanding, and very careful thought.

APPENDIX A

═══════════════

DIAGNOSTIC CRITERIA FOR THE MAJOR MOOD DISORDERS

DIAGNOSTIC CRITERIA FOR MAJOR DEPRESSIVE EPISODE

Note: A "Major Depressive Syndrome" is defined as criterion A below.

A. At least five of the following symptoms have been present during the same two-week period and represent a change from previous functioning; at least one of the symptoms is either (1) depressed mood, or (2) loss of interest or pleasure. (Do not include symptoms that are clearly due to a physical condition, mood-incongruent delusions or hallucinations, incoherence, or marked loosening of associations.)

    (1) depressed mood (or can be irritable mood in children and adolescents) most of the day, nearly every day, as indicated either by subjective account or observation by others

    (2) markedly diminished interest or pleasure in all, or almost all, activities most of the day, nearly every day (as indicated either by subjective account or observation by others of apathy most of the time)

    (3) significant weight loss or weight gain when not dieting (e.g., more than 5% of body weight in a month), or decrease or increase in appetite nearly every day (in children, consider failure to make expected weight gains)

    (4) insomnia or hypersomnia nearly every day

    (5) psychomotor agitation or retardation nearly every day (observable by others, not merely subjective feelings of restlessness or being slowed down)

    (6) fatigue or loss of energy nearly every day

(7) feelings of worthlessness or excessive or inappropriate guilt (which may be delusional) nearly every day (not merely self-reproach or guilt about being sick)

(8) diminished ability to think or concentrate, or indecisiveness, nearly every day (either by subjective account or as observed by others)

(9) recurrent thoughts of death (not just fear of dying), recurrent suicidal ideation without a specific plan, or a suicide attempt or a specific plan for committing suicide

B. (1) It cannot be established that an organic factor initiated and maintained the disturbance

(2) The disturbance is not a normal reaction to the death of a loved one (Uncomplicated Bereavement)
Note: Morbid preoccupation with worthlessness, suicidal ideation, marked functional impairment or psychomotor retardation, or prolonged duration suggest bereavement complicated by Major Depression.

C. At no time during the disturbance have there been delusions or hallucinations for as long as two weeks in the absence of prominent mood symptoms (i.e., before the mood symptoms developed or after they have remitted).

D. Not superimposed on Schizophrenia, Schizophreniform Disorder, Delusional Disorder, or Psychotic Disorder not otherwise specified.

DIAGNOSTIC CRITERIA FOR MANIC EPISODE

Note: A "Manic Syndrome" is defined as including criteria A, B, and C below. A "Hypomanic Syndrome" is defined as including criteria A and B, but not C, i.e., no marked impairment.

A. A distinct period of abnormally and persistently elevated, expansive, or irritable mood.

B. During the period of mood disturbance, at least three of the following symptoms have persisted (four if the mood is only irritable) and have been present to a significant degree:
(1) inflated self-esteem or grandiosity
(2) decreased need for sleep, e.g., feels rested after only three hours of sleep
(3) more talkative than usual or pressure to keep talking
(4) flight of ideas or subjective experience that thoughts are racing
(5) distractibility, i.e., attention too easily drawn to unimportant or irrelevant external stimuli
(6) increase in goal-directed activity (either socially, at work or school, or sexually) or psychomotor agitation
(7) excessive involvement in pleasurable activities which have a high po-

tential for painful consequences, e.g., the person engages in unrestrained buying sprees, sexual indiscretions, or foolish business investments

C. Mood disturbance sufficiently severe to cause marked impairment in occupational functioning or in usual social activities or relationships with others, or to necessitate hospitalization to prevent harm to self or others.

D. At no time during the disturbance have there been delusions or hallucinations for as long as two weeks in the absence of prominent mood symptoms (i.e., before the mood symptoms developed or after they have remitted).

E. Not superimposed on Schizophrenia, Schizophreniform Disorder, Delusional Disorder, or Psychotic Disorder not otherwise specified.

F. It cannot be established that an organic factor initiated and maintained the disturbance. **Note:** Somatic antidepressant treatment (e.g., drugs, ECT) that apparently precipitates a mood disturbance should not be considered an etiologic organic factor.

DIAGNOSTIC CRITERIA FOR CYCLOTHYMIA

A. For at least two years (one year for children and adolescents), presence of numerous Hypomanic Episodes (all of the criteria for a Manic Episode, Manic Episode . . . except criterion C that indicates marked impairment) and numerous periods with depressed mood or loss of interest or pleasure that did not meet criterion A of Major Depressive Episode.

B. During a two-year period (one year in children and adolescents) of the disturbance, never without hypomanic or depressive symptoms for more than two months at a time.

C. No clear evidence of a Major Depressive Episode or Manic Episode during the first two years of the disturbance (or one year in children and adolescents).

   Note: After this minimum period of Cyclothymia, there may be superimposed Manic or Major Depressive Episodes, in which case the additional diagnosis of Bipolar Disorder or Bipolar Disorder not otherwise specified should be given.

D. Not superimposed on a chronic psychotic disorder, such as Schizophrenia or Delusional Disorder.

E. It cannot be established that an organic factor initiated and maintained the disturbance, e.g., repeated intoxication from drugs or alcohol.

SOURCE: From American Psychiatric Association, *Diagnostic and Statistical Manual of Mental Disorders, Third Edition, Revised* (Washington, D.C.: American Psychiatric Association, 1987). Reprinted by permission of American Psychiatric Association.

CLINICAL CRITERIA FOR CYCLOTHYMIA

GENERAL

1. Onset in teens or early adulthood
2. Clinical presentation as a personality disorder (patient often unaware of "moods" *per se*)
3. Short cycles—usually days—which are recurrent in an irregular fashion, with infrequent euthymic periods
4. May not attain full syndrome for depression and hypomania during any one cycle, but entire range of affective manifestations occurs at various times
5. "Endogenous" mood changes, i.e., often wake up with mood

BIPHASIC COURSE

1. Hypersomnia alternating with decreased need for sleep (although intermittent insomnia can also occur)
2. Shaky self-esteem which alternates between lack of self-confidence and naive or grandiose overconfidence
3. Periods of mental confusion and apathy, alternating with periods of sharpened and creative thinking
4. Marked unevenness in quantity and quality of productivity, often associated with unusual working hours
5. Uninhibited people-seeking (that may lead to hypersexuality) alternating with introverted self-absorption

BEHAVIORAL MANIFESTATIONS

1. Irritable-angry-explosive outbursts that alienate loved ones
2. Episodic promiscuity; repeated conjugal or romantic failure
3. Frequent shift in line of work, study, interest or future plans
4. Resort to alcohol and drug abuse as a means for self-treatment or augmenting excitement
5. Occasional financial extravagance

SOURCE: From H.S. Akiskal, M. K. Khani, and A. Scott-Strauss, Cyclothymic temperamental disorders, *Psychiatric Clinics of North America*, 2 (1979): 527–554. Reprinted by permission of W. B. Saunders Company.

DIAGNOSTIC CRITERIA FOR HYPOMANIA

MOOD
Elevated, expansive, or irritable

PSYCHOMOTOR
More energy than usual
Physical restlessness

SPEECH
More talkative than usual

SLEEP
Decreased need for sleep

COGNITIVE
Inflated self-esteem
Sharpened and unusually creative thinking
Overoptimism or exaggeration of past achievement

BEHAVIOR
Increased productivity, often with unusual and self-imposed working hours
Uninhibited people–seeking
Hypersexuality
Inappropriate laughing, joking, punning
Excessive involvement in pleasurable activities with lack of concern for painful
   consequences, for example, buying sprees, foolish business investments, reck-
   less driving

SOURCE: Based on diagnostic criteria from American Psychiatric Association, *Diagnostic and Statistical Manual of Mental Disorders, Third Edition* (Washington, D.C.: American Psychiatric Association, 1980). Reprinted by permission of W. B. Saunders Company.

APPENDIX B

WRITERS, ARTISTS, AND COMPOSERS WITH PROBABLE CYCLOTHYMIA, MAJOR DEPRESSION, OR MANIC-DEPRESSIVE ILLNESS

POETS

- Antonin Artaud
φ • Konstantin Batyushkov
  φ Charles Baudelaire
  † Thomas Lovell Beddoes
† • John Berryman
   William Blake
   Aleksandr Blok
† Barcroft Boake
- Louise Bogan
   Rupert Brooke
   Robert Burns
   George Gordon, Lord Byron
   Thomas Campbell
† Paul Celan
† Thomas Chatterton
- John Clare
   Hartley Coleridge
   Samuel Taylor Coleridge
- William Collins
φ • William Cowper
† Hart Crane

   George Darley
† John Davidson
   Emily Dickinson
   Ernest Dowson
- T. S. Eliot[1]
† Sergey Esenin
- Robert Fergusson
φ Afanasy Fet
   Anne Finch, Countess of
     Winchilsea
   Edward FitzGerald
† John Gould Fletcher
φ • Gustaf Fröding
   Oliver Goldsmith
† Adam Lindsay Gordon
   Thomas Gray
φ Nikolai Gumilyov
   Robert Stephen Hawker
- Friedrich Hölderlin
   Gerard Manley Hopkins
   Victor Hugo

cont.

Key: • Asylum or psychiatric hospital † Suicide φ Suicide attempt

† • Randall Jarrell[2]
   Samuel Johnson
   John Keats
• Henry Kendall
• Velimir Khlebnikov
† Heinrich Von Kleist
   Walter Savage Landor
• Nikolaus Lenau
φ J.M.R. Lenz
   Mikhail Lermontov
† Vachel Lindsay
   James Russell Lowell
• Robert Lowell
• Hugh MacDiarmid
   Louis MacNeice
φ • Osip Mandelstam
   James Clarence Mangan
† Vladimir Mayakovsky
• Edna St. Vincent Millay
   Alfred de Musset
† • Gérard de Nerval

• Boris Pasternak
† Cesare Pavese
† • Sylvia Plath
φ Edgar Allan Poe
• Ezra Pound
   Alexander Pushkin
φ Laura Riding
• Theodore Roethke
• Delmore Schwartz
† • Anne Sexton
φ Percy Bysshe Shelley
• Christopher Smart
• Torquato Tasso
† • Sara Teasdale
   Alfred, Lord Tennyson
   Dylan Thomas
   Edward Thomas
φ Francis Thompson
† • Georg Trakl
† Marina Tsvetayeva
   Walt Whitman

WRITERS

   Hans Christian Andersen
   Honoré de Balzac
   James Barrie
• Arthur Benson
   E. F. Benson
   James Boswell

   John Bunyan
   Samuel Clemens
φ Joseph Conrad
   Charles Dickens
φ Isak Dinesen
   Ralph Waldo Emerson

cont.

Key: • Asylum or psychiatric hospital   † Suicide   φ Suicide attempt
Note 1: This is meant to be an illustrative rather than a comprehensive list; for systematic studies see text. Most of the writers, composers, and artists are American, British, European, Irish, or Russian; all are deceased.
Note 2: Many if not most of these writers, artists, and composers had other major problems as well, such as medical illnesses (e.g., Paul Gauguin, John Keats, Edward Lear, Nikolaus Lenau, Cole Porter, Hugo Wolf), alcoholism or drug addiction (e.g., Antonin Artaud, John Berryman, Samuel Taylor Coleridge, F. Scott Fitzgerald, Ernest Hemingway, Modest Mussorgsky, Eugene O'Neill, Raphaelle Peale, Edgar Allan Poe, Francis Thompson, Tennessee Williams), or exceptionally difficult life circumstances (e.g., Arshile Gorky, Osip Mandelstam). They are listed here as having suffered from a mood disorder because their mood symptoms predated their other conditions, because the nature and course of their mood and behavior symptoms were consistent with a diagnosis of an independently existing affective illness, and/or because their family histories of depression, manic-depressive illness, and suicide—coupled with their own symptoms—were sufficiently strong to warrant their inclusion.

- William Faulkner
- F. Scott Fitzgerald
ɸ Lewis Grassic Gibbon
  Nikolai Gogol
ɸ Maxim Gorky
  Kenneth Graham
  Graham Greene
† • Ernest Hemingway
ɸ • Hermann Hesse
  Henrik Ibsen
† • William Inge
  Henry James
  William James
- Charles Lamb
† • Malcolm Lowry

  Herman Melville
ɸ • Eugene O'Neill
  Francis Parkman
- John Ruskin[3]
  Mary Shelley
- Jean Stafford
  Robert Louis Stevenson
  August Strindberg
  Leo Tolstoy
  Ivan Turgenev
- Tennessee Williams
ɸ Mary Wollstonecraft
† • Virginia Woolf
  Emile Zola

COMPOSERS

  Anton Arensky
ɸ Hector Berlioz
- Anton Bruckner
† Jeremiah Clarke
  John Dowland
  Edward Elgar
  Carlo Gesualdo
  Mikhail Glinka
  George Frideric Handel[4]
  Gustav Holst
  Charles Ives
- Otto Klemperer[5]

  Orlando de Lassus
  Gustav Mahler
  Modest Mussorgsky
  Sergey Rachmaninoff
  Giocchino Rossini
ɸ • Robert Schumann
  Alexander Scriabin
  Peter Tchaikovsky
† Peter Warlock
ɸ • Hugo Wolf
† Bernd Alois Zimmerman

NONCLASSICAL COMPOSERS AND MUSICIANS

- Irving Berlin
  Noel Coward
  Stephen Foster
- Charles Mingus

ɸ • Charles Parker
- Cole Porter
- Bud Powell

ARTISTS

† Ralph Barton
† Francesco Bassano
- Ralph Blakelock
  David Bomberg
† Francesco Borromini
  John Sell Cotman
- Richard Dadd[6]

† Edward Dayes
  Thomas Eakins
ɸ Paul Gauguin
  Théodore Géricault
  Hugo van der Goes
† • Vincent van Gogh
† Arshile Gorky

cont.

- Philip Guston
† Benjamin Haydon
- Carl Hill
- Ernst Josephson
φ George Innes
† • Ernst Ludwig Kirchner
- Edwin Landseer[7]
  Edward Lear
† Wilhelm Lehmbruck
  John Martin
- Charles Méryon
  Michelangelo
  Adolphe Monticelli
- Edvard Munch

† Jules Pascin
- Georgia O'Keeffe
- Raphaelle Peale
- Jackson Pollock
  George Romney
φ Dante Gabriel Rossetti
† Mark Rothko
† Nicolas de Staël
† Pietro Testa
† Henry Tilson
  George Frederic Watts
  Sir David Wilkie
  Anders Zorn

Key: • Asylum or psychiatric hospital   † Suicide   φ Suicide attempt
[1] Although not formally hospitalized, Eliot had to take a three-month leave of absence (for a "nervous breakdown") in order to be treated in a Swiss clinic.
[2] See chapter 7, note 48, p. 349.
[3] Ruskin had the equivalent of psychiatric hospitalization (his doctors arranged for twenty-four hour nursing care during his psychotic episodes).
[4] See chapter 3, note 63, pp. 297–298.
[5] Primarily a conductor.
[6] See chapter 6, note 166, p. 342.
[7] Landseer was confined to the care of a physician.

NOTES

CHAPTER 1
THAT FINE MADNESS

1. Michael Drayton, "To my dearly loved Friend, Henry Reynolds, Esq.; of Poets and Poesy," lines 106–110, *The Works of Michael Drayton, Esq.*, vol. 4 (London: W. Reeve, 1753).

2. Ernest J. Lovell, ed., *Lady Blessington's Conversations of Lord Byron* (Princeton, N.J.: Princeton University Press, 1969), p. 115.

3. George Becker, *The Mad Genius Controversy: A Study in the Sociology of Deviance* (Beverly Hills, Calif.: Sage Publications, 1978), p. 73.

4. Ibid., pp. 127–128.

5. Ian Hamilton, *Robert Lowell: A Biography* (New York: Random House, 1982), p. 208.

6. George Gordon, Lord Byron, "The Lament of Tasso," line 5, *Lord Byron: The Complete Poetical Works*, ed. Jerome J. McGann (Oxford: Oxford University Press, 1986), vol. 4, p. 116.

7. Dante Alighieri, *The Comedy of Dante Alighieri: Cantica I: Hell (L'Inferno)*, canto XVII, lines 109–110, trans. Dorothy L. Sayers (Middlesex, England: Penguin, 1949), p. 177.

8. Charles Lamb, "The Sanity of True Genius," *Elia and the Last Essays of Elia* (New York: Oxford University Press, 1987), p. 213.

9. Seamus Heaney, "Elegy," lines 34–40, *Agenda: Robert Lowell Special Issue* (Autumn 1980), pp. 21–22.

CHAPTER 2
ENDLESS NIGHT, FIERCE FIRES AND SHRAMMING COLD

1. Dante, *The Comedy of Dante Alighieri: Cantica I: Hell* (*L'Inferno*), canto III, lines 86–87, p. 87.

2. Robert Lowell, "Visitors," lines 35–41, *Day by Day* (London and Boston: Faber and Faber, 1977), p. 111.

3. Robert Lowell, "For John Berryman, 1914–1972," *Collected Prose*, ed. Robert Giroux (New York: Farrar, Straus & Giroux, 1987), pp. 104–118.

4. Hamilton, *Robert Lowell*, p. 351.

5. Ernst Kretschmer, quoted in J. D. Campbell, *Manic-Depressive Disease: Clinical and Psychiatric Significance* (Philadelphia: J. B. Lippincott, 1953).

6. Eliot Slater and Martin Roth, *Clinical Psychiatry*, 3rd ed. (Baltimore: Williams & Wilkins, 1969), pp. 206–207.

7. Emil Kraepelin, *Manic-Depressive Insanity and Paranoia*, trans. R. M. Barclay, ed. G. M. Robertson (Edinburgh: E&S Livingstone, 1921; reprinted New York: Arno Press, 1976).

H. S. Akiskal, Subaffective disorders: Dysthymic, cyclothymic and bipolar II disorders in the "borderline" realm, *Psychiatric Clinics of North America*, 4 (1981): 25–46.

H. S. Akiskal, The bipolar spectrum: New concepts in classification and diagnosis, in L. Grinspoon, ed., *Psychiatry Update, Volume II* (Washington, D.C.: American Psychiatric Press, 1983), pp. 271–292.

H. S. Akiskal, A. H. Djenderendjian, R. H. Rosenthal, and M. K. Khani, Cyclothymic disorder: Validating criteria for inclusion in the bipolar affective group, *American Journal of Psychiatry*, 134 (1977): 1227–1233.

H. S. Akiskal, A. H. Bitar, V. R. Puzantian, T. L. Rosenthal, and P. W. Walker, The nosological status of neurotic depression: A prospective three- to four-year follow-up in light of the primary-secondary and unipolar-bipolar dichotomies, *Archives of General Psychiatry*, 35 (1978): 756–766.

R. A. Depue and S. M. Monroe, The unipolar-bipolar distinction in the depressive disorders, *Psychological Bulletin*, 85 (1978): 1001–1029.

B. G. H. Waters, Early symptoms of bipolar affective psychosis: Research and clinical implications, *Canadian Psychiatric Association Journal*, 2 (1979): 55–60.

R. A. Depue, J. F. Slater, H. Wolfstetter-Kausch, D. Klein,

E. Goplerud, and D. Farr, A behavioral paradigm for identifying persons at risk for bipolar depressive disorder: A conceptual framework and five validation studies, *Journal of Abnormal Psychology Monograph*, 90 (1981): 381–437.

R. A. Depue, R. M. Kleiman, P. Davis, M. Hutchinson, and S. P. Krauss, The behavioral high-risk paradigm and bipolar affective disorder, VIII: Serum free cortisol in nonpatient cyclothymic subjects selected by the General Behavioral Inventory, *American Journal of Psychiatry*, 142 (1985): 175–181.

8. Akiskal (1981), ibid.; Akiskal (1983), ibid.; Akiskal et al. (1977), ibid.; Depue and Monroe (1978), ibid.; Depue et al. (1981), ibid.

9. H. S. Akiskal, M. K. Khani, and A. Scott-Strauss, Cyclothymic temperamental disorders, *Psychiatric Clinics of North America*, 2 (1979): 527–554.

10. Akiskal et al., Cyclothymic disorder: Validating criteria (1977); R. A. Depue et al., A behavioral paradigm (1981); D. L. Dunner, F. D. Russek, B. Russek, and R. R. Fieve, Classification of bipolar affective disorder subtypes, *Comprehensive Psychiatry*, 23 (1982): 186–189.

11. A. Bertelsen, B. Harvald, and M. Hauge, A Danish twin study of manic-depressive disorders, *British Journal of Psychiatry*, 130 (1977): 330–351.

12. *Mania: An Evolving Concept*, ed. R. H. Belmaker and H. M. van Praag (New York: SP Medical and Scientific Books, 1980); *Handbook of Affective Disorders*, ed. E. S. Paykel (New York: Guilford Press, 1982); *Neurobiology of Mood Disorders*, ed. R. M. Post and J. C. Ballenger (Baltimore: Williams & Wilkins, 1984); P. C. Whybrow, H. S. Akiskal, and W. T. McKinney, *Mood Disorders: Toward a New Psychobiology* (New York: Plenum, 1984); W. Z. Potter, M. V. Rudorfer, and F. K. Goodwin, Biological findings in bipolar disorders, in *American Psychiatric Association Annual Review*, vol. 6, ed. R. E. Hales and A. J. Francis (Washington, D.C.: American Psychiatric Press, 1987), pp. 32–60; *Depression and Mania*, ed. A. Georgotas and R. Cancro (New York: Elsevier, 1988); F. K. Goodwin and K. R. Jamison, "Evolution of the Bipolar-Unipolar Concept," *Manic-Depressive Illness* (New York: Oxford University Press, 1990), pp. 56–73.

13. Robert Burns, *The Letters of Robert Burns*, vol. 1, 1780–1789 (letter 374, December 3, 1789), 2nd ed., ed. G. Ross Roy (Oxford: Oxford University Press, 1985), pp. 456–457.

14. John W. Robertson, *Edgar A. Poe: A Psychopathic Study* (New York: G. P. Putnam, 1923), p. 27; Edgar Allan Poe, *The Letters of Edgar Allan Poe*, vol. 1 (letter to John P. Kennedy, September 11, 1835), ed.

John Wand Ostrom (Cambridge: Harvard University Press, 1948), p. 73.

15. Hector Berlioz, *The Memoirs of Hector Berlioz*, trans. David Cairns (St. Albans, England: Granada, 1970), p. 142.

16. Ibid., pp. 226–228.

17. Burns, *Letters*, vol. 2, 1790–1796 (letter to Mrs. W. Riddell, December, 1793).

18. William Shakespeare, *Hamlet*, ed. T. J. B. Spencer (London: Penguin, 1980), act II, scene 2, lines 295–303, p. 112.

19. William Cowper, *The Letters and Prose Writings of William Cowper*, ed. James King and Charles Ryskamp (Oxford: Oxford University Press, 1981), vol. 2, p. 200.

20. F. Walker, *Hugo Wolf: A Biography* (London: J. M. Dent & Sons, 1968), p. 322. See also R. Pauly and H. Hecaen, [Mania and musical inspiration: Hugo Wolf's case], *Annales Médico-Psychologiques*, 97 (1939): 389–405; Hugo Wolf, *Letters to Melanie Köchert*, ed. Franz Grasberger, English ed. and trans. Louise McClelland Urban (New York: Schirmer, 1991).

21. Walker, *Hugo Wolf*, p. 361.

22. R. George Thomas, *Edward Thomas: A Portrait* (Oxford: Clarendon Press, 1985), p. 64.

23. William Cowper, *Letters of William Cowper* (letter to Lady Hesketh, January 22, 1796), ed. W. Benham (London: Macmillan, 1914), pp. 310–311.

24. F. Niecks, *Robert Schumann: A Supplementary and Corrective Biography* (London: J. M. Dent & Sons, 1925), p. 142.

25. David Cecil, *The Stricken Deer: The Life of Cowper* (1929, reprint, London: Constable, 1988), pp. 223–225.

26. F. Scott Fitzgerald, "The Crack-Up," in *The Crack-Up and Other Stories* (New York: New Directions, 1956), pp. 69–75.

27. Edward Thomas, *The Icknield Way* (London: Constable, 1913), pp. 280–283.

28. James Clarence Mangan, *Autobiography*, ed. James Kilroy (Dublin: Dolman Press, 1968), p. 26.

29. Ibid., p. 27.

30. Ibid., p. 21.

31. James Clarence Mangan, "The Nameless One," lines 5–8, 17–20, and 25–28, *Poems of James Clarence Mangan*, Centenary Ed., ed. D. J. O'Donoghue (Dublin: O'Donoghue, London: A. H. Bullen, 1903), p. 120.

32. Gerard Manley Hopkins, *Gerard Manley Hopkins, Including His Correspondence with Coventry Patmore* (letter to A. W. M. Baillie,

May 8, 1885), ed. Claude Colleer Abbott (London: Oxford University Press, 1956), p. 256.

33. Gerard Manley Hopkins, *The Letters of Gerard Manley Hopkins to Robert Bridges* (letter to Robert Bridges, September 1, 1885), ed. Claude Colleer Abbott (London: Oxford University Press, 1935), p. 222.

34. Gerard Manley Hopkins, Retreat notes dated January 1, 1888, a New Year slip for 1889, *The Sermons and Devotional Writings of Gerard Manley Hopkins*, ed. Christopher Devlin (London: Oxford University Press, 1959), p. 262.

35. Ibid.

36. Hopkins, *The Letters of Gerard Manley Hopkins to Robert Bridges* (letter to Robert Bridges, May 17, 1885), p. 219.

37. Gerard Manley Hopkins, "No Worst, There Is None," *The Poetical Works of Gerard Manley Hopkins*, ed. Norman H. Mackenzie (Oxford: Oxford University Press, 1990), p. 182.

38. Lewis Grassic Gibbon, *Cloud Howe* (1933, reprint, Edinburgh: Canongate Classics, 1988), p. 20.

39. Quentin Bell, *Virginia Woolf: A Biography* (London: Hogarth Press, 1972), p. 11.

40. Ibid.

41. Sylvia Plath, *The Bell Jar* (New York: Harper & Row, 1971), pp. 142–143.

42. Theodore Roethke, "Elegy," lines 3–4, 13–16, *The Collected Poems of Theodore Roethke* (New York: Anchor Press/Doubleday, 1975), p. 138.

43. Walker, *Hugo Wolf*, p. 359.

44. Walter Jackson Bate, *John Keats* (Cambridge: Belknap Press of Harvard University Press, 1963), p. 98.

45. Quoted in Allan Seager, *The Glass House: The Life of Theodore Roethke* (Ann Arbor: University of Michigan Press, 1991), p. 101.

46. Hamilton, *Robert Lowell*, p. 285.

47. Hamilton, *Robert Lowell*, p. 157.

48. John Rosenberg, *The Darkening Glass: A Portrait of Ruskin's Genius* (New York: Columbia University Press, 1986), p. 151.

49. Leonard Woolf, *Beginning Again: An Autobiography of the Years 1911 to 1918* (New York: Harcourt, 1964), pp. 172–173.

50. Saul Bellow, *Humboldt's Gift* (Middlesex, England: Penguin, 1976), pp. 29–31.

51. Edgar Allan Poe, "The Man of the Crowd," *The Fall of the House of Usher and Other Writings*, ed. David Galloway (London: Penguin, 1986), p. 179.

52. Joan Abse, *John Ruskin: The Passionate Moralist* (London: Quar-

tet Books, 1980), p. 302. For discussions of Ruskin's psychiatric illness see, for example, John Ruskin, Mr. Ruskin's illness as described by himself, *British Medical Journal*, 1 (1900): 225–226; L. J. Bragman, The case of John Ruskin: A study of cyclothymia, *American Journal of Psychiatry*, 91 (1935): 1137–1159; R. J. Joseph, John Ruskin: Radical and psychotic genius, *Psychoanalytic Review*, 56 (1969): 425–441.

53. Jonathan Carroll, *Outside the Dog Museum* (New York: Doubleday, 1992), pp. 16–17.

54. Hamilton, *Robert Lowell*, p. 286.

55. Ibid., p. 307.

56. Ibid., p. 218.

57. Delmore Schwartz, "May's Truth and May's Falsehood," *Selected poems (1938–1958): Summer Knowledge* (New York: New Directions, 1959) pp. 213–214.

58. Kraepelin, *Manic-Depressive Insanity and Paranoia*, p. 54.

59. John D. Campbell, *Manic-Depressive Disease: Clinical and Psychiatric Significance* (Philadelphia: J. B. Lippincott, 1953), pp. 112–113.

60. Goodwin and Jamison, "Evolution of the Bipolar-Unipolar Concept," pp. 56–60; J. R. Whitwell, *Historical Notes on Psychiatry (Early Times–End of 16th Century)* (London: H. K. Lewis & Co., 1936); S. W. Jackson, *Melancholia and Depression: From Hippocratic Times to Modern Times* (New Haven, Conn.: Yale University Press, 1986); G. Roccatagliata, *A History of Ancient Psychiatry* (New York: Greenwood Press, 1986).

61. Whitwell, *Historical Notes on Psychiatry*, pp. 163–164, from *De acut, et diut, morborum, causis, signis, et curatione* (Paris, 1554), trans. R. Moffatt.

62. Ibid., p. 175, from Trallianus Alexander, *Medici libri duodecim*, interpret. Guintherius (Basel, 1556).

63. Ibid., p. 212, from Pratensis Jason, *De cerebri morbis* (Basel, 1549).

64. Michel Foucault, *Madness and Civilization: A History of Insanity in the Age of Reason* (New York: Vintage Books, 1965), p. 132.

65. Jackson, *Melancholia and Depression*, p. 258; from Richard Mead, *The Medical Works of Richard Mead, M.D.* (London: C. Hitch et al., 1762), *pp. 485–486.*

66. M. J. Sedler, Falret's discovery: The origin of the concept of bipolar affective illness, *American Journal of Psychiatry*, 140 (1983): 1127–1133.

67. Kraepelin, *Manic-Depressive Insanity*, pp. 99–116.

68. Robertson, *Edgar A. Poe*, p. 82; Poe, *Letters*, vol. 2 (letter to George Eveleth, 1848), p. 356.

69. Donald W. Goodwin, *Alcohol and the Writer* (Kansas City: Andrews and McMeel, 1988); Tom Dardis, *The Thirsty Muse: Alcohol and the American Writer* (New York: Ticknor & Fields, 1989).

70. S. Foster Damon, *Thomas Holley Chivers: Friend of Poe* (New York: Harper, 1930), p. 170.

71. W. R. Bett, Edgar Allan Poe: The Oedipus complex and genius, in W. R. Bett, *The Infirmities of Genius* (London: Johnson, 1952), p. 74–75.

72. Ibid., p. 64; Poe, *Letters*, vol. 2 (letter to Annie L. Richmond, November 16, 1848), pp. 401 and 403.

73. Ibid., p. 218; Poe, *Letters*, vol. 1 (letter to James Russell Lowell, June 2, 1844), p. 256. Professor Kenneth Silverman, who feels that the evidence is otherwise weak for Poe's use of opium, describes Poe's suicide attempt (with an overdose of laudanum) in his recent biography *Edgar A. Poe: Mournful and Never-ending Remembrance* (New York: Harper Collins, 1991), pp. 373–374.

74. Goodwin and Jamison, "Alcohol and Drug Abuse in Manic-Depressive Illness," pp. 210–226. Review of twenty studies of rates of alcohol abuse or alcoholism in patients with manic-depressive illness, pp. 213–215.

75. Ibid., Review of thirteen studies of rates of affective illness in patients with alcohol abuse or alcoholism, pp. 215–216.

76. D. A. Regier, M. E. Farmer, D. S. Raye, B. Z. Locke, S. J. Keith, L. L. Judd, and F. K. Goodwin, Comorbidity of mental disorders with drug and alcohol abuse: Results from the Epidemiologic Catchment Area (ECA) study, *Journal of the American Medical Association*, 264 (1990): 2511–2518.

77. J. E. Helzer and T. R. Pryzbeck, The co-occurrence of alcoholism with other psychiatric disorders in the general population and its impact on treatment, *Journal of Studies on Alcohol*, 49 (1988): 219–224.

78. Goodwin and Jamison, *Manic-Depressive Illness*, review of six studies, pp. 219–220; S. Zisook and M. A. Schuckit, Male primary alcoholics with and without family histories of affective disorder, *Journal of Studies on Alcohol*, 48 (1987): 337–344.

79. Hamilton, *Robert Lowell*, pp. 300–301.

80. Goodwin and Jamison, *Manic-Depressive Illness*, pp. 222–224.

F. N. Pitts and G. Winokur, Affective disorder VII: Alcoholism and affective disorder, *Journal of Psychiatric Research*, 4 (1966): 37–50.

B. Liskow, D. Mayfield, and J. Thiele, Alcohol and affective disorder: Assessment and treatment, *Journal of Clinical Psychiatry*, 43 (1982): 144–147.

J. M. Himmelhoch, Mixed states, manic-depressive illness, and the nature of mood, *Psychiatric Clinics of North America*, 2 (1979): 449–459.

J. M. Himmelhoch, D. Mulla, J. F. Neil, T. P. Detre, and D. J. Kupfer, Incidence and significance of mixed affective states in a bipolar population, *Archives of General Psychiatry*, 33 (1976): 1062–1066.

81. Goodwin and Jamison, *Manic-Depressive Illness*, pp. 216–219; T. W. Estroff, C. A. Dackis, M. S. Gold, and A. L. C. Pottash, Drug abuse and bipolar disorders, *International Journal Psychiatry Med*, 15 (1985): 37–40.

82. Regier et al., Comorbidity of mental disorders (1990).

83. S. M. Mirin, R. D. Weiss, A. Sollogub, and J. Michael, Affective illness in substance abusers, in S. M. Mirin, ed., *Substance Abuse and Psychopathology* (Washington, D. C.: American Psychiatric Press, 1984), pp. 57–78.

T. R. Kosten and B. J. Rounsaville, Psychopathology in opioid addicts, *Psychiatric Clinics of North America*, 9 (1986): 515–532.

S. M. Mirin and R. D. Weiss, Affective illness in substance abusers, *Psychiatric Clinics of North America*, 9 (1986): 503–514.

R. D. Weiss and S. M. Mirin, Subtypes of cocaine abusers, *Psychiatric Clinics of North America*, 9 (1986): 491–501.

R. D. Weiss, S. M Mirin, M. L. Griffin, and J. L. Michael, Psychopathology in cocaine abusers: Changing trends, *Journal of Nervous and Mental Disease*, 176 (1988): 719–725.

E. V. Nunes, F. M. Quitkin, and D. F. Klein, Psychiatric diagnosis in cocaine abuse, *Psychiatry Research*, 28 (1989): 105–114.

84. E. J. Khantzian, The self-medication hypothesis of addictive disorders: Focus on heroin and cocaine dependence, *American Journal of Psychiatry*, 142 (1985): 1259–1264; F. H. Gawin and H. D. Kleber, Abstinence symptomatology and psychiatric diagnosis in cocaine abusers, *Archives of General Psychiatry*, 43 (1986): 107–113; Weiss et al., Psychopathology in cocaine abusers (1988).

85. Weiss et al. Psychopathology in cocaine abusers, (1988).

86. Regier et al., Comorbidity of mental disorders, (1990).

87. Samuel Taylor Coleridge, *Collected Letters of Samuel Taylor Coleridge*, vol. 4, 1815–1819 (letter to James Gillman, April 13, 1816), ed. Earl Leslie Griggs (Oxford: Oxford University Press, 1959), p. 1002.

88. John Haffenden, *The Life of John Berryman* (Boston: Routledge & Kegan Paul, 1982), pp. 374–375.

89. W. Read, *The Days of Dylan Thomas* (New York: McGraw-Hill, 1964).

90. Kraepelin, *Manic-Depressive Insanity*, p. 25.

91. Goodwin and Jamison, "Suicide," *Manic-Depressive Illness*, pp. 227–244.

92. O. Hagnell, J. Lanke, and B. Rorsman, Suicide rates in the Lundby study: Mental illness as a risk factor for suicide, *Neuropsychobiology*, 7 (1981): 248–253.

93. D. A. Brent, J. A. Perper, C. E. Goldstein, D. J. Kolko, M. J. Allan, C. J. Allman, and J. P. Zelenak, Risk factors for adolescent suicide: A comparison of adolescent suicide victims with suicidal inpatients, *Archives of General Psychiatry*, 45 (1988): 581–588.

94. Bruce Kellner, *The Last Dandy: Ralph Barton* (Columbia: University of Missouri Press, 1991), p. 213.

95. Goodwin and Jamison, *Manic-Depressive Illness*, pp. 231–234.

96. D. A. Regier, J. H. Boyd, J. D. Burke, Jr., D. S. Rae, J. K. Myers, M. Kramer, L. N. Robins, L. K. George, M. Karno, and B. Z. Locke, One-month prevalence of mental disorders in the United States: Based on five Epidemiological Catchment Area sites, *Archives of General Psychiatry*, 45 (1988): 977–986.

97. Norman Sherry, *The Life of Graham Greene, vol. 1, 1904–1939* (New York: Viking Penguin, 1989), p. 159; reference for Graham Greene's self-diagnosis of manic-depressive illness, Paul Theroux, "An Edwardian on the Concorde: Graham Greene as I Knew Him," *New York Times Book Review*, April 21, 1991.

98. Sherry, *The Life of Graham Greene*, p. 155.

99. George Gordon, Lord Byron, *Byron's Letters and Journals*, vol. 5, *1816–1817* (letter to Thomas Moore, January 28, 1817), ed. Leslie A. Marchand (Cambridge: Belknap Press of Harvard University Press, 1976), p. 165.

100. Lowell, "I. A. Richards 2. Death," lines 7–8, *History* (London: Faber and Faber, 1973), p. 202.

101. Lowell, "Suicide," lines 46–55, *Day by Day*, p. 16.

102. E. Robins, S. Gassner, J. Kayes, R. H. Wilkinson, and G. E. Murphy, The communication of suicidal intent: A study of 134 consecutive cases of successful (completed) suicide, *American Journal of Psychiatry*, 115 (1959): 724–733.

103. William Styron, *Darkness Visible: A Memoir of Madness* (New York: Random House, 1990), p. 62.

104. Leo Tolstoy, *Confession*, trans. David Patterson (New York: W. W. Norton, 1983), pp. 28–29.

105. A. Alvarez, *The Savage God: A Study of Suicide* (New York: Random House, 1973), p. 75.

106. Ibid., pp. 95–97.

107. Ibid., pp. 79–80.

108. Kraepelin, *Manic-Depressive Insanity*; G. R. Jameison, Suicide and mental disease: A clinical analysis of one hundred cases, *Arch Neurol Psychiatry*, 36 (1936): 1–12; G. Winokur, P. J. Clayton, and T. Reich, *Manic Depressive Illness* (St. Louis: C. V. Mosby, 1969); J. Kotin and F. K. Goodwin, Depression during mania: Clinical observations and theoretical implications, *American Journal of Psychiatry*, 129 (1972): 679–686; C. P. Miles, Conditions predisposing to suicide: A review, *Journal of Nervous and Mental Disease*, 164 (1977): 231–246.

109. Percy Bysshe Shelley, "The Retrospect: Cwm Elan, 1812," lines 25–34, *Shelley: Poetical Works*, ed. Thomas Hutchinson (London: Oxford University Press, 1970), p. 874.

110. Vladimir Mayakovsky, "It's After One," lines 1–12, in Edward J. Brown, *Mayakovsky: A Poet in the Revolution* (New York: Paragon House, 1988), p. 356.

111. Ibid.

112. George Gordon, Lord Byron, "Manfred: A Dramatic Poem," act III, lines 160–167, *Lord Byron: The Complete Poetical Works*, ed. J. J. McGann, vol. 4 (Oxford: Oxford University Press, 1986).

CHAPTER 3
COULD IT BE MADNESS—THIS?

1. Joyce Carol Oates, speech given to the Cosmos Club, Washington, D.C., Reprinted in *Cosmos Club Bulletin*, 44 (January 1991): 5.

2. Emily Dickinson, "The First Day's Night Had Come" (poem 410), lines 17–20, *The Poems of Emily Dickinson*, ed. Thomas H. Johnson, (Cambridge: Harvard University Press, 1955).

3. Robert Graves, *The Greek Myths*, vol. 1. (Middlesex, England: Penguin, 1955), p. 9.

4. Plato, *Phaedrus and the Seventh and Eighth Letters*, trans. Walter Hamilton. (Middlesex, England: Penguin, 1974), pp. 46–47.

5. Ibid., p. 48.

6. Aristotle, *Problems II: Books XXII–XXXVIII*, trans. W. S. Hett (Cambridge: Harvard University Press, 1936), pp. 155–157.

7. William Wordsworth, "Resolution and Independence," *William Wordsworth: The Poems*, vol. 1, ed. John O. Hayden (New Haven: Yale University Press, 1981), p. 553.

8. Byron, "Childe Harold's Pilgrimage," canto III, verse 7, lines 55–60, *Lord Byron: The Complete Poetical Works*, vol. 2, p. 79.

9. Benjamin Rush, *Medical Inquiries and Observations Upon the*

Diseases of the Mind. (Philadelphia: Kimber and Richardson, 1812), pp. 153–154.

10. J.-J. Moreau, *La Psychologie Morbide dans ses Rapports avec la Philosophie de l'Histoire.* (Paris: V. Masson, 1859); Cesare Lombroso, *L'Homme de Génie.* (Paris: Alcon, 1889); P. J. Möbius, "Über das Studium der Talente," *Zeitschrift für Hypnotismus,* 10 (1902): 66–74.

11. Lamb, "The Sanity of True Genius," pp. 212–213.

12. David Cecil, *A Portrait of Charles Lamb.* (London: Constable, 1983), p. 55.

13. William James, *The Varieties of Religious Experience: A Study in Human Nature* (1902; reprint, Middlesex, England: Penguin, 1982), pp. 23–24.

14. Kraepelin, *Manic-Depressive Insanity,* p. 17.

15. A. Myerson and R. Boyle, The incidence of manic-depressive psychosis in certain socially important families, *American Journal of Psychiatry,* 98 (1941): 11–21.

16. Lionel Trilling, *The Liberal Imagination: Essays on Literature and Society* (New York: Harcourt Brace Jovanovich, 1950), pp. 152–153.

17. Rudolf Wittkower and Margot Wittkower, *Born Under Saturn: The Character and Conduct of Artists: A Documented History from Antiquity to the French Revolution.* (New York: W. W. Norton, 1963), p. 100.

18. Trilling, *The Liberal Imagination,* p. 165, 170.

19. Francis Galton, *Hereditary Genius: An Inquiry Into Its Laws and Consequences.* (New York: D. Appleton & Co., 1871); J. F. Nisbet, *The Insanity of Genius,* 5th ed. (London: Alexander Moring, 1891).

20. C. Whilbey, The indiscretions of biography, *English Review,* 39 (1924): 769–772.

J. A. Garraty, The interrelations of psychology and biography, *Psychological Bulletin,* 51 (1954): 569–582.

J. A. Chambers, Relating personality and biographical factors to scientific creativity, *Science,* 145 (1964): 1203–1205;

M. B. Shapiro, The single case in clinical psychological research, *Journal of General Psychology* 74 (1966): 3–23.

M. Roff and D. F. Ricks, eds., *Life History Research in Psychopathology,* vol. 1 (Minneapolis: University of Minnesota Press, 1970).

M. Roff, L. Robins, and M. Pollack, eds., *Life History Research in Psychopathology,* vol. 2. (Minneapolis: University of Minnesota Press, 1972).

F. E. Kenyon, Pathography and psychiatry, *Canadian Psychiatric Association Journal,* 18 (1973): 63–66.

D. F. Ricks, A. Thomas, and M. Roff, eds., *Life History Re-*

search in Psychopathology, vol. 3 (Minneapolis: University of Minnesota Press, 1974).

L. Ross, The intuitive psychologist and his shortcomings: Distortions in the attribution process, in L. Berkowitz, ed., *Advances in Experimental Social Psychology*, vol. 10 (New York: Academic Press, 1977).

W. M. Runyan. A stage-state analysis of the life course, *Journal of Personality and Social Psychology*, 38 (1980): 951–962.

H. A. Murray, *Endeavors in Psychology: Selections from the Personology of Henry A. Murray*, ed. E. S. Shneidman. (New York: Harper & Row, 1981).

W. M. Runyan, *Life Histories and Psychobiography: Explorations in Theory and Method* (New York: Oxford University Press, 1984).

21. Anthony Storr, "The Sanity of True Genius," unpublished manuscript.

22. Studies of suicide in depressive and manic-depressive illness are reviewed in Goodwin and Jamison, *Manic-Depressive Illness*. See also Hagnell, Lanke, and Rorsman, Suicide rates in the Lundby study; J. A. Egeland and J. N. Sussex, Suicide and family loading for affective disorders, *Journal of the American Medical Association*, 254 (1985): 915–918.

23. For example, Galton, *Hereditary Genius*, 1871; Lombroso, *L'Homme de Génie*, 1889.

24. A. Juda, The relationship between highest mental capacity and psychic abnormalities, *American Journal of Psychiatry*, 106 (1949): 296–307.

25. C. Martindale, Father's absence, psychopathology, and poetic eminence. *Psychological Reports*, 31 (1972): 843–847; C. Martindale, *The Clockwork Muse: The Predictability of Artistic Change* (New York: Basic Books, 1990).

26. J. J. Schildkraut and A. J. Hirshfeld, Mind and mood in modern art: The New York School, *CME Syllabus and Proceedings Summary, American Psychiatric Association Annual Meeting* (New York: May 1990), pp. 255–256. J. J. Schildkraut, A. J. Hirshfeld, and J. Murphy, Mind and mood in modern art II: Depressive disorders, spirituality and early deaths in the abstract expressionist artists of the New York School, submitted for publication. The artists studied were Bradley Walker Tomlin, Adolph Gottlieb, Mark Rothko, Arshile Gorky, Clyfford Still, Willem de Kooning, Barnet Newman, James Brooks, David Smith, Franz Kline, William Baziotes, Jackson Pollock, Philip Guston, Ad Reinhardt, and Robert Motherwell.

27. W. H. Trethowan, Music and mental disorder, in *Music and the Brain*, M. Critchley and R. E. Henson (London: Heinemann, 1977), pp. 398–442.

28. A. M. Ludwig, Creative achievement and psychopathology: Comparisons among professions. *American Journal of Psychotherapy*, 46 (1992): 330–356.

29. A partial listing of autobiographical, biographical, and medical sources:

SAMUEL JOHNSON. *An Account of the life of Dr. Samuel Johnson, from his Birth to his Eleventh Year, Written by Himself*, ed. Richard Wright (London: Richard Phillips, 1805); R. Macdonald Ladell, The neurosis of Dr. Samuel Johnson, *British Journal of Medical Psychology*, (1929) 9:314–323; James Boswell, *Boswell's Life of Johnson*, 6 vols., ed. George Birkbeck Hill, rev. and enlarg. Lawrence F. Powell (Oxford: Clarendon Press, 1934–1950); *The Letters of Samuel Johnson*, 3 vols., ed. R. W. Chapman (Oxford: Clarendon Press, 1952); Paul Fussell, *Samuel Johnson and the Life of Writing* (New York: W. W. Norton, 1971); W. Jackson Bate, *Samuel Johnson* (New York: Harcourt Brace Jovanovich, 1977); R. Porter, "The Hunger of Imagination": Approaching Samuel Johnson's melancholy, in *The Anatomy of Madness: Essays in the History of Psychiatry. Volume I: People and Ideas*, ed. W. F. Bynum, Roy Porter, and Michael Shepherd (London: Tavistock, 1985).

THOMAS GRAY. Edmund Gosse, *Gray: English Men of Letters* (London: Macmillan, 1902); Samuel Johnson, "Gray," in *Lives of the English Poets*, vol. 3, ed. George Birkbeck Hill (Oxford: Clarendon Press, 1905), pp. 421–442; *The Correspondence of Thomas Gray*, 3 vols., ed. Paget Toynbee and Leonard Whibley (Oxford: Clarendon Press, 1935); William Powell Jones, *Thomas Gray, Scholar: The True Tragedy of an Eighteenth-Century Gentleman* (Cambridge: Harvard University Press, 1937); R. W. Ketton-Cremer, *Thomas Gray: A Biography* (Cambridge: Cambridge University Press, 1955); A. L. Lytton Sells, *Thomas Gray: His Life and Works* (London: George Allen & Unwin, 1980).

WILLIAM COLLINS. Samuel Johnson, "Collins," in *Lives of the English Poets*, vol. 3, ed. George Birkbeck Hill (Oxford: Clarendon Press, 1905), pp. 334–342; E. G. Ainsworth, *Poor Collins: His Life, His Art, and His Influence* (Ithaca, NY: Cornell University Press, 1937); Oliver F. Sigworth, *William Collins* (New York: Twayne, 1965); P. L. Carver, *The Life of a Poet: A Biographical Sketch of William Collins* (London: Sidgwick & Jackson, 1967); R. Wendorf, *William Collins and Eighteenth-Century English Poetry* (Minneapolis: University of Minnesota Press, 1981).

CHRISTOPHER SMART. E. G. Ainsworth and C. E. Noyes, *Christopher Smart: A Biographical and Critical Study* (Columbia: University of Missouri Press, 1943); Christopher Devlin, *Poor Kit Smart* (London: Rupert Hart-Davis, 1961); Geoffrey Grigson, *Christopher Smart* (London: Longmans, Green & Co., 1961); Arthur Sherbo, *Christopher Smart: Scholar of the University* (East Lansing: Michigan State

University, 1967); Frances E. Anderson, *Christopher Smart* (New York: Twayne, 1974).

JOSEPH WARTON.   John Wooll, *Biographical Memoirs of the Late Reverend Joseph Warton, D.D.* (London: Cadell & Davies, 1806); "Joseph Warton," in *The Dictionary of National Biography*, vol. 20, ed. Sir Leslie Stephen and Sir Sidney Lee (London: Oxford University Press, 1917), pp. 885–888; John A. Vance, *Joseph and Thomas Warton* (Boston: Twayne, 1983).

OLIVER GOLDSMITH.   James Prior, *Life of Oliver Goldsmith, M.B., from a Variety of Original Sources*, 2 vols. (London: Murray, 1837); Washington Irving, *Oliver Goldsmith: A Biography* (New York: George Putnam, 1849); John Forster, *The Life and Times of Oliver Goldsmith* (London: Bickers & Son, 1877); *The Collected Letters of Oliver Goldsmith*, ed. Katharine C. Balderston (Cambridge: Cambridge University Press, 1928); William Freeman, *Oliver Goldsmith* (London: Herbert Jenkins, 1951); Ralph M. Wardle, *Oliver Goldsmith* (Lawrence: University of Kansas Press, 1957); Ricardo Quintana, *Oliver Goldsmith: A Georgian Study* (New York: Macmillan, 1967); A. Lytton Sells, *Oliver Goldsmith: His Life and Works* (London: George Allen & Unwin, 1974); Leonard Wibberley, *The Good-Natured Man: A Portrait of Oliver Goldsmith* (New York: William Morrow, 1979).

WILLIAM COWPER.   G. B. Cheever, *Lectures on the Life, Genius and Insanity of Cowper* (London: Nisbeth, 1856); Anon., The insanity of William Cowper, *American Journal of Insanity*, 14 (1858): 215–240; Lord David Cecil, *The Stricken Deer: The Life of Cowper* (London: Constable, 1929); James Hendrie Lloyd, The case of William Cowper, the English poet, *Archives of Neurology and Psychiatry*, 24 (1930): 682–689; *The Letters and Prose Writings of William Cowper*, 5 vols., ed. James King and Charles Ryskamp (Oxford: Clarendon Press, 1979–1986); J. King, *William Cowper: A Biography* (Durham, NC: Duke University Press, 1986); J. E. Meyer and R. Meyer, Self-portrayal by a depressed poet: A contribution to the clinical biography of William Cowper, *American Journal of Psychiatry*, 144 (1987): 127–132.

JAMES MACPHERSON.   *The Poems of Ossian*, 2 vols., ed. Malcolm Laing (Edinburgh: A. Constable, 1805); Bailey Saunders, *The Life and Letters of James Macpherson* (London: Swann Sonnenschein, 1894); J. S. Smart, *James Macpherson: An Episode in Literature* (London: Nutt, 1905).

ROBERT FERGUSSON.   David Irving, *The Life of Robert Fergusson* (Glasgow: Chapman & Lang, 1799); *The Works of Robert Fergusson*, ed. A. B. Grosart (London: Fullarton, 1851); Alexander B. Grosart, *Robert Fergusson* (Edinburgh: Oliphant, 1898); Sir George Douglas,

Scottish Poetry: Drummond of Hawthornden to Fergusson (Glasgow: James Macklehose & Sons, 1911); Sydney Goodsir Smith, *Robert Fergusson: 1750–1774. Essays by Various Hands to Commemorate the Bicentenary of His Birth* (Edinburgh: Thomas Nelson and Sons, 1952); P. J. Rooney, W. Watson Buchanan, and A. L. Macneill, Robert Fergusson: Poet and patient (1750–1774), *The Practitioner*, 219 (1977): 402–407; David Daiches, *Robert Fergusson* (Edinburgh: Scottish Academic Press, 1982).

THOMAS CHATTERTON.   John Dix, *The Life of Thomas Chatterton, Including His Unpublished Poems and Correspondence* (London: Hamilton, Adams, & Co., 1837); Daniel Wilson, *Chatterton: A Biographical Study* (London: Macmillan, 1869); David Masson, *Chatterton: A Story of the Year 1770* (London: Macmillan, 1874); John H. Ingram, *The True Chatterton: A New Study from Original Documents* (London: T. Fisher Unwin, 1910); Esther Parker Ellinger, *Thomas Chatterton: The Marvelous Boy* (Philadelphia: University of Pennsylvania Press, 1930); E. H. W. Meyerstein, *A Life of Thomas Chatterton* (London: Ingpen & Grant, 1930); John Cranstoun Nevill, *Thomas Chatterton* (London: Frederick Muller Ltd., 1948); *The Complete Works of Thomas Chatterton: A Bicentenary Edition*, 2 vols., ed. Donald S. Taylor and Benjamin B. Hoover (Oxford: Clarendon Press, 1971); Linda Kelly, *The Marvellous Boy: The Life and Myth of Thomas Chatterton* (London: Weidenfield & Nicholson, 1971); Peter Ackroyd, *Chatterton* (London: Penguin, 1987); Louise J. Kaplan, *The Family Romance of the Imposter-Poet Thomas Chatterton* (New York: Atheneum, 1988).

JOHN CODRINGTON BAMPFYLDE.   Robert Southey, Esq., letter to Egerton Bridges, Esq., May 10, 1809, in S. E. Brydges, *Modern Aristocracy, Or the Bard's Reception* (Geneva: A. L. Vignier, 1831); "John Codrington Bampfylde," *The Dictionary of National Biography*, vol. 3, ed. Sir Leslie Stephen (London: Smith, Elder, & Co., 1885), p. 103; *The Poems of John Bampfylde*, ed. Roger Lonsdale (Oxford: Perpetua Press, 1988).

GEORGE CRABBE.   George Crabbe, Jr., *The Poetical Works of the Rev. George Crabbe*, 8 vols., vol. 1: *The Life of the Rev. George Crabbe, LL.B.* (London: John Murray, 1834); Lilian Haddakin, *The Poetry of Crabbe* (London: Chatto & Windus, 1955); Neville Blackburne, *The Restless Ocean: The Story of George Crabbe The Aldeburgh Poet 1754–1832* (Lavenham: Terence Dalton, 1972); Arthur Pollard, ed., *Crabbe: The Critical Heritage* (London: Routledge & Kegan Paul, 1972); Terence Bareham, *George Crabbe* (New York: Barnes & Noble, 1977); *Selected Letters and Journals of George Crabbe*, ed. Thomas C. Faulkner (Oxford: Clarendon Press, 1985).

WILLIAM BLAKE. Arthur Symons, *William Blake* (London: Archibald Constable and Co., 1907); Hubert J. Norman, William Blake, *Journal of Mental Science*, 61 (1915): 198–244; Osbert Burdett, *William Blake* (New York: Macmillan, 1926); Helen C. White, *The Mysticism of William Blake* (Madison: University of Wisconsin Press, 1927); S. Foster Damon, *William Blake: His Philosophy and Symbols* (New York: Peter Smith, 1947); Northrop Frye, *Fearful Symmetry: A Study of William Blake* (Princeton: Princeton University Press, 1947); *The Writings of William Blake*, 3 vols., ed. Geoffrey Keynes (London: Oxford University Press, 1966); Alexander Gilchrist, *Life of William Blake, With Selections from His Poems and Other Writings*, 2 vols. (New York: Phaeton Press, 1969); Kathleen Raine, *Blake and Tradition*, 2 vols. A. W. Mellon Lectures in the Fine Arts (Princeton: Princeton University Press, 1969); Alvin H. Rosenfeld, *William Blake: Essays for S. Foster Damon* (Providence, RI: Brown University Press, 1969); Algernon Charles Swinburne, *William Blake: A Critical Essay* (reprint Lincoln: University of Nebraska Press, 1970; originally published 1868); Joseph Anthony Wittreich, Jr., *Nineteenth-Century Accounts of William Blake* (Gainesville, FL: Scholars' Facsimiles & Reprints, 1970); Geoffrey Keynes, *Blake Studies: Essays on His Life and Work*, 2nd ed. (Oxford: Clarendon Press, 1971); G. E. Bentley, Jr., ed., *William Blake: The Critical Heritage* (London: Routledge & Kegan Paul, 1975); Michael Davis, *William Blake: A New Kind of Man* (London: Paul Elek, 1977); Jack Lindsay, *William Blake: His Life and Work* (London: Constable, 1978); *The Letters of William Blake*, 3rd ed., ed. Geoffrey Keynes (Oxford: Clarendon Press, 1980); Paul Youngquist, *Madness & Blake's Myth* (University Park, PA, and London: Pennsylvania State University Press, 1989); David V. Erdman, *Blake: Prophet Against Empire*, 3rd ed. (New York: Dover, 1991); James King, *William Blake: His Life* (New York: St. Martin's Press, 1991).

ROBERT BURNS. J. G. Lockhart, *The Life of Robert Burns* (Edinburgh: Constable, 1828); John MacIntosh, *Life of Robert Burns* (Paisley: Gardner, 1906); Franklin Bliss Snyder, *The Life of Robert Burns* (New York: Macmillan, 1932); *Robert Burns's Commonplace Book 1783–1785*, ed. J. C. Ewing and Davidson Cook (Glasgow: Cowans & Gray, 1938); J. De Lancey Ferguson, *Pride and Passion* (New York: Oxford University Press, 1939); David Daiches, *Robert Burns* (London: Andre Deutsch, 1966); Robert T. Fitzhugh, *Robert Burns: The Man and the Poet, A Round, Unvarnished Account* (Boston: Houghton Mifflin, 1970); Hugh Douglas, *Robert Burns: A Life* (London: Robert Hale, 1976); *The Letters of Robert Burns*, 2 vols., 2nd ed., ed. J. De Lancey Ferguson and G. Ross Roy (Oxford: Clarendon Press, 1985); Alan Bold, *A Burns Companion* (London: Macmillan, 1991).

JOANNA BAILLIE. "A Life of Joanna Baillie," in *The Dramatic and Poetical Works of Joanna Baillie* (London: Longman, Brown, Green & Longmans, 1853); Margaret S. Carhart, *The Life and Work of Joanna Baillie* (New Haven: Yale University Press, 1923); Donald Carswell, *Sir Walter: A Four-Part Study in Biography (Scott, Hogg, Lockhart, Joanna Baillie)* (London: John Murray, 1930); *Unpublished Letters of Joanna Baillie to a Dumfriesshire Laird*, ed. W. H. O'Reilly, in *Transactions of the Dumfriesshire and Galloway Natural History and Antiquarian Society*, 18 (1934): 1–18.

WILLIAM LISLE BOWLES. Memoir of the Rev. Wm. Lisle Bowles, *New Monthly Magazine*, 82 (1820): 480–484; *The Poetical Works of William Lisle Bowles, With Memoir, Critical Dissertation, and Explanatory Notes*, ed. Rev. George Gilfillan (Edinburgh: James Nichol, 1855); T. E. Casson, "William Lisle Bowles," in *Eighteenth Century Literature: An Oxford Miscellany* (Oxford: Clarendon Press, 1909, pp. 51–183); *A Wiltshire Parson and His Friends: The Correspondence of William Lisle Bowles*, ed. Garland Greever (London: Constable, 1926).

SAMUEL ROGERS. *Recollections*, ed. William Sharpe (Boston: Bartlett and Miles, 1859); Richard Ellis Roberts, *Samuel Rogers and His Circle* (London: Methuen, 1910); *Recollections of the Table-Talk of Samuel Rogers*, ed. Morchand Bishop (first collected by the Rev. Alexander Dyce) (Lawrence: University of Kansas Press, 1953); J. R. Watson, *Samuel Rogers: The Last Augustan*, in *Augustan Worlds: New Essays in Eighteenth-Century Literature*, ed. J. C. Hilson, M.M.B. Jones, and J. R. Watson (New York: Harper & Row, 1978), pp. 281–297.

WILLIAM WORDSWORTH. *The Prelude, Or growth of a Poet's Mind, An Autobiographical Poem* (London: Moxon, 1850); Raymond Dexter Havens, *The Mind of a Poet: A Study of Wordsworth's Thought* (Baltimore: Johns Hopkins University Press, 1941); Arthur Beatty, *William Wordsworth: His Doctrine and Art in Their Historical Relations* (Madison: University of Wisconsin Press, 1962); Mary Moorman, *William Wordsworth: A Biography*, 2 vols. (New York: Oxford University Press, 1965); Christopher Wordsworth, *Memoirs of William Wordsworth*, 3 vols., ed. Henry Reed. (Boston: Ticknor, Reed, and Fields, 1966); Hunter Davies, *William Wordsworth: A Biography* (New York: Atheneum, 1980); Jonathan Wordsworth, *William Wordsworth: The Borders of Vision* (Oxford: Clarendon Press, 1982); *The Letters of William Wordsworth: A New Selection*, ed. Alan G. Hill (New York: Oxford University Press, 1984); Stephen Gill, *William Wordsworth: A Life* (Oxford: Clarendon Press, 1989).

SIR WALTER SCOTT. John Gibson Lockhart, *Memoirs of the Life of Sir Walter Scott, Bart*, 10 vols. (Edinburgh: Cadell, 1839); Andrew Lang, *Sir Walter Scott* (New York: Charles Scribner's Sons, 1906); *The Letters of Sir Walter Scott*, 12 vols., ed. H. J. C. Grierson (London: Constable, 1932–1937); Sir Herbert J. C. Grierson, *Sir Walter Scott, Bart* (New York: Columbia University Press, 1938); The medical adventures of Sir Walter Scott, *Medical Journal of Australia*, II (1953): 307–308; A. Dickson Wright, Sir Walter Scott's laudanum? *Annals of the Royal College of Surgeons of England*, 32 (1963): 194–195; Arthur Melville Clark, *Sir Walter Scott: The Formative Years* (Edinburgh and London: William Blackwood, 1969); Edgar Johnson, *Sir Walter Scott: The Great Unknown*, 2 vols. (New York: Macmillan, 1970); Edward Wagenknecht, *Sir Walter Scott* (New York: Continuum, 1991).

SAMUEL TAYLOR COLERIDGE.   E. K. Chambers, *Samuel Taylor Coleridge: A Biographical Study* (Oxford: Clarendon Press, 1938); Lawrence Hanson, *The Life of Samuel Taylor Coleridge: The Early Years* (New York: Oxford University Press, 1939); *Collected Letters of Samuel Taylor Coleridge*, 6 vols., ed. Earl Leslie Griggs (Oxford: Clarendon Press, 1956–1973); J. R. de J. Jackson, ed., *Coleridge: The Critical Heritage* (London: Routledge & Kegan Paul, 1970); Samuel Taylor Coleridge, *Biographia Literaria, or Biographical Sketches of My Literary Life and Opinions*, ed. George Watson (London: J. M. Dent, 1975); Oswald Doughty, *Perturbed Spirit: The Life & Personality of Samuel Taylor Coleridge* (Rutherford, NJ: Fairleigh Dickinson University Press, 1981); John Livingston Lowes, *The Road to Xanadu: A Study in the Ways of the Imagination* (Princeton: Princeton University Press, 1986); W. Jackson Bate, *Coleridge* (Cambridge: Harvard University Press, 1987); Richard Holmes, *Coleridge: Early Visions* (New York: Viking, 1990).

ROBERT SOUTHEY.   *The Life and Correspondence of Robert Southey*, 6 vols., ed. Charles Cuthbert Southey (London: Longman, Brown, Green & Longmans, 1849); Edward Dowden, *Southey* (New York and London: Harper & Brothers, 1902); Jack Simmons, *Southey* (New Haven: Yale University Press, 1948); Geoffrey Carnall, *Robert Southey and His Age: The Development of a Conservative Mind* (Oxford: Clarendon Press, 1960); William Haller, *The Early Life of Robert Southey: 1774–1803* (New York: Octagon Books, 1966); Ernest Bernhardt-Kabisch, *Robert Southey* (Boston: Twayne, 1977).

WALTER SAVAGE LANDOR.   John Forster, *Walter Savage Landor: A Biography*, 2 vols. (London: Chapman and Hall, 1869); Sidney Colvin, *Landor* (London: Macmillan, 1881); *Letters and Other Unpublished Writings of Walter Savage Landor*, ed. Stephen Wheeler (London: Bentley, 1897); R. H. Super, *Walter Savage Landor: A Biography* (New York: New York University Press, 1954); Malcolm Elwin, *Landor: A*

Replevin (London: Macdonald, 1958); Herbert van Thral, *Landor: A Biographical Anthology* (London: George Allen & Unwin, 1973).

THOMAS CAMPBELL. *Life and Letters of Thomas Campbell*, 3 vols., ed. by William Beattie (London: Edward Moxon, 1849); Cyrus Redding, *Literary Reminiscences and Memoirs of Thomas Campbell*, 2 vols. (London: Charles J. Skeet, 1860); J. Cuthbert Hadden, *Thomas Campbell* (Edinburgh & London: Oliphant Anderson & Ferrier, 1899); *The Complete Poetical Works of Thomas Campbell*, ed. J. Logie Robertson (London: Oxford University Press, 1907).

THOMAS MOORE. *Memoirs, Journal, and Correspondence of Thomas Moore*, 8 vols., ed. Lord John Russell (London: Longman, Brown, Green & Longmans, 1853–1856); Stephen Gwynn, *Thomas Moore* (New York: Macmillan, 1905); L. A. G. Strong, *The Minstrel Boy: A Portrait of Tom Moore* (New York: Alfred A. Knopf, 1937); *The Letters of Thomas Moore*, 2 vols., ed. Wilfred S. Dowden (Oxford: Clarendon Press, 1964); Hoover H. Jordan, *Bolt Upright: The Life of Thomas Moore*, 2 vols. Salzburg Studies in English Literature, no. 38. (Salzburg: Institut für Englische Sprache and Literatur, Universität Salzburg, 1975); Terence de Vere White, *Tom Moore: The Irish Poet* (London: Hamish Hamilton, 1977).

LEIGH HUNT. *The Correspondence of Leigh Hunt*, 2 vols., ed. Thornton Hunt (London: Smith, Elder, 1862); Cosmo Monkhouse, *Life of Leigh Hunt* (London: Walter Scott, 1893); Barnette Miller, *Leigh Hunt's Relations with Byron, Shelley, and Keats* (New York: Columbia University Press, 1910); Edmund Blunden, *Leigh Hunt and His Circle* (New York: Harper & Brothers, 1930); *The Autobiography of Leigh Hunt*, ed. J. E. Morpurgo (London: Cresset Press, 1949); John R. Thompson, *Leigh Hunt* (Boston: Twayne, 1977); Ann Blainey, *Immortal Boy: A Portrait of Leigh Hunt* (London & Sydney: Croom Helm, 1985).

THOMAS LOVE PEACOCK. A. B. Young, *The Life and Novels of Thomas Love Peacock* (Norwich: privately printed, 1904); *Letters to Edward Hookham and Percy Bysshe Shelley*, ed. Richard Garnett and F. B. Sanborn (Boston: Bibliophile Society, 1910); Carl Van Doren, *The Life of Thomas Love Peacock* (New York: Dutton, 1911); *The Works of Thomas Love Peacock*, Halliford ed., 10 vols., ed. H.F.B. Brett-Smith and C. E. Jones (London: Constable, 1924–1934); J. B. Priestley, *Thomas Love Peacock* (New York: Macmillan, 1927); O. W. Campbell, *Thomas Love Peacock* (New York: Roy, 1953); Howard Mills, *Peacock: His Circle and His Age* (Cambridge: Cambridge University Press, 1969); Carl Dawson, *His Fine Wit: A Study of Thomas Love Peacock* (Berkeley and Los Angeles: University of California Press, 1970); Felix Felton, *Thomas Love Peacock* (London: George Allen & Unwin, 1973).

GEORGE GORDON, LORD BYRON.   See chapter 5.

PERCY BYSSHE SHELLEY.   *Peacock's Memoirs of Shelley with Shelley's Letters to Peacock*, ed. H. F. B. Brett-Smith (London: Henry Frowde, 1909); A. A. Moll, Shelley the invalid, *New York Medical Journal*, 110 (1919): 934–941; T. V. Moore, Percy Bysshe Shelley: An introduction to the study of character, *Psychological Monographs*, no. 141 (1922); Marjory A. Bald, The psychology of Shelley, *Contemporary Review*, 131 (1927): 359–366; Kenneth N. Cameron, *The Young Shelley: Genesis of a Radical* (New York: Macmillan, 1950); C. L. Cline, *Byron, Shelley, and Their Pisan Circle* (Cambridge: Harvard University Press, 1952); W. R. Bett, Percy Bysshe Shelley (1792–1822): Neurosis and genius, in W. R. Bett, *The Infirmities of Genius* (New York: Philosophical Library, 1952); *The Letters of Percy Bysshe Shelley*, 2 vols., ed. Frederick L. Jones (Oxford: Oxford University Press, 1964); Edward Dowden, *The Life of Percy Bysshe Shelley* (London: Routledge & Kegan Paul, 1966); Milton L. Miller, Manic depressive cycles of the poet Shelley, *Psychoanalytic Forum*, 1 (1966): 188–203; James Rieger, *The Mutiny Within: The Heresies of Percy Bysshe Shelley* (New York: Braziller, 1967); Kenneth Neill Cameron, *Shelley: The Golden Years* (Cambridge: Harvard University Press, 1974); Richard Holmes, *Shelley: The Pursuit* (London: Weidenfeld & Nicolson, 1974); Claire Tomalin, *Shelley and His World* (London: Thames & Hudson, 1980); Richard Holmes, *Footsteps: Adventures of a Romantic Biographer* (New York: Viking, 1985); Nora Crook and Derek Guiton, *Shelley's Venomed Melody* (Cambridge: Cambridge University Press, 1986); *The Journals of Mary Shelley, 1814–1844*, 2 vols., ed. Paula R. Feldman and Diana Scott-Kilvert (Oxford: Clarendon Press, 1987); William St. Clair, *The Godwins and the Shelleys: The Biography of a Family* (New York: W. W. Norton, 1989).

JOHN CLARE.   *Poems of John Clare's Madness*, ed. Geoffrey Grigson (London: Routledge & Kegan Paul, 1949); June Wilson, *Green Shadows: The Life of John Clare* (London: Hodder & Stoughton, 1951); John Tibble and Anne Tibble, *John Clare: His Life and Poetry* (London: Heinemann, 1956); Frederick Martin, *The Life of John Clare*, ed. Eric Robinson and Geoffrey Summerfield (London: Frank Cass, 1964); J. W. Tibble and Anne Tibble, *John Clare: A Life* (Totowa, NJ: Rowan and Littlefield, 1972); William Howard, *John Clare* (Boston: Twayne, 1981); *John Clare's Autobiographical Writings*, ed. Eric Robinson (Oxford: Oxford University Press, 1983); Edward Storey, *A Right to Song: The Life of John Clare* (London: Methuen, 1982); Tim Chilcott, 'A Real World & Doubting Mind': A Critical Study of the Poetry of John Clare (Hull, England: Hull University Press, 1985); *The Letters of John Clare*, ed. Mark Storey (Oxford: Clarendon Press, 1985); E. Blackmore, John Clare's psychiatric disorder and its influence on his poetry, *Victorian Poetry*, 24 (1986): 209–228.

JOHN KEATS.   Edward Thomas, *Keats*, no. 126 of *The People's Books* (London: T. C. and E. C. Jack, 1916); Amy Lowell, *John Keats*, 2 vols. (Boston and New York: Houghton Mifflin, 1925); R. L. Kitching, The medical history of John Keats, *Guy's Hospital Gazette*, 66 (1952): 396; Robert Gittings, *John Keats: The Living Year (21 September 1818 to 21 September 1819)* (Melbourne: Heinemann, 1954); W. R. Bett, John Keats (1795–1821): Tuberculosis and genius, in W. R. Bett, *The Infirmities of Genius* (New York: Philosophical Library, 1952), pp. 129–136; *The Letters of John Keats*, 2 vols., ed. Hyder Edward Rollins (Cambridge: Harvard University Press, 1958); Walter Jackson Bate, *John Keats* (Cambridge: Harvard University Press, 1963); Aileen Ward, *John Keats: The Making of a Poet* (New York: Viking, 1963); Robert Gittings, *John Keats* (Boston: Little, Brown, 1968); Stephen A. Reid, Keats's depressive poetry, *Psychoanalytic Review*, 58 (1971): 395–418; Andrew Brink, *Loss and Symbolic Repair: A Psychological Study of Some English Poets* (Hamilton, Ontario: Cromlech Press, 1977); Helen Vendler, *The Odes of John Keats* (Cambridge: Harvard University Press, 1983).

GEORGE DARLEY.   R. A. Streatfield, A forgotten poet: Darley, *Quarterly Review*, 196 (1902): 367–402; *The Complete Poetical Works of George Darley*, ed. Ramsay Colles (London: George Routledge & Sons, 1908); Claude Colleer Abbott, *The Life and Letters of George Darley* (London: Humphrey Milford, 1928); *Selected Poems of George Darley*, ed. Anne Ridler (London: Merrion Press, 1979).

HARTLEY COLERIDGE.   *Poems by Hartley Coleridge, With a Memoir of his Life by his Brother*, 2 vols. (London: Edward Moxon, 1851); Eleanor A. Towle, *A Poet's Children: Hartley and Sara Coleridge* (London: Methuen, 1912); E. L. Griggs, *Hartley Coleridge: His Life and Work* (London: University of London, 1929); H. Hartman, *Hartley Coleridge: Poet's Son and Poet* (London: Oxford University Press, 1931); *Letters of Hartley Coleridge*, ed. Grace Evelyn Griggs and Earl Leslie Griggs (London: Oxford University Press, 1941).

THOMAS HOOD.   J. C. Reid, *Thomas Hood* (London: Routledge & Kegan Paul, 1963); John Clubbe, *Victorian Forerunner: The Late Career of Thomas Hood* (Durham, NC: Duke University Press, 1968); Walter Jerrold, *Thomas Hood: His Life and Times* (New York: Greenwood Press, 1969); Lloyd N. Jeffrey, *Thomas Hood* (New York: Twayne, 1972); *The Letters of Thomas Hood*, ed. Peter F. Morgan (Edinburgh: Oliver & Boyd, 1973).

THOMAS LOVELL BEDDOES.   *The Letters of Thomas Lovell Beddoes*, ed. Edmund Gosse (London: Elkin Mathews & John Lane,

1894); *The Poems of Thomas Lovell Beddoes*, ed. Ramsay Colles (London: George Routledge & Sons, 1907); Royall H. Snow, *Thomas Lovell Beddoes: Eccentric & Poet* (New York: Covici-Friede, 1928); H. W. Donner, *Thomas Lovell Beddoes: The Making of a Poet* (Oxford: Basil Blackwell, 1935); H. K. Johnson, Thomas Lovell Beddoes, *Psychiatric Quarterly*, 17 (1943): 447–469; *Plays and Poems of Thomas Lovell Beddoes*, ed. H. W. Donner (London: Routledge & Kegan Paul, 1950); Geoffrey Wagner, Beddoes: Centennial of a suicide, *Horizon*, 19 (1949): 417–435; James R. Thompson, *Thomas Lovell Beddoes* (Boston: Twayne, 1985).

ROBERT STEPHEN HAWKER. *The Poetical Works of Robert Stephen Hawker, M.A.*, ed. Alfred Wallis (London: John Lane, 1899); Sabine Baring-Gould, *The Vicar of Morwenstow, Being a Life of Robert Stephen Hawker, M.A.* (London: Methuen & Co., 1899); Charles Edward Byles, *The Life and Letters of R. S. Hawker* (London: John Lane, 1905); Margaret Florence Burrows, *Robert Stephen Hawker: A Study of His Thought and Poetry* (Oxford: Blackwell, 1926); Piers Brendon, *Hawker of Morwenstow: Portrait of a Victorian Eccentric* (London: Cape, 1975).

JAMES CLARENCE MANGAN. *James Clarence Mangan: His Selected Poems with a Study by the Editor Louise Imogene Guiney* (London: John Lane, 1897); D. J. O'Donoghue, *The Life and Writings of James Clarence Mangan* (Dublin: M. H. Gill, 1897); *Poems of James Clarence Mangan*, ed. D. J. O'Donoghue (Dublin: O'Donoghue & Co., 1903); *The Prose Writings of James Clarence Mangan*, ed. D. J. O'Donoghue (Dublin: O'Donoghue & Co., 1904); *The Autobiography of James Clarence Mangan*, ed. James Kilroy (Dublin: Dolmen, 1968); James Kilroy, *James Clarence Mangan* (Lewisburg, PA: Bucknell University Press, 1970); Henry J. Donaghy, *James Clarence Mangan* (New York: Twayne, 1974); David Lloyd, *Nationalism and Minor Literature: James Clarence Mangan and the Emergence of Irish Cultural Nationalism* (Berkeley: University of California Press, 1987).

30. I chose the poets for study by surveying fifteen anthologies of eighteenth- and nineteenth-century verse. These anthologies included *The New Oxford Book of Eighteenth Century Verse*, *The Oxford Book of Nineteenth Century English Verse*, *The Norton Anthology of English Literature*, *Eighteenth Century Poetry and Prose*, *English Romantic Poetry and Prose*, *The Oxford Book of Scottish Verse*, *The Oxford Book of Irish Verse*, and *English Romantic Writers*.

Among the poets chosen, Samuel Johnson, Thomas Gray, William Collins, Christopher Smart, Oliver Goldsmith, William Cowper, Thomas Chatterton, George Crabbe, William Blake, Robert Burns, William Wordsworth, Sir Walter Scott, Samuel Taylor Coleridge, Robert Southey, Walter Savage Landor, Thomas Campbell, Thomas Moore,

Thomas Love Peacock, George Gordon, Lord Byron, Percy Bysshe Shelley, John Clare, John Keats, George Darley, Hartley Coleridge, Thomas Hood, and Thomas Lovell Beddoes were represented in all or virtually all of these anthologies.

A considerably smaller number were included in several collections: Leigh Hunt, James Clarence Mangan, William Lisle Bowles, James Macpherson, and Robert Fergusson. An equally small number were represented in only a few of the anthologies: Robert Stephen Hawker, Joanna Baillie, Samuel Rogers, John Codrington Bampfylde, and Joseph Warton.

31. Kathleen Jones, *Lunacy, Law and Conscience, 1744–1845* (London: Routledge & Kegan Paul, 1955); Andrew T. Scull, *Museums of Madness: The Social Organization of Insanity in 19th Century England*, doctoral diss., Princeton University, 1974; D. J. Mellett, *The Prerogative of Asylumdom: Social, Cultural, and Administrative Aspects of the Institutional Treatment of the Insane in Nineteenth Century Britain* (New York: Garland, 1982); Margaret S. Thompson, *The Mad, the Bad, and the Sad: Psychiatric Care in the Royal Edinburgh Asylum (Morningside), 1813–1894*, doctoral diss., Boston University Graduate School, 1984; W. F. Bynum, Roy Porter, and Michael Shepherd, eds., *The Anatomy of Madness: Essays in the History of Psychiatry. Vol. II: Institutions and Society* (London: Tavistock, 1985); John Crammer, *Asylum History: Buckinghamshire County Pauper Lunatic Asylum—St. John's* (London: Gaskell, Royal College of Psychiatrists, 1990).

32. Robert Burns, *Common Place Book*, quoted in W. R. Bett, *The Infirmities of Genius* (New York: Philosophical Library, 1952), p. 147.

33. N. J. C. Andreasen and A. Canter, The creative writer: Psychiatric symptoms and family history, *Comprehensive Psychiatry*, 15 (1974): 123–131; N. J. C. Andreasen and P. S. Powers, Creativity and psychosis: An examination of conceptual style, *Archives of General Psychiatry*, 32 (1975): 70–73; N. C. Andreasen, Creativity and mental illness: Prevalence rates in writers and their first-degree relatives, *American Journal of Psychiatry*, 144 (1987): 1288–1292.

34. Hagop Akiskal, letters of September 20, 1988 and February 1, 1990; H. S. Akiskal and K. Akiskal, Reassessing the prevalence of bipolar disorders: Clinical significance and artistic creativity, *Psychiatry and Psychobiology*, 3 (1988): 29s–36s.

35. Akiskal, letter, September 20, 1988.

36. K. R. Jamison, Mood disorders and patterns of creativity in British writers and artists, *Psychiatry*, 52 (1989): 125–134.

37. One study conducted at Johns Hopkins found that the diagnostic measures utilized in the Epidemiologic Catchment Area (ECA) study resulted in twice the number of people diagnosed as having major

depressive disorder compared with the rate obtained when using in-depth clinical interviews conducted by experienced psychiatrists (M. F. Folstein, A. J. Romanoski, G. Nestadt, R. Chahal, A. Merchant, S. Shapiro, M. Kramer, J. Anthony, E. M. Gruenberg, and P. R. McHugh, Brief report on the clinical reappraisal of the Diagnostic Interview Schedule carried out at the Johns Hopkins site of the Epidemiologic Catchment Area Program of the NIMH, *Psychological Medicine*, 15 [1985]) 809–814.

Other studies have found that only one person in three who meets the diagnostic criteria for a major mood disorder actually receives treatment for it.

M. M. Weissman, J. K. Myers, and W. D. Thompson, Depression and treatment in a U.S. urban community: 1975–1976, *Archives of General Psychiatry*, 38 (1981): 417–421.

S. Shapiro, E. A. Skinner, L. G. Kessler, M. Von Korff, P. S. German, G. L. Tischler, P. J. Leaf, L. Benham, L. Cotler, and D. A. Regier, Utilization of health and mental health services: Three Epidemiologic Catchment Area sites, *Archives of General Psychiatry*, 41 (1984): 971–978.

M. M. Weissman, M. L. Bruce, P. J. Leaf, L. P. Florio, and C. Holzer, Affective disorders, in L. N. Robins and D. A. Regier, eds., *Psychiatric Disorders in America: The Epidemiologic Catchment Area Study* (New York: Free Press, 1991).

38. Weissman, et al., Depression and treatment in a U.S. urban community, (1981).

39. S. Shapiro, et al., Utilization of health and mental health services, (1984).

40. R. G. McCreadie and D. P. Morrison, The impact of lithium in Southwest Scotland. I. Demographic and clinical findings, *British Journal of Psychiatry*, 146 (1985): 70–74.

41. J. I. Escobar, J. C. Anthony, G. Canino, L. Cotler, M. L. Melville, and J. M. Golding, Use of neuroleptics, antidepressants, and lithium by U.S. community populations, *Psychopharmacology Bulletin*, 23 (1987): 196–200.

42. Ibid.

43. Ibid.

44. R. L. Richards, D. K. Kinney, I. Lunde, and M. Benet, Creativity in manic-depressives, cyclothymes, and their normal first-degree relatives: A preliminary report, *Journal of Abnormal Psychology*, 97 (1988): 281–288.

45. Ibid., p. 287.

46. G. R. De Long and A. Aldershof, Associations of special abilities

with juvenile manic-depressive illness, *Annals of Neurology*, 14 (1983): 362.

47. C. Banks, V. S. Kardak, E. M. Jones, and C. J. Lucas, The relation between mental health, academic performance and cognitive test scores among chemistry students, *British Journal of Educational Psychology*, 40 (1970): 74–79; C. J. Lucas and P. Stringer, Interaction in university selection, mental health and academic performance, *British Journal of Psychiatry*, 120 (1972): 189–195.

48. Andreasen, Creativity and mental illness (1987), p. 1290.

49. Lombroso, *L'Homme de Génie*.

Galton, *Hereditary Genius*.

W. Lange-Eichbaum, *The Problem of Genius*, trans. E. Paul and C. Paul (New York: Macmillan, 1932).

Juda, The relationship between highest mental capacity and psychic abnormalities, (1949).

J. L. Karlsson, Genetic association of giftedness and creativity with schizophrenia, *Hereditas*, 66 (1970): 177–182.

T. F. McNeil, Prebirth and postbirth influence on the relationship between creative ability and recorded mental illness, *Journal of Personality*, 39 (1971): 391–406.

J. L. Karlsson, Genetic basis of intellectual variation in Iceland, *Hereditas*, 95 (1981): 283–288.

J. L. Karlsson, Creative intelligence in relatives of mental patients, *Hereditas*, 100 (1984): 83–86.

Richards et al., Creativity in manic-depressives, (1988).

Related issues and findings are reviewed in R. L. Richards, Relationship between creativity and psychopathology: An evaluation and interpretation of the evidence, *Genetic Psychology Monograph*, 103 (1981): 261–324.

N. C. Andreasen and I. D. Glick, Bipolar affective disorder and creativity: Implications and clinical management, *Comprehensive Psychiatry*, 29 (1988): 207–217.

T. J. Crow, A single locus for psychosis and intelligence in the exchange region of the sex chromosomes? In R. J. Srám, V. Bulyzhenkov, L. Prilipko, and Y. Christen, eds., *Ethical Issues of Molecular Genetics in Psychiatry* (Berlin: Springer-Verlag, 1991).

50. Karlsson, Genetic association of giftedness (1970); Karlsson, Genetic basis of intellectual variation (1981); Karlsson, creative intelligence in relatives (1984).

51. Richards, Relationship between creativity and psychopathology (1981); Andreasen and Glick, Bipolar affective disorder (1988); J. A.

Melvin and D. Mossman, Mental illness and creativity, *American Journal of Psychiatry*, 145 (1988): 908.

52. McNeil, Prebirth and postbirth influence (1971).

53. Ibid., p. 405.

54. Goodwin and Jamison, *Manic-Depressive Illness*, pp. 169–173. Studies of social class have been hampered, and the interpretation of data has been made difficult, by two major types of methodological problems: diagnostic bias (and diagnostic overinclusiveness) and treatment bias. Together these factors can contribute to incorrect and inaccurate reporting of incidence and prevalence rates of manic-depressive illness among various social classes. For example, upper- and middle-class people are more likely to be diagnosed as manic-depressive, whereas lower-class individuals, especially among poor urban black populations, are more likely to be diagnosed as schizophrenic (often mistakenly so) and are consequently treated as such. Minorities are generally underrepresented in these studies as well. Further, criteria for social class vary across studies. Some authors have used the Hollingshead and Redlich system, others used occupation alone or parental social class, and still others used only educational achievement.

Two other possible sources of error include statistical artifacts—where significant results may be secondary to other social factors, such as place of residence, marital status, and so on—and gender biases. Gender bias enters in because women often do not drop in social class through illness but retain the social class of their husbands (Ö. Ödegård, The incidence of psychoses in various occupations, *International Journal of Social Psychiatry*, 2 [1956]: 85–104).

55. C. Bagley, Occupational status and symptoms of depression, *Social Science Medicine*, 7 (1973): 327–339, p. 331.

56. U. Petterson, Manic-depressive illness: A clinical, social and genetic study, *Acta Psychiatrica Scandinavica* (suppl. 269) (1977): 1–93.

57. M. M. Weissman and J. K. Myers, Affective disorders in a U.S. urban community: The use of Research Diagnostic Criteria in an epidemiologic survey, *Archives of General Psychiatry*, 35 (1978): 1304–1311.

58. E. S. Gershon and J. H. Liebowitz, Sociocultural and demographic correlates of affective disorders in Jerusalem, *Journal of Psychiatric Research*, 12 (1975): 37–50.

59. Myerson and Boyle, The incidence of manic-depressive psychosis (1941); Bagley, Occupational status and symptoms of depression (1973).

Unlike schizophrenia, there does not appear to be "downward social drift" in manic-depressive illness. This has been attributed to aspects of the natural history of the illness: (1) It is an illness with a good prognosis and without the progressive deteriorative course that would affect earning potential; (2) the onset of the illness is usually sudden, with no prolonged prepsychotic period; (3) the onset is usually after college age so that it does not seriously interfere with opportunities for higher education; and (4) individuals with manic-depressive illness frequently have compensatory energy and ambition (C Landis and J. D. Page, *Modern Society and Mental Disease* [New York: Farrar & Rinehart, Inc., 1938]).

60. Weissman et al., Affective disorders (1991).

61. Shapiro et al., Utilization of health and mental health services (1984).

62. Harold Nicolson, The health of authors, *Lancet*, 11 (1947): 709–714.

63. W. A. Frosch, Moods, madness, and music. I. Major affective disease and musical creativity, *Comprehensive Psychiatry*, 28 (1987): 315–322. Dr. Frosch, for example, argues that Beethoven experienced "mood swings . . . was clearly eccentric . . . may even have been psychotic . . . [but] there is no evidence that he was ever manic-depressive [p. 316]." It is certainly true that eccentricity and mood swings alone do not constitute manic-depressive illness; there is at least some evidence, however, that Beethoven may have suffered from affective illness. Suggestively, Beethoven has been described by his contemporaries, as well as by scholars, as having had several "nervous breakdowns," being suicidally depressed at different times in his life, and drinking heavily (O. G. Sonneck, ed., *Beethoven: Impressions by His Contemporaries* [New York: G. Schirmer, 1925]; W. Schweisheimer, Beethoven's physicians, *Musical Quarterly*, 31 [1945]: 289–298; *Thayer's Life of Beethoven*, 2 vols., 2nd ed., Elliot Forbes [Princeton: Princeton University Press, 1967]; Edward Larkin, Beethoven's medical history, in Martin Cooper, *Beethoven: The Last Decade, 1817–27* [London: Oxford University Press, 1970], pp. 439–466; Maynard Solomon, *Beethoven* [New York: Schirmer, 1977]; Maynard Solomon, *Beethoven Essays* [Cambridge: Harvard University Press, 1988]; John O'Shea, Ludwig van Beethoven, 1770–1827, in *Music and Medicine: Medical Profiles of Great Composers*, pp. 39–65 [London: J. M. Dent, 1990]). Scholar Maynard Solomon has characterized Beethoven as having had "sudden rages, uncontrolled emotional states, suicidal tendencies, melancholic disposition, and frequent feelings of persecution" (Solomon, *Beethoven Essays*, 1988, p. 146); most of these traits and behaviors predated the onset of his deafness (Solomon, *Beethoven*, 1977). Beethoven's family history is also of interest: His paternal grandmother was an alcoholic who needed to be placed in a cloister for her care; his father, likewise, was an alcoholic; his maternal grandmother reportedly had a "psychological breakdown" of an unspecified nature; and one of his

brothers, who was himself of a violent and volatile nature, had a son who attempted suicide (Donald MacArdle, The family van Beethoven, *Musical Quarterly*, 35 [1949]: 528–550; *Thayer's Life of Beethoven*; Solomon, 1977). All these facts can be interpreted in different ways—and they have been—but the possibility that Beethoven suffered from a mood disorder cannot be dismissed out of hand.

Relatedly, the possibility that two other great composers, Handel and Mozart, may have suffered from manic-depressive illness or cyclothymia has been raised. Handel has been thought by many scholars to have been cyclothymic (E. Slater and A. Meyer, Contributions to a pathography of the musicians: 2. Organic and psychotic disorders, *Confinia Psychiatrica*, 3 [1960]: 129–145; A. Storr, *The Dynamics of Creation* [London: Secker & Warburg, 1972]; M. Keyes, Handel's illnesses, *Lancet*, 2 [1980]: 1354–1355; K. R. Jamison and R. Winter, *Moods and Music*, Program notes for a concert performed by the National Symphony Orchestra at the John F. Kennedy Center for the Performing Arts, Washington, DC [November 1988]). Dr. Frosch has disputed this view, however (W. A. Frosch, Moods, madness, and music. I. Major affective disease and musical creativity, *Comprehensive Psychiatry*, 28 [1987]: 315–322; W. A. Frosch, Moods, madness, and music. II. Was Handel insane? *Musical Quarterly*, 74 [1990]: 31–56). Although there are several strong lines of evidence that Handel did, in fact, suffer from a recurrent mood disorder, the relative lack of autobiographical materials and reliable contemporary medical accounts makes any diagnostic formulation necessarily tentative. More recently, Peter Davies has argued that Mozart had manic-depressive "tendencies," consistent with a diagnosis of cyclothymia (P. J. Davies, Mozart's manic-depressive tendencies, pts. 1 and 2, *Musical Times* [1987]: 123–126 and 191–196; P. J. Davies, *Mozart in Person: His Character and Health* [Westport: Greenwood Press, 1989]). Frosch agrees that Mozart may well have been hypomanic at times but attributes his depressed periods to physical illness (W. A. Frosch, Book review of P. J. Davies, *Mozart in Person, Musical Quarterly*, 24 [1990]: 170–173). This is consistent with Slater and Meyer's earlier formulation that, although Mozart had his "melancholic side," he was "not liable to severe depressive moods until . . . he was a dying man" (Slater and Meyer, p. 131). Davies's work brings up very important questions, however, and it will be interesting to see what develops from future research into the nature and patterns of Mozart's moods and mental states.

64. Nicolson, The health of authors (1947), p. 711.
65. Ibid.
66. Ibid.
67. Ibid.

68. Ibid.

69. S. Foster Damon, *William Blake: His Philosophy and Symbols* (New York: Peter Smith, 1947), pp. 207–208.

70. Northrop Frye, *Fearful Symmetry: A Study of William Blake* (Princeton: Princeton University Press, 1969), p. 12.

71. Hubert J. Norman, William Blake, *Journal of Mental Science*, 61 (1915): 216.

72. Max Byrd, *Visits to Bedlam: Madness and Literature in the Eighteenth Century* (Columbia: University of South Carolina Press, 1974), p. 162.

73. Norman, William Blake (1915), p. 240.

74. The relationship between "madness" and visionary, religious, or mystical states has been the topic of much speculation. William James, of course, described it beautifully in *The Varieties of Religious Experience: A Study in Human Nature* (Middlesex, England: Penguin, 1982; originally published 1902). Many other writers have described the overlap between the extreme mood states and such acute religious experiences as conversions, mystical experiences, and religious exaltation (for example, H. Maudsley, *Natural Causes and Supernatural Seemings* [London: Kegan Paul, 1886]; S. Arieti, *Creativity: The Magic Synthesis* [New York: Basic Books, 1976]; Sir Alister Hardy, *The Spiritual Nature of Man: A Study of Contemporary Religious Experience* [Oxford: Clarendon Press, 1979]). The specific relationship between manic-depressive illness, the spiritual "dark nights of the soul," and religious ecstasy—as well the possible role of mood disorders in the lives of such individuals as Martin Luther, George Fox, Sabbatai Sevi, and Emmanuel Swedenborg—is discussed further in Goodwin and Jamison, *Manic-Depressive Illness* (1990), pp. 360–364. More recently, Dr. Lawrence Foster has explored the link between manic-depressive illness and creativity in unorthodox or new religious movements (the nineteenth-century Shakers, the Mormons, and the Oneida Perfectionists). This work, which includes a detailed description of Joseph Smith's probable manic-depressive psychosis, is presented in Foster's book *Women, Family, and Utopia: Communal Experiments of the Shakers, the Oneida Community, and The Mormons* (New York: Syracuse University Press, 1991).

75. Psychoanalyst Albert Rothenberg, for example, has been critical of studies whose findings purport to show a relationship between psychopathology and artistic creativity. This is a view at odds with most of the available historical, biographical, and scientific evidence. Some of his confusion appears to be based on a lack of appreciation for the subtlety, complexity, and fluctuation in the symptom patterns of manic-depressive

and depressive illness, as well as insufficient awareness of the cyclic or episodic nature of these disorders.

76. William B. Ober, *Boswell's Clap and Other Essays: Medical Analyses of Literary Men's Affliction* (Carbondale: Southern Illinois University Press, 1979), p. 138.

77. Quoted in Louise J. Bragman, The case of John Ruskin: A study in cyclothymia, *American Journal of Psychiatry*, 91 (1935): 1137–1159, quotation on 1152–1153.

78. A. Roe, A psychological study of eminent psychologists and anthropologists, and a comparison with biological and physical scientists, *Psychological Monographs*, 67 (Number 352) (1953).

R. B. Cattell and J. E. Drevdahl, A comparison of the personality profile of eminent researchers with that of eminent teachers and administrators, *British Journal of Psychology*, 44 (1955): 248–261.

J.E. Drevdahl, Factors of importance for creativity, *Journal of Clinical Psychology*, 12 (1956): 21–26; J. E. Drevdahl and R. B. Cattell, Personality and creativity in artists and writers, *Journal of Clinical Psychology*, 14 (1958): 107–111.

D. W. MacKinnon, The nature and nurture of creative talent, *American Psychologist*, 17 (1962): 484–495.

D. W. MacKinnon, The personality correlates of creativity: A study of American architects, in G. S. Nielsen, ed. *Proceedings of the Fourteenth International Congress of Applied Psychology*, (Copenhagen: Munksgaard, 1962); vol. 2, pp. 11–39.

P. G. Cross, R. B. Cattell, and H. J. Butcher, The personality pattern of creative artists, *British Journal of Educational Psychology*, 37 (1967): 292–299.

F. Barron, *Creativity and Personal Freedom* (Princeton: Van Nostand, 1968).

F. Barron, *Creative Person and Creative Process* (New York: Holt, Rinehart & Winston, 1969).

R. B. Cattell, *Abilities and Their Structure Growth and Action* (Boston: Houghton Mifflin, 1971).

R. B. Cattell and H. J. Butcher, The prediction, selection and cultivation of creativity, in H. J. Butcher and D. E. Lomax, eds, *Readings in Human Intelligence* (London: Methuen, 1972): pp. 172–192.

Lucas and Stringer, Interaction in university selection (1972).

D. W. MacKinnon, *In Search of Human Effectiveness* (New York: Creative Education Foundation, 1978).

K. O. Götz and J. K. Götz, Personality characteristics of successful artists, *Perceptual and Motor Skills*, (1979): 919–924.

J. Mohan and M. Tiwana, Personality and alienation of creative writers: A brief report, *Personality of Individual Differences*, 8 (1987): 449.

79. Byron, *Byron's Letters and Journals*, 12 vols., ed. Leslie A. Marchand (London: John Murray, 1973–1982), vol. 8, p. 146.

80. For example, Nicolson, The health of authors (1947); Trilling, *The Liberal Imagination;* Wittkower and Wittkower, *Born Under Saturn;* A. Rothenberg, Creativity, mental health, and alcoholism, *Creativity Research Journal*, 3 (1990): 179–201.

81. Thomas Carlyle, "Goethe," in *Thomas Carlyle: Selected Writings*, ed. Alan Shelston (London: Penguin, 1971), p. 37.

82. Longinus, "On the Sublime," in *Classical Literary Criticism: Aristotle, Horace, and Longinus*, trans. T. S. Dorsch. (London: Penguin, 1965), p. 101.

83. John Keats, *The Letters of John Keats, 1814–1821*, vol. 2 (letter to Percy Bysshe Shelley, August 16, 1820), ed. Hyder Edward Rollins (Cambridge: Harvard University Press, 1958), p. 323.

84. Samuel Taylor Coleridge, *Biographia Literaria*, ed. George Watson (London: Dent, 1975), p. 3.

85. Studies of personality structure in individuals with manic-depressive illness are reviewed in Goodwin and Jamison, *Manic-Depressive Illness* (1990), pp. 281–317. Dr. Robert Hirschfeld and his colleagues have studied the role of obsessionality in mood disorders; these findings are presented in several articles and papers, including R. M. A. Hirschfeld, "Personality and bipolar disorder," paper presented at the Symposium on New Results in Depression Research, Munich, March 1985; R. M. A. Hirschfeld and G. L. Klerman, Personality attributes and affective disorders, *American Journal of Psychiatry*, 136 (1979): 67–70; R. M. A. Hirschfeld, G. L. Klerman, P. J. Clayton, M. B. Keller, P. McDonald Scott, and B. H. Larkin, Assessing personality: Effects of the depressive state on trait measurement, *American Journal of Psychiatry*, 140 (1983): 695–699.

It is relevant to note that recent studies have shown an increased rate of obsessive-compulsive disorders in patients with manic-depressive and depressive illness as well as in their families: L. N. Robins and D. A. Regier, *Psychiatric Disorders in America* (New York: Free Press, 1991); L. Bellodi, G. Sciuto, G. Diaferia, P. Ronchi, and E. Smeraldi, A family history of obsessive-compulsive patients, *Clinical Neuropharmacology*, 15 (suppl. 1, part B) (1992): 308B; P. Rocca, G. Maina, P. Ferrero, F. Bogetto, and L. Raizza, Evidence of two subtypes of obsessive-compulsive disorder, *Clinical Neuropharmacology*, 15 (suppl. 1, part B) (1992): 315 B.

86. Seamus Heaney, "Robert Lowell: A Memorial Address," *Agenda: Robert Lowell Special Issue*, 18 (Autumn 1980), p. 26.

CHAPTER 4
THEIR LIFE A STORM WHEREON THEY RIDE

1. Byron, "Childe Harold's Pilgrimage," canto III, verse 44, lines 388–396, *Lord Byron: The Complete Poetical Works*, vol. 2, p. 92.

2. Arthur Koestler, *The Act of Creation* (New York: Dell, 1971), pp. 316–317.

3. William Butler Yeats, "A Remonstrance with Scotsmen for Having Soured the Dispositions of Their Ghosts and Faeries," *The Celtic Twilight and a Selection of Early Poems* (New York: Signet Classics, 1962), pp. 106–107.

4. Sir Walter Scott, *The Journal of Sir Walter Scott*, ed. W. F. K. Anderson (Oxford: Clarendon Press,1972), p. 9.

5. E. J. Lovell (ed.), *Lady Blessington's Conversations of Lord Byron* (Princeton: Princeton University Press, 1969), p. 547.

6. Teresa Guiccioli, "Recollections of Byron," cited in *His Very Self and Voice: Collected Conversations of Lord Byron*, ed. Ernest J. Lovell, Jr. (New York: Macmillan, 1954), p. 244.

7. J. P. Guilford, Traits of creativity, in H. H. Anderson, ed., *Creativity and Its Cultivation* (New York: Harper, 1959), pp. 142–161; J. P. Guilford, A revised structure of intellect, Report of the Psychological Laboratory, University of Southern California, no. 19, 1967.

8. Frank Barron, The disposition towards originality, *Journal of Abnormal and Social Psychology*, 51 (1955): 478–485; Liam Hudson, *Contrary Imaginations: A Psychological Study of the English Schoolboy* (Middlesex, England: Penguin 1966); see also M. Dellas and E. Gaier, Identification of creativity: The individual, *Psychological Bulletin*, (1970): 55–73; D. M. Harrington, J. Block, and J. H. Block, Predicting creativity in preadolescence from divergent thinking in early childhood, *Journal of Personality and Social Psychology*, 45 (1983): 609–623.

9. Kraepelin, *Manic-Depressive Insanity*, p. 15.

10. E. Bleuler, *Textbook of Psychiatry*, English ed. A. A. Brill (New York: Macmillan, 1924 [4th German ed.]), pp. 466, 468.

11. M. E. Shenton, M. R. Solovay, and P. Holzman, Comparative studies of thought disorders: II. Schizoaffective disorder, *Archives of General Psychiatry*, 44 (1987): 21–30.

12. M. R. Solovay, M. E. Shenton, and P. Holzman, Comparative studies of thought disorders: I. Mania and schizophrenia, *Archives of General Psychiatry*, 44 (1987): 13–20.

13. Andreasen and Powers, Creativity and psychosis (1975), p. 72.

14. Ibid.

15. Ibid.

16. R. J. Larsen, E. Diener, and R. S. Cropanzano, Cognitive operations associated with the characteristic of Intense Emotional Responsiveness, *Journal of Personality and Social Psychology*, 53 (1987): 767–774.

17. D. Schuldberg, Schizotypal and hypomanic traits, creativity, and psychological health, *Creativity Research Journal*, 3 (1990): 218–230.

18. Kraepelin, *Manic-Depressive Insanity;* G. Murphy, Types of word-association in dementia praecox, manic-depressives, and normal persons, *American Journal of Psychiatry*, 79 (1923): 539–571.

19. L. Pons, J. I. Nurnberger, Jr., and D. L. Murphy, Mood-independent aberrancies in associative processes in bipolar affective disorder: An apparent stabilizing effect of lithium, *Psychiatry Research*, 14 (1985): 315–322.

20. E. F. Donnelly, D. L. Murphy, F. K. Goodwin, and I. N. Waldman, Intellectual function in primary affective disorder, *British Journal of Psychiatry*, 140 (1982): 633–636.

21. A. M. Isen, K. A. Daubman, and G. P. Nowicki, Positive affect facilitates creative problem solving, *Journal of Personality and Social Psychology*, 52 (1987): 1122–1131; T. R. Greene and H. Noice, Influence of positive affect upon creative thinking and problem solving in children, *Psychological Reports*, 63 (1988): 895–898.

22. Jamison, Mood disorders and patterns of creativity, (1989).

23. R. Richards and D. K. Kinney, Mood swings and creativity, *Creativity Research Journal*, 3 (1990): 202–217.

24. William Hazlitt, *Lectures on the English Poets*, reprinted in *English Romantic Writers*, ed. D. Perkins (San Diego: Harcourt, 1967), p. 642.

25. Quoted in W. Jackson Bate, *Coleridge* (Cambridge: Harvard University Press, 1987), p. 211.

26. Carlyle, "Coleridge," *Thomas Carlyle: Selected Writings*, pp. 315–323.

27. John Keats, *The Letters of John Keats, 1814–1821*, vol. 2 (letter to the George Keatses, 1819), ed. Hyder Edward Rollins (Cambridge: Harvard University Press, 1958), pp. 88–89.

28. John Livingstone Lowes, *The Road to Xanadu: A Study in the Ways of the Imagination* (1927; reprint, Princeton: Princeton University Press, 1986), pp. 3–4.

29. John Ruskin, *Modern Painters*, ed. David Barrie (New York: Alfred A. Knopf, 1987), p. 248.

30. Olof Lagercrantz, *August Strindberg*, trans. Anselm Hollo (New York: Farrar, Straus & Giroux, 1985), pp. 272–273. See also E. W. Anderson, Strindberg's illness, *Psychological Medicine*, 1 (1971): 104–117.

31. Michael Meyer, *Strindberg* (New York: Random House, 1985), p. 331.

32. R.A. Prentky, *Creativity and Psychopathology: A Neurocognitive Perspective* (New York: Praeger, 1980).

A. J. Rush, M. A. Schlesser, E. Stokely, F. R. Bronte, and K. Z. Altshuller, Cerebral blood flow in depression and mania. *Psychopharmacology Bulletin*, 18 (1982): 6–8.

M. E. Phelps, J. C. Mazziota, R. Gerner, L. Baxter, and D. E. Kuhl, Human cerebral glucose metabolism in affective disorders: Drug-free states and pharmacologic effects, *Journal of Cerebral Blood Flow and Metabolism*, 3 (Supplement 1) (1983): 7–8; M. S. Buchsbaum, L. E. De Lisi, H. H. Holcomb, J. Cappelletti, A. C. King, J. Johnson, E. Hazlett, S. Dowling-Zimmerman, R. M. Post, J. Morihisa, W. Carpenter, R. Cohen, D. Pickar, D. R. Weinberger, R. Margolin, and R. M. Kessler, Anteroposterior gradients in cerebral glucose use in schizophrenia and affective disorders, *Archives of General Psychiatry*, 41 (1984): 1159–1166.

M. E. Phelps, J. C. Mazziotta, L. Baxter, and R. Gerner, Positron emission tomographic study of affective disorders: Problems and strategies, *Annals of Neurology*, 15 (Supplement) (1984): 149–156.

L. R. Baxter, M. E. Phelps, J. C. Mazziotta, J. M. Schwartz, R. H. Gerner, C. E. Selin, and R. M. Sumida, Cerebral metabolic rates for glucose in mood disorders: Studies with positron emission tomography and fluorodeoxyglucose F 18, *Archives of General Psychiatry*, 42 (1985): 441–447.

R. J. Matthew, R. A. Margolin, and R. M. Kessler, Cerebral function, blood flow, and metabolism: A new vista in psychiatric research, *Integrative Psychiatry*, 3 (1985): 214–225.

R. M. Post, L. E. De Lisi, H. H. Holcomb, T. W. Uhde, R. Cohen, and M. S. Buchsbaum, Glucose utilization in the temporal cortex of affectively ill patients: Positron emission tomography, *Biological Psychiatry*, 22 (1987): 545–553.

J. M. Schwartz, L. R. Baxter, J. C. Mazziota, R. H. Gerner, and M. E. Phelps, The differential diagnosis of depression: Relevance of positron emission tomography studies of cerebral glucose metabolism to the bipolar-unipolar dichotomy, *Journal of the American Medical Association*, 258 (1987): 1368–1374.

E. A. Van Royen, J. F. de Bruíne; T. C. Hill, A. Vyth, M. Limburg, B. L. Byse, D. H. O'Leary, J. M. de Jong, A. Hijdra, J. B. Van der Schoot, Cerebral blood flow imaging with thallium-201 diethyldithiocarbamate SPECT, *Journal of Nuclear Medicine*, 28 (1987): 178–183.

H. A. Sackeim and B. L. Steif, Neuropsychology of depression and mania, in A Georgotas and R. Cancro eds., *Depression and Mania* (New York: Elsevier, 1988).

N. C. Andreasen, *Brain Imaging: Applications in Psychiatry* (Washington, D.C.: American Psychiatric Association Press, 1989).

R. M. Cohen, W. E. Semple, M. Gross, T. E. Nordahl, A. C. King, D. Pickar, and R. M. Post, Evidence for common alterations in cerebral glucose metabolisms in major affective disorders and schizophrenia, *Neuropsychopharmacology*, 2 (1989): 241–254.

R. M. Dupont, T.L. Jernigan, J. C. Gillan, N. Butlers, D. C. Delis, and J. R. Hesselink, Subcortical signal hyperintensities in bipolar patients detected by MRI, *Psychiatry Research*, 21 (1987): 357–358.

P. Silverskiöld and J. Risberg, Regional blood flow in depression and mania, *Archives of General Psychiatry*, 46 (1989): 253–259.

L. Baxter, J. M. Schwartz, M. E. Phelps, J. C. Mazziotta, B. H. Guze, C. E. Selin, R. H. Gerner, and R. M. Sumida, Reduction of prefrontal cortex glucose metabolism common to three types of depression, *Archives of General Psychiatry*, 46 (1989): 243–250.

S. P. Springer and G. Deutsch, *Left Brain, Right Brain*, 3rd ed. (New York: W. H. Freeman, 1989).

R. M. Dupont, T. L. Jernigan, N. Butters, D. Delis, J. R. Hesselink, W. Heindel, and J. C. Gillin, Subcortical abnormalities detected in bipolar affective disorder using magnetic resonance imaging: Clinical and neuropsychological significance, *Archives of General Psychiatry*, 47 (1990): 55–59.

Goodwin and Jamison, *Manic-Depressive Illness*, pp. 247–280 and pp. 503–540.

H. A. Sackeim, I. Prohovnik, J. R. Moeller, R. P. Brown, S. Apter, J. Prudic, D. P. Devanand, and S. Mukherjee, Regional cerebral blood flow in mood disorders: I. Comparison of major depressives and normal controls at rest, *Archives of General Psychiatry*, 47 (1990): 60–70.

L. L. Altshuler, A. Conrad, P. Hauser, X. Li, B. H. Guze, K. Denikoff, W. Tourtellotte, and R. Post. Reduction of temporal lobe volume in bipolar disorder: A preliminary report of magnetic resonance imaging. *Archives of General Psychiatry*, 48 (1991): 482–483.

T. J. Crow. The origins of psychosis and "The Descent of Man," *British Journal of Psychiatry*, 159 (Supplement 14) (1991): 76–82.

T. Hines, The myth of right hemisphere creativity, *Journal of Creative Behavior*, 25 (1991): 223–227.

G. A. Ojemann, Cortical organization of language, *Journal of Neuroscience*, 11 (1991): 2281–2287; M. Niaz and G. S. Denunez, The relationship of mobility—fixity to creativity, formal reasoning and intelligence, *Journal of Creative Behavior*, 25 (1991): 205–217.

M. E. Raichle, J. Fiez, T. O. Videen, P. T. Fox, J. V. Pardo, and S. E. Petersen, Practice-related changes in human brain functional anatomy, *Society for Neuroscience Abstracts*, vol. 17, pt. 1 (Washington, D.C.: Society for Neuroscience, 1991), p. 21.

L. Squire, J. Ojemann, F. Miezin, S. Petersen, T. Videen, and M. Raichle, A functional anatomical study of human memory, *Society for Neuroscience Abstracts*, vol. 17, pt. 1, (1991), p. 4.

33. Most neuropsychological studies of manic-depressive illness have focused on deficits in the performance of cognitive tasks. It is not yet understood how differences in cognitive processing between normal and affectively ill individuals might translate, if at all, into possible cognitive advantage (either from compensatory mechanisms or by altogether different pathways). Neuropsychological findings from studies of patients with affective illness are extensively reviewed in Goodwin and Jamison, *Manic-Depressive Illness* (1990), pp. 268–279. See also P. Flor-Henry, *The Cerebral Basis of Psychopathology* (Boston: John Wright, 1983); P. Flor-Henry and J. Gruzelier, *Laterality and Psychopathology* (Amsterdam: Elsevier, 1983); J. Gruzelier, K. Seymour, L. Wilson, A. Jolley, and S. Hirsch, Impairments on neuropsychiatric tests of temporohippocampal and frontohippocampal functions and word fluency in remitting schizophrenia and affective disorders, *Archives of General Psychiatry*, 45 (1988): 623–629; H. A. Sackeim and B. L. Steif, Neuropsychology of depression and mania, in *Depression and Mania*, eds. A. Georgotas and R. Cancro (New York: Elsevier, 1988), pp. 265–289.

Neuropsychological studies of patients with affective illness show a surprising degree of consistency in their findings. Patients with depressive and manic-depressive illness, as a group, typically demonstrate deficits in right hemisphere or nondominant hemisphere functioning, long associated with problems in perception, spatial relations, integration of holistic figures, and complex nonverbal tasks (K. Walsh, *Neuropsychology: A Clinical Approach*, 2nd ed. [Edinburgh: Churchill Livingstone, 1987]). Fragmented thinking and a general inability to integrate thoughts or relate elements in a complex pattern are also associated with right cortical damage (E. K. Daniels, M. E. Shenton, P.S. Holzman, L. I. Benowitz, S. Levine, and D. Levine, Patterns of thought disorder associated with right cortical damage, schizophrenia, and mania, *American Journal of Psychiatry*, 145 [1988]: 944–949). This is counterintuitive to the high rates of affective illness found in writers, but the specificity to right hemispheric impairment is most consistent and pronounced in depressed rather than manic patients (Sackeim and Steif, Neuropsychology of depression and mania [1988]). Cognitive functioning improves after effective treatment (such as electroconvulsive therapy or antidepressants) and during remission (R. D. Staton, H. Wilson, and R. A. Brumback, Cognitive improvement associated with tricyclic antidepressant treatment of childhood major depressive illness, *Perceptual and Motor Skills*, 53 [1981]: 1219–234; D. Fromm-Auch, Comparison of unilateral and bilateral ECT: Evidence for selective memory impairment, *British Journal of Psychiatry*, 141 [1982]: 608–613; D. Fromm and D. Schopflocher, Neuropsychological test performance in depressed patients before and after drug therapy, *Biological Psychiatry*, 19 [1984]: 55–72). It should be noted that hypomanic and manic patients are notoriously difficult to test, and that virtually all neuropsychological assessment to date has been carried out with the goal of determining the negative effects of psychopathology on cognitive functioning. It can be hoped that, in the future, neuroimaging techniques will allow a far more subtle and imaginative understanding of brain functioning—enhanced, diminished, or both—during depressed, manic, and normal states.

The extent to which hemispheric differences are state or trait dependent, primary or derivative, relatively more pronounced in depressive or manic-depressive illness, remains unclear. Children, for example, who have one parent with manic-depressive illness, and are therefore at an increased risk for developing the illness show significant discrepancies between their verbal and performance scores on intelligence tests (C. J. Kestenbaum, Children at risk for manic-depressive illness: Possible predictors, *American Journal of Psychiatry*, 136 [1979]: 1206–1208; P. Decina, C. J. Kestenbaum, S. Farber, L. Kron, M. Gargan, H. A. Sackeim, and R. R. Fieve, Clinical and psychological assessment of children of bipolar probands, *American Journal of Psychiatry*, 140 [1983]: 548–553). This discrepancy, reflected in verbal scores that are significantly higher than performance scores, is also found in depressed children (R. A. Brumback, Wechsler performance IQ deficit in depressed children, *Perceptual and Motor Skills*, 61 [1985]: 331–335) and is consistent with an extensive psychometric literature that demonstrates a similar pattern associated with right hemisphere damage caused by localized lesions (R. M. Reitan, Certain differential effects of left and right cerebral lesions in human adults, *Journal of Comparative and Physiological Psychology*, 48 [1955]: 474–477; H. Lansdell, Laterality of verbal intelligence in the brain, *Science*, 135 [1962]: 922–923; C. B. Blackenmore, G. Ettlinger, and M. A. Falconer, Cognitive abilities in relation to frequency of seizures and neuropathology of the temporal lobes in man, *Journal of Neurology, Neurosurgery, and Psychiatry*, 29 [1966]: 268–272; P. Satz, Specific and nonspecific effects of brain lesions in man, *Journal of Abnormal Psychol-*

ogy, 71 [1966]: 65–70; P. Satz, W. Richard, and A. Daniels, The alteration of intellectual performance after lateralized brain-injury in man, *Psychonomic Science*, 7 [1967]: 369–370; S. F. Zimmerman, J. W. Whitmyre, and F. F. J. Fieldo, Factor analytic structure of the Wechsler Adult Intelligence Scale in patients with diffuse and lateralized cerebral dysfunction, *Journal of Clinical Psychology*, 26 [1970]: 462–465; J. D. Matarazzo, *Wechsler's Measurement and Appraisal of Adult Intelligence*, 5th ed. [Baltimore: Williams & Wilkins, 1972]).

34. Ruskin, *Modern Painters*, p. 252.

35. Arthur Rimbaud, *Rimbaud: Complete Works, Selected Letters*, (letter to Paul Demeny, 15 May 1871), trans. and ed. Wallace Fowlie (Chicago: University of Chicago Press, 1966), p. 307.

36. Keats, *Letters*, vol. 1 (letter to J. A. Hessey, October 8, 1818), p. 374.

37. A. Roe, A psychological study of eminent biologists, *Psychological Monographs: General and Applied*, 65 (331) (1951).

A. Roe, A psychological study of eminent psychologists and anthropologists, and a comparison with biological and physical scientists. *Psychological Monographs: General and Applied*, 67 (352) (1953).

Cattell and Drevdahl, A comparison of the personality profile, (1955).

R. B. Cattell, The personality and motivation of the researcher from measurements of contemporaries and from biography, in C. W. Taylor and F. Barron (eds.), *Scientific Creativity: Its Recognition and Development* (New York: Wiley, 1963): pp. 119–131.

J. A. Chambers *Psychological Monographs: General and Applied*, 78 (584) (1964).

Barron, *Creativity and Personal Freedom*.

Barron, *Creative Person and Creative Process*.

Cattell, *Abilities and Their Structure*.

MacKinnon, *In Search of Human Effectiveness*.

38. John Berryman, *Writers at Work: The Paris Review Interviews*, ed. George Plimpton 4th series. (New York: Viking Press, 1976), p. 322.

39. Roethke, "In a Dark Time," lines 7–12, *The Collected Poems of Theodore Roethke*, p. 231.

40. Percy Bysshe Shelley, "Julian and Maddalo," *Shelley: Selected Poetry, Prose and Letters*, ed. A. S. B. Glover (London: Nonesuch Press, 1951), p. 641.

41. Keats, *Letters*, vol. 2 (letter to the George Keatses, April 21, 1819), p. 102.

42. Koestler, *The Act of Creation*, p. 358.

43. George Edward Woodberry, quoted in M. Wilkinson, *The Way of the Makers* (New York: Macmillan, 1925), p. 13.

44. Edgar Allan Poe, "Eleanora," *The Fall of the House of Usher and Other Writings*, ed. David Galloway (London: Penguin, 1986), p. 243.

45. Vincent van Gogh, *The Complete Letters of Vincent van Gogh* (letter 514) (Boston: New York Graphic Society, 1958) vol. 2, p. 620.

46. L. G. Sexton and L. Ames, eds., *Anne Sexton: A Self-Portrait in Letters* (Boston: Houghton Mifflin, 1977), p. 105.

47. Lowell, "A Conversation with Ian Hamilton," *Collected Prose*, p. 286.

48. Ibid., p. 287.

49. Lowell, "Home," lines 45–46, *Day by Day*, p. 114.

50. Virginia Woolf, *The Diary of Virginia Woolf*, 5 vols., ed. Anne Olivier Bell and Andrew McNeille (New York: Harcourt, 1976–1984), vol. 3, p. 112.

51. Myerson and Boyle, The incidence of manic-depressive psychosis, p. 20.

Dr. Philip Sandblom has emphasized the role of both psychological and physical suffering in the creative process and has described the effect of medical illness and mental anguish on the work of many great artists, writers, and composers. Philip Sandblom, *Creativity and Disease: How Illness Affects Literature, Art and Music* (Philadelphia: Lippincott, 1989).

52. S. E. Taylor and J. D. Brown, Illusion and well-being: A social psychological perspective on mental health, *Psychological Bulletin*, 103 (1988): 193–210; H. A. Sackheim, Self-deception, self-esteem, and depression: The adaptive value of lying to oneself, in *Empirical Studies of Psychoanalytic Theories*, ed. J. Masling (Hillsdale, N.J.: Analytic Press, 1983), vol. 1, pp. 101–157.

53. T. S. Eliot, *Murder in the Cathedral* (San Diego: Harvest/HBJ, 1935), part 2, p. 69.

54. John Freccero, *Dante: The Poetics of Conversion*, ed. Rachel Jacoff (Cambridge: Harvard University Press, 1986), p. 70.

55. Herman Melville, *Pierre: Or, The Ambiguities* (New York: Signet Classic, 1964), p. 114.

56. John Keats, "Why Did I Laugh Tonight?" lines 5–14, *The Complete Poetical Works and Letters of John Keats* (Boston and New York: Houghton Mifflin, 1899), p. 137.

57. Edward Thomas, "Melancholy," lines 7–8, *The Collected Poems of Edward Thomas*, ed. R. George Thomas (Oxford: Oxford University Press, 1978), p. 193.

58. Thomas, "Liberty," lines 24–27, *The Collected Poems of Edward Thomas*, p. 255.

59. Poe, "Romance," in *The Fall of the House of Usher and Other Writings*, p. 521.

60. Alfred, Lord Tennyson, *In Memoriam*, section 59, lines 1–8, *The Poetical Works of Alfred, Lord Tennyson* (New York: Crowell, 1897), p. 496.

61. Leon Edel, The madness of art, *American Journal of Psychiatry*, 132 (1975): 1005–1012, quote on p. 1008.

62. Ibid.

63. Randall Jarrell, "90 North," *Randall Jarrell: The Complete Poems*, lines 29–33 (New York: Farrar, Straus & Giroux, 1969), pp. 113–114.

64. Antonin Artaud, "Van Gogh, the Man Suicided by Society (1947)," *Antonin Artaud: Selected Writings*, ed. Susan Sontag (Berkeley and Los Angeles: University of California Press, 1988), p. 497.

65. Anthony Storr, *The Dynamics of Creation* (London: Secker & Warburg, 1972).

66. Edel, The madness of art (1975), p. 1010.

67. Sexton and Ames, *Anne Sexton*, p. 335.

68. Diane Wood Middlebrook, *Anne Sexton: A Biography* (Boston: Houghton Mifflin, 1991).

69. Cowper, *The Letters and Prose Writings of William Cowper*, vol. 2, 1782–1786 (letter to Lady Hesketh, October 12, 1785) (1981), pp. 382–383.

70. Hector Berlioz, letter to his father, February 13, 1830, quoted in David Cairns, *Berlioz, vol. 1, The Making of an Artist (1803–1832)* (London: André Deutsch, 1989), p. 330.

71. *BLJ*, vol. 3 (letter to Annabella Milbanke, November 29, 1813), p. 179.

72. T. S. Eliot, *Selected Essays* (London: Faber and Faber, 1950), p. 21.

73. John Donne, "The Triple Fool," *The Complete Poetry and Selected Prose of John Donne and The Complete Poetry of William Blake* (New York: Random House, 1941).

74. Tennyson, *In Memoriam*, section 5, lines 5–12, p. 481.

75. Lowell, "Near the Unbalanced Aquarium," *Collected Prose*, p. 362.

76. Lowell, "Unwanted," lines 116–117, *Day by Day*, p. 124.

77. Graham Greene, *Ways of Escape* (New York: Simon and Schuster, 1980), p. 285.

78. Dante, *The Comedy of Dante Alighieri: Cantica I: Hell (L'Inferno)*, canto 24, lines 50–51, p. 221.

79. Byron, "Childe Harold's Pilgrimage" canto III, verse 6, lines 46–54, *Lord Byron: The Complete Poetical Works*, p. 78.

80. Edel, The madness of art, p. 1012.

81. Nathaniel Hawthorne, *The House of the Seven Gables* (Toronto: Bantam Books, 1981), p. 235.

82. These lines from Paul Celan were used to close Israel Chalfen's recent biography, *Paul Celan: A Biography of His Youth*, trans. Maximilian Bleyleben (New York: Persea Books, 1991), p. 192.

83. Lowell, "Ten Minutes," lines 13–14, *Day by Day*, p. 108.

84. George Gordon, Lord Byron, *Don Juan*, ed. T. G. Steffan, E. Steffan, and W. W. Pratt (London: Penguin Books, 1982), notes to canto XVI, verse 97, p. 752.

85. Byron, *Don Juan*, canto XVI, verse 97, lines 817–824 in *Lord Byron: The Complete Poetical Works*, p. 649.

Danish writer Hans Christian Andersen, who suffered from recurrent depressions as had his father and grandfather before him (the latter became insane), described the *mobilité* of the artistic temperament as well. "I am like water," he wrote to a friend. "Everything moves me, I suppose it is part of my poetic nature, and it often brings me joy and happiness, but very often it is also a torment." (Quoted in E. Bredsdorff, *Hans Christian Andersen: The Story of His Life and Work, 1805–75* [New York: Charles Scribner's Sons, 1975], p. 287.)

86. Richard Holmes, *Coleridge: Early Visions* (New York: Viking, 1989), p. 132.

87. Virginia Woolf, *The Letters of Virginia Woolf*, 6 vols., ed. Nigel Nicolson and Joanne Trautmann (New York: Harcourt, 1975–1980), vol. 5, p. 209.

88. Keats, *Letters*, vol. 1 (letter to Richard Woodhouse, October 27, 1818), p. 387.

89. Percy Bysshe Shelley, *The Complete Works of Percy Bysshe Shelley*, 10 vols., ed. Roger Ingpen (New York: Gordian Press, 1965), vol. 1, p. 283.

90. Robert Louis Stevenson, *Dr. Jekyll and Mr. Hyde*, introduction by Vladimir Nabokov (1886; reprint, New York: Signet Classic, 1980), pp. 104–105.

91. Jerome J. McGann, *Fiery Dust: Byron's Poetic Development* (Chicago: University of Chicago Press, 1968), p. 65.

92. N. J. C. Andreasen and B. Pfohl, Linguistic analysis of speech in affective disorders, *Archives of General Psychiatry*, 33 (1976): 1361–1367.

93. J. Zimmerman and L. Garfinkle, Preliminary study of the art pro-

ductions of the adult psychotic, *Psychiatric Quarterly*, 16 (1942): 313–318.

F. Reitman, *Psychotic Art* (London: Routledge & Kegal Paul, 1950).

E. C. Dax, *Experimental Studies in Psychotic Art* (London: Faber and Faber, 1953).

C. Enâchescu, Aspects of pictorial creation in manic-depressive psychosis, *Confinia Psychiatrica*, 14 (1971): 133–142.

H. S. Wadeson and W. T. Carpenter, Jr., A comparative study of art expression of schizophrenic, unipolar depressive, and bipolar manic-depressive patients, *Journal of Nervous and Mental Disease*, 162 (1976): 334–344.

94. Robert Schumann. [Letter to Simonin de Sire, February 8, 1838].

95. William Blake, "Auguries of Innocence," lines 59–62, *The Complete Poetry and Selected Prose of John Donne and the Complete Poetry of William Blake*, p. 598.

96. Quoted in Justin Kaplan, *Mr. Clemens and Mark Twain: A Biography* (New York: Touchstone, 1966), p. 123.

97. Ibid., p. 124.

98. Ibid.

99. Virginia Woolf, *A Room of One's Own* (New York: Harcourt Brace Jovanovich, 1957).

100. Among the many writers who have emphasized the importance of the reconciliation of opposite states in the creative process are Aristotle, "On the Art of Poetry," *Classical Literary Criticism*, trans. T. S. Dorsch (London: Penguin, 1965).

Percy Bysshe Shelley, "A Defence of Poetry," *Shelley's Critical Prose*, ed. B. R. McElderry, Jr. (1821; reprint, Lincoln: University of Nebraska Press, 1967).

Maurice Bowra, *The Romantic Imagination* (Cambridge: Harvard University Press, 1950).

Barron, *Creative Person and Creative Process*.

Guilford, Traits of creativity.

Storr, *The Dynamics of Creation*.

Koestler, *The Act of Creation*

Albert Rothenberg, *The Emerging Goddess* (Chicago: University of Chicago Press, 1979).

John Carey, *John Donne: Life, Mind and Art* (London: Faber and Faber, 1981). John Carey's book contains an especially eloquent discussion of John Donne's use of opposite images and emotional states.

Karl Miller, *Doubles: Studies in Literary History* (Oxford: Oxford University Press, 1985).

101. Thomas Moore, *The Works of Lord Byron: With His Letters*

and Journals and His Life, ed. Richard Henry Stoddard (1832; reprint, London: Francis A. Nicholls, 1900), vol. 16, p. 237.

102. Ruskin, *Modern Painters*, p. 250.

103. W. Mayer-Gross, E. Slater, and M. Roth, *Clinical Psychiatry* (Baltimore: Williams & Wilkins, 1955), p. 211.

104. T. A. Wehr and F. K. Goodwin, Introduction, in T. A. Wehr and F. K. Goodwin, eds., *Circadian Rhythms in Psychiatry* (Pacific Grove: Boxwood Press, 1983), p. 5.

105. Quoted in Whitwell, *Historical Notes on Psychiatry*, p. 157.

106. Quoted in Roccatagliata, *A History of Ancient Psychiatry*, p. 143.

107. D. B. Weiner, Phillipe Pinel's "Memoir on Madness" of December 11, 1794: A fundamental text of modern psychiatry, *American Journal of Psychiatry*, 149 (1992): 725–732.

108. Kraepelin, *Manic-Depressive Insanity*, p. 139.

109. There are many sources of possible error in the collection of seasonality data. For example, hospital admission dates, although likely to be meaningful markers for the onset of manic episodes, are unlikely to reflect the true onset of depressive episodes. In fact, hospitalizations for depression are more likely to reflect severity or lethality of illness than time of onset. Clearly, however, the seasonality of maximal severity is meaningful in its own right. Voluntary admissions and hospital schedules (rotation of physician staff or holidays) also may affect reported seasonal patterns. Despite these methodological problems, the consistency of findings in the seasonality studies of both affective episodes and suicide is impressive. It gains further weight from the fact that virtually all the studies were carried out after the widespread use of lithium had begun, which may have dampened the natural pattern of seasonal variability. Dr. Trevor Silverstone has noted:

> It appears as if in more temperate climes, such as in the United Kingdom, Ireland and New Zealand . . . , or where there is little seasonal variation in temperature, as in Hawaii . . . , the peak of manic admissions occurs in summer. In places with greater temperature swings, such as Hungary . . . , Yugoslavia . . . , Greece . . . , and Australia . . . , the peak occurs in spring. These differences are unlikely to be due simply to differences in latitude, as in Ontario, which spans the latitudes of much of Europe, no seasonal variation was seen in admission rates for mania. . . . It is not known whether it is day length, the rate of temperature change, the amount of sunlight, air ionization, or relative humidity which is the critical variable in determining seasonal variation.

From T. Silverstone, Mania, *Biological Aspects of Affective Disorders*, ed. R. Horton and C. Katona (London: Academic Press, 1991), pp. 273–274.

The studies reviewed for figure 4–1 (Seasonal Variations in Peak Occurrences of Mania and Depression) included S. H. Kraines, *Mental Depressions and Their Treatment* (New York: Macmillan, 1957).

J. Angst, P. Grof, H. Hippius, W. Pöldinger, and P. Weis, La psychose maniaco-dépressive est-elle périodique ou intermittente? in *Cycles Biologiques et Psychiatrie*, ed. J. de Ajuriaguerra (Geneva: George & Cie, SA, 1968), pp. 339–351.

C. Perris, A study of cycloid psychoses, *Acta Psychiatrica Scandinavica* (suppl. 253) (1974): 1–75.

W. W. K. Zung and R. L. Green, Seasonal variation of suicide and depression, *Archives of General Psychiatry*, 30 (1974): 89–91.

M. R. Eastwood and J. Peacocke, Seasonal patterns of suicide, depression and electroconvulsive therapy, *British Journal of Psychiatry*, 129 (1976): 472–475.

V. Milstein, J. G. Small, D. Shelbourne, and I. F. Small, Manic depressive illness: Onset, diurnal temperature and season of birth, *Diseases of the Nervous System*, 37 (1976): 373–375.

R. L. Symonds and P. Williams, Seasonal variation in the incidence of mania, *British Journal of Psychiatry*, 129 (1976): 45–48.

V. Sedivec, [Effect of seasons of year on the development of pathological mood phases of affective melancholia], *Ceskoslovenska Psychiatrie*, 72 (1976): 98–103.

S. D. Walter, Seasonality of mania: A reappraisal, *British Journal of Psychiatry*, 131 (1977): 345–350.

M. R. Eastwood and S. Stiasny, Psychiatric disorder, hospital admission, and season, *Archives of General Psychiatry*, 35 (1978): 769–771.

D. H. Myers and P. Davies, The seasonal incidence of mania and its relationship to climatic variables, *Psychological Medicine*, 8 (1978): 433–440.

E. Frangos, G. Athanassenas, S. Tsitourides, P. Psilolignos, A. Robos, N. Katsanou, and C. Bulgaris, Seasonality of the episodes of recurrent affective psychoses: Possible prophylactic interventions, *Journal of Affective Disorders*, 2 (1980): 239–247.

P. A. Carney, C. T. Fitzgerald, and C. E. Monaghan, Influence of climate on the prevalence of mania, *British Journal of Psychiatry*, 152 (1988): 820–823.

110. E. Takahashi, Seasonal variation of conception and suicide, *Tohoku Journal of Experimental Medicine*, 84 (1964): 215–227; G. Parker and S. Walter, Seasonal variation in depressive disorders and suicidal deaths in New South Wales, *British Journal of Psychiatry*, 140 (1982): 626–632.

111. A. J. Lewy, T. A. Wehr, F. K. Goodwin, D. A. Newsome, and N. E. Rosenthal, Manic-depressive patients may be supersensitive to light, *Lancet*, 1 (1981): 383–384; A. J. Lewy, J. I. Nurnberger, Jr., T. A. Wehr, D. Pack, L. E. Becker, R. Powell, and D. A. Newsome, Supersensitivity to light: Possible trait marker for manic-depressive illness, *American Journal of Psychiatry*, 142 (1985): 725–727. Some researchers have found the opposite pattern in seasonal affective illness, that is, subsensitivity to light: C. Reme, M. Terman, and A. Wirz-Justice, Are deficient retinal photoreceptor renewal mechanisms involved in the pathogenesis of winter depression? *Archives of General Psychiatry*, 47 (1990): 878–879; R. W. Lam, C. W. Beattie, A. Buchanan, R. A. Remick, and A. P. Zis, Low electrooculographic ratios in patients with seasonal affective disorder, *American Journal of Psychiatry*, 148 (1991): 1526–1529.

Interestingly, there is evidence that lithium reduces sensitivity to light in patients with manic-depressive illness: P. A. Carney, J. Seggie, M. Vojtechovsky, J. Parker, E. Grof, and P. Grof, Bipolar patients taking lithium have increased dark adaptation threshold compared with controls, *Pharmacopsychiatry*, 21 (1988): 117–120; J. Seggie, P. A. Carney, J. Parker, E. Grof, and P. Grof, Effect of chronic lithium on sensitivity to light in male and female bipolar patients, *Progress in Neuro-Psychopharmacology and Biological Psychiatry*, 13 (1989): 543–549.

112. J. I. Nurnberger, Jr., W. Berrettini, L. Tamarkin, J. Hamovit, J. Norton, and E. S. Gershon, Supersensitivity to melatonin suppression by light in young people at high risk for affective disorder: A preliminary report, *Neuropsychopharmacology*, 1 (1988): 217–223.

113. S. Kasper, T. A. Wehr, J. J. Bartko, P. A. Gaist, and N. E. Rosenthal, Epidemiological findings of seasonal changes in mood and behavior, *Archives of General Psychiatry*, 46 (1989): 823–833.

114. M. R. Eastwood, J. L. Whitton, P. M. Kramer, and A. M. Peter, Infradian rhythms: A comparison of affective disorders and normal persons, *Archives of General Psychiatry*, 42 (1985): 295–299.

115. These are reviewed in the pathophysiology chapters of Goodwin and Jamison, *Manic-Depressive Illness*.

116. D. Kimura and C. Toussaint, Sex differences in cognitive function vary with the season, *Society for Neuroscience Abstracts*, vol. 17, part 1 (Washington, D.C.: Society for Neuroscience, 1991), p. 868. Many neurobiological systems of relevance to mood disorders show pronounced seasonal patterns; these include thyroid functioning, central nervous system transmitters, metabolism, and sleep and temperature regulators. A. Wirz-Justice, W. Pühringer, G. Hole, and R. Menzi, Monoamine oxidase and free tryptophan in human plasma: Normal variations and their implications for biochemical research in affective disorders, *Pharmakopsy-*

chiatr Neuropsychopharmakol, 8 (1975): 310–317; A. G. H. Smals, H. A. Ross, and P. W. Kloppenborg, Seasonal variation in serum T3 and T4 levels in man, *Journal of Clinical Endocrinology and Metabolism,* 44 (1977): 998–1001; G. H. McLellan, W. J. Riley, and C. P. Davies, Season variation in serum-thyroxine, *Lancet,* i (1979): 883–884; A. Wirz-Justice and R. Richter, Seasonality in biochemical determinations: A source of variance and a clue to the temporal incidence of affective illness, *Psychiatry Research,* 1 (1979): 53–60; A. Wirz-Justice, G. A. Groos, and T. A. Wehr, The neuropharmacology of circadian time-keeping in mammals, in *Vertebrate Circadian Systems: Structure and Physiology,* ed. J. Aschoff, S. Daan, and G. A. Groos (Berlin: Springer-Verlag, 1982).

117. N. E. Rosenthal, D. A. Sack, J. C. Gillin, A. J. Lewy, F. K. Goodwin, Y. Davenport, P. S. Mueller, D. A. Newsome, and T. A. Wehr, Seasonal affective disorder: A description of the syndrome and preliminary findings with light therapy, *Archives of General Psychiatry,* 41 (1984): 72–80.

118. Delmore Schwartz, "The Deceptive Present, The Phoenix Year," lines 1–19, *Selected Poems (1938–1958): Summer Knowledge,* p. 212.

119. T. S. Eliot, "Little Gidding," lines 4–14, *Four Quartets* (London: Faber and Faber, 1944), p. 41.

120. Lombroso, *L'Homme de Génie;* C. Lombroso, Pensiero e meteore, *Biblioteca scientifica internazionale,* vol. 16 (Dumolard, Milan, 1872).

121. Jamison, Mood disorders and patterns of creativity (1989).

122. Quoted in J. W. and A. Tibble, *John Clare: A Life* (Totowa, N.J.: Rowman and Littlefield, 1972), p. 168.

123. K. R. Jamison and R. J. Wyatt, Van Gogh: Ménière's Disease? Epilepsy? Psychosis? *Journal of the American Medical Association,* 265 (1991): 723–724.

124. M. E. Tralbaut, *Vincent van Gogh* (New York: Viking Press, 1969); Jan Hulsker, *Vincent and Theo van Gogh: A Dual Biography* (Ann Arbor, Mich.: Fuller Publications, 1990).

125. Van Gogh's physician in Arles, Dr. Urpar, diagnosed van Gogh as suffering from "acute mania with generalized delirium" (Tralbaut, *Vincent van Gogh*), and recorded that he "was affected by a severe nervous attack, accompanied by complete mania and general derangement" (Hulsker, *Vincent and Theo Van Gogh,* p. 352); it was Dr. Peyron, in his admitting note of May 1889, who mentioned epilepsy as well. Van Gogh, he concluded, had been "affected by a severe nervous attack, accompanied by hallucinations of sight and hearing," and was "subject to attacks of epilepsy, far distanced from each other" (ibid.).

126. The diagnosis of Ménière's disease (a peripheral vestibular disorder) was proposed by Dr. Arenberg and his colleagues in 1990 (I. K. Arenberg, L. F. Countryman, L. H. Bernstein, and G. E. Shambaugh, *Journal of the American Medical Association*, 264 (1990): 491–493. Sharp rebuttals appeared several months later in the Letters to the Editor section of the *Journal of the American Medical Association*. Dr. Wyatt and I (Jamison and Wyatt, Van Gogh: Ménière's Disease? [1991]) were among many others who disputed the validity of a diagnosis of a disease of the inner ear. The lack of substantiating symptoms for Ménière's disease was brought up by several authors. We argued that it was difficult to fathom focusing so exclusively on a few, ill-defined somatic complaints when the preponderance of van Gogh's symptomatology was psychiatric in nature. Clearly psychosis, violence, institutionalization in an insane asylum for over a year, and suicide are extremely unlikely to be the result of Ménière's disease alone. The letter cited by the authors as evidence that van Gogh suffered a hearing loss in fact contained no evidence for that at all. Indeed, van Gogh described in that letter, as well as others, an increased sensory sensitivity—hyperacusis—which is a common symptom in manic-depressive illness. Van Gogh also described visual as well as auditory changes in the same letter. The evidence for a diagnosis of manic-depressive illness, or, conceivably, manic-depressive illness and complex partial seizures, is, on the other hand, compelling.

In the same Letters to the Editor section of the journal (*Journal of the American Medical Association*, 265 [1991]: 723), Dr. Richard Kunin outlined an argument that van Gogh might have suffered instead from acute intermittent porphyria, a genetic disease characterized by gastrointestinal, neurological, and psychiatric symptoms. Slightly less than a year later Drs. Loftus and Arnold wrote an article in the *British Medical Journal* also arguing for a diagnosis of porphyria (L. Loftus and W. Arnold, Vincent van Gogh: acute intermittent porphyria? *British Medical Journal*, 303 [1991]: 1589–1591).

Dr. Wyatt and I wrote another letter, this time to the editor of the *British Medical Journal* (304 [1992]: 577), again arguing for a diagnosis of manic-depressive illness. We felt there were several reasons why the latter diagnosis was far more probable than porphyria (although porphyria is certainly a more plausible diagnosis than Ménière's disease). First, although there is marked variability in the psychiatric symptomatology of porphyria (T. N. Cross, Porphyria—a deceptive syndrome, *American Journal of Psychiatry*, 112 [1956]: 1010–1014), manic-depressive illness is one of the most clearly and reliably diagnosed of psychiatric disorders. Of ten cases of porphyria admitted to Bellevue Hospital, Roth found that "none showed symptoms typical of manic-depressive psychosis" (N. Roth, The neuropsychiatric aspects of porphyria, *Psychosomatic Medicine*, 7 [1945]: 291–301; likewise, Tishler and his colleagues found that none of the porphyria patients in their survey of 3,867 psychiatric inpatients met *DSM-III* criteria for bipolar illness (P. V. Tishler, B. Woodward, J. O'Connor, D. A. Holbrook, L. J. Seidman, M. Hallett, and D. J. Knighton, High prevalence of intermittent acute porphyria in a psychiatric patient population, *American Journal of Psychiatry*, 142 [1985]: 1430–1436). Drs. Loftus and Arnold ruled out bipolar illness in van Gogh's case on the basis of the "facile reversibility and relatively short duration of Vincent's crises"; however, short duration and reversibility are perfectly consistent with a diagnosis of manic-depressive illness.

Second, although the authors present van Gogh's family history as an argument for porphyria, it is far more of an argument for manic-depressive illness. Porphyria is autosomal dominant for the enzyme deficiency, but up to 90 percent of those with the deficiency remain clinically free of the disease (A. Kappas, S. Sassa, R. A. Galbraith, and Y. Nordmann, The porphyrias, in *The Metabolic Basis of Inherited Disease, 6 ed.*, ed. C. R. Scriver, A. L. Beaudet, W. S. Sly, and D. Valle (New York: McGraw-Hill, 1989), pp. 1305–1365). On the other hand, bilineality as a result of assortative mating is common in manic-depressive illness, not infrequently giving rise to a large number of affected family members. In the one study that systematically investigated psychiatric illness in first-degree relatives of patients with porphyria, only one relative was found to have a history of mental illness; this relative's symptoms and course were not consistent with a diagnosis of manic-depressive illness (B. Ackner, J. E. Cooper, C. H. Gray, and M. Kelly, Acute porphyria: A neuropsychiatric and biochemical study, *Journal of Psychosomatic Research*, 6 [1962]: 1–24). The authors focus on the physical symptoms experienced by van Gogh's brother Theo at the end of his life, but it should be noted that both Theo and Vincent wrote about melancholia as their shared constitutional malady. Vincent's occasional gastrointestinal symptoms could have been due to far more probable causes than porphyria (for example, poor nutrition, influenza, or depression itself); his convulsive disorder may have been precipitated by absinthe abuse or due to a coexisting complex partial seizure disorder. The nature and extent of both van Gogh's absinthe use and convulsive disorder remain unclear (Hulsker, *Vincent and Theo van Gogh*); in any event, van Gogh's affective symptomatology clearly predates any history of seizures, and his family history is more consistent with manic-depressive illness.

Third, both Vincent and his brother Cor committed suicide.

Suicide is a very uncommon behavior in the general population, and there is no indication of elevated rates of suicide in porphyria. On the other hand, 15 to 20 percent of untreated manic-depressives commit suicide, 70 to 80 percent of all suicides are associated with affective illness, and suicides tend to cluster in families with strong histories of manic-depressive illness (see chapter 6).

Fourth, manic-depressive illness is far more common in highly creative artists and writers than in the general population; porphyria shows no such relationship. Indeed, although Drs. Wetterberg and Österberg found that cognitive functioning (except memory) was normal in porphyria (L. Wetterberg and E. Österberg, Acute intermittent porphyria: A psychometric study of twenty-five patients, *Journal of Psychosomatic Research*, 13: [1969]: 91–93), others have shown significant neuropsychological impairment (Tishler, High prevalence of intermittent acute porphyria [1985]) as well as extremely poor functioning on tests of manual dexterity (Ackner, Acute porphyria [1962]).

Finally, manic-depressive illness is a common illness, occurring in at least one percent of the population. Porphyria, on the other hand, occurs in only 0.001 to 0.008 percent (Tishler, High prevalence of intermittent acute porphyria [1985]; Kappas, The porphyrias [1989]). Even in studies of psychiatric inpatients the prevalence of porphyria is rare, ranging from 0.16 to 0.48 percent (Tishler, High incidence of intermittent acute porphyria [1985]). It is a basic truth in clinical medicine that when one hears hoofbeats it is unlikely to be a zebra. This admonition against diagnosing rare disorders when a common disease equally, or better, fits the symptoms and course of an illness, is particularly apt in the case of Vincent van Gogh.

127. Van Gogh, *The Complete Letters*; Jan Hulsker, *Complete Van Gogh Paintings, Drawings and Sketches* (New York: H. N. Abrams, 1980).

128. Van Gogh, *The Complete Letters* (letter 504, June 1888), vol. 2, pp. 598–599.

129. Lombroso, *L'Homme de Génie*.

130. John Clare, *The Letters of John Clare*, ed. J. W. and A. Tibble (London: Routledge & Kegan Paul, 1951).

131. Rosamond Harding, *An Anatomy of Inspiration* (Cambridge: W. Heffer & Sons, 1948), p. 70.

132. For further discussion of the importance of the rate of change of light, see Wehr and Goodwin, 1983; N. E. Rosenthal, D. A. Sack, J. C. Gillin, A. J. Lewy, F. K. Goodwin, Y. Davenport, P. S. Mueller, D. A. Newsome, and T. A. Wehr, Seasonal affective disorder: A description of the syndrome and preliminary findings with light therapy, *Archives of*

General Psychiatry, 41 (1984): 72–80; Goodwin and Jamison, *Manic-Depressive Illness* (1990).

133. Lucretius, "Meteorology and Geology," *On the Nature of the Universe*, trans. R. E. Latham (London: Penguin, 1951), p. 228.

134. E. Slater and A. Meyer, Contributions to a pathography of the musicians: 1. Robert Schumann, *Confinia Psychiatrica*, 2 (1959): 65–94.

135. Sorley MacLean, "Glen Eyre," lines 49–60, *Spring Tide and Neap Tide: Selected Poems 1932–72* (Edinburgh: Canongate, 1977), p. 70.

136. George Gordon, Lord Byron, "Manfred," act III, scene 1, lines 138–145, *Lord Byron: The Complete Poetical Works*, vol. 4, ed. Jerome J. McGann (Oxford: Clarendon Press, 1986), p. 92.

CHAPTER 5
THE MIND'S CANKER IN ITS SAVAGE MOOD

1. Byron, "The Lament of Tasso," lines 5–10, *Lord Byron: The Complete Poetical Works*, vol. 4 (1986), p. 116.

2. Leslie A. Marchand, *Byron: A Biography*, 3 vols. (New York: Alfred A. Knopf, 1957), p. 131.

3. *Byron's Letters and Journals*, 12 vols., ed. Leslie A. Marchand (London: John Murray, 1973–1982), vol. 9, p. 37. Hereafter cited as *BLJ*.

4. Byron, "The Corsair," canto II, verse 10, lines 328–30, *Byron: The Complete Poetical Works*, vol. 3, p. 182.

5. Moore, *The Works of Lord Byron*, vol. 13, p. 24.

6. *BLJ*, vol. 3, p. 119.

7. Julius Millingen, *Memoirs of the Affairs of Greece* (London, 1831), p. 16.

8. Byron, *Don Juan*, canto XVII, stanza 11, *Lord Byron: The Complete Poetical Works*, vol. 5, p. 660.

9. Lovell, Blessington, *Lady Blessington's Conversations*, p. 220. (Originally published in 1834 as the *Journal of the Conversations of Lord Byron* by the Countess of Blessington.)

10. Ibid., p. 72.

11. Byron, "Manfred," act I, scene 2, lines 40–41, *Bryon: The Complete Poetical Works*, vol. 4, p. 63.

12. Ibid., line 41.

13. Ibid., line 42.

14. Percy Bysshe Shelley, "A Defence of Poetry," *Shelley's Prose*, ed. David Lee Clark (New York: New Amsterdam, 1988), p. 295.

15. Ibid.

16. Keats, *Letters* (letter to his brothers, December 1817), p. 193.

17. Keats, *Letters* (letter to Richard Woodhouse, October 27, 1818), p. 386.

18. Byron, "Childe Harold's Pilgrimage," canto III, stanza 44, *Lord Byron: The Complete Poetical Works*, vol. 2, p. 92.

19. Lovell, *Lady Blessington's Conversations*, p. 179.

20. Kraepelin, *Manic-Depressive Insanity*; A. P. Zis, P. Grof, M. Webster, and F. K. Goodwin, Prediction of relapse in recurrent affective disorder, *Psychopharmacology Bulletin*, 16 (1980): 47–49.

J. Angst, Course of affective disorders, in H. M. van Praag, M. H. Lader, O. J. Rafaelsen, and E. J. Sachar, eds., *Handbook of Biological Psychiatry* (New York: Marcel Dekker, 1981), pp. 225–242.

F. K. Goodwin and K. R. Jamison, The natural course of manic-depressive illness, in R. M. Post and J. C. Ballenger, eds., *Neurobiology of Mood Disorders* (Baltimore: Williams & Wilkins, 1984), pp. 20–37.

P. Roy-Byrne, R. M. Post, T. W. Uhde, T. Porcu, and D. Davis, The longitudinal course of recurrent affective illness: Life chart data from research patients at the NIMH, *Acta Psychiatrica Scandianvica* 71 (Suppl. 317) (1985): 1–34; Goodwin and Jamison, "Course and Outcome," *Manic-Depressive Illness*, pp. 127–156.

21. Kraepelin, *Manic-Depressive Insanity*.

F. I. Wertham, A group of benign psychoses: Prolonged manic excitements: With a statistical study of age, duration and frequency in 2000 manic attacks, *American Journal of Psychiatry*, 9 (1929): 17–78.

C. Perris, The course of depressive psychoses, *Acta Psychiatrica Scandinavica*, 44 (1968): 238–248.

A. W. Loranger and P. M. Levine, Age at onset of bipolar affective illness, *Archives of General Psychiatry*, 35 (1978): 1345–1348.

M. Baron, N. Risch, and J. Mendlewicz, Age at onset in bipolar-related major affective illness: Clinical and genetic implications, *Journal of Psychiatric Research*, 17 (1983): 5–18.

Goodwin and Jamison, "Childhood and Adolescence," *Manic-Depressive Illness*, pp. 186–209.

22. Goodwin and Jamison, Peak incidence of affective episodes by month: Review of 13 studies, "Epidemiology," *Manic-Depressive Illness*, pp. 157–185. See discussion of seasonality in chapter 4.

23. Kraepelin, *Manic-Depressive Insanity*.

Zis et al., Prediction of relapse (1980).

Angst, Course of affective disorders.

R. M. Post, D. R. Rubinow, and J. C. Ballenger, Conditioning, sensitization, and kindling: Implications for the course of affective illness, in Post and Ballenger, *The Neurobiology of Mood Disorders*, pp. 432–466.

R. M. Post, D. R. Rubinow, and J. C. Ballenger, Conditioning and sensitization in the longitudinal course of affective illness, *British Journal of Psychiatry*, 149 (1986): 191–201.

Roy-Byrne et al., The longitudinal course of recurrent affective illness (1985).

Goodwin and Jamison, "Course and Outcome," *Manic-Depressive Illness*, pp. 127–156; M. Maj, F. Veltro, R. Pirozzi, S. Lobrace, and L. Magliano, Pattern of recurrence of illness after recovery from an episode of major depression: A prospective study, *American Journal of Psychiatry*, 149 (1992): 795–800.

24. *Lady Blessington's Conversations of Lord Byron*, "Journal," p. 55.

25. *BLJ* (letter from Byron to Countess Teresa Guiccioli, October 1, 1820), vol. 7, p. 189.

26. *BLJ*, (letter from Byron to John Murray, September 20, 1821), vol. 8, p. 216.

27. Quoted in Malcolm Elwin, *Lord Byron's Wife* (New York: Harcourt, Brace & World, 1962), p. 252.

28. John Nichol, *Byron* (New York: Harper & Brothers, 1880), p. 12.

29. Marchand, *Byron*, p. 3.

30. Ibid.

31. Violet Walker, *The House of Byron: A History of the Family from the Norman Conquest, 1066–1988* (London: Quiller Press, 1988), p. 113.

32. Ibid., p. 45.

33. Ibid., p. 44.

34. Ibid., p. 45.

35. Nichol, *Byron*, p. 5; Marchand, *Byron*, p. 6; Walker, *The House of Byron*, p. 118.

36. Ibid., p. 170.

37. Nichol, *Byron*, p. 7.

38. Walker, *The House of Byron*, p. 118.

39. Ibid.

40. Ibid., p. 174.

41. Ibid., p. 172.

42. André Maurois, *Byron*, trans. Hamish Miles (1930, reprint, London: Constable, 1984), pp. 23–24.

43. Walker, *The House of Byron*, p. 158.

44. A. L. Rowse, *The Byrons and Trevanions* (London: Weidenfeld and Nicolson, 1978), p. 138.

45. Ibid., p. 139.

46. Ibid.

47. Doris Langley Moore, *Lord Byron: Accounts Rendered* (New York: Harper & Row, 1974), p. 16.

48. Doris Langley Moore, *The Late Lord Byron: Posthumous Dramas* (Philadelphia: J. B. Lippincott, 1961), p. 133.

49. Moore, *Lord Byron: Accounts Rendered*, p. 29.

50. Maurois, *Byron*, p. 33; Moore, *The Late Lord Byron*, p. 82; J. G. Kiernan, "Degeneracy Stigmata," *Alienist Neurologist*, 22 (1898) [1901]: 50–57, 287–304.

51. Maurois, *Byron*, pp. 26–27.

52. Marchand, *Byron*, p. 18.

53. Maurois, *Byron*, p. 27; see also Byron's account of his grandfather's death, *BLJ* & letter from Byron to John Murray, September 20, 1821), vol. 8, p. 217.

54. *BLJ* (letter from Byron to John Murray, September 20, 1821), vol. 8, p. 217.

55. Moore, *The Works of Lord Byron*, vol. 12, p. 15.

56. *BLJ*, (letter from Byron to Augusta Byron, November 2, 1804), vol. 1, p. 54.

57. *BLJ*, (letter from Byron to Augusta Byron, November 11, 1804), vol. 1, pp. 55–56.

58. Ibid., p. 56.

59. *BLJ*, (letter from Byron to Augusta Byron, June 5, 1805), vol. 1, p. 68.

60. *BLJ*, (letter from Byron to Augusta Byron, August 18, 1805), vol. 1, p. 75.

61. Moore, *The Works of Lord Byron*, vol. 12, pp. 99–100.

62. Quoted in Marchand, *Byron*, p. 920.

63. Ibid., p. 923.

64. *BLJ*, (letter from Byron to Augusta Leigh, August 2, 1816), vol. 6, p. 62.

65. Joan Baum, *The Calculating Passion of Ada Byron* (Hamden, Conn.: The Shoe String Press, 1986), p. 40.

66. Ibid., p. xvi.

67. *BLJ*, (letter from Byron to Augusta Leigh, February 23, 1824), vol. 11, p. 121.

68. *BLJ*, (letter from Byron to John Murray, December 10, 1821), vol. 9, p. 77.

69. Baum, *The Calculating Passion*, p. 65.

70. Ibid., p. 57.

71. Ibid., p. 65.

72. Ibid.

73. Doris Langley Moore, *Ada, Countess of Lovelace: Byron's Legitimate Daughter* (London: John Murray, 1977), p. 154.

74. Ibid., p. 219

75. Ibid., p. 217

76. "Childe Harold's Pilgrimge," canto III, stanza 118, lines 1094–1096, *Lord Byron: The Complete Poetical Works*, vol. 2, p. 119.

77. *BLJ*, "Cephalonia Journal" (15 February 1824), vol. 11, p. 113.

78. B. S. Abeshouse, *A Medical History of Lord Byron* (Norwich, N.Y.: Eaton Laboratories, 1965), 30 pp.

79. *BLJ*, "Cephalonia Journal," vol. 11, p. 113.

80. Moore, *The Works of Lord Byron*, vol. 12, p. 11.

81. Ibid.

82. Ibid., p. 18.

83. *BLJ*, "Journal of 1813–1814," vol. 8, p. 258.

84. Ibid.

85. Moore, *The Works of Lord Byron*, vol. 12, p. 255.

86. John Cam Hobhouse, *Journal*, 16 May 1824, quoted in Moore, *The Late Lord Byron*, p. 15.

87. *BLJ*, (letter from Byron to Augusta Byron, April 9, 1804), vol. 1, p. 48.

88. Ibid.

89. *BLJ*, (letter from Byron to Augusta Byron, April 4, 1805), vol. 1, pp. 62–63.

90. Moore, *The Works of Lord Byron*, vol. 13, p. 447.

91. Ibid.

92. George Gordon, Lord Byron, "The Deformed Transformed," part I, scene 1, lines 313–318, *Lord Byron: The Complete Poetical Works*, vol. 6 (1991), p. 531.

93. Marchand, *Byron*, p. 113.

94. *BLJ*, (letter from Byron to Augusta Byron, December 27, 1805), vol. 1, p. 86.

95. Marchand, *Byron*; Moore, *The Works of Lord Byron*, vol. 13.

96. *BLJ*, (letter from Byron to Augusta Byron, January 7, 1806), vol. 1, p. 87.

97. Marchand, *Byron*, p. 125.

98. *BLJ*, (letter from Byron to Earl of Clare, February 6, 1807), vol. 1, p. 106.

99. *BLJ*, (letter from Byron to Edward Noel Long, April 16, 1807), vol. 1, p. 114.

100. *BLJ*, (letter from Byron to Elizabeth Bridget Pigot, October 26, 1807), vol. 1, pp. 135–136.

101. Moore, *Lord Byron: Accounts Rendered*, p. 29.

102. Quoted in Marchand, *Byron*, p. 923.

103. *BLJ*, (letter from Byron to R. C. Dallas, January 20, 1808), vol. 1, p. 146.

104. *BLJ*, (letter from Byron to John Cam Hobhouse, February 27, 1808), vol. 1, p. 158.

105. *BLJ*, (letter from Byron to Hobhouse, March 14, 1808), vol. 1, p. 160.

106. *BLJ*, (letter from Byron to Francis Hodgson, May 5, 1810), vol. 1, p. 241.

107. *BLJ*, (letter from Byron to Hobhouse, August 23, 1810), vol. 2, p. 13.

108. *BLJ*, (letter from Byron to Hobhouse, June 19, 1811), vol. 2, p. 48.

109. *BLJ*, (letter from Byron to Hobhouse, November 26, 1810), vol. 2, p. 29.

110. *BLJ*, (Byron note to himself, May 22, 1811), vol. 2, pp. 47–48.

111. *BLJ*, (letter from Byron to Hobhouse, June 19, 1811), vol. 2, p. 51. A *calenture* is a tropical delirium characterized by an intensely feverish or passionate state.

112. Moore, *The Works of Lord Byron*, vol. 3, p. 446; Marchand, *Byron*, p. x.

113. *BLJ*, (letter from Byron to Henry Drury, July 7, 1811), vol. 2, p. 59.

114. *BLJ*, "Ravenna Journal," vol. 8, p. 24.

115. *BLJ*, (letter from Byron to R. C. Dallas, August 21, 1811), vol. 2, p. 75.

116. *BLJ*, (letter from Byron to Francis Hodgson, October 13, 1811), vol. 2, pp. 111–112.

117. *BLJ*, (letter from Byron to Hobhouse, October 22, 1811), vol. 2, pp. 117–118.

118. *BLJ*, (letter from Byron to Francis Hodgson, March 5, 1812), vol. 2, p. 167.

119. Marchand, *Byron*, p. 345.

120. Ibid., p. 335.

121. Marchand, *Byron*, p. 328.

122. *BLJ*, (letter from Byron to Lady Caroline Lamb, May 19, 1822), vol. 2, p. 177.

123. *BLJ*, (letter from Byron to Lady Melbourne, August 14, 1812), vol. 2, p. 188.

124. Marchand, *Byron*, p. 382.

125. *BLJ*, (letter from Byron to Lady Melbourne, November 4, 1813), vol. 3, p. 157.

126. *BLJ*, "Journal" (December 10, 1813), vol. 3, p. 236.

127. *BLJ*, "Journal" (February 27, 1814), vol. 3, p. 246.

128. Byron, "Manfred," act II, scene 1, lines 24–27; act II, scene 2, lines 105–109, *Lord Byron: The Complete Poetical Works*, vol. 4, pp. 68, 74.

129. *BLJ*, (letter from Byron to Lady Melbourne, April 25, 1814), vol. 4, p. 105.

130. *BLJ*, (letter from Byron to Thomas Moore, May 31, 1814), vol. 4, p. 121.

131. Ibid.

132. *BLJ*, (letter from Byron to Thomas Moore, August 3, 1814), vol. 4, p. 153.

133. *BLJ*, (letter from Byron to Lady Melbourne, October 18, 1812), vol. 2, p. 231.

134. Moore, *The Late Lord Byron*, p. 251.

135. Quoted in Elwin, *Lord Byron's Wife*, p. 119.

136. *BLJ*, (letter from Byron to Augusta Leigh, August 30, 1811), vol. 2, p. 85.

137. John Cam Hobhouse, *Recollections of a Long Life*, 6 vols. (London: John Murray, 1909–1911), vol. 1, p. 196.

138. Quoted in Marchand, *Byron*, p. 547.

139. Quoted in Elwin, *Lord Byron's Wife*, p. 328.

140. Ibid., p. 256.

141. Ibid., p. 344.

142. Ibid., p. 413.

143. Marchand, *Byron*, p. 543.

144. Marchand, *Byron*, p. 569.

145. Byron, "Don Juan," canto I, stanzas, 26–27, *Byron: The Complete Poetical Works*, vol. 5, pp. 16–17.

146. Quoted in Elwin, *Lord Byron's Wife*, p. 382.

147. *BLJ*, (letter from Byron to Sir Ralph Noel, February 2, 1816), vol. 5, p. 20.

148. Moore, *The Works of Lord Byron*, vol. 15, pp. 105–108.

149. Sir Walter Scott, *The Letters of Sir Walter Scott* (letter to J. B. S. Morritt, November 22, 1816), ed. H. J. C. Grierson (London: Constable, 1933), p. 297.

150. Shelley, *Complete Works*, vol. 9, (letter from Shelley to Peacock, July 17, 1816), p. 181.

151. George Gordon, Lord Byron, *The Works of Lord Byron, Let-*

ters and Journals, 6 vols., ed. Rowland E. Prothero (London: John Murray, 1899), vol. 3, pp. 347–348.

152. *BLJ*, (letter from Byron to Douglas Kinnaird, December 17, 1816), vol. 5, p. 140.

153. *BLJ*, (letter from Byron to Augusta Leigh, December 18, 1816), vol. 5, p. 141.

154. *BLJ*, (letter from Byron to Thomas Moore, March 25, 1817), vol. 5, p. 187.

155. John Cam Hobhouse, 14 October 1817, quoted in Norman Page, *Byron: Interviews and Recollections* (Atlantic Highlands, N.J.: Humanities Press, 1985), p. 54.

156. Marchand, *Byron*, p. 717.

157. *BLJ*, (letter from Byron to Hobhouse, May 19, 1818), vol. 6, p. 40.

158. Shelley, *Complete Works*, vol. 9 (letter from Shelley to Peacock, October 8, 1818), p. 334.

159. Ibid. (letter from Shelley to Peacock, December 22, 1818), p. 12.

160. Mary Shelley, *The Letters of Mary Wollstonecraft Shelley*, (letter from Mary Shelley to Hunt, April 6, 1819), ed. Betty T. Bennett (Baltimore: Johns Hopkins University Press, 1980), vol. 1, p. 92.

161. *BLJ*, (letter from Byron to John Murray, August 24, 1819), vol. 6, p. 216.

162. *BLJ*, (letter from Byron to Hobhouse, August 23, 1819), vol. 6, p. 214.

163. *BLJ*, (letter from Byron to Teresa Guiccioli, September 28, 1820), vol. 7, p. 185.

164. *BLJ*, (letter from Byron to Teresa Guiccioli, September 29, 1820), vol. 7, p. 186.

165. *BLJ*, "Ravenna Journal" (January 6, 1821), vol. 8, p. 15.

166. Ibid. (February 2, 1821), vol. 8, p. 42.

167. *BLJ*, (letter from Byron to Thomas Moore, October 1, 1821), vol. 8, p. 230.

168. *BLJ*, "Detached Thoughts," vol. 9, p. 47.

169. Dr. James Alexander, quoted by Marchand, *Byron*, p. 1052.

170. Ibid.

171. Moore, *The Works of Lord Byron*, vol. 14, p. 464.

172. Lovell, *Lady Blessington's Conversations*, "Journal," p. 92.

173. Ibid., p. 80.

174. James Hamilton Brown, quoted in Marchand, *Byron*, p. 1111.

175. Ibid., p. 1112.

176. Byron, "On This Day I Complete My Thirty-Sixth Year," in Jerome McGann, ed., *Byron* (Oxford: Oxford University Press, 1986), pp. 969–970.

177. Page, *Byron: Interviews and Recollections, 1985*, p. 152.

178. Millingen, *Memoirs of the Affairs of Greece*, p. 119.

179. Ibid., p. 141.

180. Pietro Gamba, *A Narrative of Lord Byron's Last Journey to Greece* (London: John Murray, 1825), p. 263.

181. Marchand, *Byron*, p. 1260.

182. "Childe Harold's Pilgrimage," canto IV, stanza 137, lines 1225–1233, *Lord Byron: The Complete Poetical Works*, vol. 2, p. 170.

183. Quoted in Angus Calder, *Byron* (Milton Keynes, England: Open University Press. 1985), p. 66.

184. Quoted in David Perkins, *English Romantic Writers* (San Diego: Harcourt Brace Jovanovich, 1967), p. 697.

185. Ibid., p. 696.

186. Ibid.

187. William Allingham, *The Diaries*, ed. H. Allingham and D. Radford; intro. John Julius Norwich (London: Folio Society, 1990), p. 324.

188. Quoted in Truman Guy Steffan, *Lord Byron's Cain: Twelve Essays and a Text with Variants and Annotations* (Austin: University of Texas Press, 1968), p. 324.

189. John Ruskin, *Praeterita: The Autobiography of John Ruskin*, intro. Kenneth Clark (Oxford: Oxford University Press, 1978), p. 134.

190. Ibid.

191. Ibid.

192. W. H. Auden, *Byron: The Making of a Comic Poet*, 1966.

193. Ronald Stephenson, "Byron as Lyricist: The Poet Among the Musicians," in Alan Bold, *Byron: Wrath and Rhyme* (London: Vision Press Ltd., 1983), pp. 78–79; Stephen Coote, *Byron: The Making of a Myth* (London: Bodley Head, 1988).

194. Moore, *The Works of Lord Byron*, vol. 13, pp. 385–386.

195. Leslie A. Marchand, "Byron and the Modern Spirit," in *The Major English Romantic Poets: A Symposium in Reappraisal* (Carbondale: Southern Illinois University Press, 1957), p. 164.

196. Moore, *The Late Lord Byron*, p. 4.

197. *BLJ*, (letter from Byron to Lady Byron, December 31, 1819), vol. 6, p. 261.

198. Bold, *Byron: Wrath and Rhyme*, p. 13.

199. Byron, "Manfred," act II, scene 4, lines 160–161, *Lord Byron: The Complete Poetical Works*, vol. 4, p. 86.

200. "Childe Harold's Pilgrimage," canto III, stanza 77, lines 726–732, *Lord Byron: The Complete Poetical Works*, vol. 2, p. 105.

CHAPTER 6
GENEALOGIES OF THESE HIGH MORTAL MISERIES

1. Herman Melville, *Moby-Dick: or The Whale* (1851; reprint, Berkeley: University of California, 1979), pp. 473–474.

2. Robert Burton, *The Anatomy of Melancholy*, "Parents a Cause by Propagation," ed. J. K. Peters (New York: Frederick Unger, 1979), p. 39.

3. Edgar Allan Poe, *The Fall of the House of Usher and Other Writings* (1839; reprint, London: Penguin Books, 1986), pp. 138–145.

4. Detailed reviews of this important but very complicated field of research can be found in Julien Mendlewicz, Genetics of depression and mania, in Anastasios Georgotas and Robert Cancro, eds., *Depression and Mania* (New York: Elsevier, 1988) pp. 197–213; E. S. Gershon's chapter on genetics, in Goodwin and Jamison, *Manic-Depressive Illness*, pp. 373–401; Ming T. Tsuang and Stephen V. Faraone, *The Genetics of Mood Disorders* (Baltimore: The Johns Hopkins University Press, 1990); George Winokur, *Mania and Depression: A Classification of Syndrome and Disease* (Baltimore: The Johns Hopkins University Press, 1991).

5. Bertelsen et al., A Danish twin study of manic-depressive disorders (1977); A. Bertelsen, A Danish twin study of manic-depressive disorders, in M. Schou and E. Strömgren, eds., *Origin, Prevention and Treatment of Affective Disorders* (London: Academic Press, 1979), pp. 227–239. Reviews of twin studies can be found in J. I. Nurnberger, Jr., and E. S. Gershon, Genetics; in E. S. Paykel, ed., *Handbook of Affective Disorders* (New York: Guilford Press, 1982) pp. 126–145; Mendlewicz, Genetics of depression; Gershon, in Goodwin and Jamison, *Manic-Depressive Illness*; and Tsuang and Faraone, *Genetics of Mood Disorders*.

6. Gershon, ibid., p. 377. Drs. Larry Rifkin and Hugh Gurling of the Molecular Psychiatry Laboratory of University College and Middlesex School of Medicine in London have recently summarized the even stronger evidence for concordance in monozygotic twins: "Two series of twins selected on the basis of BP [bipolar] disorder probands have been the most thoroughly investigated over a particularly long time. These are the twins investigated by Bertelsen and those at the Maudsley Hospital. A recent reassessment of the Maudsley twins has now shown that the concordance for all subtypes of affective disorder in the co-twins is 100% [(A. Reveley, 1990, personal communication]. Bertelsen [1988, personal communication] has also followed up his series of

twins and if a diagnosis of suicide is counted as a case then the concordance amongst MZ twins is also 100%." L. Rifkin and H. Gurling, Genetic aspects of affective disorders, *Biological Aspects of Affective Disorders*, in ed. R. Horton and C. Katona (London: Academic Press, 1991), pp. 305–334; quoted on p. 313.

7. J. Price, Neurotic and endogenous depression: A phylogenetic view, *British Journal of Psychiatry*, 114 (1968): 119–120.

8. The many family studies of manic-depressive illness are reviewed by Gershon in Goodwin and Jamison, *Manic-Depressive Illness*. Recent, well-controlled studies include E. S. Gershon, J. Hamovit, J. J. Guroff, E. Dibble, J. F. Leckman, W. Sceery, S. D. Targum, J. I. Nurnberger, Jr., L. R. Goldin, and W. E. Bunney, Jr., A family study of schizoaffective, bipolar I, bipolar II, unipolar, and normal control probands, *Archives of General Psychiatry*, 39 (1982): 1157–1167.

M. M. Weissman, E. S. Gershon, K. K. Kidd, B. A. Prusoff, J. F. Leckman, E. Dibble, J. Hamovit, W. D. Thompson, D. L. Pauls, and J. J. Guroff, Psychiatric disorders in the relatives of probands with affective disorders: The Yale–National Institute of Mental Health collaborative study, *Archives of General Psychiatry*, 41 (1984): 13–21.

M. T. Tsuang, S. V. Faraone, and J. A. Fleming, Familial transmission of major affective disorders: Is there evidence supporting the distinction between unipolar and bipolar disorders? *British Journal of Psychiatry*, 146 (1985): 268–271.

9. Gershon et al. (1982).

W. Coryell, J. Endicott, T. Reich, N. Andreasen, and M. Keller, *British Journal of Psychiatry*, 145 (1984): 49–54.

J. Endicott, J. Nee, N. Andreasen, P. Clayton, M. Keller, and W. Coryell, Bipolar II: Combine or keep separate? *Journal of Affective Disorders*, 8 (1985): 17–28.

J. R. De Paulo, Jr., S. G. Simpson, J. O. Gayle, and S. Folstein, Bipolar II disorder in six sisters, *Journal of Affective Disorders*, 19 (1990): 259–264.

10. Gershon, in Goodwin and Jamison, *Manic-Depressive Illness*, p. 398.

11. J. A. Egeland, D. S. Gerhard, D. L. Pauls, J. N. Sussex, K. K. Kidd, C. R. Allen, A. M. Hostetter, and D. E. Housman, Bipolar affective disorders linked to DNA markers on chromosome 11, *Nature*, 325 (1987): 783–787.

12. M Baron, N. Risch, R. Hamburger, B. Mandel, S. Kushner, M. Newman, D. Drumer, and R. H. Belmaker, Genetic linkage between X-chromosome markers and bipolar affective illness, *Nature*, 326 (1987), 289–292; J. Mendlewicz, P. Simon, S. Sevy, F. Charon, H. Brocas, S.

Legros, and G. Vassart, Polymorphic DNA marker on X chromosome and manic depression, *Lancet*, i (1987): 1230–1232.

13. S. Hodgkinson, R. Sherrington, H. Gurling, R. Marchbanks, S. Reeders, J. Mallet, M. McInnis, H. Pertursson, and J. Brynjolfsson, Molecular genetic evidence for heterogeneity in manic depression, *Nature*, 325 (1987): 805–806.

E. S. Gershon, S. D. Targum, S. Matthysse, and W. E. Bunney, Jr., Color blindness not closely linked to bipolar illness, *Archives of General Psychiatry*, 36 (1979): 1423–1430.

J. R. Kelsoe, E. I. Ginns, J. A. Egeland, D. S. Gerhard, A. M. Goldstein, S. J. Bale, D. J. Pauls, R. T. Long, K. K. Kidd, G. Conte, D. E. Housman, and S. M. Paul, Re-evaluation of the linkage relationship between chromosome 11p loci and the gene for bipolar affective disorder in the Old Order Amish, *Nature*, 342 (1989): 238–243.

W. H. Berrettini, L. R. Golden, J. Gelernter, P. V. Gejman, E. S. Gershon, and S. Detera-Wadleigh, X-chromosome markers and manic-depressive illness: rejection of linkage to Xq28 in nine bipolar pedigrees, *Archives of General Psychiatry*, 47 (1990): 366–373.

J. Mendlewicz, M. Leboyer, A. De Bruyn, A. Malafosse, S. Sevy, D. Hirsch, C. van Broeckhoven, and J. Mallet, Absence of linkage between chromosome 11p15 markers and manic-depressive illness in a Belgian pedigree, *American Journal of Psychiatry*, 148 (1991): 1683–1687.

G. Vassart and P. Simon, Manic-depression locus on X-chromosome, *Lancet*, 338 (1991): 821–822.

14. Pat Conroy, *The Prince of Tides* (New York: Banham, 1987), p. 52.

15. Alfred Tennyson, "Maud," Part I, lines 1–8 and 53–56, Susan Shatto, ed., *Tennyson's Maud: A Definitive Edition* (London: Athlone Press, 1986), pp. 41–42, 47.

16. Hallam, Lord Tennyson, *Alfred Lord Tennyson: A Memoir* (London: Macmillan, 1897), p. 396.

17. In addition to autobiographical writings and letters, biographical information for the pedigree is based on ibid.; Harold Nicolson, *Tennyson's Two Brothers: The Leslie Stephen Lecture 1947* (Cambridge: Cambridge University Press, 1947); Sir Charles Tennyson and Hope Dyson, *The Tennysons: Background to Genius* (London: Macmillan, 1974); Robert Bernard Martin, *Tennyson: The Unquiet Heart* (Oxford: Clarendon Press, 1980); Hallam Tennyson, ed., *Studies in Tennyson* (London: Macmillan, 1981); Christopher Ricks, *Tennyson*, 2nd ed. (London: Macmillan, 1989).

18. Tennyson and Dyson, *The Tennysons*, p. 184.

19. Nicolson, The health of authors (1947), p. 5.

20. "Dr. Tennyson's breakdown: 1820–1827," *Tennyson: The Unquiet Heart*, pp. 32–51.

21. Ibid., p. 64.

22. Ricks, *Tennyson*, pp. 59–60.

23. Ibid., p. 62.

24. Martin, *Tennyson: The Unquiet Heart*, p. 378.

25. Ibid., p. 506.

26. Ibid., p. 523.

27. Nicolson, The health of authors (1947), p. 7.

28. Tennyson and Dyson, *The Tennysons*, p. 125.

29. Ibid., pp. 195–196.

30. T. S. Eliot, "In Memoriam," *Selected Prose of T. S. Eliot* (New York: Harcourt Brace Jovanovich, 1975), p. 246.

31. Niecks, *Robert Schumann*, p. 290.

32. Niecks, *Robert Schumann*, p. 10.

33. Ibid., p. 27.

34. Ibid.

35. In addition to autobiographical writings and letters, biographical and medical information for the pedigree is based on F. H. Garrison, the medical history of Robert Schumann and his family, *Bulletin of the New York Academy of Medicine*, 10 (1934): 523–538.

Eliot Slater and Alfred Meyer, Contributions to a pathography of the musicians: Robert Schumann, *Confin. Psychiat.*, 2 (1959): 65–94.

The New Grove Dictionary of Music and Musicians, 20 vols., ed. Stanley Sadie (London: Macmillan, 1980), pp. 831–870.

Ronald Taylor, *Robert Schumann: His Life and Work* (London: Granada, 1982).

Peter F. Ostwald, Robert Schumann and his doctors, *American Journal of Social Psychiatry*, 3 (1983): 5–14.

Peter Ostwald, *Schumann: The Inner Voices of a Musical Genius* (Boston: Northeastern University Press, 1985).

Nancy B. Reich, *Clara Schumann: The Artist and the Woman* (Ithaca: Cornell University Press, 1985).

36. Quoted in Ostwald, Robert Schumann and his doctors (1983), p. 6.

37. J. Hermand and J. Steakley, eds., *Writings of German Composers* (New York: Continuum, 1984).

38. Quoted in R. H. Schauffler, *Florestan: The Life and Work of Robert Schumann* (New York: Henry Holt & Co., 1945), p. 42.

39. Ibid.

40. Robert Schumann (letter from Leipzig, 1828), quoted in T. Dowley, *Schumann: His Life and Times* (New York: Hippocrene, 1982), p. 24.

41. Schumann (letter to Clara Wieck, 1837), quoted in ibid., p. 58.

42. Robert Schumann (letter to Clara Wieck, February 11, 1838) *Early Letters of Robert Schumann*, trans. May Herbert (London: George Bell and Sons, 1888; reprint, Mich.: St. Clair Shores, Scholarly Press, 1970), pp. 182–184.

43. Quoted in Taylor, *Robert Schumann: His Life and Work*, p. 87.

44. Quoted in Niecks, *Robert Schumann*, p. 219.

45. Ibid.

46. Quoted in ibid., p. 244.

47. Frank Cooper, Operatic and dramatic music, in *Robert Schumann: The Man and His Music*, ed. Alan Walker (New York: Harper & Row, 1972), p. 339.

48. Quoted in Taylor, *Robert Schumann: His Life and Work*, p. 271.

49. Quoted in ibid., p. 285.

50. M. Tchaikovsky, *The Life and Letters of Peter Tchaikovsky* (London: John Lane, Bodley Head, 1906).

51. Quoted in Niecks, *Robert Schumann*, p. 25.

52. Ostwald, *Schumann: The Inner Voices*, p. 305.

53. Quoted in Taylor, *Robert Schumann: His Life and Work*, p. 314.

54. Quoted in ibid., p. 206.

55. Henry James, Sr., *Substance and Shadow* (Boston: Ticknor & Fields, 1863), p. 75.

56. William James, *The Varieties of Religious Experience*, p. 136.

57. Henry James, The art of fiction, in *Partial Portraits* (New York: Haskell, 1968), pp. 375–408, quotation on p. 388.

58. Henry James, *Autobiography* (Princeton: Princeton University Press, 1983), p. 396. Originally published as *A Small Boy and Others* (1913), *Notes of a Son and Brother* (1914), and *The Middle Years* (1917).

59. F. O. Matthiessen, *The James Family: Including Selections from the Writings of Henry James, Senior, William, Henry, & Alice James* (New York: Alfred A. Knopf, 1947), p. 14.

60. Ibid., p. 5.

61. Ibid., p. 18.

62. Ibid., p. 161.

63. J. F. Nisbit, *The Insanity of Genius* (London: Grant Richards, 1900), p. 299.

64. H. Maudsley, *Natural Causes and Supernatural Seemings* (London: Kegan Paul, 1886), pp. 241–242.

65. Henry James, *Autobiography*, p. 265.

66. Jean Strouse, *Alice James: A Biography* (Boston: Houghton Mifflin, 1980), p. 25.

67. Matthiesen, *The James Family*, p. 213.

68. Jacques Barzun, *A Stroll with William James* (New York: Harper & Row, 1983), p. 8.

69. William James, *Varieties of Religious Experience*, pp. 160–161.

70. Matthiesen, *The James Family*, p. 303.

71. Leon Edel, *Henry James: A Life* (New York: Harper & Row, 1985), p. 665.

72. Strouse, *Alice James*, p. 112.

73. R. W. B. Lewis, *The Jameses: A Family Narrative* (New York: Farrar, Straus Giroux, 1991), p. 581.

74. Ibid., p. 580.

75. Matthiesen, *The James Family*, p. 267.

76. Lewis, *The Jameses*, p. 415.

77. Henry James, *Autobiography*, p. 261.

78. Alice James, *The Diary of Alice James* (October 26, 1890) (Middlesex, England: Penguin, 1982), p. 149.

79. Ibid., (June 28, 1889), pp. 40–41.

80. Strouse, *Alice James*, p. 58.

81. In addition to autobiographical writings and letters, biographical information for the pedigree is based on Matthiessen, *The James Family*; J. Strouse, *Alice James*; Barzun, *A Stroll with William James*; Jane Maher, *Biography of Broken Fortunes: Wilkie and Bob, Brothers of William, Henry, and Alice James* (Hamden, Conn.: Archon Books, 1986); Henry James, *Autobiography; Alice James, The Diary*; Gerald E. Myers, *William James: His Life and Thought* (New Haven: Yale University Press, 1986); Leon Edel, *The Life of Henry James*, 5 vols. (Philadelphia: J. B. Lippincott, 1953–1972); Lewis, *The Jameses*.

82. Myerson and Boyle, The incidence of manic-depressive psychosis in certain socially important families. (1941), p. 19.

83. Melville, *Pierre: Or, The Ambiguities*, p. 199.

84. Neal L. Tolchin, *Mourning, Gender, and Creativity in the Art of Herman Melville* (New Haven: Yale University Press, 1988), p. 2.

85. Leon Howard, *Herman Melville: A Biography* (Berkeley: University of California, 1952), p. 7.

86. Edwin Haviland Miller, *Melville* (New York: George Braziller, 1975), p. 75.

87. Ibid., p. 284.

88. Michael Paul Rogin, *Subversive Genealogy: The Politics and Art of Herman Melville* (Berkeley: University of California, 1985), p. 20.

89. Miller, *Melville*, p. 324.

90. Ibid., p. 287.

91. Melville, *Moby-Dick*, p. 2.

92. Herman Melville, *The Letters of Herman Melville*, ed. M. R. Davis and W. H. Gilman (letter to E. A. Duyckinck, 5 April 1849) (New Haven: Yale University Press, 1960), p. 83.

93. Miller, *Melville*, p. 101.

94. Melville, *Moby-Dick*, pp. 465–466.

95. Samuel Taylor Coleridge, "The Rime of the Ancient Mariner," part VI, lines 422–429, *Samuel Taylor Coleridge (The Oxford Authors)*, ed. H. J. Jackson (Oxford: Oxford University Press, 1985), p. 59.

96. Sara Coleridge, letter to H. N. Coleridge, 3 November 1836. Quoted in Bradford Keyes Mudge, *Sara Coleridge: A Victorian Daughter: Her Life and Essays* (New Haven: Yale University Press, p. 92).

97. Holmes, *Coleridge: Early Visions*, p. 3.

98. Samuel Taylor Coleridge, *Collected Letters of Samuel Taylor Coleridge*, ed. E. L. Griggs, vol. 1: 1785–1800 (letter to Thomas Poole, 16 October 1797) (Oxford: Oxford University Press, 1959), p. 91.

99. Holmes, *Coleridge: Early Visions*, pp. 49–52.

100. Ibid., p. 58.

101. Coleridge, *Collected Letters of Samuel Taylor Coleridge* (letter to George Coleridge, 23 February 1794), vol 1, p. 36.

102. Holmes, *Coleridge: Early Visions*, p. 143.

103. Coleridge, *Collected Letters of Samuel Taylor Coleridge*, vol. 3: 1807–1814 (letter to Joseph Cottle, 26 April 1814), p. 919.

104. Holmes, *Coleridge: Early Visions*, p. 3.

105. Hartley Coleridge, *Poems by Hartley Coleridge* (London: Edward Moxon, 1851); Sara Coleridge, *Memoir and Letters of Sara Coleridge*, ed. her daughter (New York: Harper & Brothers, 1874); E. L. Griggs, *Hartley Coleridge: His Life and Work* (London: University of London, 1929); H. Hartman, *Hartley Coleridge: Poet's Son and Poet* (London: Oxford University Press, 1931); Hartley Coleridge, *Letters of Hartley Coleridge*, ed. G. E. Griggs and E. L. Griggs (London: Oxford University Press, 1936).

106. Mudge, *Sara Coleridge*, p. 210.

107. Sara Coleridge, *Memoir*, p. 49.

108. Mudge, *Sara Coleridge*, p. 58.

109. Ibid., p. 205.

110. Ibid., p. 208.

111. Ibid., pp. 215–216.

112. Virginia Woolf, "Sara Coleridge," *The Death of the Moth and Other Essays* (New York: Harcourt Brace Jovanovich, 1974), p. 114.

113. Ibid.

114. Bell, *Virginia Woolf*, p. 226.

115. Thomas Caramagno, *The Flight of the Mind: Virginia Woolf's Art and Manic-Depressive Illness* (Berkeley: University of California Press, 1992).

116. Biographical information for pedigree based on Woolf, *The Letters of Virginia Woolf*; Virginia Woolf, *The Diary of Virginia Woolf*, eds. Anne Olivier Bell and Andrew McNeillie, 5 vols. (New York: Harcourt, 1976–1984); Virginia Woolf, *Moments of Being: Unpublished Autobiographical Writings*, ed. Jeanne Schulkind (New York: Harcourt, 1985), 2nd ed.; Leonard Woolf, *Beginning Again*; Bell, *Virginia Woolf*; Catherine Peters, *Thackeray's Universe: Shifting Worlds of Imagination and Reality* (London: Faber and Faber, 1987); Caramagno, *The Flight of the Mind*.

117. Woolf, *Moments of Being*, p. 133.

118. Thomas, "Old Man," lines 25–32, in *The Collected Poems of Edward Thomas*, pp. 19, 21.

119. Virginia Woolf, "Moments of Being," in *A Haunted House and Other Short Stories* (New York: Harcourt, 1944), pp. 104–105.

120. Woolf, *The Letters of Virginia Woolf*, vol. 4, p. 180.

121. Virginia Woolf, *"The Moment" and Other Essays* (New York: Harcourt, 1948), p. 14.

122. Ernest Hemingway, canceled passage from *Green Hills of Africa*, quoted in Kenneth S. Lynn, *Hemingway* (New York: Simon & Schuster, 1987), p. 415.

123. In addition to autobiographical writings and letters, biographical information for the pedigree is based on ibid.; Paul Hendrickson, "Papa's Boys," *Washington Post*, July 29 and 30, 1987; I. Yalom and M. Yalom, Ernest Hemingway—A psychiatric view, *Archives of General Psychiatry*, 24 (1971): 485–494; Carlos Baker, *Ernest Hemingway: A Life Story* (New York: Avon Books, 1980).

124. Lynn, *Hemingway*, p. 36.

125. Ibid., p. 592.

126. Hendrickson, "Papa's Boys."

127. Ibid.

128. Lynn, *Hemingway*, p. 99.

129. Mary Wollstonecraft, *A Short Residence in Sweden, Norway and Denmark*, ed. Richard Holmes (Middlesex, England: Penguin, 1987), p. 152.

130. Mary Shelley, *Frankenstein Or, The Modern Prometheus* (New York: Penguin, 1983), p. 53.

131. Richard Holmes, *Footsteps: Adventures of a Romantic Biographer* (New York: Viking, 1985), p. 91.

132. William Godwin, *Memoirs of the Author of the Rights of Woman*, ed. Richard Holmes (Middlesex, England: Penguin, 1987), p. 250.

133. Holmes, *Footsteps*, p. 91.

134. Mary Shelley, *The Journals of Mary Shelley: 1814–1844*, vol. 2, *1822–1844*, ed. P. R. Feldman and D. Scott-Kilvert (Oxford: Oxford University Press, 1987), p. 563.

135. Mary Shelley, *The Letters of Mary Wollstonecraft Shelley*, vol. 2, ed. B. T. Bennett (letter to Leigh Hunt, 20 July 1839) (Baltimore: Johns Hopkins University Press, 1983), p. 318.

136. Mary Shelley, *The Journals of Mary Shelley*, vol. 2 (26 February 1841), p. 572.

137. W. Jackson Bate, *Samuel Johnson* (San Diego: Harvest/HBJ, 1979), p. 383.

138. James Boswell, *Life of Johnson*, ed. L. F. Powell (1770; reprint, Oxford: Oxford University Press, 1934), vol. 2, p. 121.

139. Bate, *Samuel Johnson*, p. 119.

140. R. Porter, 'The Hunger of Imagination': Approaching Samuel Johnson's melancholy, in W. F. Bynum, R. Porter, and M. Shepherd, eds., *The Anatomy of Madness: Essays in the History of Psychiatry* (London and New York: Tavistock, 1985), pp. 63–88.

141. Bate, *Samuel Johnson*, p. 121.

142. Ibid., p. 348.

143. Ibid.

144. Ibid., p. 371.

145. M. Harris, *The Heart of Boswell: Highlights from the Journals of James Boswell* (New York: McGraw-Hill, 1981); Henry R. Kranzler, Boswell's affective illness: A reappraisal, *Connecticut Medicine*, 53 (1989): 225–228.

146. William B. Ober, *Boswell's Clap and Other Essays: Medical Analyses of Literary Men's Afflictions* (Carbondale: Southern Illinois University Press, 1979); Kranzler, Boswell's affective illness (1989).

147. Van Gogh, *The Complete Letters* (letter 521, August 1888), vol. 3, p. 8.

148. Tralbaut, *Vincent van Gogh*, p. 286.

149. Hulsker, *Vincent and Theo Van Gogh*, p. 12.

150. Ibid., p. 454.

151. Ibid., p. 458.

152. Tralbaut, *Vincent van Gogh*, p. 276.

153. David Sweetman, *Van Gogh: His Life and His Art* (New York: Crown, 1990), p. 53.

154. Van Gogh, *The Complete Letters* (letter 481, May 1888), vol. 2, p. 557.

155. THÉODORE GÉRICAULT (1791–1824), French Romantic painter, had a tumultuous emotional existence, alternating between periods of ardent energy and activity and deep melancholia (including paranoid delusions and at least one reported suicide attempt). His paintings, characterized by their violent but evocative beauty, often had macabre themes, including severed heads and limbs, decaying corpses, murder and suicide, and insanity. Lorenz E. A. Eitner, in his book *Géricault: His Life and Work* (London: Orbis Publishing 1983), comments on the extensive history of insanity in Géricault's family: "A strain of mental illness ran through four generations of Géricault's family on his mother's side. His grandfather, J. V. Charles Caruel, was confined to an asylum in 1773 and died insane in 1779; his uncle François J. L. Caruel, was confined in 1770 and died insane in 1805; his cousin, Louis-Sylvestre Caruel, was institutionalized in 1845 and died insane in 1885; and his own son, Georges-Hippolyte Géricault, by his aunt Alexandrine-Modeste Caruel who was also the mother of Louis-Sylvestre, died in 1882 under circumstances that suggest he was not of sound mind" (p. 322).

156. GUSTAV MAHLER (1860–1911), Austrian composer, was the second eldest of a large family. Of the five children who lived through the age of risk for developing manic-depressive illness, Gustav was cyclothymic, his brother Otto committed suicide, his sister Justine had recurrent death hallucinations and often hovered on the verge of a nervous breakdown, and his brother Alois misrepresented himself in grandiose ways as well as manifesting an exceptionally extravagant life-style. (Alma Mahler, *Gustav Mahler, Memories and Letters*, 2nd ed. trans. Basil Creighton [London: John Murray, 1968]; Henry-Louis de La Grange, *Mahler*, vol. 1 [London: Victor Gollancz, 1974]; Egon Gartenberg, *Mahler: The Man and His Music* [New York: Schirmer Books, 1978]; Knud Martner, *Selected Letters of Gustav Mahler*, trans. by Eithne Wilkins and Ernst Kaiser [New York: Farrar, Straus & Giroux, 1979]; Donald Mitchell, *Gustav Mahler: The Early Years* [London: Faber and Faber, 1980]; Norman Lebrecht, *Mahler Remembered* [London: Faber and Faber, 1987].)

157. ROBERT LOWELL (1917–1977), American poet, was hospitalized repeatedly for manic and depressive episodes. His great-uncle, poet James Russell Lowell, also suffered from extended periods of severe depression, heavy drinking, paranoia, and fears of going mad. James Russell Lowell's mother was institutionalized at McLean Psychiatric Hospital (as

was Robert Lowell, many times), his sister Rebecca suffered from severe mood swings and other symptoms that were similar to those of their mother, and his brother Charles reportedly suffered from the same illness as did their mother and sister. (C. David Heymann, *American Aristocracy: The Lives and Times of James Russell, Amy, and Robert Lowell* [New York: Dodd, Mead, 1980]; Hamilton, *Robert Lowell: A Biography*; Jeffrey Meyers, *Manic Power: Robert Lowell and his Circle*, (New York: Arbor House, 1987; Lowell, *Collected Prose*).

158. JOHN BERRYMAN (born John Allyn Smith, Jr., in 1914) was a fellow poet and friend of Robert Lowell. His father shot and killed himself and one of his father's sisters also committed suicide. In 1972, after years of struggling with manic-depressive illness and alcoholism, John Berryman jumped to his death from a bridge over the Mississippi River. (Haffenden, *The Life of John Berryman*; E. M. Halliday, *John Berryman and the Thirties: A Memoir* [Amherst: University of Massachusetts Press, 1987]; Paul Mariani, *Dream Song: The Life of John Berryman* [New York: William Morrow, 1990].)

His father's suicide haunted Berryman, and he described its lasting and disturbing effects in many of his poems. In *The Dream Songs* he wrote:

> The marker slants, flowerless, day's almost done,
> I stand above my father's grave with rage,
> often, often before
> I've made this awful pilgrimage to one
> who cannot visit me, who tore his page
> out: I come back for more,
>
> I spit upon this dreadful banker's grave
> who shot his heart out in a Florida dawn
> O ho alas alas
> When will indifference come . . .

(John Berryman, "384: The Marker Slants," lines 1–10, *The Dream Songs* [New York: Farrar, Straus and Giroux, 1969], p. 406.)

159. ANNE SEXTON (1928–1974), American poet, had a strong family history of mental illness and suicide. Her maternal great-aunt was hospitalized and received electroshock therapy for a major "nervous breakdown"; her paternal grandfather was also hospitalized for a nervous breakdown. Her father was an alcoholic, and his sister committed suicide. One of Anne's sisters also committed suicide. (Sources are Sexton and Ames, *Anne Sexton: A Self-Portrait in Letters* [Boston: Houghton Mifflin Company, 1977]; Diane Wood Middlebrook, *Anne Sexton: A Biography*. [Boston: Houghton Mifflin Company, 1991].)

Although Anne Sexton does not appear to have been given the diagnosis of manic-depressive illness (the primary diagnostic emphasis was placed on the depressive side of her illness, as well as her alcoholism, "hysteria," and other personality difficulties), the case for manic-depressive illness is very strong. In addition to Sexton's extensive family history of suicide and mental illness, as well as her own suicide, her symptoms—pronounced swings and lability in mood, expansiveness, impulsivity, anger, altered sleep and energy patterns, seasonal variations in mood—are highly characteristic of manic-depressive illness. So, too, are her alcoholism and the worsening, rapidly cycling quality of the course of her illness. Sexton's "hysterical" symptoms may well have been hysterical; they also may have been a manifestation of the emotional extremes and lability that go along with manic-depressive illness. Women who have affective illness not uncommonly are diagnosed as "borderlines" or "hysterics" and, in Sexton's case, she may well have had both a personality disorder and manic-depressive illness.

Sexton reportedly was given lithium in 1972, but without therapeutic effect (Diane Wood Middlebrook, personal communication, letter, September 1991). She was, however, drinking heavily at the time, which may well have undermined both the drug's efficacy and her compliance in taking the medication as prescribed. Likewise, nonresponsiveness to lithium by no means rules out a diagnosis of manic-depressive illness, even assuming lithium was given (and taken) in the necessary amount for the necessary period of time. Given the nature and duration of Sexton's psychiatric illness, by the time she was prescribed lithium it is quite likely that anticonvulsants and/or thyroid medication would have been necessry to effect a change in her clinical condition.

160. AUGUST STRINDBERG (1849–1912), Swedish playwright and novelist, suffered from severe manic-depressive psychosis, characterized by extreme mood swings, grandiose and paranoid delusions, and hallucinations. His mother was described as being of "nervous temperament," his sister Elisabeth had severe persecution mania, recurrent depressions, and had to be admitted to a mental hospital, and Strindberg's daughter Kerstin was paranoid and "mentally unbalanced." Primary sources for biographical information about Strindberg are Lagercrantz, *August Strindberg* (1985); and Meyer, *Strindberg: A Biography*, as well as A. Brett, Psychological abnormalities in August Strindberg, *Journal of English and German Philology*, 20 (1921): 4–98; B. M. E. Mortensen and B. W. Downs, *Strindberg: An Introduction to his Life and Work* (London: Cambridge University Press, 1949); E. Sprigge, *The Strange Life of August Strindberg* (London: Hamilton, 1949); S. Hedenberg, August Strindberg: Opinions of German psychiatrists. Criticism of studies by

Jaspers, Rahmer and Storch, *Acta Psychiatrica Neurologica*, suppl. 34 (1959): 325–339; E. W. Anderson, Strindberg's illness, *Psychological Medicine*, 1 (1971): 104–117.

161. EUGENE O'NEILL suffered from severe recurrent depressions, was an alcoholic, often suicidal, and attempted suicide when he was in his mid-twenties. His mother was a morphine addict (she used morphine, she said, for her "nerves'), his father a heavy drinker, and his brother an alcoholic. One of O'Neill's sons was hospitalized for "shock," was a narcotics addict and an alcoholic, and on more than one occasion tried to kill himself. Another son, who had been a professor of Greek drama at Yale, committed suicide at the age of forty. See Croswell Bowell, with the assistance of Shane O'Neill, *The Curse of the Misbegotten: A Tale of the House of O'Neill* (New York: McGraw-Hill, 1959); Louis Sheaffer, *O'Neill: Son and Playwright* (New York: Paragon, 1968); Arthur Gelb and Barbara Gelb, *O'Neill*, enlarged ed. (New York: Harper & Row, 1973).

162. TENNESSEE WILLIAMS's "deep nervous problems" began when he was sixteen years old. Throughout his life he suffered from what he described as his "dreadful depressions," as well as from alcoholism and drug abuse. At one point he had to be committed involuntarily to a psychiatric ward. His sister was also committed to a psychiatric hospital as a result of a severe psychosis; eventually she underwent a lobotomy. Williams's mother was hospitalized for psychosis as well, and Williams wrote in his *Memoirs* that on both sides of her family there had been "alarming instances of mental and nervous breakdowns." Tennessee Williams, *Memoirs* (New York: Doubleday, 1972), quotation on p. 116; Dakin Williams and Shepherd Mead, *Tennessee Williams: an Intimate Biography* (New York: Arbor House, 1983); Donald Spoto, *The Kindness of Strangers: The Life of Tennessee Williams* (New York: Ballantine Books, 1985); *Tennessee Williams, Five O'Clock Angel: Letters of Tennessee Williams to Maria St. Just: 1948–1982* (New York: Alfred A. Knopf, 1990).

163. VICTOR HUGO, who had very real difficulties with his own moods, had both a brother and a daughter who were committed to institutions because of "incurable insanity."

164. The role of genetics in suicide is reviewed in S. Kety, Genetic factors in suicide, in A. Roy, ed., *Suicide* (Baltimore: Williams & Wilkins, 1986), pp. 41–45; A. Roy, Genetics of suicide, in J. Mann and M. Stanley, ed., *Psychobiology of Suicidal Behavior* (New York: New York Academy of Sciences, 1986), pp. 97–105; Mendlewicz, Genetics of depression and mania, p. 207; A. Roy, N. L. Segal, B. S. Centerwell, and C. D. Robinette, Suicide in twins, *Archives of General Psychiatry*, 48 (1991): 29–32.

165. Egeland and Sussex, Suicide and family loading for affective disorders (1985).

166. Although British painter RICHARD DADD is usually characterized as having suffered from paranoid schizophrenia, it is in fact more
likely that he suffered from a severe, relatively unremitting form of manic-
depressive illness. First, his extremely strong family history of psychiatric
illness (of seven children from his father's first marriage, three became
insane and a fourth required a "private attendant") is more consistent
with what is known about the genetics of manic-depressive than with
schizophrenic illness. Second, his pre-illness personality and social ad-
justment were more like those seen in manic-depressive illness. Third,
his age at the onset of his illness and the fact that his psychosis coincided
in time with prolonged exposure to light (in fact, his contemporaries
attributed his insanity to sunstroke) suggest a possible bipolar vulnerability. Fourth, his symptoms of violent behavior, extreme restlessness,
paranoia, religious preoccupations (he murdered his father under the
influence of the delusion that his father was the devil or the devil's agent),
and feverish excitements, along with the episodic nature of at least the
early course of his illness, are also consistent with manic-depressive illness. Hallucinations and delusions can occur in both schizophrenia and
manic-depressive illness. After Dadd was admitted to Bethlem Hospital,
and later transferred to Broadmoor Hospital for the Criminally Insane, his
illness showed some signs of remission; in any event, it did not appear to
deteriorate further. It seems, from the hospital records, that he remained
deluded, but clinical observations were infrequent and inadequate (for
example, entries of "no change," written every six months). Examination
of Dadd's letters and other writings reveals a strongly manic quality to
many of them.

167. Andreasen, Creativity and mental illness (1987); McNeil, Prebirth and postbirth influence (1971); Richards, Creativity in manic-
depressives (1988); Karlsson, Genetic basis of intellectual variation (1981);
Karlsson, Creative intelligence (1984).

168. Drs. Ming Tsuang and Stephen Faraone of Harvard University
have summarized the risk of major mood disorders among relatives of
manic-depressive probands and concluded:

> Overall, family studies of bipolar probands strongly support the hy-
> pothesis that their first degree relatives are at greater risk of bipolar
> disorder than is the general population. The risk to relatives ranges
> from a low of 1.2 percent to a high of 24.9 percent. All of these values
> are greater than the general population risk of 0.5 percent suggested
> by epidemiologic studies. . . . More important, each of the three
> double-blind, controlled studies found high rates of bipolar disorder
> among relatives of bipolar probands in comparison to control probands

[one study found a 4.5 percent risk in the relatives and 0 percent risk in the controls; the other two studies found ten to twenty times the risk]. Tsuang and Faraone, *Genetics of Mood Disorders*, p. 47.

A recent review of studies found that the morbid risk of bipolar disorder in first-degree relatives of bipolar patients ranged between 5.8 and 7.8 percent, again showing a greatly increased risk over that found in the general population (L. Rifkin and H. Gurling, Genetic aspects of affective disorders, in *Biological Aspects of Affective Disorders*, ed. R. Horton and C. Katona (London: Academic Press, 1991), pp. 305–334.

169. Herman Melville, *White-Jacket or The World in a Man-of-War* (Oxford: Oxford University Press, 1990), pp. 402–403. Originally published in 1850.

CHAPTER 7
THIS NET THROWNE UPON THE HEAVENS

1. John Donne, *The Epithalamions, Anniversaries and Epicedes*, ed. W. Milgate (Oxford: Oxford University Press, 1978), p. 30.
2. Quoted in Thomas, *Edward Thomas: A Portrait* (letter to Gordon Bottom, 21 May 1908) p. 162.
3. Quoted in Ragna Stang, *Edvard Munch: The Man and His Art*, trans. Geoffrey Culverwell (New York: Abbeville Press, 1979), p. 107.
4. M. Schou, P.C. Baastrup, P. Grof, P. Weis, and J. Angst, Pharmacological and clinical problems of lithium prophylaxis, *British Journal of Psychiatry*, 116 (1970): 615–619.
5. P. Polatin and R. R. Fieve, Patient rejection of lithium carbonate prophylaxis, *Journal of the American Medical Association*, 218 (1971): 864–866; R. G. Fitzgerald, Mania as a message: Treatment with family therapy and lithium carbonate, *American Journal of Psychotherapy*, 26(1972): 547–553; T. Van Putten, Why do patients with manic-depressive illness stop their lithium? *Comprehensive Psychiatry*, 16(1975): 179–183; R. J. Kerry, Recent developments in patient management, in F. N. Johnson and S. Johnson, ed., *Lithium in Medical Practice* (Baltimore: University Park Press, 1978), pp. 337–353.
6. K.R. Jamison, R. H. Gerner, and F. K. Goodwin, Patient and physician attitudes toward lithium: Relationship to compliance, *Archives of General Psychiatry*, 36 (1979) 866–869; K.R. Jamison and H.S. Akiskal, Medication compliance in patients with bipolar disorders, *Psychiatric Clinics of North America*, 6(1983): 175–192.
7. These studies are reviewed in Goodwin and Jamison, "Person-

ality and Interpersonal Behavior," and "Maintenance Medical Treatment," *Manic-Depressive Illness* pp. 281–317, 665–724.

8. Ibid. pp. 293–297.

9. M. Schou, Special review of lithium in psychiatric therapy and prophylaxis, *Journal of Psychiatric Research*, 6(1968): 67–95, quotation on p. 78.

10. L. L. Judd, B. Hubbard, D. S. Janowsky, L. Y. Huey, and P. A. Attewell, The effect of lithium carbonate on affect, mood, and personality of normal subjects, *Archives of General Psychiatry*, 34 (1977): 346–351.

11. D. Kropf and B. Müller-Oerlinghausen, Changes in learning, memory, and mood during lithium treatment: Approach to a research strategy, *Acta Psychiatrica Scandinavica*, 59 (1979): 97–124.

12. R. H. Belmaker, R. Lehrer, R. P. Ebstein, H. Lettik, and S. Kugelmass, A possible cardiovascular effect of lithium, *American Journal of Psychiatry*, 136 (1979): 577–579; K. White, R. Bohart, K. Whipple, and J. Boyd, Lithium effects on normal subjects: Relationships to plasma and RBC lithium levels, *International Pharmacopysychiatry*, 14 (1979): 176–183.

13. U. Bonetti, F. Johansson, L. Von Knorring, C. Perris, and E. Strandman, Prophylactic lithium and personality variables: An international collaborative study, *International Pharmacopsychiatry*, 12 (1977): 14–19.

14. M. F. Folstein, J. R. De Paulo, Jr., and K. Trepp, Unusual mood stability in patients taking lithium, *British Journal of Psychiatry*, 140 (1982): 188–191; J. R. De Paulo, Jr., E. I. Correa, and M. F. Folstein, Does lithium stabilize mood? *Biological Psychiatry*, 18 (1983): 1093–1097.

15. D. Kropf and B. Müller-Oerlinghausen, The influence of lithium long-term medication on personality and mood, *Pharmacopsychiatry*, 18 (1985): 104–105.

16. G. N. Christodoulou, A. Siafakas, and P. M. Rinieris, Side effects of lithium, *Acta Psychiatrica Belg*, 77 (1977): 260–266; summaries of published and unpublished findings on the subject are reviewed in Goodwin and Jamison, *Manic-Depressive Illness*, pp. 760–762.

17. Goodwin and Jamison, "Thought Disorder, Perception, and Cognition," *Manic-Depressive Illness*, pp. 247–280.

18. A. Coppen, C. Swade, and K. Wood, Platelet-5-hydroxytryptamine accumulation in depressive illness, *Clin Chim Acta*, 87 (1978): 165–168; M. T. Abou-Saleh and A. Coppen, Subjective side effects of amitriptyline and lithium in affective disorders, *British Journal of Psychiatry*, 142 (1983): 391–397; F. Engelsmann, J. Katz, A. M. Ghadirian, and D. Schachter, Lithium and memory: A long-term follow-up study, *Journal of Clinical Psychopharmacology*, 8 (1988): 207–212.

19. See Goodwin and Jamison, "Thought Disorder, Perception, and Cognition."

20. C. J. Kestenbaum, Children at risk for manic-depressive illness: Possible predictors, *American Journal of Psychiatry*, 136 (1979): 1206–1208; P. Decina, C. J. Kestenbaum, S. Farber, L. Kron, M. Gargan, H. A. Sackeim, and R. R. Fieve, Clinical and psychological assessment of children of bipolar probands, *American Journal of Psychiatry*, 140 (1983): 548–553.

21. These issues have been reviewed by E. D. Shaw, J. J. Mann, P. E. Stokes, and A. Z. Manevitz, Effects of lithium on associative productivity and idiosyncrasy in bipolar outpatients, *American Journal of Psychiatry*, 143 (1986): 1166–1169; J. Anath, A. M. Ghadirian, and F. Engelsmann, Lithium and memory: A review, *Canadian Journal of Psychiatry*, 32 (1987): 312–316; L. L. Judd, L. R. Squire, N. Butters, D. P. Salmon, and K. A. Paller, Effects of psychotropic drugs on cognition and memory in normal humans and animals, in H. Y. Meltzer, ed., *Psychopharmacology: The Third Generation of Progress* (New York: Raven Press, 1987), pp. 1467–1475; E. D. Shaw, P. E. Stokes, J. J. Mann, and A. Z. A. Manevitz, Effects of lithium carbonate on the memory and motor speed of bipolar outpatients, *Journal of Abnormal Psychology*, 96 (1987): 64–69.

22. Anath, et al., Lithium and memory (1987).

23. J. W. Jefferson, J. H. Greist, D. L. Ackerman, and J. A. Carroll, *Lithium Encyclopedia for Clinical Practice*, 2nd ed. (Washington, D.C.: American Psychiatric Press, 1987); Judd et al., Effects of psychotropic drugs (1987).

24. Ibid., p. 1468.

25. L. L. Judd, B. Hubbard, D. S. Janowsky, L. Y. Huey, and K. I. Takahashi, The effect of lithium carbonate on the cognitive functions of normal subjects, *Archives of General Psychiatry*, 34 (1977): 355–357; I. G. G. Karniol, J. Dalton, and M. H. Lader, Acute and chronic effects of lithium chloride on physiological and psychological measures in normals, *Psychopharmacology* (Berlin), 57: 289–294, (1978); Kropf and Müller-Oerlinghausen, Changes in learning, memory, and mood (1979); H. Weingartner, M. V. Rudorfer, and M. Linnoila, Cognitive effects of lithium treatment in normal volunteers, *Psychopharmacology* (Berlin), 86 (1985): 472–474; P. W. Glue, D. J. Nutt, P. J. Cowen, and D. Broadbent, Selective effect of lithium on cognitive performance in man, *Psychopharmacology* (Berlin), 91 (1987): 109–111.

26. Studies reporting detrimental effects of lithium on cognitive abilities and speed of performance include, among others, R. G. Demers and G. R. Heninger, Visual-motor performance during lithium treatment: A

preliminary report, *Journal of Clinical Pharmacology*, 11 (1971): 247–279; V. I. Reus, S. D. Targum, H. Weingartner, and R. M. Post, Effect of lithium carbonate on memory processes in bipolar affectively ill patients. *Psychopharmacology* (Berlin), 63 (1979): 39–42; Y. Lund, M. Nissen, and O. J. Rafaelsen. Long-term lithium treatment and psychological functions, *Acta Psychiatrica Scandinavica*, 65 (1982): 233–244; L. Pons, J. I. Nurnberger, Jr., and D. L. Murphy, Mood-independent aberrancies in associative processes in bipolar affective disorder: An apparent stabilizing effect of lithium, *Psychiatry Research*, 14 (1985): 315–322; Shaw et al., Effects of lithium on associative productivity (1986); Shaw et al., Effects of lithium carbonate (1987); P. Jauhar, Cognitive impairment in long-term lithium therapy, *Clinical Neuropharmacology*, 15 (Supplement 1, Part B) (1992): 211B.

Studies reporting no significant effect of lithium on memory or other cognitive abilities include R. Telford and E. P. Worrall, Cognitive functions in manic-depressives: Effects of lithium and physostigamine, *British Journal of Psychiatry*, 133 (1978): 424–428; B. F. Kjellman, B. E. Karlberg, and L. H. Thorell, Cognitive and affective functions in patients with affective disorders treated with lithium, *Acta Psychiatrica Scandinavica*, 62 (1980): 32–46; A. M. Ghadirian. F. Engelsmann, and J. Anath, Memory functions during lithium therapy, *Journal of Clinical Psychopharmacology*, 3 (1983): 313–315; Engelsmann et al., Lithium and memory (1988).

27. Polatin and Fieve, Patient rejection of lithium, p. 864.

28. M. H. Marshall, C. P. Neumann, and M. Robinson, Lithium, creativity, and manic-depressive illness: Review and prospectus, *Psychosomatics*, 11 (1970): 406–488; M. Schou, Artistic productivity and lithium prophylaxis in manic-depressive illness, *British Journal of Psychiatry*, 135 (1979): 97–103.

29. Schou, Artistic productivity and lithium prophylaxis (1979).

30. Judd et al., The effect of lithium carbonate (1977).

31. Shaw et al., Effects of lithium on associative productivity (1986).

32. Pons et al., Mood-independent aberrancies (1985).

33. Goodwin and Jamison, Review of thirteen studies (1,094 patients) investigating lithium side effects, *Manic-Depressive Illness*, pp. 760–762.

34. Ibid.

35. Reviews of efficacy studies of carbamazepine and valproate are in Goodwin and Jamison, *Manic-Depressive Illness*, pp. 712–713. See, for instance, R. M. Post, J. C. Ballenger, T. W. Uhde, and W. E. Bunney, Jr., Efficacy of carbamazepine in manic-depressive illness: Implications for underlying mechanisms, in *Neurobiology of Mood Disorders*, ed.

R. M. Post and J. C. Ballenger (Baltimore: Williams and Wilkins, 1984), pp. 777–816; J. R. Calabrese and G. A. Delucchi, Spectrum of efficacy of valproate in 55 rapid-cycling manic-depressives, *American Journal of Psychiatry*, 147 (1990): 431–434; H. G. Pope, S. L. McElroy, and P. E. Keck, Jr., Valproate in the treatment of acute mania, *Archives of General Psychiatry*, 48 (1991): 62–68; J. R. Calabrese, P. J. Markovitz, S. E. Kimmel, and S. C. Wagner, Spectrum of efficacy of valproate in 78 rapid-cycling bipolar patients, *Journal of Clinical Psychopharmacology*, 12 (suppl. 1) (1992): 53S–56S; R. H. Gerner and A. Stanton, Algorithm for patient management of acute manic states: Lithium, valproate, or carbamazepine? *Journal of Clinical Psychopharmacology*, 12 (suppl. 1) (1992): 57S–63S; S. L. McElroy, P. E. Keck, Jr., H. G. Pope, Jr., and J. I. Hudson, Valproate in the treatment of bipolar disorder: Literature review and clinical guidelines, *Journal of Clinical Psychopharmacology*, 12 (suppl. 1) (1992): 42S–52S.

36. S. D. Cochran, Preventing medical noncompliance in the outpatient treatment of bipolar affective disorders, *Journal of Consulting and Clinical Psychology*, 52 (1984): 873–878;

I. D. Glick, J. F. Clarkin, J. H. Spencer, G. L. Maas, A. B. Lewis, J. Peyser, N. DeMane, M. Good-Ellis, E. Harris, and V. Lestelle, A controlled evaluation of inpatient family intervention: Preliminary results of the six-month follow-up, *Archives of General Psychiatry*, 42(1985): 882–886.

D. J. Miklowitz, M. J. Goldstein, K. H. Nuechterlein, K. S. Snyder, and J. Mintz, Family factors and the course of bipolar affective disorder, *Archives of General Psychiatry*, 45 (1988): 225–231.

37. M. J. Goldstein, E. H. Rodnick, J. R. Evans, P. R. A. May, and M. Steinberg, Drug and family therapy in the aftercare of acute schizophrenia, *Archives of General Psychiatry*, 35 (1978): 1169–1177.

38. A. Coppen and C. Swade, Reduced lithium dosage improves prophylaxis: A possible mechanism, in H. Hippius, G. L. Klerman, and N. Matussek, ed., *New Results in Depression Research* (Berlin: Springer-Verlag, 1986), pp. 126–130.

P. Vestergaard and M. Schou, Prospective studies on a lithium cohort, I. General features, *Acta Psychiatrica Scandinavica*, 78 (1988): 421–426.

A. J. Gelenberg, J. M. Kane, M. B. Keller, P. Lavori, J. F. Rosenbaum, K. Cole, and J. Lavelle, Comparison of standard and low serum levels of lithium for maintenance treatment of bipolar disorder, *New England Journal of Medicine*, 321 (1989): 1490–1493.

39. Shaw, et al., Effects of lithium on associative productivity (1986).

40. P. Plenge, E. T. Mellerup, T. G. Bolwig, C. Brun, O. Hetmar,

J. Ladefoged, S. Larsen, and O. J. Rafaelsen, Lithium treatment: Does the kidney prefer one daily dose instead of two? *Acta Psychiatrica Scandinavica*, 66(1982): 121–128.

41. H. V. Jensen, K. Olafsson, A. Bille, J. Andersen, E. Mellerup, and P. Plenge, Lithium every second day, A new treatment regimen? *Lithium*, 1 (1990): 55–58, p. 353; P. Plenge and E. T. Mellerup, W. H. O. Cross-cultural study on lithium every second day, *Clinical Neuropharmacology*, (Supplement 1, Part A): (1992) 487A–488A. This experimental regimen of lithium dosing is now being tested in ten different centers worldwide with the specific hope that side effects such as "lack of initiative and emotional colour" will be minimized.

42. Ralph Waldo Emerson, *Emerson in His Journals*, ed. Joel Porte (Cambridge: Belknap Press of Harvard University Press, 1982), p. 430.

43. Gelenberg et al., Comparison of standard and low serum levels (1989); Goodwin and Jamison, "Maintenance Medical Treatment," *Manic-Depressive Illness*, pp. 665–724; T. Suppes, R. J. Baldessarini, G. L. Faedda, and M. Tohen, Risk of recurrence following discontinuation of lithium treatment in bipolar disorder, *Archives of General Psychiatry*, 48 (1991): 1082–1088.

44. Antonin Artaud, *Anthology* (San Francisco: City Light Books, 1965), pp. 27–28 (passage translated by David Ossman).

45. See F. N. Johnson, ed. *Depression and Mania: Modern Lithium Therapy* (Oxford: IRL Press, 1987); A. Georgotas and R. Cancro, eds., *Depression and Mania* (New York: Elsevier, 1988); Goodwin and Jamison, "Maintenance Medical Treatment," *Manic-Depressive Illness*, pp. 665–724.

      Patients taking lithium make fewer suicide attempts and commit suicide less often than manic-depressive patients not taking lithium: D. W. K. Kay and U. Petterson, Mortality, in U. Petterson, Manic-depressive illness: A clinical, social, and genetic study, *Acta Psychiatrica Scandinavica* (Supplement 269) (1977): 55–60; A. J. Poole, H. D. James, and W. C. Hughes, Treatment experiences in the lithium clinic at St. Thomas' Hospital, *Journal of the Royal Society of Medicine*, 71 (1978): 890–894; H. Hanus and M. Zapletalek, Sebevrazedna aktivita nemocnych afektivnimi poruchami v prubehu lithioprofylaxe, *Ceskoslovenska Psychiatrie*, 80 (1984): 97–100; B. Causemann and B. Müller-Oerlinghausen, Does lithium prevent suicides and suicidal attempts? in *Lithium: Inorganic Pharmacology and Psychiatric Use*, ed. N. J. Birch (Oxford: IRL Press, 1988), pp. 23–24; A. Coppen, J. Bailey, G. Houston, and P. Silcocks, Lithium and mortality: A 15 year follow-up, *Clinical Neuropharmacology*, 15 (Supplement 1, Part A) (1992): 448A.

46. Robert Burns, *Common Place Book*, March 1784, quoted in

David Daiches, *Robert Burns* (London: André Deutsch, 1966), p. 67.

47. Lowell, "A Conversation with Ian Hamilton," in *Robert Lowell: Collected Prose*, ed. Robert Giroux (New York: Farrar, Straus & Giroux, 1987), pp. 267–290, quotation on p. 286.

48. There remains uncertainty about whether Randall Jarrell's death—he was hit by an oncoming car at night—was an accident or a suicide. Several of his friends (including Robert Lowell and Peter Taylor), as well as biographer Jeffrey Meyers, believe he did commit suicide; the occupants of the car that hit Jarrell described the poet as having "lunged" in front of the car. Jarrell's wife, and biographer William Pritchard, disagree, and the medical examiner concluded that the death was accidental, with a "reasonable doubt" about its being a suicide. Of relevance to the discussion is the fact that he had been hospitalized for both mania and depression several months earlier and, at the time of his death he was still recouperating from having attempted suicide by slashing his wrists (J. Meyers, The death of Randall Jarrell, *The Virginia Quarterly Review* [Summer 1982]: 450–467; *Randall Jarrell's Letters*, ed. Mary Jarrell [Boston: Houghton Mifflin, 1985]; W. H. Pritchard, *Randall Jarrell: A Literary Life* [New York: Farrar, Straus and Giroux, 1990]).

49. Van Gogh, *The Complete Letters* (May 1890, letter 630), vol. 3, p. 263.

50. Lowell, *Collected Prose*, pp. xiii–xiv.

51. R. M. Post, Transduction of psychosocial stress into the neurobiology of recurrent affective disorder, *American Journal of Psychiatry*, 149 (1992): 999–1010; R. J. Wyatt and R. M. Post, Early and sustained intervention alters the course of schizophrenia and affective disorders, submitted for publication.

52. Lewis Thomas, "The Wonderful Mistake," *The Medusa and the Snail: More Notes of a Biology Watcher* (New York: Viking Press, 1979), pp. 27–30.

53. Some of these potential problems are shared by most genetic diseases. Drs. Eric Juengst and James Watson have outlined three general sets of ethical issues that are relevant to the study of human disease: issues involved in the integration of new genetic tests into health care (for example, insuring the accuracy of genetic tests), issues involved in educating and counseling individuals about the results of genetic tests, and issues of privacy concerning the results of genetic tests (that is, maximizing confidentiality of test results by protecting accessibility to employers, researchers, and insurance providers). E. T. Juengst and J. D. Watson, Human genome research and the responsible use of new genetic knowledge, *International Journal of Bioethics*, 2 (1991): 99–102. Many articles

and books have been written about the tremendously important ethical issues surrounding genetic research. These include:

W. F. Anderson and J. C. Fletcher, Gene therapy in humans: when is it ethical to begin? *New England Journal of Medicine*, 303 (1980): 1293.

United States President's Commission for the Study of Ethical Problems in Medicine and Biomedical and Behavioral Research, *Screening and Counseling for Genetic Conditions* (Washington, D.C.: Government Printing Office, February 1983).

Jonathan Glover, *What Sort of People Should There Be? Genetic Engineering, Brain Control, and Their Impact on Our Future World* (New York: Penguin, 1984).

W. F. Anderson, Prospects for human gene therapy, *Science*, 226 (1984): 401–409.

Le Roy Walters, Ethical issues in intrauterine diagnosis and therapy, *Fetal Therapy*, 1 (1986): 32–37.

Le Roy Walters, The ethics of human gene therapy, *Nature*, 320 (1986): 225–227.

F. D. Ledley, Somatic gene therapy for human disease: Background and prospects, Part II, *Journal of Pediatrics*, 110 (1987): 167–174.

H. Pardes, C. A. Kaufmann, H. A. Pincus, and A. West, Genetics and psychiatry: Past discoveries, current dilemmas, and future directions, *American Journal of Psychiatry*, 146 (1989): 435–443.

Le Roy Walters, Genetics and reproductive technologies, in *Medical Ethics*, ed. R. M. Veatch (Boston: Jones and Bartlett, 1989), pp. 201–228.

Z. Bankowski and A. M. Capron, *Genetics, Ethics, and Human Values: Human Genome Mapping, Genetic Screening and Gene Therapy* (Geneva: Council for International Organizations of Medical Sciences, 1991).

J. A. Robertson, Issues in procreation liberty raised by the new genetics, *Legal and Ethical Issues Raised by the Human Genome Project*, ed. M. A. Rothstein (Houston: University of Houston, 1991).

D. J. Kevles and L. Hood, *The Code of Codes: Scientific and Social Issues in the Human Genome Project* (Cambridge: Harvard University Press, 1992).

54. D. Suzuki and P. Knudtson, *Genethics: The Clash Between the New Genetics and Human Life* (Cambridge: Harvard University Press, 1990), pp. 183–184.

55. Goodwin and Jamison, "Manic-Depressive Illness, Creativity, and Leadership," *Manic-Depressive Illness*, pp. 332–367.

56. M. Hammer and J. Zubin, Evolution, culture, and psychopathology. *Journal of General Psychology*, 78 (1968): 151–164; L. F. Jarvik

and B. S. Deckard, *Neuropsychobiology*, 3 (1977): 179–191; L. Sloman, M. Konstantareas, and D. W. Dunham, The adaptive role of maladaptive neurosis, *Biological Psychiatry*, 14 (1979): 961–972; J. S. Price and L. Sloman, The evolutionary model of psychiatric disorder, *Archives of General Psychiatry*, 41 (1984): 211; J. M. Himmelhoch and M. E. Garfinkel, Sources of lithium resistance in mixed mania, *Psychopharmacology Bulletin*, 22 (1986): 613–620.

57. Dr. Leon Kass has discussed at length the arguments against abortions based on information derived from genetic tests (L. R. Kass, *Toward a More Natural Science: Biology and Human Affairs* [New York: Free Press, 1988]). Here he summarizes succintly his own views, which, although certainly controversial, are important to note:

> I have failed to provide myself with a satisfactory intellectual and moral justification for the practice of genetic abortion. Perhaps others more able than I can supply one. Perhaps the pragmatists can persuade me that we should abandon the search for principled justification, that if we just trust people's situational decisions or their gut reactions, everything will turn out fine. Maybe they are right. But we should not forget the sage observation of Bertrand Russell: "Pragmatism is like a warm bath that heats up so imperceptibly that you don't know when to scream." Before we submerge ourselves irrevocably in amniotic fluid, we should note its connection to our own baths, into which we have started the hot water running. (p. 98)

58. Interview with Dr. Francis Collins, "Tracking down killer genes," *Time*, September 17, 1990, p. 12.

59. Committee on Mapping and Sequencing the Human Genome: Board on Basic Biology, Commission on Life Sciences, National Research Council, *Mapping and Sequencing the Human Genome* (Washington, D.C.: National Academy Press, 1988).

60. Larry Gostin, quoted in *Designing Genetic Information Policy: The Need for an Independent Policy Review of the Ethical, Legal, and Social Implications of the Human Genome Project*. Sixteenth report by the Committee on Government Operations (Washington, D.C.: U.S. Government Printing Office, 1992), p. 24.

61. B. Onuf, The problem of eugenics in connection with the manic-depressive temperament, *New York Journal of Medicine*, 3 (1920): 402–412, 461–465.

Glover, *What Sort of People Should There Be?* (1984).

D. J. Kevles, *In the Name of Eugenics: Genetics and the Uses of Human Heredity* (New York: Alfred A. Knopf, 1985).

E. K. Nichols, *Human Gene Therapy* (Cambridge: Harvard University Press, 1988).

Congress of the United States Office of Technology Assessment. *Mapping Our Genes: Genome Projects: How Big? How Fast?* (Baltimore: Johns Hopkins University Press).

Z. Bankowski and A. M. Capron, ed., *Genetics, Ethics and Human Values: Human Genome Mapping, Genetic Screening and Gene Therapy* (Geneva: Council for International Organizations of Medical Sciences, 1991).

62. Kevles, *In the Name of Eugenics*, p. 10.

63. N.D. Kristof, "Parts of China Forcibly Sterilizing the Retarded Who Wish to Marry," *New York Times*, August 15, 1991, pp. A1 and A8. (Although the title of this article refers to the policies affecting the mentally retarded, policies affecting those with hereditary mental illness are also reported in the article.)

64. Kevles, *In the Name of Eugenics.*

65. H. Luxenberger, Berufsglied und soziale Schichtung in den Familien erblich Geisteskranker, *Eugenik*, 3 (1933): 34–40.

66. Myerson and Boyle, The incidence of manic-depressive psychosis in certain socially prominent families, (1941): 20.

67. John W. Robertson, *Edgar A. Poe: A Psychopathic Study* (New York: G. P. Putnam, 1923), p. 145.

68. A few of the basic strategies for human gene therapy have been summarized by Suzuki and Knudtson in their book *Genethics:*

1. *Gene Insertion.* The most straightforward approach to gene therapy would be *gene insertion*, which involves the simple insertion of one or more copies of the normal version of a gene into the chromosomes of a diseased cell. Once expressed, these supplementary genes could produce sufficient quantities of a missing enzyme or structural protein, for example, to overcome the inherited deficit.

2. *Gene Modification.* A more delicate feat, *gene modification*, would entail the chemical modification of the defective DNA sequence right where it lies in the living cell, in an effort to recode its genetic message to match that of the normal allele. In principle, this approach would be less likely to disrupt the intricate geographical layout of genes on chromosomes, thereby reducing the possibility of unwanted side effects.

3. *Gene Surgery.* Even more daring would be bona fide *gene surgery*—the precise removal of a faulty gene from a chromosome, followed by its replacement with a cloned substitute. The notion of transplanting freshly synthesized DNA sequences to replace defective ones is the ultimate dream of gene therapy. But it would demand a mastery of human genetics that, for the moment at least, simply exceeds the geneticist's grasp.

69. See notes 53, 57, and 58.

70. Davis, *Mapping the Code*, pp. 252–253.

71. James D. Watson, quoted in ibid., p. 262.

72. Lewis Thomas, "Notes of a biology watcher: to err is human," B. Dixon, ed., *From Creation to Chaos: Classic Writings in Science*, (Oxford: Basil Blackwell, 1989), pp. 199–201.

73. John Keats, "Lamia," lines 234–237, *The Poetical Works of John Keats* (Cambridge Edition), rev. P. D. Sheats (Boston: Houghton Mifflin, 1975), p. 156.

74. Walker Percy, *The Second Coming* (New York: Washington Square Press/Pocket Books, 1981), p. 314.

75. Byron, *Don Juan*, canto X, verses 2–4, lines 10–32, *Lord Byron: The Complete Poetical Works*, vol. 5, pp. 437–438.

In our own time, Sorley MacLean has described this with grace and power:

> Who is this, who is this in the night of the heart?
> It is the thing that is not reached,
> the ghost seen by the soul,
> A Cuillin rising over the sea.
>
> Who is this, who is this in the night of the soul,
> following the veering of the fugitive light?
> It is only, it is only the journeying one
> seeking the Cuillin over the ocean.

From Sorley MacLean, "The Cuillin," Part VII, lines 164–183, in *From Wood to Ridge* (Manchester, England: Carcanet Press Ltd., 1991).

ACKNOWLEDGMENTS

Several biographers were kind enough to read early drafts of my book and make very helpful comments. Professor Leslie Marchand, preeminent biographer of Lord Byron, was especially generous in taking time with my work; Professor Jerome McGann, editor and scholar of Byron's poetry, also reviewed early chapters and made several thought-provoking comments about Byron's psychological life and temperament. Professor Robert Bernard Martin, whose outstanding biography of Alfred Tennyson I found invaluable, read not only my material on Lord Tennyson but what I had written about Gerard Manley Hopkins as well. He generously sent me an advance copy of his recent biography of Hopkins, and we spent a delightful afternoon in Oxford discussing our mutual fascination with the life, poetry, and moods of this extraordinary poet. I was also particularly helped by conversations and correspondence with the eminent Hopkins scholar, and editor of his poetry, Professor Norman MacKenzie. Professor Robert Winter kindly reviewed what I had written about Beethoven and Professor Diane Middlebrook of Stanford University, biographer of Anne Sexton, read early drafts of four chapters and made several useful suggestions that I took to heart. Professor Kenneth Silverman looked over what I had written about Edgar Allan Poe and provided me with a very interesting perspective, as well as useful information about Poe's drug use and his suicide attempt. Dr. Tom Caramagno, who has recently written a book about Virginia Woolf and her manic-depressive illness is, as I have noted in the text, responsible for fastidious and important research into Woolf's family psychiatric history. Her pedigree, drawn up in chapter 6, is based largely on his work. I am especially indebted to Dr. Iain McGilchrist for making extremely detailed and helpful comments on my manuscript. His background as a physician, as well as a former lecturer in English literature at the University of Oxford, made his observations particularly meaningful. Professor Peter Sacks of the Johns Hopkins University Department of English was likewise helpful and encouraging in his remarks.

Several other individuals also read early drafts of the book. I am extremely indebted to Dr. Anthony Storr, who has been a tremendous friend and colleague; his book *The Dynamics of Creation* remains a classic in the field, and I have found our many conversations about artistic creativity and psychopathology very helpful. John Julius Norwich has given me much encouragement over the years and made many useful comments. On occasion he suggested several poets, long dead, whom he thought "perhaps a bit odd." They were, in fact, more than a bit odd, and I am grateful to him for his leads. J. Carter Brown read an early draft of the manuscript and made several very helpful suggestions; I am indebted to him as well for having made me more aware of the poem from which I took the book's title. Dr. James Watson, Director of the Cold Spring Harbor Laboratory, was kind enough to take the time to read an early draft; his usual clarity of thought was extremely useful and much appreciated. Molecular biologists Francis Collins, of the University of Michigan, and Samuel Barondes, of the University of California, San Francisco, reviewed the genetics sections and made several very helpful comments. My editor, Erwin Glikes, understood long before I did what I wanted to say, and believed there was a point in saying it. He has a clear, yet marvelously dendritic mind, and his help was enormously important. Editing supervisor Edith Lewis and copy editor Sue Llewellyn made many useful suggestions and improvements. Art director Nancy Etheredge took my original ideas for illustrations and turned them into a beautifully designed book.

It is my pleasure to express my appreciation to the staffs of the William H. Welch Medical Library of the Johns Hopkins University School of Medicine, the Georgetown University Library, the Clinical Center Library of the National Institutes of Health, the National Library of Medicine, the Radcliffe, Bodleian, and Merton College Libraries of the University of Oxford, and the National Gallery of Art Library in Washington, D.C. The warm and wonderful atmosphere of the London Library defies description; it is, without question, the nicest place I have ever found to read, write, or procrastinate.

I am grateful to Oxford University Press for permission to use material previously published in *Manic-Depressive Illness*, a book I wrote with Dr. Frederick Goodwin, Director of the National Institute of Mental Health. All the material used was based on chapters that I had written, or sections that I had written for other chapters (for example, material about the cognitive side effects of lithium, which appeared in a chapter about maintenance medical treatment), except for a brief discussion of biological rhythms in normal and affectively ill populations. Dr. Goodwin was kind enough to grant me permission to use this material, which is based on his work with Dr. Thomas Wehr. Drs. Audrey Burnam and Myrna Weissman provided assistance with epidemiologic findings. The study of mood disorders in British writers and artists, discussed in chapter 3, was originally published in the journal *Psychiatry*; I remain grateful to the many outstanding writers and artists who participated and gave their time and thoughts. Portions of my remarks about Virginia Woolf in chapter 6 were first published in the Afterword I wrote for Dr. Tom Caramagno's book *The Flight of the Mind: Virginia Woolf's Art and Manic-Depressive Illness*, published in 1992 by the University of California Press. The description of Robert Schumann's life, also in chapter 6, was taken from a biographical sketch I wrote in program notes for "Moods & Music," a concert performed by the National Symphony Orchestra at the John F. Kennedy Center for the Performing Arts in Washington, D.C. The concert was produced with pianist and music scholar Robert Winter.

For their friendship over the years I am deeply indebted to Dr. Daniel B. Auerbach, without whom this book could not have been written; David Mahoney, who has been a particularly close and supportive friend for many years; and Alain Moreau, who did the artwork for the cover and two illustrations in the book. Lucie Bryant, Judy Hoyer, Dr. Audrey Burnam, Dr. Barbara Parry, Dr. Jeremy Waletzky, Dr. Harriet Braiker, Professor Andrew Comrey, Dr. Raymond De Paulo, Dr. Robert Faguet, Dr. Robert Gerner, Dr. Michael Gitlin, the late Lt. Colonel David Laurie, Royal Army Medical Corps, the late Professor William McGlothlin, Professor Paul McHugh, Ben Magliano, Victor and Harriet Potik, Dr. Robert Post, Professor Mogens Schou, and Professor Louis Jolyon West provided friendship and encouragement as well. Mr. William Collins typed the entire manuscript with intelligence, style, and consistently good-humored ability to work around my last-minute deadlines.

I owe my family and Frances Lear my greatest debt. My father, Dr. Marshall Jamison—a meteorologist and former pilot in the United States Air Force—gave me a love for that which is vast, beautiful, and turbulent. My sisters share this inheritance. The kindness and understanding of my mother, Dell Jamison, have deeply affected not only me but everyone who knows her. She is responsible for my lifelong interest in biography and psychology. My brother Dr. Dean Jamison, sister-in-law Dr. Joanne Leslie, nephews Julian and Eliot, and niece Leslie have been more than one could ask for in a family.

Frances Lear, a remarkable and generous friend, has given new meaning to the lines from William Butler Yeats:

> *Think where man's glory most begins and ends,*
> *And say my glory was I had such friends.*

INDEX

About the Author

Kay Redfield Jamison, Ph.D., is professor of psychiatry at the Johns Hopkins University School of Medicine and co-author of the definitive medical text *Manic-Depressive Illness*. Dr. Jamison is a member of the National Advisory Council for Human Genome Research. She is also the executive producer and writer for a series of award-winning public television specials about manic-depressive illness and the arts.